A Companion to the Study
of St. Augustine

A Companion to the Study

OF

ST. AUGUSTINE

EDITED BY

ROY W. BATTENHOUSE

BAKER BOOK HOUSE
Grand Rapids, Michigan

Library of Congress Catalog
Card Number: 55-6253
ISBN: 0-8010-0760-7

PHOTOLITHOPRINTED BY CUSHING - MALLOY, INC.
ANN ARBOR, MICHIGAN, UNITED STATES OF AMERICA
1 9 7 9

Preface

THE SIXTEEN HUNDREDTH ANNIVERSARY, this year, of St. Augustine's birth is a fitting occasion for renewed attention to his life and work. His appeal has never been more pertinent, probably, than today. Our own twentieth-century tensions, bred of a secularized society in torment, find a close parallel in his fourth-century Mediterranean world. Augustine was then the interpreter of such tensions, the analyst at a profound level of the spiritual deficiencies and cultural decay which characterized Roman life and indirectly were disturbing the Christian community. By his personal involvements in the situation, along with an acute vision of its deeper meanings, he made of the crisis an exercise of transition to new foundations. The significant features of his total accomplishment, therefore, deserve periodic review by all thoughtful people.

The present book is offered as a tribute to St. Augustine's importance, and as a guide to the study of his works. It is written to aid, as a kind of companion, the appreciation of his varied contributions and of their enduring significance. The method here is that of fresh review, analysis, and evaluation. The story of his life is first resurveyed; individual chapters are then devoted to major writings; and finally certain important aspects of his thought are put under investigation and criticism.

Since the book is intended primarily as an introduction, for new readers as well as for old, the coverage is adjusted, in the progressive sections, to three levels of approach. The early chapters are broadly comprehensive, and mainly informative, merely to suggest St. Augustine's range and riches. The middle section undertakes something more advanced—and scarcely to be found in any one modern book on Augustine—namely, a systematic exposition of the contents of his chief works (excepting his sermons and scriptural commentaries), with critical appraisal at important points. This section should help especially the student of the history of ideas. Third, a section entitled 'Special Aspects of St. Augustine's Thought' includes essays in which evaluation is predominant. Here each chapter, in drawing widely from a variety of works, offers interpretations and critical judgments. It is our hope that even the specialist scholar will find something of fresh value in this section.

Sixteen college and seminary teachers are the authors of this volume. Each is immediately responsible only for his own chapter, yet the work as a whole has emerged as a project which has had the benefit of group discussion as its continuing context. All the authors (as well as a few others not contributing to the volume) are members of a small theological society known as the *Duodecim*, which for a dozen years has met semi-annually to hear papers and to debate their contents. Five such meetings during the years 1945–7 were devoted solely to St. Augustine. Out of this experience, immensely beneficial to the members themselves, arose the plan and purpose of the present book. All of the original papers have been recast or revised, and new essays have been added. The supervision of this effort has been the responsibility of the editor. He has sought to remove overlapping, in so far as is practicable, and to guide the proportions of the treatment. But the final product is a group accomplishment.

The central theme of our book is the continuing vitality of Augustinian wisdom. The reader will find occasional differences of interpretation by the contributors, particularly in reference to the degree of influence Neoplatonism continued to hold on Augustine. He will also find Augustine's occasional deficiencies noted and variously probed. Nevertheless, in the composite perspective of the volume there is conveyed a common awareness of Augustine's signal value for our understanding of

Western culture and for our grappling with present-day issues. Furthermore, the book as a whole is directed more toward the learner than the specialist. In planning the book we thought of it as useful in college courses in the humanities as well as for advanced courses in philosophy and history. We shall be especially pleased if teachers are helped by this volume to introduce into the university curriculum, as a normal offering, a semester course on Augustine. At the same time, we believe the book will have appeal generally for the average clergyman, teacher, or man of letters.

Four of the essays in this volume have already been separately published in professional journals. For permission to reprint these essays we are indebted to *The Journal of Religion* (essays 4 and 15), to *Church History* (essay 11), and to *The Harvard Theological Review* (essay 12). We also wish to acknowledge with gratitude the encouragement given us by the Hazen Foundation, which has supplied grants-in-aid for our meetings and for some stenographic services as well. The editor could not have succeeded, moreover, without a self-denying willingness on the part of each author to carry through this project despite a multitude of other claims on time and labor. And virtually all the *Duodecim* members have given aid, at one time or another, as editorial consultants. The editor owes particular thanks to Albert C. Outler, Cyril C. Richardson, James H. Nichols, and the society's Executive Secretary, Paul Ramsey. Finally, Mrs. Battenhouse has, inevitably but graciously, helped with the chores of correspondence and with the index.

ROY W. BATTENHOUSE

Bloomington, Indiana
August, 1954

Contributors

DANIEL D. WILLIAMS: Professor of Christian Theology, University of Chicago; author of *God's Grace and Man's Hope*, 1949, and *What Present-Day Theologians Are Thinking*, 1950; Associate Director, Study of Theological Education, 1954–5.

ROY W. BATTENHOUSE: Associate Professor of English, Indiana University; author of *Marlowe's 'Tamburlaine,'* 1941, and of essays on Shakespeare; formerly Associate Professor of Church History, Episcopal Theological School, Cambridge, Mass.

JOSEPH B. BERNARDIN: Rector, St. Andrew's Church, Maryville, Tennessee; author of *The Intercession of Our Lord*, 1933, and *An Introduction to the Episcopal Church*, 1940; Chaplain, U.S.A.R.

DAVID E. ROBERTS: Hartley Professor of the Philosophy of Religion, Union Theological Seminary; author of *Liberal Theology* (with H. P. Van Dusen), 1942, and *Psychotherapy and a Christian View of Man*, 1950.

T. S. K. SCOTT-CRAIG: Professor of Philosophy, Dartmouth College; formerly Assistant Professor of English, Hobart College; author of *Christian Attitudes to War and Peace*, 1938; Chairman of Faculty Work in the Episcopal Church, 1952–4.

STANLEY ROMAINE HOPPER: Professor of Christian Philosophy and Letters, Drew University, Madison, N.J.; author of *Crisis of Faith*, 1944; editor of *Spiritual Problems in Contemporary Literature*, 1952.

FREDERICK W. DILLISTONE: Chancellor of Liverpool Cathedral, England; formerly Professor of Theology, Episcopal Theological

School, Cambridge, Mass.; author of *The Structure of the Divine Society*, 1951, and *Jesus Christ and His Cross*, 1953.

PAUL LEHMANN: Colwell Professor of Applied Christianity, Princeton Theological School; author of *Forgiveness*, 1940, and of essays in *Christianity and Property* (ed. J. Fletcher), 1947, and *Christian Faith and Social Action* (ed. J. Hutchison), 1953; formerly Associate Professor of Biblical History, Wellesley College.

CYRIL C. RICHARDSON: Washburn Professor of Church History, Union Theological Seminary; author of *The Church through the Centuries*, 1940, and *Early Christian Fathers*, 1953.

EDWARD R. HARDY, JR.: Professor of Church History, Berkeley Divinity School; formerly tutor at the General Theological Seminary; author of *Militant in Earth: Twenty Centuries of the Spread of Christianity*, 1940, and *Christian Egypt*, 1952.

ROBERT E. CUSHMAN: Professor of Systematic Theology, Duke University; formerly Professor of Religion, University of Oregon; author of essays in the fields of Christian ethics, the history of doctrine, and Plato studies.

WILLIAM A. CHRISTIAN: Associate Professor of Religion, Yale University; author of essays on philosophy of religion; formerly Associate Professor of Religion, Smith College.

ALBERT C. OUTLER: Professor of Theology, Perkins School of Theology, Southern Methodist University; formerly Professor of Theology, Yale University; author of *Psychotherapy and the Christian Message*, 1954, and of a new translation of Augustine's *Confessions and Enchiridion*, 1955.

THOMAS J. BIGHAM: Instructor in Christian Ethics, General Theological Seminary; associate in University Seminars, Columbia University; former Chairman, Commission on Religion and Health, National Council of Churches.

ALBERT T. MOLLEGEN: Professor of New Testament Language and Literature, Virginia Theological Seminary.

ROGER HAZELTON: Abbot Professor of Christian Theology, Andover Newton Theological Seminary; author of *Renewing the Mind*, 1949, and *On Proving God*, 1952; formerly Dean of the Chapel and teacher, Colorado College.

OTHER MEMBERS OF *DUODECIM*

Professors Joseph Haroutunian, McCormick Theological Seminary; Paul Minear, Andover Newton Theological School; James H. Nichols, University of Chicago; W. Norman Pittenger, General Theological Seminary; Samuel Terrien, Union Theological Seminary; Julian Hartt, Yale University Divinity School; Paul Ramsey, Princeton University; George Johnston, Emmanuel College, University of Toronto; Hugh T. Kerr, Jr., Princeton Theological Seminary; Franz Hildebrandt, Drew University; and Mr. Burns Chalmers, American Friends Service Committee.

Contents

Preface, v

Contributors, ix

xiii

Part One

Introduction

Some Dates in Augustine's Life

A.D.

354 (13 November) Augustine is born at Tagaste.

370 Goes to Carthage to study rhetoric.

373 Becomes associated with Manichees.

374 Begins teaching rhetoric in Carthage.

383 Leaves Carthage for Rome. Abandons Manicheism.

384 Goes to Milan as public rhetorician.

386 Experiences conversion; resigns professorship. Composes at Cassiciacum his earliest surviving treatises.

387 (25 April) Is baptized at Milan by St. Ambrose.

388 Begins writing against the Manichees. Returns to Tageste; sets up monastery.

391 Is ordained priest in Hippo; preaches; monastery is transferred there.

396 Becomes sole Bishop of Hippo. Debates with Donatist bishop.

400 Finishes the *Confessions;* begins *On the Trinity;* brings his anti-Manichean writings to a climax; writes *On Baptism,* his chief work against the Donatists.

410 Rome is sacked by Goths under Alaric.

413–26 Writes the *City of God.*

412–30 Writes many treatises against Pelagianism.

426 Lists and reviews his works in the *Retractations.*

430 Dies while Hippo is under siege from the Vandals.

THE SIGNIFICANCE OF

ST. AUGUSTINE TODAY

Daniel D. Williams

Why is Augustine, who was born 1600 years ago, so widely read in the twentieth century by those who are trying to understand human problems? An astonishing variety of people — mystical seekers after God and rationalist philosophers, Protestants and Catholics of many theological persuasions, political scientists and educators, statesmen in search of social justice — all are to be found among those who turn repeatedly to Augustine. Wherever men discuss the meaning of good and evil, or human love and the love of God, or the nature of justice, or the unity of the Church and the relations of Church and State, the argument often turns on references to Augustine's thought. Why is this so?

In part the answer is that a reading of St. Augustine belongs to the discovery of our own intellectual and spiritual ancestry. It was he who in the fourth century gave to Western civilization the formative ideas which have guided it for centuries. As we recall Professor Whitehead's remark that Western philosophy is a series of footnotes to Plato, we can say with equal justice that theology in Western Christianity has been a series of footnotes to Augustine. These footnotes which later thinkers made to both Plato and Augustine display a wide variety, and many have offered strong dissent. Yet Augustine's writings remain among the dominant peaks in the range of Christian thought, so that no serious thinker can fail to reckon with them. In the medieval period St. Anselm and St. Thomas Aquinas directly depended upon him. In the Protestant Reformation Luther and Calvin reaffirmed Augustinian conceptions of God and of man's need for God's grace. Modern idealistic philosophy since Descartes has been indebted to aspects of Augustine's thought, while other sides of his doctrine have given support to such seminal thinkers as Pascal and Newman, and in our own day to Jacques Maritain, Reinhold Niebuhr, Paul Tillich, and Karl Barth. Whoever would know the structural ideas of the Christian tradition and Western philosophy which have shaped our minds for fifteen centuries must know St. Augustine.

But we read Augustine today for something more than historical understanding. The temper of our own times and the form of our own problems bear a close kinship to those of the age in which he wrote. One of our astute political analysts calls him 'the one great thinker who lived in a period which in some respects resembled our own more than any other in recorded history.' [1] His thought was hammered out amid the shattering of a great civilization. Ours, too, is a time of world-shaking struggle, of revolutionary forces let loose. The values that have informed Western civilization are threatened, and hope for neat solutions has crumpled. With the weapons created by science, destruction is possible on a scale never before imagined. The militant faith of communism proposes to build a new City of Man without benefit of faith in God or humility before Him. Among those who reject the communist utopia there are some who welcome the mood of existentialist philosophies in which nothing is left for man but his naked freedom. They see us as anxious individ-

4

uals adrift in a world that gives us no support. But St. Augustine understands this anguish: 'Is not man's heart an abyss? For what abyss is deeper . . . It is night, because here the human race wanders blindly.' [2] When we read on to find, as we do in Augustine, hope for a transformed world, we know that his hope was not cheaply won. He once stood where we stand.

Along with this kinship in crisis which we have with Augustine, his relevance for us must be found in his specific ideas and convictions. An account of these, and of his way of arriving at them, makes up the substance of this book. In this introductory chapter we can underline and illustrate one fundamental characteristic of Augustine's thought. His importance does not lie in a 'system,' for he has no system such as we find in St. Thomas' *Summa Theologica* or in John Calvin's *Institutes of the Christian Religion*. What we do find instead is the rational expression of a faith that brings a new perspective on all human problems. What makes Augustine so important for us and at the same time constitutes the perennial fascination of his thought is that he held together in his own mind disparate elements of thought and experience which we so often tend to pull apart. Faith and reason, for example, are today often found split into warring factions. Augustine held them together. Or again, we let ourselves become subjectivists without standards of good or truth, or rationalists who understand everything except our own experience. But in Augustine's mind personal experience and rational structure are kept in constant interplay. So also the lonely search of the individual soul for God and the discovery of the Church as the community through which God's grace becomes available are for Augustine two sides of one continuous story.

I. The Problem of Reason's Status

We shall begin with faith and reason. In our day philosophies of life seem divided into two irreconcilable camps. On one side is scientific reason with its objectivity, its faithfulness to evidence gathered through patient experiment, and its theory organized in a rational system. If we make a philosophy out of this outlook we see the world as a collection of processes whose structures can be measured mathematically and described rationally. For some, science in this strict sense marks the limit of our knowledge. But there is a widespread protest against this kind of rationalism, a protest which has found powerful voices in modern literature and art as well as philosophy. One of its manifestations is found in various kinds of existentialism, some of whose upholders deny that there are any objective rational principles of truth or value. They find no meaning in life beyond what man creates for himself. Within Christian thought such extremes are avoided; but the joining of faith and reason has often been accomplished with an uneasy sense of compromise. Which comes first, faith or reason, and what are the limits of each? These remain the difficult questions.

Now, St. Augustine takes up a quite different 'stance' with respect to this problem from that of much modern thought. For him faith and reason are never to be opposed to one another or kept apart from each other. The cardinal feature of our search for truth is that we who do the seeking are not disembodied minds but persons with feelings and wills as well as mental processes. Only when the whole person turns toward the truth does it become available to him. This means that faith in the sense of personal trust and belief is prior to understanding. 'Unless we believe we shall never understand' is the Augustinian formula.

This priority of faith does not mean that all questions are answered dogmatically before we reason about them. Rather, faith means that we lay hold upon the positive reality of our existence and our relationship to God. Once we have been turned toward this real truth, rather than some figment of disordered imagination, we are released to inquire into every question with all our rational powers. Augustine daringly champions the view that God Himself is intelligible. God is the truth, and some degree of understanding of God can be ours. Hence rational analysis of any problem is always for Augustine a step in the pilgrimage of the mind toward God. There is scarcely a question about human life he does not discuss. Do men have free will? If so why do they do evil? Is matter evil in itself, or is the cause of evil to be found in the mind or soul? In what way is God's nature analogous to human personality? The reader of Augustine finds himself caught up into the movement of thought as if he were entering into a searching conversation. Augustine proves to us by his method of teaching what he deeply believed, that the teacher does not give wisdom to the student, but lifts the student's eyes to the living Truth above them both.

As Christian philosopher Augustine insists on the importance of the arts and liberal disciplines in the education of the Christian. Through his own skills in rhetoric and logic he established a pattern of learning which became the foundation of the first universities. His conception of education is full of suggestions for us today, as a modern educator has pointed out. Dr. G. F. Leckie, following Augustine, develops the view that when we discover principles that give us a basis for organizing knowledge we can go on to give meaningful interpretation to all the diverse materials in the wide range of experience. The discovery of unifying principles is essential to freedom, for freedom in this educational context means the power to understand experience according to the basic principles of our human nature.[3]

This search for intelligibility is never finished in this life. Augustine always makes a final reservation as he leads us closer to the vision of God. God is infinite and our finite minds cannot wholly comprehend Him even when God Himself illumines our understanding. 'He whom thou comprehendest is not God' is a primary Augustinian motto. In this humility concerning the limits of reason Augustine takes up a position which is relevant to our own day. Those who resist rigid dogmatizing either of traditional faiths or of the results of science find him a liberating influence. The wise believer knows the mystery of God and distrusts all neatly packaged systems. For all Augustinians the infinite God is a continual source of freedom for new reflection.

II. Human Freedom

Augustine's attempt to understand the depth of sin in man, and yet to affirm both man's responsibility and the possibility of his redemption, was born out of his own experience. The story of his own struggle is told in his great *Confessions.* He tells of the years spent trying to extricate himself from bondage to sensuality and pride, of his relationships to his mother, his friends, and his teachers, of his breakthrough out of intellectual darkness into the sunlight of Neoplatonism, and finally his conversion to the Christian faith. It was this Augustine, the religious individual, recounting the story of his own inward combat with sin, who was rediscovered in the Renaissance period. He became the inspiration for countless mystics, philosophers, and poets, who rejoiced in a new sense of personal religious awakening. Above all, the lonely desperate seekers after God's power to lift the burden of moral guilt, those who may be called the 'wrestlers with Christ,' find St. Augustine second only to St. Paul as their companion and their guide.

Augustine is a chief defender of the doctrine that without God's help men are unable to choose good instead of evil. One of his greatest debates was carried on with the Pelagians over this issue. Later Christians who have emphasized that they can find peace only in God's forgiveness have always looked to him. St. Thomas Aquinas, in spite of his high estimate of human freedom, does not significantly qualify Augustine's conception of grace as the power which makes possible our right use of freedom. Martin Luther, it is important to recall, was a monk in the Augustinian order. He came a long way toward his even more radical doctrine of grace through his training in the thought of Augustine.

Divine grace upholds and fulfills a right use of freedom; it does not destroy freedom. This is Augustine's view. For him a right understanding of grace and freedom rests upon a true understanding of how God's spirit works. Grace is infused into human life with transforming power. If, as Reinhold Niebuhr has recently argued, Augustine does not altogether solve the problem of grace and freedom he has nevertheless set the terms of it for those who try to understand the mystery of human responsibility for good and evil.[4] In rather recent times Augustine's emphasis on man's sinfulness has seemed too pessimistic; but in our day we are seeing even more clearly that a faith which does not recognize the evil of which man is capable cannot cope with our world of concentration camps, mass slaughter, and widespread hopelessness. In a time when plays like *Death of a Salesman* and *A Streetcar Named Desire* express our estimate of the disorder in the human soul, we are ready to understand Augustine when he says that we are involved in an evil from which moral effort alone will never extricate us.

When Christian theologians today set forth with renewed vigor the faith that only through God's forgiveness can man be redeemed, they do so in a conscious dependence upon Augustine. Karl Barth, who has done so much to call theology back to the evangelical theme, refers constantly to Augustine. Much of the structure of Barth's Biblical interpretation of Christian faith stems directly from Augustinian sources.[5]

The impression should not be given that Augustine sees nothing in man but evil. Astute psychologist that he was, he had a profound insight into human development. His description of four stages in man's growth shows a striking parallel to modern psychological theories which trace development from the unconscious 'id' to spontaneous self-expression.

This same Augustine who understands the inner life is also the churchman and political theorist, the first comprehensive philosopher of history. Although Augustine once said that he cared to know nothing but God and his own soul, the search for this knowledge led him to give an account of the course of history and of the place of State and Church within that history. It became decisive for subsequent Christian thought that Augustine's Platonism, with its doctrine of God as immutable and eternal, did not for him destroy the significance of creation as the beginning of the world with its real history. For him time is real; and his view that time can be understood only as we look within our own processes of memory and anticipation is one of his distinctive contributions to modern philosophy.[6] In the Christian assertion that God has acted in a decisive and unique way in Jesus Christ at a given point in history, Augustine sees Christianity declaring a truth which Platonic philosophy can never understand.

With his vision of history as constituted by two cities, the City

9

of God and the earthly city, Augustine develops one of the supreme conceptions which molded medieval civilization and which has influenced all later philosophies of history. The earthly city is determined by self-love, whereas the City of God is constituted by the love of God. The Church on earth is the City of God in essence and intent, though it is mixed with much earthly evil. For Augustine every human community is determined by the kind of love which gives it its fundamental bond. He defines a people as 'a multitude of rational creatures associated in common agreement as to the things which it loves.' [7] Here he shows himself profounder than those political theorists who have tried to find the basis of the State in purely rational values and individualistic rights. Further, Augustine does not regard earthly communities as without value. The two cities are mingled in many ways. Men need the minimal values of justice and order that the secular State provides. At the same time Augustine has a realistic view of the degree of force and injustice that underlies every community in which self-love is uncorrected. One of the leading theologians of our day, who is also a profound political analyst, Reinhold Niebuhr, has emphasized again this realistic element in Augustine's political theory. He says that Augustine can help us to guard against the utopian illusion that the perfect society can be built by revolutionary effort or by gradual education. Niebuhr says: 'A generation which finds its communities imperiled and in decay, from the smallest and most primordial community, the family, to the largest and most recent, the potential world community, might well take counsel of St. Augustine in solving its perplexities.' [8]

Practical demonstration of Augustine's insight for the meeting of our political problems is given in Miss Hannah Arendt's study *The Origins of Totalitarianism*. While Miss Arendt refers directly to St. Augustine only once, the reference comes at a crucial point, when she is interpreting the breakdown of the human community and the dissolution of human rights. She quotes St. Augustine's dictum that only love can create the other person as one whose being I am willing to accept and to affirm. She believes we must grasp the truth Augustine saw, that man is a 'new beginning within himself,' if we are to understand what is happening to us today, and are not to put a false reliance on methods of social analysis which overlook the mystery of man and fail to comprehend the extent of his creative power both for good and for evil.[9]

III. God and the World

Augustine's influence on philosophic thought is bound up with his characteristic teaching about God and the world. The dominant theme of his philosophy is that our human knowledge of truth involves our participation in God's being itself as that is reflected in His creation. For Augustine there is no ultimate abyss between God and His creatures. He elaborates the Platonic metaphor of the participation of all earthly goods and beauties in God. Created things are images of their Author. Wherever in our culture since Augustine we find philosophers working with the idea that our minds have a direct knowledge of 'being itself' there his influence is surely present.

Augustine's thought passed into the medieval period, having been articulated by Gregory the Great in a theological and ecclesiastical system. The greatest medieval Augustinians, though by no means the only ones, were St. Anselm, with his ontological argument for the existence of God, and St. Bonaventura, who sought to organize all knowledge within the unity of the mystical vision of God. When Anselm sets out to show that if we clearly understand the idea of God as the 'greatest being' we must see that God exists, he is working with a thoroughly Augustinian conception of reason and truth. Further, he begins his argument with a version of the formula, 'I believe in order to understand.'

Descartes, who stands at the beginning of modern philosophy, developed his metaphysics in close relationship to Augustinianism. His exercise in radical doubt leading to the famous dictum, 'I think, therefore I am,' is akin to Augustine's argument against the skeptic, 'I err, therefore I am.' We cannot doubt without acknowledging the existence of truth.[10] Most modern commentators friendly to Augustine point out that Descartes' rationalism led him to discount the personalistic elements in knowledge which Augustine emphasized. Further, Descartes does not observe Augustine's cautious restraint with respect to the limits of human knowledge. Had he done so, many believe, modern philosophy might have taken a more satisfactory course.

The ontological argument has had a long history in modern philosophy since Descartes. Hegel, and other idealists in our own day, such as William E. Hocking and Charles Hartshorne, sought to reinstate it after Immanuel Kant's powerful assault. Back of all forms of the argument there lies the Augustinian faith that reason leads us directly to ultimate reality.

There is a special affinity between such idealism and some aspects of modern science, especially in mathematics and physics. As a good Platonist Augustine thought of nature as a multitude of creatures that behave according to the fundamental harmonies of number. Some of the medieval scientific schools, especially Chartres and Oxford, were saturated with Augustinian philosophy as they investigated the nature of light. While modern physics has certainly gone far beyond the ancient world view, its picture of a nature that exhibits mathematical structure and its use of mathematical hypothesis as a step in scientific method are matters which St. Augustine not only would have understood but which he helped to prepare.

Other followers of Augustine have stressed the more personalistic side of his thought. Pascal, for example, accepted the radical doctrine of man's depravity in the Jansenist movement, an extreme Augustinianism of the seventeenth century. Many of Pascal's concepts in ethics and theology are derived at least indirectly from Augustine. While Pascal is more skeptical, there remains a certain balance in his estimate of man's greatness and misery which is Augustinian in spirit. In the nineteenth century we can see in Cardinal Newman a reincarnation of Augustine's method and doctrine, both in Newman's subtle appreciation of the intertwining of faith and reason and in his social philosophy.

The question of the relation of Augustine's thought to that of St. Thomas Aquinas is extraordinarily complex. Many Roman Catholics, while recognizing the difference in perspective and materials of the Christian Platonist as compared with the Christian Aristotelian, hold that St. Thomas so delicately adjusted his Aristotelianism within the Augustinian framework that the two theologians must be said to share a genuine and unbreakable unity of outlook. Other Roman scholars like Przywara hold that these two stand for rather different types of adjustment of faith to reason.[11]

Paul Tillich, a leading Protestant theologian, finds in Augustine's assertion that our minds have direct access to God's being a solid foundation for both faith and culture. In Tillich's words: 'The ontological approach to philosophy of religion as envisaged by Augustine and his followers . . . if critically interpreted by us, is able to do for our time what it did in the past, both for religion and culture, to overcome as far as it is possible by mere thought, the fateful gap between religion and culture, thus reconciling concerns which are not strange to each other but have been estranged from each other.' [12]

This assertion that Augustine offers possibilities of reconciling positions that have been set against each other leads to a final comment. In spite of his grim doctrine of the depth of sin in man Augustine remains realistically hopeful because he believes in the reality of God's grace as the power which redeems and transforms life. Richard Niebuhr has recently used St. Augustine as a classic exponent of the faith that Christ is 'the transformer of culture.'[13] Augustine's profound reflection on the nature of love, in which he seeks a synthesis of Christian love and rightly directed human love, suggests the vision of a civilization in which Christian faith and cultural values support one another. Anders Nygren has criticized Augustine's doctrine of love because Nygren sees in such a synthesis the danger of watering down the New Testament conception of love as God's unmerited forgiveness.[14] While Nygren thus raises a basic issue for Augustinians, it is plain that Christianity must show how the love which God has revealed in Christ can become the guiding and ordering spirit for our common life. Augustine never lets go of the attempt to show that this is in some measure possible.

Those who seek reconciliation within the divided soul of man, or between divided Christian churches, or within our strife-torn society, will continually turn to St. Augustine. He does not solve every problem; but he remains after fifteen centuries one of the most alive, most richly equipped, and most penetrating of all interpreters of the Christian faith with its Gospel of healing and wholeness for mankind.

FOR FURTHER READING

M. C. D'Arcy, *et al.*, *A Monument to St. Augustine* (New York, 1930).

Roger Hazelton, *Renewing the Mind* (New York, 1949).

NOTES

1. Hannah Arendt, 'Understanding and Politics,' *The Partisan Review* (July–August 1953), p. 390.
2. *Enarrations on the Psalms,* XLI. 13. 9.; CXXXVIII. 16.
3. Introduction to his edition of Augustine, *Concerning the Teacher* (New York, 1938).
4. *The Nature and Destiny of Man* (New York, 1943), II, 134–48.
5. It is significant that Barth regards his book on Anselm as decisive for his own development. Barth's *Church Dogmatics* already contains hundreds of references to Augustine.
6. Cf. Bertrand Russell, *The History of Western Philosophy* (New York, 1945), pp. 353–5; also C. Hartshorne and W. Reese, *Philosophers Speak of God* (Chicago, 1953), pp. 85–96.
7. *City of God*, XIX. 24.
8. *Christian Realism and Political Problems* (New York, 1953), p. 146.
9. *The Origins of Totalitarianism* (New York, 1951), p. 296. Cf. her article, 'Understanding in Politics,' cited earlier, and her book, *Der Liebesbegriff bei Augustin* (Berlin, 1929).
10. Whether Descartes knew Augustine's works directly is a debated question. See Nigel Abercrombie, *St. Augustine and French Classical Thought* (Oxford, 1938), and E. Gilson, *Introduction à l'étude de Saint Augustine* (Paris, 1931).
11. E. Przywara, *Polarity* (London, 1935), esp. pp. 116ff. See Przywara's essay and others in *A Monument to St. Augustine* (New York, 1930); cf. Alan Richardson, *Christian Apologetics* (New York, 1947).
12. Paul Tillich, 'The Two Types of Philosophy of Religion,' *Union Seminary Quarterly Review,* vol. I, no. 4 (1946).
13. Richard Niebuhr, *Christ and Culture* (New York, 1951), ch. 6.
14. Anders Nygren, *Agape and Eros* (London, 1939), Part II, vol. II. Cf. Paul Ramsey, *Basic Christian Ethics* (New York, 1950) for another evaluation of Augustine's doctrine of love.

II

THE LIFE OF ST. AUGUSTINE

Roy W. Battenhouse

T HE LIFE of Augustine began on 13 November, A.D. 354 and
closed on 28 August, A.D. 430, and for these seventy-five years
his career was focused around six geographical points: Tagaste,
Madaura, Carthage, Rome, Milan, and Hippo. Yet, in any telling of his full story, the categories of chronology and geography
must yield to the more ultimate ones of crisis and homecoming.
For these latter are central to the *Confessions,* in which Augustine sees his own life in terms of the parable of the Prodigal Son.
The story begins with a 'heart restless till it find its rest' in God,
and closes with Augustine's return home to Tagaste, midway in
his journey of life, to begin anew. His almost forty years afterward as priest and bishop at Hippo have nothing to do with
globe-trotting, though much to do with exploring two mystical
cities which are spread throughout the world.

I. The *Confessions* as Biography

In Augustine's *Confessions* the reader is presented with a special kind of writing, unique in the literature of antiquity. The

life story is told in a spirit of meditation; and the meditation, in contrast to that of the classic Marcus Aurelius, is not self-centered. It seeks self-knowledge, but only where such knowledge can fairly be found, within the light of a knowledge of God. This perspective means that the categories of sin and grace emerge as necessary dimensions for understanding a man's life. It means also that, because all life is acknowledged to be under the providence of God, no event can be dismissed as entirely accidental. The vision of the biographer therefore is profoundly historical in its scrutiny of process and of significant detail, yet theological in interpretation. Augustine's method is that of radical empiricism.

Moreover, Augustine's autobiography has an integration which stems from his grasp of the meaning of time. His analysis of this concept, which occurs in Book xi of the *Confessions,* is one of his great contributions to Christian thought. Time, he points out, is not measured only by the movement of the heavenly bodies, as in Greek science; for the truer measure of past and future is to be found not in things but in the soul. The past is the soul's remembrance; the future is its expectation; and the present is its attention. Time is therefore spiritual extension: the impression which is made by things upon the soul in passing by and which remains when they have passed — 'this I measure when I measure times.' [1] We must expect Augustine's story of his own life, therefore, to focus on the dimensions of spiritual change, and on its form as extended along the memory.

When a biography is thus written it has unusual depths, but also some omissions which may disappoint the modern reader. We must remember that the work is written as a long prayer, with spiritual pilgrimage as its theme. Augustine does not give us surface details such as might help us visualize, for example, his father's business, or his own childhood companions, or the mistress he acquired at Carthage. On the other hand, his youthful participation in a pear-stealing prank with a neighborhood gang is magnified, almost as if it were the apple-stealing in Genesis, to which, indeed, it is related. For Augustine is probing, by way of his own experience, a universal logic in the human story —

much as T. S. Eliot has done in *The Family Reunion* when he focuses on events that happen 'on the under side of things.' And therefore instead of being given full naturalistic detail by which we may picture the crime, we are given just those features of action which are pertinent to an intricate analysis of the sin. In this way Augustine can reveal in his own story something of every man's story. Petrarch could exclaim after reading the *Confessions:* 'I account myself to be reading the narrative not of another man's pilgrimage but of my own.' Yet readers who are accustomed to the conventions of present-day naturalistic biography may feel ill at ease when confronted with Augustine's different, though deliberately chosen, methods.

Failure to take into account the form in which the *Confessions* is cast has misled certain critics at another point. In studying Augustine's state of mind at Cassiciacum immediately after his conversion, they are unable to reconcile the story given in the *Confessions* with the impression they get from reading the philosophical dialogues composed at Cassiciacum. Evidence of Christian language in these dialogues is scant. Yet do these not constitute our most reliable picture of the 'authentic' Augustine of the years 386–7? The contrasting tone of the *Confessions,* written just before A.D. 400, must mean that Augustine forgot some of what really happened, that he telescoped his memories, reading back into his earlier experience more Christian piety than had really been there. Such has been the contention of Harnack, Loofs, and Alfaric. Augustine was 'still living wholly in philosophical problems at Cassiciacum,' says Harnack; and he infers, as others have argued more at length, that the 'conversion' was not yet to Christianity but largely to Neoplatonism. These critics underestimate the fact that Augustine was a master of rhetoric. Surely no one knew better than he that every type of expression has its fitting style, prescribed by the approach chosen and by the nature of its intended audience. The Cassiciacum dialogues are set in a traditional form, no less proper for Augustine than for the pagan Plato or, later, the Christian Boethius. In this type the appeal throughout is to reason. Even though a Christian writer in this genre himself accepts another authority than reason, the authority of doctrine specifically Christian is not proper here, since by convention the conclusions are to be argued from the world of nature. The discussion is directed to human ears, believing and unbelieving alike. The *Confessions* presents a different picture, partly perhaps because in looking back the author has more accumulated wisdom for understanding the original events, but more importantly because he is writing now within a different set of conventions as he addresses himself to God. Thus each literary mode which Augustine uses reflects but one form, not the whole, of the author's world of experience.

In making the point, however, we must not encourage an opposite kind of misunderstanding. We must not suppose that there was no development in Augustine between Cassiciacum and the days of his episcopate. The conversion was, after all, but a kind of commencement. It brought an end to the moral torments of his divided life by turning his flight from Christ into a submission. It meant that progress in understanding could begin afresh from principles now fixed and certain. Yet the implications of those principles were not all immediately recognized; some were to be appreciated only as Augustine was challenged by the Donatist and Pelagian heresies.

The successive stages in the maturing of Augustine's Christian faith have been well delineated, I think, in Karl Adam's fine essay.[2] He observes that Augustine's concern during the period immediately after his conversion was in Christianity as the 'true philosophy,' and in faith as an aid to intellectual activity; but that after his ordination in 391 a closer study of Scripture revealed the meaning of faith as an act of the will, together with the importance of love as the deepest of all realities. In this second period, however, love was still regarded by Augustine as simply an 'infusion,' effected in the soul by God; and faith was thought of as the work of man himself, though supported by God's grace. A third period began after Augustine's elevation to the episcopate. Through closer study of Galatians and Romans he came to see love as an aspect of membership in the Mystical Body of Christ, and faith as itself the gift of God's grace to an otherwise helpless creature. We may say, then, that Augustine was a Christian from the days of his conversion, but one who was inclined to interpret his faith in a Neoplatonic fashion. His subsequent development consisted of an evolution by which his thinking was progressively freed from the limitations of the Neoplatonic categories. This is not to say, with Loofs, that Augustine's Christianity was 'simply Neo-Platonism with a Christian tint'; it is to agree rather with Gilson, who calls it more aptly 'a Christianity tinted with Neo-Platonism.'

To review Augustine's later life and thought will require our going outside and beyond the *Confessions*. But for the early years, his period of storm and stress before he reached a haven in baptism, we can not do better than to summarize, for the most part, from his *Confessions*.

II. Augustine's Boyhood

Augustine was born in Tagaste, an agricultural village in North Africa. His father, Patricius, was of the middle class — a 'poor freeman' the *Confessions* calls him — employed in the Roman administration of the village. He was a pagan in faith and in morals. His infidelities and his temper tantrums were a hardship for Monnica, his young Christian wife. Monnica bore his lapses with patience, however; and her example, we are told, was not without its winning effect. Neighbors' wives were amazed at her self-control and were instructed by her virtue; and Patricius was at last baptized, just before his death in 370. It was much later that Augustine, the son whose Christian nurture was Monnica's special anxiety, was brought through her tears and prayers to the church font at Milan.

From the beginning, however, the mother's concern for her son was by no means of an exclusively religious nature. She recognized the child's talents and was desirous of his worldly advancement. Here her hopes coincided with those of Patricius. Both parents wished to provide the boy with a good education and to delay his marriage till he might have had time to achieve some distinction in learning. They also delayed his baptism — presumably because Patricius had no interest in it, while Monnica thought it better to allow a season first for the sins of youth.[3] She was content simply to enroll the child as a catechumen.

It is pertinent to remark here that in the fourth century the custom of infant baptism was not yet widespread. A chief reason was the lack of a well-developed system of private penance for the washing away of sins after baptism; instead, the Church had a process involving public disabilities, a system ill suited to youths and strenuously avoided by most adults. It was intended to be strict to prevent the major crimes. The Church's reputation for high morality — which had been of such influence in converting the Empire — was at stake. But the system naturally discouraged baptism, since a delay both postponed the heavier moral obligations of membership and kept baptism in reserve as the one simple means of shedding past sins. We know, for example, that Constantine was baptized only on his deathbed. Thus he had helped write the creed of Nicea, and even preached, without being, strictly speaking, a member of the Church. And Augustine's contemporary, St. Ambrose, though Christian in his family background, was not baptized until after his election as bishop. The next three centuries, however, were to see an important shift in custom. As the Church faced the problem of disciplining hordes of converts from barbarism, early baptism was increasingly insisted on, for it put the newcomers immediately under Christian law and Christian nurture. At the same time, to supplement baptism the practice of private and regular penance, even for the minor sins, was encouraged by popularizing certain handbooks of penance, first developed in the monasteries of Ireland. As this system of penance relieved baptism of some of its customary importance, baptism could be directed more conspicuously to cleansing the sin which Augustine's theology had shown as man's most truly troublesome one, namely, Original Sin. For further comment about Augustine's contribution on this point, the reader is referred to Chapter VIII.

When Augustine was about eleven, he was sent off to Madaura. He was ready for advanced studies; and Madaura, twenty miles to the south of Tagaste, had excellent schools. The pagan poet

Apuleius had flourished there two centuries earlier, and the town
had continued to be renowned for its literary culture. At Madaura the young Augustine acquired a groundwork for his extensive knowledge of the classical poets and orators. Though he
never mastered Greek, he became increasingly skillful in Latin
grammar and its niceties of construction. He remained in Madaura until his sixteenth year, which he had to spend at home for
lack of funds. After a year of idleness he was off to school once
again, this time to the metropolis of Carthage, aided by money
provided by Romanianus, a wealthy townsman of Tagaste. Great
things henceforth were expected of the brilliant youth, and he
did not disappoint his sponsors. He was soon, we are told, 'chief
in the rhetoric school' at Carthage.

Such are the material facts of Augustine's early years. But the
story as told in the *Confessions* probes deeper, exploring an inner
history which he came to know only later by reflection in the light
of faith.[4] Attention is focused on his restlessness of heart. The
young Augustine, we are told, needed God but did not know it.
Homeless as regards fellowship with God, he was not able to feel
quite at home in the world of things. Failing to see things as
having their being and beauty from God, he went 'plunging amid
those fair forms.' He tasted them and continued to hunger,
touched them and went on burning for peace. Surrounded and
supported by good things, he did not know how to take them,
because he did not know what to will, except as his own will, a
deformed will, urged him.

Examples, some of them inferences from later observation, are
adduced to substantiate this reading of his secret life. As an infant — so Augustine surmises — he flung himself about at ran-
dom in the effort to get his will obeyed, and avenged himself with
tears when that will was thwarted. As a boy, he learned to talk
from his elders, but not so much out of obedience to their teaching as out of a desire to express his private will. Yes, he learned to
say prayers; but were the fetters of his tongue to be loosed for
this, that he might pray to escape at school the beatings his idleness deserved? The mockery of such learning! And why did he
hate such truly useful studies as reading, writing, and arith-

metic? Why did he dote, instead, on the empty fictions of the Latin poets? 'O thou torrent of human custom . . . How long roll the sons of Eve in that huge and hideous ocean?'

The ways of youthful beguilement, he notes, are made easier by the applause given them by one's elders. It was to win their approbation that he neglected the reading of God's Scripture and studied instead the arts of declamation. Furthermore, if he neglected honesty, it was because by committing petty thefts he found he could win favor with his schoolmates. Thus, for the sake of others' praise, he became shameless. 'Behold,' says Augustine, 'with what companions I walked the streets of Babylon and wallowed in its mire.' 'I was torn piecemeal,' and 'I lost myself among a multiplicity of things.' Yet during this time Patricius did nothing to check his son, caring little how chaste the boy was so long as he was making progress in the arts of speech.

We come then to the famed episode of the pear-stealing. Augustine uses it as a climax to illustrate the extent of his youthful iniquity. The significance of the escapade lies in the fact that he engaged in it out of sheer sport in the theft. He was neither hungry for the pears nor interested in selling them for money. Indeed, he flung away the pears uneaten, caring to taste no sweetness except that of the sin itself. He loved the deed exactly because it was forbidden. In the name of liberty he was glorying in wanton destruction. The act was significant, he tells us, as illustrating the perverse way in which we strive to imitate God's omnipotence at the very moment when we are fleeing from Him. We thus 'mimic a maimed liberty,' obtain a shadow, and make of life a 'depth of death.'

No reader can afford to take lightly such an analysis. It is what makes the biography great, because it illuminates both its subject and ourselves. The last words of this chapter — 'and I became to myself a barren land' — have furnished T. S. Eliot the title for *The Waste Land*. Eliot's apocalyptic poem on modern life grows toward a climax in the lines:

> *To Carthage then I came*
> *Burning burning burning burning* . . .

The allusion is to Augustine's experience as described in the opening words of Book III of the *Confessions*. But the words are also — and so Eliot intends them — a true confession of modern love.

III. Life at Carthage

Augustine found Carthage a sumptuous city, gorgeous and dissipated. This was the city, was it not, where Dido had made love and inspired poetry? Love and poetry were what he, too, most craved. 'There sang all around me in my ears,' he tells us, 'a cauldron of unholy loves. I was not yet in love, but I loved the idea of love.' Before long he had found the actual taste of it and acquired a mistress. By his eighteenth year she had borne him a son, whom he named Adeodatus, 'Given of God,' a pious name in any case. At the same time Augustine's hunger for poetry was drawing him frequently to the theater. There his emotions were engrossed by the imaginary joys and sorrows of stage lovers. He tells us that, sighing after their fictitious felicities and groaning with their pictured griefs, he was wholly uncritical of the wickedness of their behavior.

Augustine's judgment of what today we might call the 'sin of the theater' is interesting. He would have agreed with those critics who feel that an obsession for movies on the part of the young can be demoralizing, not, however, because he ever came to regard art as in itself wicked but because bad art can become a substitute for life. The shadows of the screen sometimes surround us with a false world of illusion, in which we lose sight of reality. The colorful world of stage events can drug like daydreams. The drama of Carthage, Augustine says, instead of purging his emotions merely irritated them, like the scratching of a wound; it stimulated to no purpose, draining off his native capacity for emotion into barren sands of inactivity.[5]

The young Augustine, fortunately, was delivered from the Carthage theater by discovering philosophy. In the midst of his prison of shadows, there shone on his mind suddenly a gleam of truth. This happened in his nineteenth year. He was reading along in Cicero's *Hortensius* (a book now lost), with an eye to observing the techniques of the master's eloquence, when in a flash his eyes were opened to the beauty of Cicero's ideas. It was a stirring experience, a crisis in Augustine's career. The 'burning' with which he had come to Carthage was now in part transmuted; there arose what John Donne would have called a 'hydroptic immoderate desire' for wisdom. As in Donne's case it involved exchanging the tumult of the senses for the ecstasy of thought. Augustine describes himself as yearning to embrace Truth, 'not this or that sect, but wisdom itself whatever it were' — here, too, voicing a cry like that of the celebrated Dean of St. Paul's.

Other eyes may see here the start of Augustine's movement toward the Catholic faith. Yet the kind of catholicity to which Augustine now began to be drawn was the psuedo-catholicity of the Manichees. He by-passed the Christian Scriptures, thinking them forbidding and unintelligible. The books of the Manichees, by contrast, seemed to offer a cosmopolitan and rational piety purified of superstition. The Manichees boasted of being able to harmonize the principles of natural science with 'the essence' of Christ's teaching. This pleased Augustine, for his mother's words had implanted in him a kind of natural affection for the name Christ. Indeed, the fact that Cicero nowhere invoked Christ's name had even dampened his enthusiasm for Cicero. But the young scholar was equally delighted with another claim of the Manichees, namely, that their truth could be proved without invoking the terrors of authority. Christ as handled critically by the Manichees seemed much more acceptable than the Christ proclaimed dogmatically by the Catholics.

In particular, Augustine was ensnared by the Manichean methods of higher criticism of the Old Testament. This great collection of books, they declared, had been corrupted and needed to be refined. Its crudities were manifest: for 'is God bounded by a bodily shape, and has [He] hairs and nails?' And how can one believe that the bigamies of the patriarchs were righteous? Or the suicide of Samson? Or the spoiling of the Egyptians by the departing Israelites? Questions of this sort, seemingly so perspicacious, fascinated Augustine. They provided him easy victories in de-

24

bates with unskillful Christians. Actually, had Augustine but known it, such cavils were nothing but the stock-in-trade of all the more clever critics of Christianity since Marcion, Celsus, Porphyry, and Julian the Apostate. Effective answers may be found in the writings of Irenaeus and Origen. But Augustine, of course, had not yet read the Church Fathers. He eagerly fed on the Manichean 'empty husks' and thus like the prodigal was 'brought down to the depths of hell.'

As Augustine remarks with irony, a chief reason for his impiety lay in his 'piety.' Because he wanted so much to believe in a 'good' God completely dissociated from evil, he accepted the Manichean notion of evil as an independent principle; he therefore 'conceived two masses contrary to one another, both unbounded.' It seemed to him 'very unseemly' for God to have the shape of human flesh. How much more proper was the Manichean understanding of God as a mass of lucid substance extended in space like a great sea. How much more reverent to believe Him bounded only on one side, that side where the mass of evil lay, than to believe Him bounded on all sides by the form of a human body. The real difficulty, we can see, arose from Augustine's inability to think of God in incorporeal terms.

Moreover, Manichean dualism offered the young intellectual a soothing explanation for his own sense of moral frustration. He knew himself to be self-divided, torn between a love of philosophy and an equally intense love of popular fame; between aspirations after purity and the strong tug of the passions of the flesh. Manicheism accounted for this tension by its theory of two eternally warring principles. It assured him that the contraries within him were not his responsibility. They were fated and he need feel no guilt about them; he needed only to observe them.

But while the Manichean faith thus flattered Augustine's reason and drugged his conscience, it offered no remedy for his restlessness. It merely kept him floundering for nine long years, as he laments in his *Confessions,* 'deceived and deceiving, in divers lusts; openly, by sciences they call liberal; secretly, with a false-named religion.' Lured by a hope of piercing to the hidden secrets of fate, Augustine even stubbornly courted for a considerable time certain fortunetellers and stargazers. But meanwhile, he confesses, he dared not gaze within on himself. He tells us very little about his teaching career during this period — he taught a year in Tagaste, and then for eight years in Carthage — except that at Carthage he won a poetry prize, and that (around A.D. 380) he published his first treatise, *On the Fair and the Fit.* What we are told, mostly, is that he was inwardly miserable. 'My error was my God,' is his theme. 'Whither should I flee from myself?'

At Tagaste the sudden death of a dear friend and companion had first exposed to Augustine his real wretchedness. The fellowship of this friend had become Augustine's chief happiness, the very life of his soul. Could death, now, so rob life as to leave man nothing at all? Ignorant as Augustine was of the fellowship of God, he found himself utterly desolate. And the fables of the Manichees were no comfort. They did nothing to teach him what he afterward learned from Christianity, that human souls, like all other forms of created beauty, must be loved in God, since in themselves they are mutable. A merely mutable good was claiming Augustine's whole heart. His soul was bound by love to beauty's self, not beauty's Giver. In a vain effort to understand beauty's meaning, he wrote his *On the Fair and the Fit,* ambitiously dedicating it to Hierius, a famous orator in Rome. But while thus writing on beauty, he felt his life to be increasingly ugly and hateful. He despaired, torn by this paradox, and found only in tears, he says, a little refreshment. Meanwhile his mother, too, was in tears — over his heresies. Discovering them during his year of teaching at Tagaste, she had for a time forbidden him to live under her roof. The poet Francis Thompson has pictured Monnica at this time:

> *At the cross thy station keeping*
> *With the mournful Mother weeping*
> *Thou, unto the sinless Son,*
> *Weepest for thy sinful one.*

Prayer and study finally broke the bonds of Augustine's captivity to the Manichees. 'But let him alone awhile,' the bishop had said to the despairing Monnica; 'only pray for him, he will himself by reading find out what that error is.' The bishop, who had himself formerly been a Manichee, was right in this prediction. The more Augustine read in the standard works of academic learning, the more he began to doubt the fables of his co-religionists. The Manichees prided themselves on their knowledge of the heavens and of the curious ways of the planets; but on these very matters Augustine found contrary calculations — and, by his own observation, more accurate ones — in the books of other writers. What if the Manichees should be proved wrong in these matters of natural science? Could one then trust their authority in deeper matters?

When Augustine put these questions to his companions in the cult they could not answer but were sure that their leader Faustus could. Augustine then looked forward most anxiously to the promised visit of this great man. Faustus came finally, but alas did not clarify the troublesome issues. He shrank, rather, from the burden of attacking what he regarded as matters too intricate. His modesty, to be sure, was winsome but his ignorance was distressing. Augustine's zeal was effectively blunted.

IV. Rome and Milan

It was now time for a change. Disappointed in Manicheism, Augustine was also by this time weary of putting up with the classroom rowdyism of his Carthage pupils. In Rome, so it was reported to him, students were better behaved. So he set sail for Rome, secretly in the middle of the night, while Monnica was on her knees by the shore, praying God to keep her son from leaving her. The prayer, as Augustine remarks, was to be answered in a deeper sense than she intended — 'Thou regardest not what she then asked, that Thou mightest make me what she ever asked.' The mother, frantic next day with sorrow, 'knew not how great joy Thou wert about to work for her out of my absence.' By this comment Augustine foreshadows the final turn of his flight.

Soon after arriving at Rome, Augustine fell ill. During the illness he was lodged with a Manichean friend, and true to Manichean principles never considered baptism. 'Though in such danger,' says Augustine, 'I did not then want to be baptized; alas, how much better I was when I was ill as a boy, for then I begged for baptism.'

While keeping up friendship with the Manichees in Rome, Augustine began after his recovery to favor the opinions of the New Academy. These contemporary skeptics seemed to him wiser, in that they pretended to less. Truth, so they were reported as teaching, can never be surely known by man. Man must be content to be a searcher rather than a finder, with probability as his only guide. It is unlikely that Augustine ever fully accepted this position. One restraining factor was his natural reluctance to give up belief in God, which he retained from his mother's teaching. Yet he tells us in his *Against the Academics,* written a few years later, that for a time he yielded to 'probability,' until he came to see that a man can be in error not only by following the wrong path but also by 'not following the right one.' [6] He formulated also, later, a philosophic argument in refutation of ultimate skepticism: 'It is beyond question that I exist, and that I know that existence. In these truths there is nothing to fear from the argument of the Academics: what if you are mistaken? Even if I am mistaken, I am. One who does not exist cannot possibly be mistaken.' [7] Meanwhile, however, during the brief stay in Rome of which we are speaking, skepticism helped emancipate Augustine from the empty dogmatisms of Manichean doctrine.

Presently we find him in Milan, where other intellectual currents complete the liberation. The circumstances of this move to Milan are interesting. Augustine had found his pupils at Rome very unsatisfactory. Though they paid attention better than those in Carthage had, they were careless about paying their fees. Now Milan at this time was seeking a teacher of rhetoric to be paid at public expense, so Augustine made application through his Manichean friends for recommendation by Symmachus, the prefect of Rome; and he was appointed to the post. The transaction was to prove delightfully ironic, for at Milan Augustine was to meet Ambrose — the one man who at this very time was thwarting the attempts of Symmachus to revive paganism at Rome by restoring to its Senate house the altar of Victory; the one man, also, whose speech was both eloquent enough to attract the pagan Augustine and learned enough to be able to free him from the figments of the Manichees.

In A.D. 384, when Augustine arrived at Milan, Ambrose had been bishop for ten years. He had just completed writing a treatise on the Incarnation, a topic most scandalous to Manichees. Moreover, his courage in public affairs stood out in noble contrast to Augustine's vacillation. Augustine had not even stood up against unruly boys but had fled from them. Nor had he the honesty to come to terms with his own mother, having in one instance deceived her in order to steal off by night. But here in Ambrose was a man of forthright resolution, not sicklied with the pale cast of thought.

The young teacher of rhetoric visited Ambrose's church to study the bishop's renowned elocution — and came away having heard The Word. To begin with, what impressed Augustine most as he listened was the reasonable way in which he heard explained the two matters he had thought most obnoxious in Christianity: the authority of the Church, and the divine inspiration of the Old Testament. These had been the very target of Manichean barbs; and now he saw how far those barbs had miscarried. God does not expect us, so Ambrose taught, to submit our faith to Him without reason, but the very limits of reason make faith a necessity; the Church therefore testifies to certain things which have not been demonstrated by reason but which nevertheless show themselves credible in experience. Thus authority does not supplant reason but precedes it and supplements it. And second, as for the supposed absurdities of the Old Testament, Augustine found to his chagrin that they were due simply to the narrow literalism of his own reading. When Ambrose expounded the texts there was nothing at all censurable. Plainly the Church had never taught those things which the Manichees made such sport of. 'I blushed,' says Augustine, 'at having so many years barked not against the Catholic faith, but against the fictions of carnal imaginations.'

Two barriers, however, still hindered Augustine's conversion, one philosophic and the other moral. The first had to do with his conception of God. He could not think of God in other than corporeal terms, for he could not imagine a spiritual substance. The second had to do with the beguilements of worldly living. To quote the words of his later confession, he 'panted after honours, gains, marriage.' Though he regarded the Church now with open sympathy and respect, he required to have his mind enlightened and his heart disburdened.

The intellectual difficulty was resolved by Augustine's discovery of Neoplatonism. Victorinus, the late professor of rhetoric at Rome, had translated into Latin some books of Plotinus. As Augustine read these he began for the first time to understand how deity can be infinite and yet not diffused through finite or infinite space. God could be beyond all space and time, and above all corporeal being as a transcendent source. The Platonists had, moreover, a convincing alternative to Manichean dualism. Evil, they taught, was no substance at all but simply a defection in substance. Evil had no being whatever apart from good, for all things are good in so far as they exist. What constituted evil was the imperfection in their existence, the corruption of their goodness. Starting from this premise, Augustine then inquired of his own experience 'what iniquity was, and found it to be no substance, but the perversion of the will, turned aside' from God.

While Augustine was studying Plotinus he was also reading the Holy Scriptures. As he compared the two he was much excited by the measure of congruence he seemed to discern. Plotinus had a doctrine of the logos which, so far as it went, appeared to coincide with that of St. John in the prologue to his Gospel. In both accounts the creative Word was understood as in no sense material but rather the transcendental author of all things of flesh and blood. Only the doctrine of the Incarnation of the logos was lacking in Plotinus — and also the mystery of the Cross. Later Augustine was to realize how very important these two omissions can be; at the moment, however, they seemed irrelevant. He was wholly absorbed in rereading St. Paul and discovering how many of the Apostle's supposed contradictions vanished when read along with the books of the Platonists.

Augustine benefited not only from the reasoning of the Platonists but even more from their method. He learned to use 'the eye of the soul,' to look within and study his own experience as an avenue to truth. Introspection became henceforth his most characteristic mode of philosophic inquiry. It may be remarked, however, that this Platonic approach to the facts of Christian revelation involved Augustine in certain limitations. The Christianity that with its help he laid hold of was somewhat partial, being more a matter of understanding Christ-the-Truth than of imitating Christ-the-Way. The Vicarious Redeemer of Christian story was neglected for an absorbing interest in the Exemplary Teacher.

V. The Struggle for Conversion

Meanwhile the moral hurdle was proving for Augustine much harder to surmount than the intellectual. It must not be forgotten that Augustine was a man of sensuous temperament and emotional warmth. He had worldly ambitions, moreover, in which even his mother encouraged him. If she persuaded him now at this time to put away his mistress, it was because she had found a young girl of better social station, to whom it would be advantageous to have him married. Still, Augustine could not endure the two years' wait for this bride, and therefore took another concubine. 'I thought it should be too miserable,' he says, 'unless folded in female arms.' He intended, he tells us elsewhere, to cast himself ultimately 'into the bosom of true wisdom' — but not until he had obtained his hopes of marriage and honors.

The company of his pagan friends, the intelligentsia of Milan, also had a strong hold on him. For a time he toyed with the idea of establishing, with some ten of them, a kind of pantisocracy, much like that of Coleridge's dream many years later. He and his friends were to retire from the bustle of the world and devote themselves to philosophy, living as one household and sharing all goods — particularly the goods of the wealthy Romanianus. Inevitably, the plan fell to pieces when the men began to consult their wives or prospective wives. The collapse of the project highlighted for Augustine the nature of his dilemma. How was he to give himself to his love of wisdom and to his love of woman, too? The tugs seemed to pull in opposite directions, and the tension was increasing steadily.

Here Augustine's Platonism was more a hindrance than a help. As Karl Adam has pointed out, it merely aggravated Augustine's moral difficulty, making his conversion a severer trial than it need have been. For the *Enneads* of Plotinus foster an exaggerated spiritualism; they put too sharp an antagonism between the life of the intellect and that of the body. Plotinus is overeager for the destruction of the sensible world, rather than its transformation. Augustine's outlook in the year 386 was biased by this spirit: it was a matter of conscience for him to renounce every form of woman's love, and hence the marriage his mother suggested seemed to him a compromise with moral duty. Purity as he conceived it required a trampling down of his sensuous nature. As he sought to achieve such a victory there arose a fierce conflict within him, which paralyzed his soul.

In this extremity rational arguments ceased to be of aid. Augustine was being tossed and tormented by two wills, one self-indulgent, the other severely ascetic. What he needed most was the inspiration of Christian example to win and strengthen the nobler of his two wills. Fortunately, such example was close at hand. Monnica, by her faithful attendance at Mass, her constant prayers for her son, and above all her serenity of heart, provided Augustine both a rebuke and a challenge. Bishop Ambrose, too, as we have already remarked, must have had a strong appeal, for his character displayed superbly that unity of will and imagination Augustine lacked. In the Lenten season of 386, Augustine saw Ambrose encounter opposition from no less a personage than the Empress Justina. When the Empress demanded one of the Christian basilicas for the use of her Arian faction, Ambrose refused, preached fearlessly, and shepherded his people wisely — even turning poet to compose hymns for their spiritual support. His victory demonstrated the hidden resources of Christian power. Though Augustine had, naturally, little opportunity to discuss his own difficulties with so busy a bishop, yet an assistant, the venerable Simplicianus, was easily available and seemed by his saintly character to promise sympathetic counsel. Simplicianus had been sent to Milan by the Pope at the time of Ambrose's elevation to serve Ambrose as guide and instructor. Might he not also have a wise word for Augustine? So Augustine went to him, and found in him a skilled confessor, whose artful instruction makes up one of the most winning chapters of the *Confessions*.

At this time Augustine was exploring concurrently Christian faith and Platonic philosophy. Simplicianus, it so happened, was also an admirer of the Platonists. But wisely he did not engage Augustine in a discussion of the relative merits of Plotinus and Christ, for he sensed that the visitor's difficulties were not primarily intellectual. When Augustine mentioned Victorinus, Simplicianus had his cue: he had known while at Rome the famous professor of rhetoric, had witnessed the man's conversion, and could tell the story. He recounted how Victorinus, hesitating to abandon his pagan friends, yet drawn by the Christian Scriptures, had often remarked privately to him, 'Understand I am already a Christian'; to which statement Simplicianus had replied each time, 'I will not believe it, nor will I rank you among Christians, unless I see you in the Church of Christ.' Then one day Victorinus came to announce his decision and to make an open profession. In the sight of all he stood up boldly, reciting in meekness the Apostles' Creed! At that moment, how the Christian congregation rejoiced, and with what rapture they whispered his name! As Simplicianus related all this, Augustine's heart was set on fire. The similarity to his own case was unmistakable.

Yet how difficult it was to gain strength enough for a decision. Augustine describes his situation in a passage of remarkable analysis:

[For an opportunity like that of Victorinus] I was sighing, bound as I was, not with another's irons, but by my own iron will. My will the enemy held, and thence had made a chain for me, and bound me. For of a froward will was a lust made; and a lust served, became custom; and custom not resisted, became necessity. By which links, as it were, joined together (whence I called it a chain) a hard bondage held me enthralled.[8]

Or again, Augustine speaks of himself at that time as a man in sleep, who hearing the call to rise is able to answer only with the drowsy words 'anon' and 'tomorrow.' He knew what he wanted, but he had not the strength to will it. His longing heart seemed imprisoned. Made captive by his old affections, he needed the intervention of grace to release him.

Help came by chance from Pontitianus, a fellow countryman of Augustine's, who introduced him to Christian monasticism. Augustine apparently had never heard of the monks. This is not particularly surprising, for although their communities had been flourishing for more than a century in Egypt, they were still quite a novelty in Italy. When Athanasius had brought two hermits to Rome at the time of his exile from Alexandria in the year 340, their appearance had created some stir but no following. Only very recently, since the monk Jerome's return to Rome in 382 from the Syrian desert, had the ascetic ideal received public notice and a few disciples. Jerome had won a number of the capital city's pleasure-weary aristocracy, including the Lady Paula and her daughters. But unfortunately one of the daughters presently took sick and died, and the pagan population, blaming the rigors of fasting, ran Jerome out of town — that is, their scandal-venomed tongues persuaded him to depart, shaking the dust of 'Babylon' from his feet. Jerome then settled as a monk at Bethlehem. Meanwhile, in Cappadocia, St. Basil was drawing up a Rule and giving monasticism its first real organization outside Egypt.

At Milan the monastic ideal was being championed by Ambrose and practiced by his sister, a professed nun. Ambrose had written some treatises in defense of virginity and, in addition, was sponsoring a small community of monks just outside the city. But Augustine knew nothing of them until Pontitianus informed him, describing with awe their holy ways. Pontitianus added also, as chief object of wonder, the story of a recently deceased Egyptian hermit, St. Anthony. A book telling St. Anthony's story, he related, had been chanced on by two courtier friends and had brought about their conversion. Though high in the imperial service, these men had renounced their positions in favor of a monastic cottage. Moreover, they had done this though young and affianced to brides.

To Augustine such words were like an arrow at the heart. Here were heroes who rejoiced in making the very resignation he so much feared. While Pontitianus was speaking, says Augustine, God was 'turning me round toward myself, taking me from behind my back, where I had placed me, unwilling to observe myself; and setting me before my face.' The revelation was dismaying. Augustine was most vividly conscious now of how foul his past life had been. He recalled with shame his youthful prayer, 'Give me chastity and continency, only not yet.' He lashed his soul with scourges of condemnation. Yet he found in himself still two minds; his will was divided, and he could not command it. In a fever of longing he strained forward to attain to newness of life. Beckoning him on was the chaste figure of Continency, 'her holy hands full of multitudes of good examples.' Holding him back were his habitual 'mistresses,' plucking at the fleshly garment and whispering in his ear.

The tumult in his breast had hurried him from the house into a garden. There under a fig tree he now cast himself down, weeping. Then a voice, as if a child's from a neighboring house, was heard chanting over and over again: '*Tolle lege,*' 'Take up and read.' The words were not, Augustine reflected, those of any child's game; they must be God's. For had not God, in just such a manner, converted St. Anthony, directing him to the Scriptures, where an oracle awaited him? Augustine hastened to his Bible. It fell open for him at Romans 13:13: 'Not in rioting and drunkenness, not in chambering and wantonness, not in strife and envying: but put ye on the Lord Jesus Christ, and make not provision for the flesh, to fulfil its lusts.' As Augustine read this text, a light as it were of serenity infused his heart; all doubt vanished.

VI. Retirement for Study

The conversion was final, but its implications were developed gradually. Nothing was done in haste. Monnica, of course, was immediately told the news; and close friends were let in on the secret that Augustine was enrolling among those preparing for baptism. But he resigned from his teaching post only after first finishing the school term and then going through the late summer vacation. The following Easter, when the baptism would take place, was many months away. He desired to devote the intervening period to quiet conversation with a few associates and with God. For this purpose, Verecundus, a friend, lent his villa at Cassiciacum, about fifty miles from Milan. There Augustine passed the time in reading from the Psalms and (since no convert easily abandons his old tools) in explaining to companions the poetry of Vergil and engaging them in philosophic discussions. The party included Monnica, Adeodatus, and Navigius, Augustine's brother, in addition to a few pupils and friends.

On certain occasions, when a formal problem was being discussed, a writer of shorthand took down the conversation of the group. The result, when polished by Augustine's revision, was a series of dialogues modeled after the Tusculan Disputations of Cicero. First to be produced was the dialogue, *Against the Academics,* a refutation of skepticism. Next came *On the Happy Life,* setting forth Augustine's view that happiness is to be found only in wisdom, which is available only in God. Discussion of this topic took place in mid-November as a way of celebrating Augustine's thirty-third birthday. A third dialogue, *On Order,* is an effort to vindicate Divine Providence from a responsibility for evil. Along the way it records Augustine's conviction that God and the human soul are the two ultimate themes for human reflection, the two realities which man must seek to know. This same concern is repeated in the *Soliloquies,* where a long prayer to God prefaces an interior dialogue between Augustine and his Reason. The self-examination occupies two books, breaking off unfinished. It is interesting that the first translation of this work into English was by King Alfred the Great, his translation including much commentary of his own.

Because of the largely philosophic character of these literary productions of the Cassiciacum period, various critics have called in question the genuineness of Augustine's conversion. We have already touched on reasons for seeing in his thought a continuing Platonism, and they will be examined in later chapters of our book. But there is little warrant, I think, for doubting the genuineness of a new center of reference. Augustine was henceforth seeking to appreciate with his understanding certain aspects of truth which faith was beginning to make available to him.[9] He was resolved, he tells us in the *Soliloquies,* never to depart from the authority of Christ; but at the same time he was following out 'an unbounded desire to apprehend truth not only by believing it but by understanding it.' He adds, it is true, that he is confident of finding among the Platonists 'what is not opposed to the teaching of our religion.' But might not many a Christian philosopher say the same?

Two other treatises were begun in this period but finished later in Africa, *On the Immortality of the Soul* and *On Music.* They were interrupted by Augustine's baptism — along with that of his son Adeodatus and of his friend Alypius — by Ambrose at Easter, 387, and by the resolution then made to return with Monnica to Africa.

The mother was anxious to get home to her native land; and her son, with a few like-minded friends, thought to establish there a retreat for ascetic devotion and Christian study. The journey was begun. But at Rome's seaport, Ostia, while they waited for a boat, Monnica took a fever and after nine days died, in her fifty-sixth year. Her death was one of singularly happy contentment. She had remarked to her son, scarcely five days before, that the world held no further delight for her now that her hopes of his becoming a Christian had been accomplished. The conversation of mother and son on that occasion makes one of the most memorable passages in the *Confessions.* Standing by a window looking out on the garden, they viewed earth's beauties as the handiwork of God, and in their contemplation they were lifted above all things of sense to the fountain of life — to 'that region of never-failing plenty where *Thou feedest Israel* for ever with the food of truth, and where life is the *Wisdom by whom all things are made*.' When Monnica died, it seemed unfitting to weep. Instead, Evodius sang a Psalm, and Augustine gave a discourse; and without tears they carried her corpse to the grave. Two years later, at Tagaste, the gifted young Adeodatus also died.

But before going on to North Africa, Augustine returned to Rome for more than a year. Here he encountered his former co-religionists, the Manichees. For their benefit, and perhaps to allay embarrassment, he wrote two books: *On the Morals of the Manichees* and *On the Morals of the Catholic Church*. These treatises are not merely a refutation of Manichean doctrine, folly, and immorality; they constitute also a vigorous apology for the authority of Holy Scripture, and for the superiority of the Christian way of life. The soul rightly seeks virtue, Augustine now tells the Manichees, not in itself, where it is not, but in God — 'in following after whom we love well, and in reaching whom we love both well and happily.' Moreover, since he now regards virtue as 'nothing else than perfect love of God,' he offers a Christian redefinition of the four classical virtues in terms of 'four forms of love.' [10]

By the end of the year 388 Augustine had returned to Tagaste, his birthplace. Gathered about him were a few associates, sharing with him a communal life, presumably on Augustine's patrimony. The days were spent in study, particularly of the Scriptures, and in writing. To former associates, such as Nebridius, Augustine addressed long letters answering inquiries on speculative points. He was eager to convert the companions he had once misled. For the benefit of his patron Romanianus, whom he had formerly converted to Manicheism, he now wrote an antidote, *On True Religion*. In it he insisted on the vanity of trying to find 'the whole truth' outside the Christian Church; and he urged the appropriateness of the Christian doctrines of the Trinity and the Incarnation. He defended Church authority as being not in conflict with reason but necessary because reason is slow. Faith must be prior in time, though not in nobility. The writing of *On Genesis: Against the Manichees* also dates from this period. During almost three years of monastic seclusion at Tagaste, Augustine was testing out the reasonableness of his faith.

VII. From Monk to Bishop

In 391 Augustine happened to make a trip to Hippo Regius. His purpose was to visit a friend who seemed by his inquiries to be a likely candidate for the monastery at Tagaste. Augustine's one hope at this time was to go on spending his years in monastic society. Because he shrank from the responsibilities of the priesthood, he had heretofore been cautious to avoid all occasions that might precipitate him, like Ambrose, into a position involving pastoral duties. But at Hippo for a moment his vigilance relaxed. With his friend he attended church, thinking himself safe enough, since there was already a bishop in charge. Unfortunately for Augustine's hopes the bishop, Valerius, recognized his visitor and also the unusual opportunity thus presented him of providing himself with an assistant. Valerius took for his sermon the need for a priest in the parish and invited the people to search about them for a candidate. The people, knowing Augustine's reputation, at once seized him and thrust him forward. There seemed to be no escape, so Augustine yielded.

It had not been customary in Africa for a presbyter to preach in a church where the bishop resided. But Valerius suspended the rule. He himself was a Greek who could not speak easily in Latin and apparently knew no Punic; a trained orator such as Augustine, fluent in Latin and acquainted with Punic, could help greatly. So while Valerius allowed Augustine to found a monastery near the church, giving him a garden for the purpose, he also insisted that he preach. The new priest's sermons attracted attention. By October of 393, when there was a Synod at Hippo under the presidency of Archbishop Aurelius of Carthage, the bishops asked to have Augustine deliver the sermon. He took as his subject, *On Faith and the Creed,* a brief survey of Christian doctrine.

In his monastery Augustine set up a school for training the

secular clergy. He also set up a writing desk for himself. From that desk were to come within the next five years various works, including pieces against the Manichees and against the Donatists. *On the Profit of Believing,* in 392, was aimed at the first of these groups, being addressed to Honoratus, a friend whom Augustine had led into Manicheism and now longed to recover. Indirectly it served also to counteract the persuasive teaching of a certain Fortunatus, Manichean priest at Hippo. Presently, Augustine was petitioned to engage in public debate with Fortunatus. On the second day of the debate Fortunatus was brought to admit his ignorance, and soon thereafter disappeared from Hippo for good. The Donatists could not be so easily harried, since in Hippo, as in most parts of Africa, they outnumbered the Catholics. But at least Catholic faith could be safeguarded. For this purpose Augustine composed in 393 an *ABC Ballad against the Donatist Party,* which reviewed their history and errors in verses to be sung. He encouraged his parish congregation to memorize this ballad as an extension of their catechism.

Though controversy with the Pelagians came twenty years later, there are foreshadowings of it even in this period. On a visit to Carthage he was asked his opinion on certain discussions then current regarding the Epistle to the Romans. As an answer he wrote, when he got home in 394, three brief treatises. They are of interest as setting forth a view of divine predestination which the semi-Pelagians were later to seize on and force Augustine to reconsider. For in these treatises the interpretation is made that the first steps in faith proceed from ourselves. Not without divine grace, of course — this is the qualification Augustine adds later when called to account for his earlier statement.

Meanwhile, the priesthood brought for Augustine many responsibilities other than doctrinal. Merely as one example, we may mention here his concern, as early as 392, in the reformation of a popular Church custom, feastings held at the chapels of martyrs. These 'jollifications' in honor of the saints had become occasions for excess in eating and drinking. Augustine followed Ambrose in preaching against them. More than that, he made his preaching effective both by having such frolics prohibited by the acts of Church councils and by engaging the people in the substitute activity of psalm singing.

By 395 the watchful Valerius, growing old, was also growing alarmed lest Hippo lose its prize possession. Other sees were angling to get Augustine as their bishop. Valerius determined to forestall them. He wrote to Aurelius, the Archbishop of Carthage, suggesting that Augustine be consecrated a coadjutor bishop of the see at Hippo. The plan was approved, and it was done. Why, it may be asked, did no one point out that the act was in violation of Canon VIII of the Council of Nicea, which forbids 'two bishops in one city'? Probably because no one in Africa at the time knew of this Canon. Augustine, we know, was hesitant to allow the procedure, since it was unusual; but he submitted when precedents were quoted to him. He was persuaded also 'through the love of Valerius and the importunity of the people.' As it happened, Valerius died within a year of the consecration, leaving Augustine sole bishop. He was now unalterably fixed at Hippo for the rest of his life, for the African church had a rule strictly forbidding the translation of bishops.

Augustine made little Hippo famous. In the thirty-five years of his episcopate he became the Western Church's leading spokesman and an important figure in its affairs. His efforts were unbending against Manichees, Donatists, and Pelagians. By the works of his pen, and his voice at councils, he repeatedly rallied the forces of conscience and orthodoxy. Some account of his major contributions is now needed to complete our sketch, even though we will be anticipating thereby themes treated in more detail in later chapters of this book.

VIII. Against the Manichees

Augustine's case against the Manichees had accumulated during the stages of his conversion. The course of his disenchantment we have already traced. Once Christian baptism had set its seal on his new-found faith, he began combatting Manichean errors. He had composed no fewer than ten tracts against them before he published the *Confessions*. Then, about A.D. 400, the whole debate reached a kind of summary so far as Augustine was concerned in his *Reply to Faustus the Manichean* in thirty-three books.

A crucial issue was the integrity of Scripture. Were the Scriptures reliable as a whole, or only where they recommended themselves to the free-thinking critic? Faustus claimed to revere Christ but claimed also the privilege of denying the Incarnation. In addition, he insisted that morals, not dogma, were the heart of the gospel. And to support his own interpretations of morality he argued that the text of Scripture was often uncertain, so that the reader was justified in exercising preference, in discarding some passages as spurious and regarding others as evidence of the Apostle's transient opinion rather than his permanent belief. On this point Augustine answered Faustus:

> It is one thing to reject the books as a whole . . . as the pagans reject our Scriptures . . . and it is another thing to say, 'This holy man wrote only the truth, and this is his epistle, but some verses are his and some are not.' And when you are asked for a proof, instead of referring to more correct or more ancient manuscripts . . . your reply is, 'This verse is his because it makes for me; and this is not his because it is against me.' Are you the rule of truth? [11]

Such a method, rather, is but the last gasp of a heretic in the grip of truth. More broadly, Augustine undertook to answer Faustus by appealing to common sense and to the authority of the Church. Against arbitrary doubt he held up the need for respecting testimony, and against individual rulings he applied the rule of faith.

It is interesting to notice also, in passing, Augustine's answer to Manichean censures on the wars of the Old Testament. Faustus had presumed to criticize Moses for his killing of an Egyptian and for his zeal in military conquest. Augustine replies that the wars of Moses were legitimate because ordained of God, and that God in ordaining such actions was not cruel but giving to every man his due. In God's providence war is a means for chastising guilty kings and peoples, and also a means for putting to the test the virtue of just and faithful peoples. To wage war out of obedience to God is a very different thing from waging it for personal gain. But even when wars are caused by human selfishness they can be profitable to the faithful by giving them an exercise in patience, humbling their souls, and teaching them to bear the paternal discipline of God.

IX. Against the Donatists

Skirmishing with the Donatists offered a more delicate problem, for the Donatists were schismatics rather than heretics, the lineal descendants of a separatist movement that had split the African Church. The error represented by them was more of the heart than of the head. What the Donatists needed, Augustine realized, was not so much destruction by argument as reconstruction by increase of charity. And this was not easy. A century of schism had established an elaborate network of vested interests. Moreover, it had ingrained fanatical loyalties not easy to correct by persuasion.

The history of Donatism reached back to the year 311, when Cecilian had been consecrated bishop of Carthage. An opposition party had disputed his right to the office, allegedly because one of his consecrators had been a *traditor,* that is, a surrenderer of the Scriptures to the state police during the recent persecution under Diocletian. Other factors were also involved, including the ambition of an able bishop named Donatus and the pique of a wealthy woman named Lucilla. The Donatists stigmatized their opponents as supporters of an apostate hierarchy, while advertising themselves as the true Church, the 'Church of the martyrs.' They throve on official opposition. In fact, the Donatist leaders both invited and provoked the intervention of the law, and then charged 'persecution.' The attentive ear given to their grievances by several Councils, and by the Emperor Constantine in person, failed to mollify the insurgents, inasmuch as almost every formal decision went against them.

By Augustine's day the nub of the Donatist argument lay in their insistence on a 'perfectionist' church. As the Manichees had contended for a religion cleansed of 'superstition,' so the Donatists insisted on a church purged of every offender or supposed offender. Publicly recognized sinners, the Donatists declared, have no place in the Church; they must be rigorously excluded. If any are allowed to remain in the priesthood, the baptism they pretend to administer is actually invalid. For baptism cannot be efficacious unless the priest's conduct is exemplary. By this standard Cecilian's sacramental acts were declared to be invalid, along with those of his supporters.

Augustine undertook to confute this theory. The sacrament of baptism, he declared, is not the minister's but Christ's, who employs the minister as His instrument. Unworthiness in the instrument cannot destroy the act. Indeed, what Donatist can be sure that his own minister's conscience is without stain of sin? Moreover, a further point is involved: the Donatists misunderstand the nature of the Church. It is not a collection of saints but a community in which sanctification is offered and at work. The presence of unworthy members in the Church cannot destroy its holiness, for the essence of that Church is not in its members but in its Head, who has provided doctrine and sacraments and ministers for the work of sanctifying the members. In the last day they will be judged, and only the just will then be accepted; but in the meantime sinners may dwell *in* the Church without being *of* the Church, even as Christ allowed the tares in the field of the Kingdom.

Holding out a hand of welcome to the separated Donatists, Augustine took care to stress both the ease and the profit of reunion. He pointed out to them that they could return to Catholic communion without being rebaptized; there would be only the regularizing of an untenable status, in order to set the stage for a blessing denied them in their isolation. As long as they remained schismatics they might retain, let it be admitted, an unspotted faith; yet this faith must suffer partial paralysis for lack of a vivifying charity. Their baptism, though valid, could not be fruitful for salvation when detached from the unity of the world-wide Church.

What moved Augustine to make his appeals was the familiar sight at Hippo of households divided over religion. They have their meals in common, he complained, but not the Table of

Christ; the children have 'one father's house, [but] not one Heavenly Father's home.' Augustine hoped by a patient examination of Scripture to dispel narrowness and thus to make an end of such tragic alienation.

But the results of persistent discussion and debate were disappointing. Some Donatists were persuaded but lethargic. Others, refusing to face reasoning, countered Augustine's efforts by a resort to violence. Catholics in North Africa found themselves beset by a wave of vandalism. Groups of marauding peasants were abetted, if not directly led, by Donatist bishops. Law and order, not merely of the Church but of the State, were being flouted. An attempt by the Catholic bishops to hold a decisive debate with the Donatists at the Synod of Carthage in 403 fell through because the latter declined to participate. Thereupon the Catholics petitioned the emperor to enforce against the Donatists certain neglected penal laws. Augustine accepted this decision.

The emperor responded with a series of decrees including fresh laws against the Donatists, singling them out by name for suppression. The Donatist leaders taunted the Catholics with using force to support religion; but Augustine was more impressed by the spectacle of wholesale conversions which the pressure of the laws was effecting. Not only was civil order being improved but Church schism was being overcome. The spiritual disorder of the Donatists, against which discussion alone had availed little, was being shaken into taking new order. Augustine could not be unthankful when he saw this taking place. The stimulus, admittedly, was fear; but the use of fear, he now felt, could be defended as instigating a closer investigation into truth and furnishing an incentive for throwing off the chains of old custom.

How many there are [he writes] who thought the sect of Donatus was really the true Church because sheer heedlessness made them too sluggish, disdainful and lazy to recognize Catholic truth! How many, again, who thought it did not matter to what sect a Christian belonged, and who stayed

among the Donatists simply because they were born among
them and because no one compelled them to quit it and pass
over to the Catholic Church.[12]

Augustine wrote these words in 417, after more than twenty
years of experience in dealing with the problem. In that time
he had written against the Donatists no fewer than eight formal
tracts, in addition to many passages of comment in letters and
sermons. In the process his views had undergone revision. He
had come to believe that love and legal constraint were not
incompatible. He argued this conclusion by two analogies —
that of the father who punishes out of love for his child, and
that of a guard who restrains by force a delirious patient; and he
invoked the gospel text, 'Compel them to come in.' The attitude
of the new converts from Donatism, however, offered Augustine
his strongest argument: instead of complaining of coercion, they
expressed themselves as glad to be rid of intimidation.

Augustine's defense of coercion by the secular power has
brought on him the reproof of many modern critics. If only he
had adhered to his earlier views, he could have stood in history
as a great Apostle of religious liberty. Perhaps so. Yet it may
be wondered whether Augustine's critics here have examined
the meaning of liberty as carefully as he had occasion to do, particularly by reason of his controversy with the Pelagians. Perhaps, like Pelagius, the modern mind takes the Christian doctrine of the Fall somewhat superficially and lacks therefore
Augustine's assessment of man's actual situation. Often liberty
is viewed apart from its context in a fallen world. But Augustine
saw vividly the handicap of Original Sin, which robbed man of
full liberty, so that government by civil law is appropriate as a
restraint upon evil and as a curb against man's tendency to abuse
his free will. It is well to remember, also, that the Protestant
reformers, no less than the Roman Catholics, turned to Augustine's reasoning when in the sixteenth century they had to deal
with the Anabaptists. Against them they invoked the old laws
against rebaptism which originally had been formulated against
the Donatists. Nor did these latter-day churchmen always disap-

prove the death penalty; but we find Augustine asking for a more merciful penalty.

On this controversial and delicate issue, however, the reader of our volume will want to consider the divergent comments of our contributors in Chapters III, VII, and XIV.

X. Against the Pelagians

In 412, just before beginning the *City of God,* Augustine found himself launching out on what was to become the most significant of all his controversies, that with Pelagianism. Intermittently it occupied his attention until his death. Unlike the Donatist problem, Pelagianism was not merely a local matter. The British-born Pelagius, who had just visited Italy and North Africa on his way to Palestine, spread his doctrine wherever he went. Augustine, immediately alert to its heresy, preached against it at Hippo and soon was dispatching letters and tracts to warn outsiders. Within a few years the whole Christian Church was aroused, including St. Jerome at Bethlehem, Pope Innocent and later Pope Zosimus, and the Emperor Honorius at Constantinople. Councils were held, and by 418 Pelagius and his disciple Coelestius were almost everywhere condemned.

Nevertheless the controversy continued. Julian of Eclanum, one of the nineteen bishops banished from Italy for Pelagianism, arose to defend what has often been called semi-Pelagianism, though some scholars would reserve this term for the theology of another contemporary, John Cassian. The saintly monk Cassian, however, never directly opposed Augustine. The urbane Julian most certainly did. No ascetic, but a scholarly bishop and a skilled dialectician, Julian felt that Augustine was barbarizing Scripture by foisting upon it the crude doctrine of Original Sin. He chose to regard Augustine as the inventor of this doctrine. He attacked his opponent in a dozen books of loquacious argument, branding his views as Manichean and calling him 'most stupid of men.' Augustine in turn saw in Julian 'the architect of the Pelagian heresy.' He therefore did him the honor of answering his books one by one — until, with but two still unanswered, death cut short the debate.

47

Pelagianism, as Augustine was quick to perceive, undermined a central pillar of Christian theology. In positing for man a native competency to accomplish, of his own choice and doing, a completely good life, Pelagius was calling in question man's need of divine grace in the acting of every good deed. Pelagius was, as we might say today, something of a 'romantic': he believed in man's innocence and perfectibility. He denied any inherited bias in man, any transmitted disposition impairing the liberty of operation of man's free will. Insisting that God had given man free will, he saw its character or present state as that of unconditioned freedom. Augustine could not accept this view. Scripture was against it, as well as his own experience. What motion toward the good could any man make, even with the benefit of commandments and teaching, unless God also draw the will? Had the free will of Saul of Tarsus, or of the young Augustine, actually been as indifferent as a pair of well-balanced scales? Would either of them ever have arrived at conversion merely by invoking the free will which by nature God had given them?

Against Pelagianism Augustine argued for the truth of Original Sin, human insufficiency, complete predestination, prevenient grace, and regenerative baptism. Moreover, he insisted on investigating human free will not as an abstract problem in metaphysics but as a fact having historical context. The man about whom we are inquiring, he said, is the man whom 'the thieves' have left half dead on the road, or who, if he is not in 'the inn,' is still in the process of cure. He needs the initial intervention and the continuing providence of the gracious Good Samaritan. It will be seen from this that Augustine's controversy with Pelagius was bound to involve at one time or another the whole circuit of Christian theory, not merely the focal issue of free will. Interpretations of man and of God, of the Church and its sacraments, of ethics and of history, all become pertinent to the discussion. In following out such a range of considerations Augustine deepened and enlarged his thinking.

We honor Augustine as the Doctor of Grace, for this title marks his genius as a theologian. It has been rightly said that 'not to Aquinas but to Augustine has been given the profoundest insights into the help that comes from above as soon as man realizes he cannot lift himself by his own bootstraps.' [13] For grasping this issue, Augustine's personal experience of human weakness was providential. But equally so was the challenge posed by Pelagius; for heresy is, proverbially, a theologian's whetstone.

XI. Pastor and Apologist

But we must not suppose that controversy was Augustine's only activity during the years of his episcopate. Amid vast literary production he still managed to carry on the routine tasks of monastery, parish, and diocese. In his clerical school he trained many for the work of the Church, including twelve who became bishops. He sat in Church courts until he was worn out from hearing disputes. Occasionally he appeared in the civil courts to ask mercy for criminals. He cared for the poor diligently. He looked after Church lands and their many tenants. The round of his daily interests will be described in Chapter III.

Whenever there was occasion, Augustine preached. His sermons comment on almost every part of the Bible, each season of the Church year, and many saints. There have come down to us, in addition to his two great series of sermons on the Gospel of St. John and the Psalms, 396 of his ordinary sermons. These last were taken down by shorthand writers from extemporaneous delivery. Moreover, .in order to instruct a young deacon in the art of religious education, Augustine wrote (about the year 400) a treatise called *On Catechising the Uninstructed*. He also brought to completion in A.D. 426 a handbook on the art of teaching, begun thirty years earlier, entitled *On Christian Instruction*. In it he describes the Scriptures as 'a narrative of the past, a prophecy of the future, and a description of the present.' [14] He advises teachers to read the whole of Scripture through, and more than once, using the plain passages to throw light on the obscure passages, that the soul 'may drink in eternal light' and not be 'put in subjection to the flesh by the blind adherence to the letter' of the text. [15] For preaching he counsels eloquence, but never at the expense of truth. Let St. Paul's practice be observed: 'Wisdom is his guide, eloquence his attendant; he follows the first, the second follows him, and yet he does not spurn it when it comes after him.' [16]

In addition to such teaching and preaching, and quite unconnected with any of the three great controversies we have mentioned, Augustine was composing the three works that have brought his most enduring fame. The most popular of them, the *Confessions,* was a long prayer in thirteen books, deriving its title from Psalm 32:5, 'I will confess my transgressions unto the Lord.' His life, with its sins, was laid bare before God and in the sight of men, even at the risk of his new episcopal dignity. Augustine had a few enemies, naturally, who later delighted to cast in his teeth the more scandalous of the revelations; but most Christian readers were stirred by them to a deeper piety—perhaps after taking to heart the incontrovertible wisdom of such a jeweled sentence as 'Thou hast commanded of us not continency alone, that is, from what things to refrain our love, but righteousness also, that is, whereon to bestow it, and hast willed us to love not Thee only, but our neighbor also.' [17]

As he was finishing the *Confessions,* about A.D. 400, Augustine began his monumental treatise *On the Trinity.* Its fifteen books — of which the earliest began to circulate immediately without his authorization — were completed finally after twenty years. They round out the contribution made by Athanasius a century earlier. They defend and expound the doctrine which in Augustine's eyes was the foundation of all Christian theology, basic for a true understanding of nature and man as well as of God. The first seven books are exegetical, deducing the doctrine from Scripture; the other eight books explore rational arguments for the doctrine by invoking analogies from nature in general and from the human soul in particular. Augustine's statement of the important principle of analogy occurs in the sentence: 'In so far, therefore, as anything that is, is good, in so far plainly it has still some likeness of the supreme good, at however great a distance'; and he adds, 'For even souls in their very sins strive after nothing else but some kind of likeness of God.' [18] In Books III,

IV, and XIII, there is valuable incidental discussion of the doctrines of Creation *ex nihilo* and the Atonement.

The signal event, in A.D. 410, of the sack of Rome by Alaric the Goth aroused pagan criticism of Christianity and called forth in reply Augustine's great work of popular apologetics, *The City of God*. Extending its course through twenty-two books, it developed into a theological account of all human history. The writing of it took Augustine thirteen years, off and on; but it became a standard textbook of the next millennium.

The Romans, like the Jews, had thought of their capital as an eternal city. The pilgrimage of Aeneas as told by Vergil was as significant to them as the pilgrimages of Abraham and Moses were to the Jews. Aeneas was understood as having founded, by his piety and self-discipline, a city dedicated to a dream of ideal order. But this city had fallen, sapped from within, so its patriots claimed, by foreigners devoted to other faiths, especially Christianity. Augustine's task in *The City of God* is to correct this misjudgment. He does it by calling for an objective review of Rome's disaster. Like a careful student he makes certain neglected data the basis for a fresh analysis, and thus offers his readers a new understanding of their own history.

The first fact he uncovers for his opponents' attention is in a sense the key to his vision of society. The Christian altars, he points out, were the one place of safety in a world inundated by violence. Romans who fled to the tombs of the martyrs found there a rock of refuge; for the barbarians respected the sanctuary of Christian churches, while recognizing no restraints elsewhere. Here is a fact, so Augustine shows, quite new in Roman history. The 'just' Romans in their own wars had not spared churches or priests; nor had the teachers of the Romans, the Greeks, spared the priest Priam at Troy — he was butchered at his own altar. And then Aeneas had carried away in his hands to Rome Priam's impotent gods, which the Romans had since been foolishly trusting to protect their city. How much better to understand that there is but one eternal city, the 'city of God' of Psalm 46, whose tabernacles are a refuge and strength in trouble, a help in times when the nations rage and kingdoms are moved.

Calamity, then, has proved a blessing in disguise. Though it has fallen on good men and bad men alike, its significance is not the same for all. A punishment for some, it is but a time of testing and teaching for others, who may become by means of it more ultimately prosperous, as did Job. The Romans misvalue temporal losses. Who shall say there is not profit both for the pagan and for the Christian in times of tribulation?

> For as the same fire causes gold to glow brightly, and chaff to smoke; and under the same flail the straw is beaten small, while the grain is cleansed; and as the lees are not mixed with oil, though squeezed out of the vat by the same pressure, so the same violence of affliction proves, purges, clarifies the good, but damns, ruins, exterminates the wicked. And thus it is that in the same affliction the wicked detest God and blaspheme, while the good pray and praise. So material a difference does it make, not what ills are suffered, but what kind of a man suffers them. For stirred up with the same movement, mud exhales a horrible stench, and ointment emits a fragrant odor.[19]

I have quoted the passage to illustrate not only Augustine's logic but his eloquence; such words can kindle the will as well as the intellect. As Christian stylist Augustine stands supreme among the Fathers. The later Schoolmen may have surpassed him in the refinements of definition, but the very gains which they thereby made for science are attended by a withering away of the power of the spoken word. Their voices do not cry aloud to the hearts of men as Augustine's does.

And in the heart and will of man, so Augustine thinks, lies the secret of man's fate. Ultimately there are only two communities: one, the city of those whose wills are submissive to God; the other, the city of those who will to rival Him. The first consults the common welfare for the sake of a celestial fellowship; the other grasps at selfish control for the sake of arrogant dominance. By their loves men distinguish and declare their separate destinies. Those who love the good of the neighbor as much as the good of the self and therefore live according to God will grow in peace and at last reign eternally with Him; while the city of those who love self above the neighbor and live according to man will be self-divided by wars and suffer eternal punishment with the devil. Here, in the course of time, these two mystical cities are intermingled; but their careers are diverse, and they shall be openly distinguished at the Last Judgment. Such is Augustine's major theme, set forth particularly in the fifteenth book of his treatise.

On such thinking was the mind of the Middle Ages nourished. It gave men the will to build toward order amid disorder. It gave them an otherworldly set of values by which to revalue the worldly. Perhaps no point has been so commonly misunderstood as the 'otherworldliness' of medieval Christianity. It is imagined as having taught men to despise the world of nature and to neglect the human body. Almost the contrary, however, is Augustine's view [20] as seen in the first book of his *City of God*. Why do Christians take such care for the bodies of the saints? Because 'the body is not an extraneous ornament or aid, but a part of man's very nature.' That is why, as Augustine goes on to argue so brilliantly, it is always wrong to commit suicide: suicide is self-murder — not self-liberation, as Cato and Lucretia, those heroes of Roman morality, have imagined. Right here at their 'noblest' is where Roman standards of virtue must be overhauled in the light of a more exacting analysis, and replaced by a genuinely supernatural standard, which alone can guarantee justice to the natural life of man. We must understand that man's life in the body is morally good as long as man's will is good. Or to state the same point in words taken from the fourteenth book: 'it is not the corruptible flesh that makes the soul sinful, but the sinful soul that makes the flesh corruptible . . . For it is not by having flesh (which the devil had not) but by living according to himself — that is, according to man — that man became like the devil.' [21]

XII. A Concluding Estimate

There is no need to mention here Augustine's many other works of lesser importance. When about 426 he wrote his *Retrac-*

tations to correct for posterity some of the passages in his earlier writings, his literary output had amounted to 97 separate works consisting of 232 books. In addition, about 220 letters written by him have been preserved, some of them containing elaborate comment on ecclesiastical and speculative questions. One of Augustine's correspondents, the bishop of Milevis, speaks of him as 'God's truly busy bee, building up for us combs full of heavenly nectar.'

Augustine and after him Heraclius, whom he chose as his successor in 426, seem to have been the last bishops of Hippo. Augustine's parishioners were scattered or slain by the Vandals within a few months of his death; and two centuries after the Vandals, the Mohammedans took over and they have possessed the country to the present day. Yet Augustine's work did not perish. The seeds of his achievement survived the autumn of African civilization to find in Europe their springtime and harvest. The civilization of medieval Christendom was to owe more to him than to any other of the Church Fathers. Gregory the Great turned to him for Scriptural commentary and theology, Charlemagne for political theory, Bonaventura for mysticism, and Aquinas for elements of scholastic philosophy. Later, with the coming of the Reformation, Luther and Calvin became his disciples and, after them, Pascal — each gathering from the bishop of Hippo fresh stimulus for revitalizing Christian piety.

This breadth of influence has been possible because Augustine's thought has so many aspects, and because it represents the work of a disciplined thinker. He 'saw Christianity as a whole, with a completeness beyond anything any of his philosophical predecessors had known.' [22] At the same time, he set forth his vision with the art of a master of rhetoric and dialectic. At home in all the liberal arts and in each of the many functions of Christian evangelism, Augustine was in a sense the completely equipped missionary. His philosophy, it is true, emerged in a great variety of contexts and applications, and thus was not presented as a system; yet it was comprehensively fruitful in exploring the implications of the Christian starting point. He relied increasingly and steadfastly on a close study of the Scriptures in order that he might expose the values of Christian insight for the life of man; and his own personal experience interpreted by the Holy Spirit enabled him to penetrate those Scriptures afresh and thus rehabilitate their intrinsic and implicit meaning.

No doubt his chief contribution was in developing a synthesis of Christianity with classical learning. To do this he had to discover first the dimensions of classical culture and its characteristic forms, and he had to discern, as he progressed, its positive values together with the radical defect of its secular first principle. He had to assess both the genius of Christianity and the stature of her neighbors. Beginning with his conversion, the pre-Christian arts, poetry, and thought were baptized and devoted to another kind of humanism. By Christian inspiration, he then gradually forged from the salvaged resources of Hellenism a new philosophy in which old problems were redefined and old concepts reshaped. Christian revelation, once accepted on the authority of the Church and through the witness of his own experience, became for him no mere capstone to a philosopher's quest but in fact a beginning in wisdom.

FOR FURTHER READING

St. Augustine, *Confessions.*

There are several available English translations: that of William Watts (1631), retouched by W. H. D. Rouse for the Loeb edition (1912); that of E. B. Pusey (1838, rev. 1843, the Oxford *Library of the Fathers*), reprinted in the Everyman and Modern Library editions; that of J. G. Pilkington (1876, T. & T. Clark), reprinted in *Nicene and Post-Nicene Fathers;* that of F. J. Sheed (Sheed and Ward, 1943); and, most recently, that of Albert Outler (Westminster Press, 1955).

Vernon J. Bourke, *Augustine's Quest of Wisdom* (Milwaukee, 1945).

The author, a trained Roman Catholic philosopher, traces in fourteen very readable chapters Augustine's spiritual and mental journey toward God. A survey rather than a critical discussion, this work is well organized, well annotated, and encyclopedic.

Charles N. Cochrane, *Christianity and Classical Culture* (London, 1940), Chaps. X–XII.

Here is brilliant analysis and exposition of the contribution of St. Augustine to Christian thought, setting him against the background both of earlier Christian writing and of the philosophical problems posed by classical culture. For advanced students, this lifetime work of a professor of classics at the University of Toronto will prove immensely stimulating.

Etienne Gilson, *Introduction à l'étude de Saint Augustine* (3rd edition, Paris, 1949).

For advanced students, this book interprets in exact detail St. Augustine's position on major philosophical issues. Of particular value is the 30-page bibliography of works on Augustine up to 1943.

NOTES

1. *Conf.*, XI. 27. 36.
2. *St. Augustine: The Odyssey of his Soul,* tr. McCann (New York, 1932).
3. Tertullian, in the third century, reports as current practice the principle that adults ought not to be baptized unless settled in either the married or the celibate state. *De Baptismo,* 18.
4. Compare T. S. Eliot, *The Dry Salvages:*
   We had the experience but missed the meaning
   But approach to the meaning restores the experience
   In a different form.
5. For Augustine's view of the Greco-Roman stage, see the excellent analysis by C. N. Cochrane, *Christianity and Classical Culture* (London, 1940), pp. 391–2.
6. III. 15. 34.
7. *De Civ. Dei,* IX. 26.
8. *Conf.,* VIII. 5. 10. Pusey's translation.
9. On this point, see Sister Mary P. Garvey, *St. Augustine: Christian or Neoplationist?* (Milwaukee, 1939).
10. *De Moribus Eccles. Cath.,* 6 and 15.
11. *Contra Faustum,* XI. 2.
12. *Ep.* 185. 16.
13. Fulton J. Sheen, in his Introduction to the *Confessions* (Modern Library), pp. xi–xii.
14. III. 10.
15. III. 5.
16. IV. 7.
17. *Conf.,* X. 37. 61.
18. XI. 5.
19. *De Civ. Dei,* I. 8. (Dods)
20. But for another interpretation of Augustine's views, see Chapter XIV of our volume.
21. *De Civ. Dei,* XIV. 3. (Dods)
22. Philip Hughes, *A History of the Church,* II (New York, 1935), 25.

III

ST. AUGUSTINE AS PASTOR

Joseph B. Bernardin

S T. AUGUSTINE possessed the pastoral instinct from an early age. While still a catechumen, he gathered a small group to live with him at the villa of Cassiciacum; and he brought two of the group, Alypius and his own son Adeodatus, to be baptized along with himself at Milan in 387. He was still a layman when he established on his family estate at Tagaste a small semi-monastic community. Here, according to Possidius, he occupied himself 'in fastings and prayers and good works, meditating day and night in the law of the Lord. And the things which God revealed to him through prayer and meditation, he taught both those present and absent in his sermons and books.' [1] So zealously was he engaged that his friend Nebridius wrote inquiring: 'Is it true, my beloved Augustine, that you are spending your strength and patience on the affairs of your fellow-citizens, and that the leisure from distractions which you so earnestly desired is still withheld from you?' [2] Such a concern for the welfare of others undoubtedly owed much to Monnica, whose whole life had been one of service — well illustrated when, on her voyage to join her son in Italy, she had comforted the mariners during a storm at sea.

When Augustine was ordained to the priesthood, it is told that he wept as he thought of the great responsibilities he was being forced to assume. Yet some thought that his tears were from wounded pride at not having been made a bishop.[3] As a matter of fact, he had carefully avoided visiting any church without a bishop, for fear of being forcibly consecrated to that office. Forcible ordination was not unknown in the early Church — St. Ambrose, St. Martin of Tours, and St. Chrysostom being among the more notable instances. Augustine did not consider the clerical profession a sinecure. To his superior, Valerius, the bishop of Hippo, he wrote soon after the ordination:

> First and foremost, I beg your wise holiness to consider that there is nothing in this life, and especially in our own day, more easy and pleasant and acceptable to men than the office of bishop or priest or deacon, if its duties be discharged in a mechanical or sycophantic way; but nothing more worthless and deplorable and meet for chastisement in the sight of God: and, on the other hand, that there is nothing in this life, and especially in our own day, more difficult, toilsome, and hazardous than the office of bishop or priest or deacon; but nothing more blessed in the sight of God, if our service be in accordance with our Captain's orders.[4]

He then mentions a knowledge of the Scriptures, prayer, and study as being essential for the task of the ministry. Later, before he himself was raised to the episcopate, he commented: 'I do not propose to spend my time in the empty enjoyment of ecclesiastical dignity, but I propose to act as mindful of this — that I must give an account of the sheep committed unto me.'[5]

Being a many-sided man, Augustine was also a very busy man. He wrote once to a heathen official: 'When I consider how a bishop is distracted and overwrought by the cares of his office clamoring on every side, it does not seem to me proper for him suddenly, as if deaf, to withdraw himself from all these, and devote himself to the work of expounding to a single student some unimportant questions in the *Dialogues* of Cicero.' [6] And another time he remarked: 'When I obtain a little leisure from the urgent necessary business of those men who so press me into their service that I am neither able to escape them nor at liberty to neglect them, there are always subjects to which I must in dictating to my amanuenses give the first place, because they are so connected with the present hour as not to admit of being postponed.' [7] Hence Augustine is found referring to the episcopate as 'an office of labor, and not of honor'; for when constrained to go one mile to help anyone, he felt himself bound to go two. [8]

A bishop in those days was more like a rector of a large, modern, city parish than like a present-day diocesan. The city with its immediately surrounding countryside was his diocese; and often there was only one large church within it. As cities grew, however, other churches were erected which were cared for by presbyters. These were frequently visited by the bishop, and particularly by Augustine, in spite of the fact that he did not like to travel. Five Catholic churches are known to have existed at Hippo at this time. In each of them Augustine must have baptized, confirmed, married, absolved, counseled, administered the Holy Communion, and buried the dead; for such were the bishop's responsibilities. He was the chief pastor, an overseer of souls, the father in God of the whole community, Catholics, heretics, schismatics, and pagans. He was the principal teacher and preacher in a day when sermons were not limited to Sundays. He ruled his congregation firmly in love, rebuked and punished their errors, and provided for their needs. His particular care was the protection of the weak, especially widows, orphans, and the poor. Bishops were very numerous in North Africa in the fourth century, and were held in esteem as great personages. The faithful approached them with lowly respect, bowing the head in obeisance. To Augustine and the other bishops they often presented themselves to receive blessing and to ask for intercessions with the Lord. [9]

The chief characteristic of Augustine as a pastor would seem to be his penetrating insight into both divine and human nature, and his use of this insight in his dealings with the contemporary world and its problems. His advice and activity were conspicuous for sound common sense, breadth of view, psychological acumen, generosity, and fairness. He was tactful, yet direct. There was a natural dignity to all his actions. Men and women eagerly consulted him in person and by letter; and he had the respect of pagans and heretics as well as of his fellow Christians. He was the spiritual father not only of North Africa; his parish, like John Wesley's, was the world of his day.

In considering St. Augustine's almost forty years as a pastor, it is well to look at it under several large headings. The sources for such a study are chiefly his letters; second, his sermons; and third, the *Life of St. Augustine* by his close friend Possidius, bishop of Calama in North Africa, written probably in 432, two years after Augustine's death. The *Confessions,* since they come to a stop with his conversion, have little of interest for the pastoral aspect of his life. The majority of his treatises have only occasional and quite incidental references.

I. Administrator of the Sacraments

Augustine has left comments upon all but one of the present seven sacraments, no reference to unction being found.[10] In his day there was no fixed number of sacraments. However, the term *sacramentum* is used by him in connection with Baptism, Penance, Holy Communion, Orders, and Matrimony. In his view, the sacraments of the old law were abolished because they had been fulfilled; and others had been instituted which were 'more efficacious, more useful, easier to administer and to receive, and fewer in number.' [11] He held that sacraments when administered by those separated from the unity of Christ's Body may give the form of godliness but that the invisible and spiritual power of godliness can in no wise be in them; for schism partly suspends the grace of the sacraments, without altogether nullifying it, and it becomes fully effective only upon reconciliation to the Catholic Church.[12]

Baptism. Augustine regarded Baptism as a sacrament of fundamental importance. He exhorted people to come to it, declaring that there is no salvation without the Church (*salus extra ecclesiam non est*).[13] For this reason he was insistent that infants should be baptized [14]; and in consequence infant slaves were often brought to Baptism by their masters, who acted as sponsors. Sometimes children were brought for superstitious reasons, such as to recover bodily health; nevertheless Augustine insisted that the intention of the sponsors does not affect the validity of the sacrament.[15] The sacrament, in fact, could benefit the sponsors as well as the child: 'Now the regenerating Spirit is possessed both by the parents who present the child, and by the infant that is presented and is born again; wherefore, in virtue of this participation in the same Spirit, the will of those who present the infant is useful to the child.' [16] Moreover, the act of the sponsors is not so much that of the presenters as of the whole society of saints and believers. It is done 'by the whole mother Church, which is in the saints, because the whole Church is the parent of each one of them.' The child 'is healed at the words of another, because it was wounded by the deed of another.' [17]

The normal administrator of Baptism was the bishop himself; presbyters were required to have formal authorization to baptize.[18] The usual time of administration was Easter Eve, and it was still performed in secret, that is, with none but Christians present. Those to be baptized repeated the Creed beforehand, without which Augustine did not consider it a true Baptism, and the Lord's Prayer afterward; they were then signed with the sign of the cross on their foreheads.[19] In the case of adults, Baptism was preceded by a long period of testing and instruction known as the catechumenate.

Augustine maintained that all sins are forgiven in Baptism,[20] and that one can be validly baptized only once. Hence he was much opposed to the Donatist custom of rebaptizing Catholic Christians who became Donatists. He held that Baptism confers a permanent spiritual state: 'The soul of an apostate, which was once similarly wedded unto Christ and now separates itself from Him, does not, in spite of its loss of faith, lose the sacrament of faith, which it has received in the waters of regeneration.' [21]

Confirmation. Augustine seldom mentions Confirmation, presumably because it was a sacrament which at that time followed immediately upon Baptism by the bishop, forming with it but one ceremony in the case of both infants and adults. Augustine is, however, alluding to the gifts of Confirmation when he writes: 'Is it now expected that they upon whom hands are laid should speak with tongues? Or when we imposed our hand upon these children, did each of you wait to see whether they would speak with tongues? And when they did not speak with tongues, was any of you so perverse of heart as to say: "These have not received the Holy Spirit"?' [22]

Penance. In regard to Penance, Augustine warned men not to listen to 'those who deny that the Church of God has power to forgive all sins'; for sins are not forgiven out of the Church, but by that Spirit by whom the Church is gathered into one.[23] And in one of his sermons he said: 'Let no one say: "I do penance secretly; I perform it in the sight of God, and He who is to pardon me knows that in my heart I repent." Was it then said to no purpose: "What you shall loose upon earth shall be loosed in heaven"? Was it for nothing that the keys were given to the Church?'[24] Bishops, he remarked, often know and reprove in secret many sins of which the public is not aware, to the end that souls may be gained. This *secreta correptio* was evidently an intermediate stage in the development from public to private penance. At this time penance in public preceded absolution, but did not necessarily include a public avowal of sins.[25] Furthermore, all Christians convicted of crimes by the State, whether punished or pardoned, still had to undergo ecclesiastical penance.[26] Public penance was required for notorious mortal sins; venial sins were purged by prayer and almsgiving; and the Church was not quite certain how to deal with mortal sins that were not notorious. This was where the secret counseling came in, which was later to develop into private confession and absolution, with a milder penance following the absolution. As in the case of the other sacraments, the bishop was the administrator.

Augustine instructed his people to do penance for the misdeeds of the past, and warned them not to put off repentance until tomorrow. He believed that sins are purged by alms and prayers, particularly by the daily saying of the Lord's Prayer with its petition: 'Forgive us our debts.' [27] He taught, however, that Penance did not end the suffering attached to sin: 'Man is forced to suffer even after his sins are forgiven, though it was sin that brought down on him this penalty. For the punishment outlasts the guilt, lest the guilt should be thought slight, if, with its forgiveness, the punishment also came to an end.' [28] In a letter to Bishop Auxilius he wrote that, though he had often been sorely tried by wicked men, he had never excommunicated anyone.[29]

Holy Communion. The Holy Communion, or Eucharist, was the principal service of the Church. From Augustine's writings a fairly good outline of its form may be obtained. The service was divided into two parts, which might even occasionally be held in different church buildings. The preparatory service consisted of a lesson from the Old Testament, a lesson from one of the Epistles, the chanting of a psalm, a lesson from one of the four Gospels, and a sermon, ending with an ascription. The catechumens were then dismissed. The Eucharist proper began with the 'prayers of the faithful,' consisting of the bishop's bidding, his own prayer, and the common prayer enjoined by the proclamation of the deacon. Then came the offering of the bread and the wine by the people, during which a psalm was sung. Then followed a recital of the names of the deceased local martyrs, *sanctimoniales* (nuns), and diocesan bishops, after which came a general commemoration of the faithful departed. Next came the salutation and *Sursum Corda,* the consecration, followed by the *Amen* of the people, the fraction, the Lord's Prayer, the kiss of peace, the blessing of the people with the laying on of hands, the communion, during which a psalm was sung, and the concluding thanksgiving. Although there was this fixed outline, the actual words of the prayers were not as yet in all cases stereotyped.[30]

Beginning in the fourth century there was a falling off in the frequency with which Christians received the Holy Communion, although in many places, such as Hippo, it was still celebrated daily early in the morning before the first meal,[31] and with only the faithful permitted to be present for the second part of the service. The days belonging to the imported saints, however, were never so popular as those of the local martyrs. To a small congregation in the heat of a Tunisian August on the feast of the Roman St. Lawrence, Augustine once said: 'The martyrdom of the blessed Lawrence is famous — but at Rome, not here, so few of you do I see before me this morning! . . . So your little gathering shall hear only a little sermon, for I myself am feeling too tired and hot to manage a long one.' [32] Augustine left the matter of daily Communion to the free choice of the individual, but he advised: 'So live, that you may receive every day.' Infants, as well as adults, received the Communion,[33] as they do today in the Orthodox Churches. The bishop, as *sacerdos,* surrounded by his presbyters and attended by his deacons, was ordinarily the one who offered the Sacrifice once every day on behalf of all the members of the local church.

In regard to the varying eucharistic customs, Augustine maintained a doctrine of common sense:

> There are other things, however, which are different in different places and countries: some fast on Saturdays, others do not; some partake daily of the Body and Blood of Christ, others receive it on stated days: in some places no day passes without the Sacrifice's being offered; in others it is only Saturday and the Lord's Day, or it may be only on the Lord's Day. In regard to these and all other variable observances which may be met anywhere, one is at liberty to comply with them or not as he chooses; and there is no better rule for the wise and serious Christian in this matter, than to conform to the practice which he finds prevailing in the Church to which it may be his lot to come. For such custom, if it is clearly not contrary to the faith or to sound morality, is to be held as a thing indifferent, and ought to be observed for the sake of fellowship with those among whom we live.[34]

The usual custom then was to fast before receiving Communion, but Augustine advised that those who partook of Communion on Maundy Thursday in the evening without fasting were not to be censured.[35]

The petition in the Lord's Prayer for daily bread, Augustine taught, was for both material and spiritual food; the daily Eucharist was man's daily bread.[36] To come to the Communion, one must have charity as well as chastity; for it can be received unworthily unto damnation, unless it is eaten by faith.[37] 'Converted Jews,' he said more than once, 'come to the Lord's Table and in faith drink the Blood which in their fury they have shed.' [38]

Following Tertullian and Cyprian, and in contrast to Ambrose, Augustine maintained the distinction between the visible elements or sign of the Communion and the invisible *res* or thing signified — the so-called dyophysite view. The sacrament was not, however, an empty sign. It conveyed a gift of life.[39] The eucharistic sacrifice of the Church was identified with the self-oblation of the faithful, who make up the Body of Christ and are offered through the great High Priest, as being the body of which He is the Head. 'There you are upon the table, there you are in the chalice,' Augustine once said to the newly confirmed at their first Easter Communion.[40] And in another sermon: 'If you have received well, you are that which you receive.' [41] Augustine also spoke of the Eucharist as 'the Sacrifice of the Body and Blood of Christ,' related it to the sacrifice of the Cross, and spoke of its having propitiatory value, especially in connection with its offering for the departed.[42]

Holy Matrimony. Augustine had much to say about marriage. He opposed any double standard for husband and wife. 'As you would have them come to you, such ought they also to find you.' [43] He considered conjugal affection, and not concupiscence, to be the bond of marital union, and believed that marital intercourse should be for the procreation of children.

But he who exceeds the limits which this rule prescribes for the fulfilment of this end of marriage, acts contrary to the very contract by which he took his wife. The contract is read — read in the presence of all the attesting witnesses; and an express clause is there that they marry for the procreation of children; and this is called the marriage contract

65

(*tabulae matrimoniales*). If it was not for this that wives were given and taken to wife, what father could without blushing give up his daughter to the lust of any man? . . . Is it not a sin in married persons to exact from one another more than this design of the procreation of children renders necessary? It is doubtless a sin, though a venial one.[44]

Augustine urged a life of continence even on married people, but was against its being undertaken without mutual consent; for one wife whom he knew drove her husband to adultery by adopting it without his consent.[45]

Inasmuch as Christian marriage was a sacrament, Augustine regarded it as indissoluble. 'Among all people and all men the good that is secured by marriage consists in the offspring and in the chastity of married fidelity: but in the case of God's people it consists, moreover, in the holiness of the sacrament by reason of which it is forbidden, even after a separation has taken place, to marry another as long as the first partner lives.' [46] Civil marriage was recognized by Christians at this time; but the usual procedure was for the couple to make their vows before the congregation, and to be blessed by the bishop. Hence, mixed marriages were disapproved, even though they could not be altogether prevented, particularly those between Catholics and Donatists.[47]

Holy Orders. Men were chosen for ordination sometimes by the congregation (which generally meant all the Christians of the city), and sometimes by the bishop; but in each case the consent of the other was obtained. From the group with which Augustine surrounded himself, first at Tagaste and later at Hippo, there came twelve North African bishops, as well as other prominent clergy of the time.[48] The clergy often married, and their sons frequently were ordained.[49] Ordination often took place suddenly; there was no regular course of study, preparation, or examination required; and no such thing as a Candidate for Holy Orders. Men were not infrequently consecrated to the episcopate *per saltum,* that is, without first having been made a deacon and a priest, with the occasional unhappy result, as in the case of

66

the consecration of Antoninus by Augustine, that they proved unfit for the office, demonstrating that the injunction to lay hands suddenly on no man is apposite. In the case of Antoninus, Augustine's decision was to deprive him of his see, but not to depose him.[50] Bishops might resign; but translation of bishops was strictly forbidden.[51] It was not unusual for bishops to pick their successors, as Valerius had done in the case of Augustine; and as he in turn chose the deacon Heraclius for his, although he refused to have him consecrated until after his death.[52]

At this period Orders were not thought of as a hierarchical ladder which one must climb, step by step, starting at the lowest rung. Commonly a man was ordained directly to the function he was best fitted to perform. The diaconate more often than the presbyterate was the steppingstone to the episcopate. Also, since Orders were conceived without reference to the congregation in which they were exercised, they might be exercised anywhere and were not limited to the ordaining church, for their validity was dependent solely upon the pedigree of the ordainer, who must always be a bishop. Ordination conferred a *character indelebilis.*

> Priests are ordained to gather a Christian community, and even though no such community be formed, the sacrament of Orders still abides in those ordained; or just as the sacrament of the Lord, once it is conferred, abides even in one who is dismissed from his office on account of guilt, although in such a one it abides unto judgment.[53]

Upon repentance and penance, however, a deposed clergyman might be restored to the exercise of his office, as happened in the case of a presbyter deposed for heresy, whom Augustine converted to orthodoxy.[54]

II. Minister to the Afflicted

The Sick. Possidius relates that Augustine 'in his visitations adhered to the rule set forth by the apostle (Jas. 1:27) and visited only widows and orphans in their afflictions. Yet whenever it happened that he was requested by the sick to come in person and pray to the Lord for them and lay his hand upon them, he went without delay. But the monasteries of women he visited only in extreme emergencies.' [55] Augustine believed in divine healing. While he was still a layman, he knelt with the clergy to pray for the recovery of his host at Carthage, and on the next morning when the clergy came again with the surgeons for the operation, the man was found healed. Many miraculous cures of which Augustine had personal knowledge had been performed through prayer, or by the reception of the sacraments, or through the touching of holy objects or relics.[56]

The Bereaved. Several of Augustine's letters of condolence have been preserved. In one, to the Lady Italica on the death of her husband, he wrote:

> You ought not to consider yourself desolate while you have Christ dwelling in your heart by faith; nor ought you to sorrow as those heathen who have no hope, seeing that in regard to those friends who are not lost, but only called earlier than ourselves to the country whither we shall follow them, we have hope, resting on a most sure promise, that from this life we shall pass into that other life, in which they will be to us more beloved as they will be better known, and in which our pleasure in loving them will not be alloyed by any fear of separation.[57]

One of his sermons touches on practices and beliefs in regard to the dead, which later were used to support the medieval doctrine of purgatory, the origin of which actually lies earlier within New Testament times.

> The pomp of funerals, the large crowds at the rites, the costly care of burial, the rich construction of monuments are solaces, such as they are, for the living, not aids to the dead. But it is not to be doubted that by the prayers of Holy Church, and the saving Sacrifice, and alms which are expended for their souls, the dead are aided, that the Lord should deal more mercifully with them than their sins have deserved.[58]

68

The Church from the very first prayed for its departed members and remembered them, particularly its martyrs, in the Communion service, and still considered them members of God's Church.[59]

Orphans. The care of orphans was another of the bishop's responsibilities. As legal guardian Augustine wrote four letters refusing permission for one of his young wards to marry a pagan. 'The protection which God is giving her in the Church is a protection against wicked men; not an opportunity to give her to any one that I choose, but an opportunity to defend her from seizure by any unsuitable person.' [60] Orphans without property were raised and provided for from the funds of the Church. The practice of exposing infants, either because they were illegitimate or because their parents were unwilling to support them, was strongly condemned by Augustine.[61] He was happy when charitable persons presented young orphans for baptism and acted as their sponsors.[62]

The Poor. Possidius states that Augustine 'was ever mindful of his fellow poor, and for them he spent from the same funds from which he spent for himself and all who lived with him; that is, either from the revenues from the possessions of the Church or from the offerings of the faithful.' [63] Because in many places the Donatists outnumbered the Catholics, the North African Church at this time was not so rich as in other parts of the world, and its charities were not so elaborate or extensive, nor its giving very generous. Nevertheless, it influenced contemporary life more by charitable enterprises than in any other way, for a state system of poor relief was lacking. At Hippo the Church was particularly accustomed to providing clothing for the poor.

Augustine's sermons contain many exhortations to the rich to give to the poor. Apparently there were not many tithers among his congregation. He reminded them that they are always beggars to God, no matter how rich they are; that riches are just as much a burden as poverty, that rich and poor should help to bear one another's burdens; and that when they give to the poor they give to Christ. 'He receives it, who bade you give it.' He enjoined the duty of hospitality, and of giving to the poor what is

69

saved by fasting; and even more, if physically unable to fast, of giving to the poor to compensate for the dispensation. The perfect state was to possess nothing material; but if one does, one must take care to be the master of one's possessions, not letting them be the master. Being rich itself is not sinful, but the desire to be rich is; for avarice is insatiable. Usurers in particular were roundly denounced. So also was a wealthy woman who gave away her estate to some questionable mendicant monks without her husband's permission, causing him to leave her and commit adultery.[64]

The poor also were warned of pride. 'You are more of you poor than rich. Do you then, at least, receive what I say; yet give heed. Whoever of you boasts of your poverty, beware of pride, lest the humble rich surpass you; beware of impiety, lest the pious rich surpass you; beware of drunkenness, lest the sober rich surpass you. Do not glory of your poverty, if they must not glory of their riches.' [65]

The Persecuted. At this time in Africa Christians were liable to attack upon their persons and property by invading barbarians, such as the Vandals; by heathen Romans and Africans; by heretics, such as the Arian Goths; and by schismatics, such as the Donatists, and especially by their fanatical adherents known as Circumcellions, 'herds of abandoned men,' most of them wandering and undisciplined monks, who often stirred up the slaves to revolt, and destroyed both secular and ecclesiastical property. They were from the dregs of society, but their leaders were often Donatist clergy.[66] Hence comfort to the persecuted was a frequent pastoral office.

In regard to the question of whether the clergy should remain at their posts or flee before persecutors in accordance with the dominical saying: 'When they persecute you in one city, flee to another' (Matt. 10:23), Augustine had much to say in a letter written to Bishop Honoratus about 428, although he himself was apparently indifferent to the barbarian invasions:

However small may be the congregation of God's people among whom we are, if our ministry is so necessary to them that it is a clear duty not to withdraw from them, it remains for us to say to the Lord: 'Be Thou to us a God of defense and a strong fortress' . . . . Perhaps some one may say that the servants of God ought to save their lives by flight when such evils are impending, in order that they may reserve themselves for the benefit of the Church in more peaceful times. This is rightly done by some, when others are not wanting by whom the service of the Church may be supplied and the work is not deserted by all, as we have stated that Athanasius did.[67]

If it is a question of some fleeing and some remaining, he believed that it should be determined by lot. He gave a vivid picture of the crowded churches in time of danger, when flight was impossible.

An extraordinary crowd of persons of both sexes and of all ages is wont to assemble in the church — some urgently asking baptism, others reconciliation [absolution], others even the doing of penance [leading to absolution later], and all calling for consolation and strengthening through the administration of the sacraments. If the ministers of God be not at their posts at such a time, how great perdition overtakes those who depart from this life either not regenerated or not loosed from their sins! [68]

Augustine felt that when any one of the Christian body suffers, the whole body suffers with him; and that on such occasions the Christians have their own peculiar consolations, as well as the hope of the world to come.[69] He warned them: 'Beware and teach others to beware of murmuring against God in these trials and tribulations,' for 'prosperity is God's gift when He comforts us; while adversity is God's gift when He is warning us.' He wrote that if Christians will pray fervently unto God, 'He will stand by them, as He has been wont ever to stand by His own, and will either not permit their chaste bodies to suffer any wrong from the lust of their enemies; or if He permit this, He will not lay sin to their charge in this matter.' [70]

Prisoners. Prisoners and those in trouble with the law were a special concern of the clergy, and the episcopal right of intercession on their behalf had been recognized since early in the fourth century. Augustine tried to avoid interceding; but often it became necessary, and then he did it with such fairness, tact, and humility that he earned for himself the praise of the officials.[71] His intercession was not limited to Catholics, for he wrote in regard to some Donatists convicted of murder: 'As to the punishment of these men, I beseech you to make it something less severe than sentence of death, although they have by their own confession been guilty of such grievous crimes. I ask this out of regard both for your own consciences and for the testimony thereby given to Catholic clemency.'[72] And in a similar instance he wrote: 'Do not send for the executioner after finding out the crime, when to find it out you did not use the services of the torturer,'[73] which consisted of the rack, burning, pincers, and beating with rods.

Since custom allowed accused persons to take sanctuary in the churches pending episcopal intervention, Augustine became indignant when one who had done so and was there awaiting Augustine's interposition was abducted. He wrote to a neighboring bishop to take the matter up with the magistrate. On another occasion, when a member of the Church at Hippo sought sanctuary there to escape arrest for debt, Augustine borrowed the necessary amount from one of his own friends; but the debtor failed to repay as promised. So Augustine asked the Church to take up a collection, apologizing for not having done so at Pentecost, when there was a large crowd, and directing the presbyters to make up any deficiency out of the Church's revenue.[74]

III. Preacher and Writer

Most of Augustine's sermons were extemporaneous and taken down by shorthand reporters among the hearers. The sermons were simple, direct, and to the point. They covered a wide variety of subjects and of texts. In addition to those concerned with Christian living, there were also many having to do with

Christian doctrines, wherein Augustine undertook to overthrow the false beliefs and heresies of the period. A digression in one of his sermons attacking a Manichean error resulted in a merchant's coming to see him and asking him to intercede for his sins, declaring that it was the digression in the sermon which had converted him.[75]

Augustine felt deeply the sacred responsibility of the preaching office. Hence he spoke of the danger of elation and pride that comes to a preacher. 'He is a vain preacher of the Word of God without, who is not a hearer within.' He noted that the hearers of sermons stood in a safer place than the preachers, remarking to them: 'You do that now, which then we shall all do. For in the next world there will be no teacher of the Word, but the Word will be the Teacher.' Nevertheless, he emphasized the danger to the hearers in not doing what they had heard.[76]

The writings of Augustine were principally of two kinds: formal treatises and letters, of which some of the latter were in the nature of tracts. Writing letters formed a large part of his pastoral activity, even though he was always pressed for time for his correspondence. His letters were dictated to amanuenses, written by them as a general rule on papyrus, and occasionally on parchment, and signed by him, or sealed with his ring. Generally they were carried by some one of his own clergy or friends, or else given to the person who had brought Augustine the letter to which he was replying. Sometimes long periods intervened before letters were received. In the famous instance of his correspondence with St. Jerome about the interpretation of the Epistle to the Galatians, the letter was nine years in reaching Jerome in Bethlehem, and in the meantime its contents had become known through other means. Letters were also miscarried; there was often no way of knowing whether a letter had been received. On the other hand, there were instances of letters being forged. Augustine preserved copies of the letters which he sent, as well as those which he received.[77]

His letters encompassed a wide field of subjects, and were often quite long. They were sent to Italy, Gaul, Sicily, Jerusalem, and all parts of North Africa. He numbered more than thirty-four bishops among his correspondents. Some of his letters were devoted to answering philosophical questions (such as *Ep.*, 7 on memory). Some had to do with moral questions; some with Church practices, or Church doctrine, or the interpretation of the Bible; others with the refutation of heresy, or with the administration of the Church and its discipline. There were letters of felicitation, intercession, condolence, commendation, and the recognition of communicant status for clergy and laity setting out on journeys.

Although Augustine was an artist in the use of language, he never ceased to be critical of his own efforts, and he welcomed those persons who pointed out errors to him. Through expressing in writing what knowledge he had, he made further progress in understanding. Because of his desire to avoid erroneous statements, many of his works were not released for publication until long after his friends wished.

Libraries existed in many of the churches, and there was one at Hippo, as well as in the convent there. Books went out on loan even over great distances; at other times scribes were sent to copy the work desired.[78]

IV. Judge

In accordance with St. Paul's advice (1 Cor. 6:1), bishops were regularly called upon by Christians to decide judicial questions, both of an ecclesiastical nature and of a secular nature. This service was also extended to non-Christians, probably as an accommodation to the poor. These episcopal courts became extremely popular, and were sanctioned by the Roman government for cases not involving capital punishment. Augustine was frequently occupied the whole day in hearing cases about such matters as gold, silver, land, and cattle; and when doing so he took the opportunity to instruct the litigants in the truth of the divine law, as well as in the matter before him.[79] But he always begrudged the time which this took from his other duties, and in 426 asked that he might be excused from it and that the burden be assumed by his designated successor, Heraclius. He warned Christians to avoid lawsuits whenever possible, since these dis-

tracted them from more important matters. He gave great thought
to his judgments, and once remarked: 'How deep and dark a
question it is to adjust the amount of punishment so as to prevent the person who receives it not only from getting no good,
but also from suffering loss thereby.' [80]

Augustine was also called upon to discipline his clergy, as in
the case of a presbyter whom he deposed for embezzlement and
immorality.[81] In cases of suspicion he tried to keep the matter
from the public until there was proof. A presbyter of his own
household fell under public suspicion, but as there was no proof
of his guilt and Augustine believed him innocent, he refused to
discipline him; but he would not allow the layman involved to be
ordained, as there were sufficient grounds from the layman's own
conduct to warrant refusal.[82] In another instance, he refused to
admit a presbyter to Communion until his excommunication was
lifted by the bishop who imposed it; but he informed the man
that he would be personally received with all charity. Furthermore, Augustine would not receive deposed Donatist clergy unless
they submitted the same proofs of penitence as would have been
acceptable to the Donatists. He commented on the fact that any
clerical scandal makes men of ill will think evil of all clergy. He
further remarked: 'I have hardly found any men better than
those who have done well in monasteries; so I have not found any
worse than monks who have fallen.' [83]

Upon occasion Augustine rebuked his fellow bishops, singling
out one for living vainly and extravagantly, and another who
was young and new for hastily excommunicating a public official
and his family for something the officer had done which the
bishop did not like. The family of the officer was not involved,
as Augustine saw the matter, and should not have been penalized;
also the punishment of the officer was too severe.[84] 'If any believer
have been wrongfully excommunicated, the sentence will do
harm rather to him who pronounces it than to him who suffers
this wrong. For it is by the Holy Spirit dwelling in holy persons
that any one is loosed or bound, and He inflicts unmerited
punishment on none.' [85] This point of view was later to give
both comfort and support to the Jansenists.

To Augustine the Catholic Church was not only the supreme authority upon earth; it was also infallible and hence to be obeyed. Yet he was never certain wherein to locate the Church's infallibility, for bishops are corrected by other bishops, and local and provincial councils by plenary councils, and earlier plenary councils by later ones.[86] Whenever he was able Augustine attended the provincial councils, not to further his own interests but to see that the Faith was rightly defined and that justice was done to the clergy whose cases were under judgment.

V. Administrator of Church Property

The title and control of Church property was vested in the bishop, and its revenues were his to administer. Augustine referred to 'the bishops, whose authority is visibly pre-eminent, and who are supposed to use and enjoy as owners and lords the property of the Church.'[87] Not many centuries later this practice was to make bishops into feudal lords, and to turn many of them into warrior and prince bishops. Augustine had no desire for such authority. He once wrote:

> God is my witness that it is only because of the service which I owe to the love of my brethren and the fear of God that I put up with all of the administration of the Church's business over which I am supposed to love the exercise of lordship, and that I have so little liking for it that I should wish to do without it, if it could be done without unfaithfulness to my office.[88]

Because Augustine subordinated administration to pastoral activity, he assigned the care of the Church's buildings and all its property to some of the more capable clergy and had them keep the accounts. The land was rented out to tenants for cultivation. Augustine would not go out and buy property for the Church, but waited for it to be given. He was opposed to accepting trusts, wishing all gifts to be outright. Occasionally he refused legacies which he thought should belong to the families themselves. On the other hand, he was indignant with a leading citizen for turning over his property to the Church and later withdrawing it. He was also not interested in erecting new buildings; but he did not restrain others from doing so, provided they were not extravagant. Augustine estimated the land belonging to the Church at Hippo as about twenty times as large as his own paternal estate, which consisted of a few small fields. Sometimes when the Church treasury was empty, he would announce to the congregation that he had nothing to give to the poor; and when the situation became desperate, he had the holy vessels melted and sold, and the proceeds given to the needy or used to ransom captives. There is reason to believe that at this period the Church treasures were often treated more as capital consisting of precious metal than as holy objects to be preserved for sacred use.[89]

VI. Opponent of Heresy and Paganism

A not inconsiderable part of Augustine's time was occupied in opposing heresy — the Manicheans, the Donatists, and the Pelagians chiefly claiming his attention. His opposition was carried on partly by learned and long treatises refuting their errors and partly by debates, sermons, letters, and personal interviews. In a debate at Hippo he confounded Fortunatus the Manichee. He also overcame in debate the Donatist bishop Emeritus, whose position he once characterized as 'this schism, which is such a grevious scandal, causing Satan to triumph and many souls to perish.'[90] Augustine would not, however, debate with the Donatists in the presence of soldiers. 'On our side there will be no appeal to men's fear of the civil power; on your side let there be no intimidation by a mob of Circumcellions.'[91] Neither would he allow a Catholic father to compel his daughter, who had become a Donatist, to return to the Church.[92]

All the emperors from Constantine on, except Julian, had issued decrees against the Donatists, and in 405 Honorius had made Donatism a penal offense. Nevertheless, a large part of the African population was Donatist, as the schism had become identified with nationalist feeling and social discontent. Augustine urged the large Catholic landowners to bring about the conversion of their Donatist tenants [93]; and he wrote that he would welcome the return of the Donatist clergy to the Catholic fold. A fifth of all his letters were concerned with Donatism. Whereas in the early years of his episcopate Augustine was opposed to the use of force or of the civil power in dealing with schismatics and heretics, by 408 his opinion had changed. He now believed that the Scripture teaches: 'Compel them to come in' (Luke 14:23); that God in His love corrects men; that of chief consideration is the nature of the thing they are coerced to do; and that the imperial edicts had been instrumental in bringing the majority of Hippo over from Donatism to Catholicism. 'How many of them, now rejoicing with us, speak bitterly of the weight with which their ruinous course formerly oppressed them, and confess that it was our duty to inflict annoyance upon them, in order to prevent them from perishing under the disease of lethargic habit, as under a fatal sleep.' [94] At the same time Augustine wished penal measures to be applied mercifully; for 'we desire their repentance, not their death, in order that they may be saved from falling into the penalties of the eternal judgment. We do not wish to see them quite absolved from punishment nor, on the other hand, visited with the torments which they deserve. Check their sins, therefore, in such a way as to produce repentance in at least a few.' [95] Though this teaching of Augustine was later to result in and be used to justify the Inquisition, it would be unfair to lay the abuses of that system at his door.

Augustine labored against Pelagianism, which appealed chiefly to the more privileged classes and to the clergy, for almost ten years by means of treatises, letters, and sermons. He wrote to a prominent Christian lady not to be taken in by it, and to Pope Sixtus thanking him for his help in denouncing it,[96] and recommended punishment of wholesome severity for those who held the error, lest they corrupt the weaker brethren. Toward the close of Augustine's life he was brought up against the Arian heresy through the Gothic invasion. The Arians mentioned in his letters are all persons of rank or distinction.[97]

Augustine also had friendly relations and correspondence with many pagans.[98] The Christian matters most difficult for these pagans to accept were the Incarnation and Resurrection of Christ; His teaching on retribution; the late period in history at which Christianity arose; and the book of Jonah.[99] Augustine attempted to convert the high-minded and noble pagans through letters and the writing of *De Civitate Dei;* the humbler through preaching and by sending them presbyters who spoke Punic.

His championing of orthodoxy and opposing of heterodoxy was unusually successful. According to Possidius,

> unity and peace were established in the part of the Church around Hippo over which he had special jurisdiction, and then in other parts of Africa, either by his own efforts or by others, and through priests whom he himself had furnished. Moreover, he found joy in seeing the Church of the Lord increase and multiply, and in seeing the Manicheans, Donatists, Pelagians, and pagans for the most part diminishing and becoming united with the Church of God.[100]

VII. Spiritual Director

A large part of Augustine's pastoral activity was the giving of advice on moral and spiritual questions through interviews, letters, and sermons. So numerous were his callers, however, that he was forced to make a public agreement with his congregation that no one should intrude upon him five days of each week, in order that he might finish some Scriptural study which the bishops had asked him to undertake at councils both at Numidia and at Carthage. But later he wrote: 'For a short time the agreement was observed by you; afterwards it was violated without consideration, and I am not permitted to have leisure for the work which I wish to do: forenoon and afternoon alike I am involved in the affairs of other people demanding my attention.'[101] Possibly because he remembered the weakness of his early life, he was extremely circumspect in his relations with women, and would never see them without other clergy being present, even if the matter was one of secrecy.[102]

The religious situation at this time was not a heartening one.

The population was still partly pagan and innumerable barbarians were still unevangelized. The vices and immorality of
paganism still dominated society. In addition, there was religious
strife everywhere. A low Christian moral tone was general; but in
spite of this, or rather because of it, there were striking evidences
of asceticism here and there. There were both widows and vir-
gins who had consecrated themselves to lives of chastity, prayer,
and the service of the Church, and married couples who had
undertaken to live together continently.[103] In some of these cases
they had taken actual vows. Furthermore, throughout North
Africa the union of the clerical and monastic life became quite
common. In addition, many of the highest Roman officials were
good Christians and eminent for their virtuous lives.

The Christian Life. Concerning the three kinds of life — active,
contemplative, and the mean between both — Augustine taught
that although one may keep the Faith in any of these courses,
'yet there is a difference between the love of truth and the duties
of charity. One may not be so given to contemplation that he
neglect the good of his neighbour, nor so far in love with action
that he forget divine speculation.' [104] Both activity and contemplation were to be for the benefit of others. Furthermore, he
taught that the Christian life was a life of discipline. 'There is
an order: if we observe it in this life, we shall come to God.' [105]
Such discipline required humility, and caused him to say: '*diffi-
dam mihi, fidam in te*' ('let me distrust myself, that I may trust in
Thee'). In addition, perservance was also needed for spiritual
growth. There was nothing static or magical about the Christian
life. 'We must walk, must make progress, must grow, that our
hearts may be capable of receiving those things which at present
we are not capable of receiving.' [106] The reward of God was God
Himself.

Prayer. Augustine wrote to a distinguished Roman lady named
Proba a long letter covering many of the aspects of prayer.[107]
Often he mentioned prayer in his sermons. Christians first learn
to believe and then to pray, and they are enjoined to pray that
unbelievers may believe. The Lord's Prayer is the prayer of
Christ's brethren, and several sermons are devoted to its exposi-

tion.[108] It was to be imparted to none but the faithful. The regular use of the prayer with its petition for forgiveness is a kind of daily baptism. 'Prayer is the soul's affectionate quest after God.' God Himself is the end of prayer. 'Whoever seeks from God aught besides God, does not seek God chastely.' [109] Prayer also is mystical communion with God. 'We pray to Him and through Him and in Him.' Before God can answer prayer, man must first listen and then obey, for 'he that would be heard of God, let him first give ear to God.' [110]

The Creed. At this time the creed was considered to be secret and was not to be written down, and was recited only in the baptismal service, and not in the Communion service. Apparently Augustine still used the creed of his youth, that of the Church of Milan, and not the form used in North Africa, for his sermons expounding it are all based on the former. He recommended that believers say the creed daily.[111]

Fasting. The practice in regard to fasting varied in different churches, and Augustine advised, quoting St. Ambrose:

'When I visit Rome, I fast on Saturday; when I am here I do not fast. On the same principle, do you observe the custom prevailing in whatever Church to which you come, if you desire neither to give offense by your conduct, nor to find cause of offense in another's' . . . For often I have perceived with extreme sorrow many disquietudes caused to weak brethren by the contentious pertinacity or superstitious vacillation of some who, in matters of this kind which do not admit of final decision by the authority of Holy Scripture, or by the tradition of the universal Church, or by their manifest good influence on manners, raise questions, it may be from some crotchet of their own, or from attachment to the custom followed in one's own country, or from preference for that which one has seen abroad, supposing that wisdom is increased in proportion to the distance which men travel from home; and agitate these questions with such keenness, that they think that all is wrong except what they do themselves.[112]

Oaths. The question of taking an oath has bothered Christians in all ages. Augustine taught that it is not a sin to take an oath, only to take a false oath; but to break an oath is utterly wrong, even when it is obtained by force. Once he rebuked the wealthy Pinianus for not keeping his oath to remain in Hippo when the congregation there tried to force him to become a presbyter.[113]

War. War is also perennially a moot question with Christians. Augustine's views on this subject laid the foundation for the teaching of the Church formulated later. He remarked that war has been and may be waged by God's commandment; and that it is possible to please God while in military service.[114] In one of his letters he wrote: 'If the Christian religion condemned wars of every kind, the command given in the Gospel to soldiers asking counsel as to salvation would rather be to cast away their arms and withdraw themselves wholly from military service.' [115] Discussing in this same letter the Sermon on the Mount in regard to non-resistance, he concluded that it demands simply an inward disposition of good will toward an aggressor. He did not approve of killing others in order to defend one's own life, however, unless one was a soldier or public official acting in defense of others in accordance with a lawful commission. To Augustine 'war is waged that peace may be obtained'; 'but it is a greater glory to slay war with a word than men with a sword, and to gain and maintain peace by means of peace, not by means of war.' [116]

Drunkenness. Drunkenness was prevalent in ancient times, and particularly so in North Africa, occurring often in connection with religious celebrations. Pagan feasts had been accompanied with drinking, and also rioting; and the custom was brought over to the Christian feasts and martyrs' days when the empire recognized Christianity and a great number of pagans entered the Church. At first the Church condoned the practice, in order not to discourage the pagans from becoming Christians. But Augustine thought that 'it was now high time for such as had not the courage to deny that they were Christians, to begin to live according to the will of Christ, casting behind them, now that they were Christians, the concessions made to induce them to become Christians.' [117] The practices alluded to were survivals of the *Parentalia* or *Feralia* held on the tombs of the dead, and caused Augustine to write: 'At least let such a disgraceful practice be removed from the cemeteries where the bodies of the saints are laid, and from the place where the sacraments are celebrated, and from the house of prayer.' [118] In dealing with drunkenness, Augustine showed himself a great Christian psychologist when he wrote, in 392, the second year of his ministry:

> It is not by harshness, in my opinion, or by severity or by overbearing methods that such evils are removed, but by education rather than by formal commands, by persuasion rather than by intimidation. That is the kind of treatment to use with men in the mass, while severity should be employed against the sins of individuals. If there be any intimidation, let it be done with sorrow by the threats of future punishment from the Scriptures; then the fear which we inspire will not be of ourselves or of our authority, but of God's speaking to us. In this way an impression will first be made on the spiritually-minded or on those most nearly so, and by their influence and gentle, but urgent, expostulation the rest of the crowd will be subdued.[119]

Heathen Practices. Although there had been little open practice of paganism since the time of Gratian's imperial decrees,[120] still the civilized world at this time was not yet wholly Christian, and many Christians were bothered about the heathenism which persisted around them. Augustine was opposed to the destruction of idols without proper legal authority, as leading to lawlessness and invading the private property of others. He said: 'When the power has not been given us, we do not do it; when it has, we do not neglect it.' [121] He received a long letter from a Roman senator named Publicola inquiring about the propriety of accepting oaths made to heathen gods, eating food that may have been offered to idols, and using articles that may have been employed in heathen worship. To this Augustine replied that it was worse to swear falsely by the true God than to swear truly by false gods; 'for not only on the frontier, but throughout all the provinces, the security of peace rests upon the oaths of barbarians.' [122] He treated Publicola's other questions liberally in the manner of St. Paul. Elsewhere, he condemned astrologers and sacrifices to pagan gods for the healing of children.[123]

Modesty. In his personal life Augustine was both a practicer and an inculcator of modesty. His clothing was neither too fine nor too mean; his table was frugal and sparing, with occasional meat for his guests and weaker brethren; his table appointments were adequate, but not costly. As for women, he did not believe that they should be over-hastily forbidden to wear ornaments or fine clothes; but he was opposed to their having their heads uncovered, and he considered the painting of their faces immoral deceit. He condemned as an accursed superstition the wearing of amulets and earrings to cure disease.[124]

Actors, particularly the pantomine actors, came in for severe censure from Augustine for portraying by obscene gestures and dances the immoralities of the pagan gods. So also did the singers and dancers, and those who provided so luxuriously for the upkeep of the actors.[125]

VIII. Monastic Director

Augustine established a semi-monastic community at Tagaste while he was still a layman, then moved it to Hippo Regius on his being made a presbyter, and finally into the episcopal residence itself on his becoming diocesan. One of its objects was to train younger men for the ministry, although he did not consider every monk qualified for it. The community rule was what he conceived apostolic practice to have been — that all things should be held in common and distributed to each as he had need; hence the household was fed and clothed at the common expense. Augustine was given to hospitality; yet the table conversation was always serious, and gossip was forbidden. Sometimes the brothers were read to as they ate. None of the members was under vows. Two other monasteries were established near Hippo during Augustine's lifetime. The monks at Capraria he described as laboring diligently in prayer, fasting, and almsgiving; as for-

giving injuries and subduing evil habits; as chastening the body
and bearing tribulation; and as singing praises to God.[126]

Augustine also founded in Hippo a nunnery for women, of
which his sister was the first head. They wore no distinctive
garb but always kept their hair covered, and never less than
three together were allowed to go out in public. Under his
sister's successor it fell into dissension; and Augustine then drew
up in 423 a set of rules and principles for the regulation of the
convent.[127] These, afterward taken over and adapted for male
communities, are the source and basis of the later Augustinian
Rule. His famous sermons on 'The Life and Customs of His
Clergy' [128] set forth the ideal of poverty and community property
in accordance with the account in Acts 2:44-6 and as practiced
in his own household. These sermons and his letters influenced
St. Benedict and St. Caesarius of Arles in the formation of their
rules, as well as many later founders of monastic orders.

During Augustine's last illness, he allowed visitors only when
the doctors came or food was brought. The rest of his time was
spent in prayer and in the repetition of the penitential psalms.
After his soul had departed, the Holy Sacrifice was offered and
he was buried. Possidius records that he made no will, because
as a poor man of God he had nothing from which to make it.
'He left to the Church a fully sufficient body of clergy, and monasteries of men and women with their continent overseers, together
with the library and books containing treatises of his own and
of other holy men. By the help of God one may find therein how
great he was in the Church; and therein the faithful may always
find him living.' [129]

Augustine's pre-eminent influence as a theologian and doctor
of the Church has been felt in each age since and has overshadowed his greatness as a pastor, the influence of which was
experienced chiefly during his lifetime. The remarkable fact,
however, is that in spite of the time taken up by his literary
work in defining the theory of the life within the Church, he
himself actively practiced what he taught. He is as fine an example of the true and great chief pastor of souls as is to be

found in the course of Christian history. Because he loved God with his whole being, with his heart and hands as well as with his head, he loved and served his fellow men. He knew his sheep and was known of them.

FOR FURTHER READING

W. J. Sparrow-Simpson, *The Letters of St. Augustine*. London, 1919.

Sister Mary Emily Keenan, *The Life and Times of St. Augustine as Revealed in His Letters*. Washington, 1935.

J. G. Cunningham, ed. and tr., *Letters of St. Augustine*. 2 vols., Edinburgh, 1872–5.

J. H. Baxter, ed. and tr., *St. Augustine: Select Letters*. London, 1930.

H. T. Weiskotten, *Sancti Augustini Vita Scripta a Possidio Episcopo*. Princeton, 1919.

NOTES

1. *Vita,* 3.
2. *Ep.,* 5.
3. *Vita,* 4; *Ep.,* 21. 2.
4. *Ep.,* 21. 1.
5. *Ep.,* 23. 6.
6. *Ep.,* 118. 2.
7. *Ep.,* 139. 3; cf. *Ep.,* 48. 1; 110. 5.
8. *Civ. Dei,* XIX. 19; *Ep.,* 48. 1.
9. *Ep.,* 33. 5; 179. 4.
10. Some think that the practice is referred to by Possidius: 'Yet whenever it happened that he was requested by the sick to come in person and pray to the Lord for them and lay his hand upon them, he went without delay.' (*Vita,* 27).
11. *Faust.,* XIX. 13; cf. *Ep.,* 54. 1.
12. *Serm.,* 71. 32; *Bapt.,* I. 12.
13. *Serm.,* 132. 1; *Bapt.,* IV. 17.
14. *Serm.,* 174. 7; *Ep.,* 98. 9, 10; 166. 10, 21.
15. *Ep.,* 98. 5, 6.
16. *Ep.,* 98. 2.
17. *Ep.,* 98. 5; *Serm.,* 294.12.
18. *Bapt.,* III. 18.
19. *Serm.,* 58. 1; *Bapt.,* VI. 25; *Serm.,* 160. 6.
20. *Serm.,* 56. 12.

21. *Nupt. et Conc.,* I. 10.
22. *Ep. Ioan.,* VI. 10; cf. Acts 19:6.
23. *Agone,* 33; *Serm.,* 71. 28.
24. *Serm.,* 392. 3.
25. *Serm.,* 82. 11.
26. *Ep.,* 153. 6.
27. *Serm.,* 56. 11.
28. *Ioan.,* CXXIV. 5.
29. *Ep.,* 250. 2.
30. *Serm.,* 325. 2; *Ep.,* 64. 3; *Serm.,* 34.9; 67. 1; 272; 362.31; 132. 4; *Ep.,* 217; *Retract.,* II. 11; *Serm.,* 159. 1; 325. 1; *Civ. Dei,* XXII. 10; *Virg.,* 46; *Ep.,* 149. 16; 175. 5; 179. 4; 217; *Serm.,* 227.
31. *Serm.,* 128. 4.
32. *Serm.,* 303.1.
33. *Serm.,* 174. 7; *Pecc. Merit.,* I. 20.
34. *Ep.,* 54. 2; cf. *Ep.,* 55. 35.
35. *Ep.,* 54. 7.
36. *Serm.,* 56. 10; 57. 7; 58. 5; 59. 6.
37. *Serm.,* 90. 6; 132. 4; 71. 17; 112. 4.
38. *Serm.,* 77. 4; 80. 5; 87. 14; 89. 1.
39. *Serm.,* 131. 1.
40. *Civ. Dei,* X. 6, 20; XXII. 10; *Serm.,* 229.
41. *Serm.,* 227; cf. also *Serm.,* 57. 7; 272.
42. *Anima,* I. 11; II. 15; *Conf.,* IX. 12; *Enchir.,* 110; *Serm.,* 172. 2; *Faust.,* XX. 18, 21; *Ep.,* 98. 9.
43. *Serm.,* 132. 2.
44. *Serm.,* 51. 22.
45. *Ep.,* 220. 12; 262. 2.
46. *Bono Coniug.,* 32; cf. also *Nupt. et Conc.,* I. 10.
47. *Ep.,* 23. 5; 33. 5.
48. *Vita,* 11.
49. *Ep.,* 101. 4; 158. 1.
50. *Ep.,* 209. 3, 5.
51. *Ep.,* 69. 1; 209. 7.
52. *Ep.,* 213.
53. *Bono Coniug.,* 32.
54. *Ep.,* 219.
55. *Vita,* 27.
56. *Civ. Dei,* XXII. 8.
57. *Ep.,* 92. 1; cf. *Ep.,* 263.
58. *Serm.,* 172. 2.
59. *Civ. Dei,* XX. 9.
60. *Ep.,* 252–5; *Ep.,* 254; cf. *Serm.,* 176. 2.
61. *Ep.,* 98. 6; 194. 32.

62. *Ep.*, 98. 6.
63. *Vita*, 23.
64. *Ep.*, 36. 7; *Serm.*, 123. 5; 164. 9; 86. 3; 111. 2; 150. 7; 125. 7; 177. 6; *Ep.*, 262. 6, 7.
65. *Serm.*, 85. 2.
66. *Ep.*, 185. 15; 88. 1, 6; 111. 1; 133. 1.
67. *Ep.*, 228. 1, 10.
68. *Ep.*, 228. 8.
69. *Ep.*, 99. 2; 111. 2; cf. *Serm.*, 105. 13.
70. *Ep.*, 111. 6, 9; 210. 1.
71. *Vita*, 20; cf. *Ep.*, 152–5.
72. *Ep.*, 139. 2; cf. *Vita*, 12.
73. *Ep.*, 133. 2.
74. *Ep.*, 115; 151. 3; 250. 1; 268.
75. *Vita*, 15.
76. *Serm.*, 179.
77. *Ep.*, 15. 1; 31. 2; 104. 1; 139. 3; 239. 29; 118. 34; 59. 2; 149; 166. 1; 28; 71. 2; 40. 8; 68. 1; 93. 1; 164. 22.
78. *Ep.*, 75. 19; 118. 9; 231. 7; 211. 13; 18. 1; 169. 13; 264. 3.
79. *Ep.*, 33. 5; *Vita*, 19.
80. *Ep.*, 95. 3.
81. *Ep.*, 65.
82. *Ep.*, 78.
83. *Ep.*, 64. 2; 35. 3; 78. 9.
84. *Ep.*, 85; 250.
85. *Ep.*, 250A.
86. *Bapt.*, II. 3.
87. *Ep.*, 125. 2.
88. *Ep.*, 126. 9.
89. *Vita*, 24; *Ep.*, 126. 7.
90. *Vita*, 14; *Ep.*, 23. 5.
91. *Ep.*, 23. 7.
92. *Ep.*, 35. 4.
93. *Ep.*, 57; 58; 89; 112.
94. *Ep.*, 93.
95. *Ep.*, 100. 1.
96. *Ep.*, 188; 191.
97. *Ep.*, 170; 185; 220; 238–42.
98. *Ep.*, 132; 136; 138; 233–5; 251. 9.
99. *Ep.*, 102.
100. *Vita*, 18.
101. *Ep.*, 213. 5.
102. *Vita*, 26.
103. *Ep.*, 150; 212; 25; 31. 5, 6; 127. 1; 200. 3.

104. *Civ. Dei*, XIX. 19.
105. *Ord.*, I. 9.
106. *Ioan.*, LIII. 7; cf. *Serm.*, 169.
107. *Ep.*, 130.
108. *Serm.*, 56–9.
109. *Serm.*, 9. 3; 137. 9; cf. *Serm.*, 331. 4.
110. *En. in Ps.*, 85. 1; *Serm.*, 17. 4.
111. *Serm.*, 212–14; 58. 13.
112. *Ep.*, 54. 3; cf. *Ep.*, 55. 35.
113. *Serm.*, 180. 2; *Ep.*, 125. 3; 126.
114. *Faust.*, XXII. 74–6; *Ep.*, 189. 4.
115. *Ep.*, 138. 15.
116. *Ep.*, 47. 5; 189. 6; 229. 2.
117. *Ep.*, 29. 9; cf. *Serm.*, 64. 4.
118. *Ep.*, 22. 3; cf. *Ep.*, 199. 37.
119. *Ep.*, 22. 5.
120. Pagan worship was openly practiced at Madaura in Augustine's time (*Ep.*, 232. 1), and the tribes adjoining the empire were still not Christian, as Augustine learned from the prisoners whom the Romans brought in as slaves (*Ep.*, 199. 46).
121. *Serm.*, 62. 17.
122. *Ep.*, 46; 47. 2.
123. *Ep.*, 55. 12; 246. 2; 98. 1.
124. *Serm.*, 356; *Vita*, 22; *Ep.*, 245.
125. *Ep.*, 55. 12; 91. 5; 138. 14.
126. *Ep.*, 60. 1; *Vita*, 5; 25; 22; *Ep.*, 48. 3.
127. *Ep.*, 210; 211.
128. *Serm.*, 355; 356.
129. *Vita*, 31.

Part Two

A Critical Guide

to the Major Works

IV

THE EARLIEST WRITINGS

David E. Roberts

Dᴜʀɪɴɢ the years leading up to his conversion, Augustine's restless search for truth prompted him to examine or entertain most of the major theories then available. These included Manichean dualism, Academic skepticism and Neoplatonic monism. The books that are to be examined in this essay form a bridge between his early intellectual pilgrimage and the haven which he reached in the Catholic faith; and like a bridge they can be looked at from either of two perspectives. They are connected with the philosophical ideas which lead up to this point, and they are also connected with the territory of Christian doctrine which lies ahead.

After the experience in the garden, Augustine decided to resign his professorship in Milan, partly because a physical ailment made it difficult for him to fulfill his duties and partly because he needed an opportunity to reflect upon his new religious outlook. Verecundus, a grammarian of Milan, placed at his disposal a villa at Cassiciacum some miles north of the city. Here Augus-

tine stayed from the autumn of 386 until Lent in 387 in the
company of his mother (Monnica), his son (Adeodatus), his
brother (Navigius), two cousins (Lastidianus and Rusticus), two
pupils (Licentius and Trygetius), and a friend (Alypius). Although the group performed some manual labor, the main interest of each day centered in study and philosophical discussions. These discussions were recorded by a stenographer, and
Augustine then revised the notes, fashioning dialogues on the
model of Plato and Cicero. Except for an essay, *De pulchro et
apto,* which he wrote while he was a teacher of rhetoric in Carthage and which was soon lost, the three Cassiciacum dialogues [1]
were his earliest works. During the sojourn at the villa he also
supervised the instruction of his two pupils, and he probably
kept a sort of devotional diary which provided the basis for the
Soliloquies.

I. The Happy Life

The dialogue *On the Happy Life (De beata vita)* begins on
Augustine's thirty-third birthday. In looking back on his early
intellectual pilgrimage, he likens the search for truth to a tem-
pestuous voyage, and he declares that intellectual pride is the
chief obstacle to reaching a safe haven. As we shall see more
fully in a moment, he is thinking primarily of the fact that the
rationalistic promises of Manicheism prevented him for many
years from learning to think of God and the soul as incorporeal.
The obstacle has now been removed, partly through studying
Platonism and partly through listening to the sermons of Ambrose.

As the discussion proceeds, Platonic influences quickly become
evident. The soul is depicted as needing nourishment (knowledge), and its 'hunger,' which is the source of all vices, is attributed to a *lack.* This Neoplatonic thesis that evil is privative
and therefore springs ultimately from nonbeing plays an important role in Augustine's subsequent discussions of the problem of evil. A second Platonic assumption appears when the
group agrees that virtuous men possess beatitude despite pain
and misfortune, while vicious men are really miserable because

of the condition of their souls, no matter how much wealth, sensual pleasure, or fame they may enjoy. The clue to the difference between these two types of men is that the former have directed their desires toward an abiding object that is not dependent upon fate or the vicissitudes of temporal existence, while the latter, directing their desires toward temporal goods, can never be free from anxiety because they can always lose what they love.

The problem arises, however, as to whether the happy life is to be equated merely with seeking this abiding object (God) or with actually possessing it. This question is closely related to the next dialogue because the Academic skeptics identified wisdom with the quest for truth instead of with the attainment of it. The upshot of the discussion in *The Happy Life* is that no man is really left in the misery of seeking a knowledge of God which remains in principle unattainable. The primary obstacles to such knowledge are regarded as moral ones which can be removed by directing desire away from inordinate attachment to temporal goods. Wisdom is a condition *within,* whereby the soul maintains its equilibrium; but wisdom is also divine, for, according to an authoritative Christian teaching, the Son of God, who is truly God, is called the Wisdom of God. Therefore the happy life consists in having God within the soul, that is, in beholding the source of truth. Since Augustine and his friends are still seeking, they cannot yet regard themselves as wise and happy; but this dialogue has served to define the goal and to indicate steps which may be undertaken with faith and hope.

II. Skepticism and Truth

At the end of *Against the Skeptics (Contra Academicos)*, Augustine gives an interesting account of how, according to his information, the Platonic Academy descended into skepticism. Plato taught that the Forms can be apprehended only through pure reasoning and that sensory perception provides mere 'opinion'; the best he could say of the latter is that it is 'truthlike.' Because an understanding of his philosophy could not be grasped without rigorous training in dialectic and other disciplines, his followers were anxious to safeguard it from being bandied about by the ignorant and the unwise. Accordingly, when Zeno the Stoic studied at the Academy and began promulgating his materialistic theories there, Arcesilas, the head of the school, concealed the true Platonic teaching and devoted himself to the one-sided task of attacking Zeno by means of skepticism concerning sense data. In succeeding generations this skepticism became sharpened in continuing controversy with the Stoics, reaching its climax in Carneades. Not until Plotinus appeared was a return to the true Platonic position made possible.

While in Rome, Augustine came under the influence of Academic skepticism, and the experience taught him that so long as a man regards attainment of the truth as impossible he is blocked at the threshold of faith and thought.[2] In Neoplatonism he found one extension of Plato's influence that could be used against the other. As we have already seen, Neoplatonism attracted him because it takes account of moral as well as intellectual obstacles to knowledge; it insists that even the most acute reasoning is insufficient unless the soul has been cleansed of errors connected with sensuality. Hence in Augustine's mind it is easily joined with the Christian conception of the Incarnation, whereby God sent 'the authority of the divine intellect down even to a human body, and caused it to dwell therein, so that souls would be aroused not only by divine precepts but also by divine acts.'[3]

Thus the two influences which he follows against skepticism are reason and faith; but there is much debate among scholars about how far he had been carried at this time into the latter. In this dialogue his leading ideas are purely philosophical, and no attempt is made to elaborate the distinctive doctrines of Christianity. No one doubts that Neoplatonism prepared him for Christianity by enabling him to think of God and the soul as spiritual; but neither are there any grounds for doubting the sincerity of his acceptance of the authority of the Bible and the Catholic Church, even though his knowledge of Christian doctrine was so rudimentary that he could employ the loose, Apollinarian-sounding language just quoted. We must simply accept at face value his assertion that, although he is 'resolved never to deviate in the least from the authority of Christ,' [4] he also desires, so far as possible, to comprehend the truth by means of reason. And we should note the bearing of this assertion not merely upon Augustine's future career but upon the ideal of harmonizing faith and reason which dominated the thinking of the Middle Ages. By 426, when he wrote a general review of his writings (the *Retractations*), Augustine had abandoned the assumption that Neoplatonism and Christianity are wholly compatible and contended that the latter must defend itself against 'gross errors' in the former. For example, the Platonic conception of the soul conflicts with Pauline teaching concerning a resurrected body in the future life. But Augustine never abandoned the general principle of a concordat between faith and reason.

Against the Skeptics is addressed to Romanianus, a fellow-townsman who had aided him in obtaining an education at Carthage and who, fifteen years later in Milan, had offered financial support for a plan to establish a philosophical community which Augustine had discussed with a few of his friends. (The plan fell through because of disagreement over whether wives should be allowed to join the group.) Romanianus followed Augustine into Manicheism and, one stage behind his mentor, is now troubled by skepticism. *De vera religione* is another and later attempt to lead this friend toward Christianity via philosophy. In the present dialogue it is Romanianus' brilliant son Licentius who defends the skeptical position against the other pupil, Trygetius.

The two boys have been studying Cicero's *Hortensius,* and Licentius is able to quote a passage which suggests that the *search* for truth, without the finding, is sufficient for wisdom. He is willing to admit that possibly after the soul has departed from the prison of the body [5] it may reach truth, but holds that so long as we are living on earth perfect knowledge transcends our grasp. Under such circumstances happiness dictates that we should not try to overleap our natural limitations. So long as a man is engaged in ceaseless inquiry, he is employing the best means for avoiding error; thus he is headed in the right direction even though he never reaches the goal. Against this case for skepticism

Trygetius is unable to do much except to make clear that the knowledge which, as he contends, a wise man must actually *possess* should include an understanding of moral values and rational principles; in other words, he admits that a man might possess special bits of knowledge without being wise and good.

When the conversation is resumed (Book II) after an interruption of several days, Augustine sets a trap for Licentius by asking whether he still thinks the skeptical position is true. Warned by a smile from Alypius, who has just joined the group, the boy replies that he regards it as 'probable.' This answer reflects the fact that the Academics, in order to avoid the shirking of practical duties, had developed the theory that a wise man can be guided by probability in action even though he cannot reach certainty in thought. Augustine points out, however, that for anything to be probable it must be 'like' the truth and that in order to know that something is like the truth one must know the truth itself. He also lays down an important distinction between what might be called 'smart-aleck' skepticism and honest doubt. In connection with the latter he acknowledges that an earnest concern not to claim anything as certain unless it really is so makes an important contribution to intellectual integrity; but, against the former, he reminds the group that the question at issue seriously affects 'our life, our morals and the soul,' [6] since only through comprehension of the truth can reason establish control over inordinate desires.

Alypius comes forward as an advocate of the serious, instead of the flippant, form of skepticism; but he quickly falls into the very unskeptical attitude of declaring that nothing higher than the authority of the Academic philosophers can be found. These philosophers declared that wisdom involves withholding assent, and he finds himself in the contradictory position of giving *unqualified* assent to their thesis.

Since the skepticism they are dealing with is based primarily on the deceptiveness of the senses, Augustine seeks to show that even if sense data are completely untrustworthy — though he grants this only momentarily for the sake of the argument — another area remains in which certainty is possible. This area we would now call formal logic, wherein (analytic) propositions are necessarily true the instant that the definitions involved are accepted. With regard to any such proposition one knows that it is (a) true, (b) false, or (c) either true or false, even when he does not know which. For example, any thinker can be certain that 'either there is only one world or there are more worlds than one.' [7] The rejoinder that such knowledge avails little is irrelevant. For if Augustine has succeeded in showing that a philosopher can know one thing with certainty, he has refuted the thesis that judgment should be suspended on all philosophical questions.

He then goes on, however, to attack the assumption that sense perception is wholly untrustworthy. We can have certainty that a world exists by defining 'world' as 'whatever the senses present,' and a skeptic cannot deny that the senses present *something* without undermining his own complaint that they are deceptive. Nor can the fact that men make mistakes in interpreting their sensations be used legitimately as the basis for a universal skepticism; for the notion 'mistaken' presupposes the notion 'valid,' with which the former must be contrasted. Indeed, from one standpoint, whatever the senses present is absolutely true. Take the famous example of the oar that seems bent when half of it is dipped in water. One makes a mistake if he thinks that the oar is 'really' bent, but the laws of refraction would be violated if the oar did not *appear* bent. Hence, so long as one confines himself to immediate sense data, what they present cannot be mistaken and there is no deception. This kind of certainty may be inferior to what pure reasoning provides, as Plato has said; nevertheless it is obtainable.

When we pass over into the field of ethics, we find notorious disagreements among various schools, but here also the applicability of formal principles provides certainty so long as we remain within the area they cover. Augustine admits, however, that practical decisions force one to venture out beyond a priori reasoning and that for some time he espoused the guidance of 'probability' in this connection. But he came to see that 'a man is in error, not only when he is following the wrong path, but also when he is not following the right one.' [8] In the first place, it is possible for a credulous person to hit upon the truth by a kind of good luck. And in the second place, a man who uses 'probability' in avoiding all mistakes due to hasty assent may nevertheless fall into another kind of mistake, namely, that of refusing to give his assent to the true way of life. Thus Augustine was forced to recognize that 'probabilism' does not enable a person to take an adequate stand against immorality. If one really believes that men do not sin so long as they do what seems to them to be 'probably' right, he will be compelled to condone or to suspend judgment about many evil acts. Catiline's orations amply illustrate how such acts can be defended by probable arguments.

His last words in the dialogue show that Augustine is able to combine moral earnestness with intellectual humility, for he advises his students to read the Academics for themselves, forming their own judgments as to whether he has succeeded in refuting them or whether their ideas, when thoroughly studied, demolish his arguments.

III. Divine Providence

As a young man he was attracted into Manicheism because it claimed to provide a rational solution to the problem of evil. The solution was a dualism in which the world was viewed as the battleground between a good and an evil principle, and, by attributing immorality to the operations of the latter, Augustine saw some prospect of escaping personal responsibility for it. Having renounced Manicheism, he must ask whether his Christian Platonism can meet the dilemma that is as old as human reflection on monotheism: Granting that evil is real, then either God is not omnipotent or He wills evil. At the outset of *Divine Providence and the Problem of Evil* (*De ordine*), Augustine declares that both horns of this dilemma are impious; but he adds that if one must choose, it is better to regard God as limited than to regard Him as cruel.

The main purpose of the dialogue, however, is to seek a way that genuinely leads out of the dilemma. The discussion begins in a picturesque manner. One night as he lay awake in thought

Augustine noticed that the sound of water flowing outside at the rear of the baths was louder than usual. His students were awake also, and Licentius suggested that autumn leaves might have blocked the outlet so that when the pressure of the water was enough to break through, the sudden rush of the stream caused a noise. This incident leads the boy to a vision of the orderliness of all events, which he confidently undertakes to demonstrate. Trygetius slyly remarks that he is not quite so cock-sure as his friend, the erstwhile skeptic.

First of all, Augustine lays down a distinction between physical evils, such as natural catastrophes, and moral evils, in which the human will is involved. He deals with the former by means of an argument similar to the last of five theistic 'proofs' which Thomas Aquinas used several centuries later. If we consider those aspects of natural order which are not attributable to human activity, then only two explanations are available. Either such order is due to purpose, or it is not. Now some natural events so surpass anything man can produce in regularity and ingenuity that it seems impossible to attribute them to chance; the only alternative is to accept a conception of superhuman purpose. Serious difficulty arises, however, in connection with those natural events which seem *to us* to be quite pointless, even though we admit that they must have some kind of cause. In such instances it is hard for us to believe that the cause is divine purpose. Augustine and his pupils deal with this difficulty by agreeing that our outlook may be too anthropocentric. Unless an occurrence fits in with our human purposes, we refuse to regard it as purposive at all. The remedy is to take a more comprehensive view of the universe. Instead of generalizing on the basis of details that are painful to us personally, we should see our own misfortunes in the light of a universal plan.[9] Such a remedy involves a certain purification of the soul; for, unless one has achieved inward unity by turning away from the multiplicity of sensuous distractions, he is hardly in a position to grasp the 'integral fittingness' of the universe. More will be said about this spiritual purification later.

The implications of this 'more comprehensive' outlook can be grasped only if we recall the privative theory of evil which Augustine has learned from Neoplatonism. Plotinus held that all things are good in so far as they exist and that they are evil only in so far as they lack something. He also maintained, however, that the universe cannot be perfect unless every possible level of being is, so to speak, filled up. While goodness supplies the positive content of each level, the negative role of evil is indispensable to the total scheme, since otherwise there would be no gradations at all. As Augustine later recognized more fully, it is extremely difficult to reconcile this monistic ontology with the Christian doctrine of creation. On the one hand, Plotinus' teaching regards finitude and temporality as having an intrinsically evil aspect; on the other hand, it denies the ultimate reality of evil by attributing its origin to nonbeing and by regarding evil as making an indispensable contribution to the perfection of the whole. In our dialogue the influence of this paradoxical scheme leads to some curious consequences. From a starting point that looks emphatically ethical the discussion moves to a conclusion where mystical acceptance of the perfection of the universe is ominously difficult to distinguish from a sort of ruthless complacency toward evil.

Let us examine in more detail how this transition occurs. Augustine and his friends begin by agreeing that, unless there was a contrast between good and evil, the very notion of divine justice would be meaningless. A difficulty is encountered when they realize that, if God has always been just, then it seems to follow that evil is co-eternal with Him. Trygetius tries to meet this by holding that God could be 'just' from all eternity in the sense of being *capable* of discriminating between good and evil even before they arose. But whether evil is regarded as eternal or as having a beginning in time, the basic dilemma remains. How can all events fall within the scope of divine providence if God is not the cause of evil? Neoplatonism furnishes an answer. For if evil has its origin in nonbeing, then God does not cause it, but neither does anything 'positively real' fall outside divine providence. Augustine's illustrations indicate, however, that one has to pay a high and dangerous price in accepting this answer. In the famous scene in which the group watches a fight between barnyard cocks, he professes to find beauty even in the condition of the vanquished fowl because the whole struggle takes place in accordance with nature's laws. Later on he cites other instances of things which are evil when considered by themselves but which are seen to fit into an orderly pattern when viewed from an inclusive perspective: the cruelty of the hangman is bad, yet it can contribute to the order of a well-regulated state; prostitution is an evil, but its abolition might lead to worse results; isolated blemishes in a literary work can make the whole more delightful by setting off the brilliant passages to advantage. Probably no one doubts that some evils are contributory to good. The central question raised by such illustrations is this: What happens to ethical distinctions if we say concerning *all* evils that their occurrence contributes to a perfection which their nonoccurrence would destroy?

In fact, it should be recognized that *Divine Providence and the Problem of Evil* is interesting not because of the satisfactoriness of its conclusions but because of the manner in which it touches upon problems that were destined to loom large in medieval thinking. For example, in their efforts to find a middle course between (*a*) an omnipotence which wills evil and (*b*) a limited God, Augustine and his pupils ask whether God is the founder of order or is Himself governed by order. This is closely allied to the problem of whether the good is determined by God or God is determined by the good. The first alternative makes the will of God arbitrary; a thing is 'good' simply because He so decrees and for no other reason. The second alternative subordinates God to a principle or a Platonic Idea (the Form of the Good) 'above' Him. In our dialogue the discussion is interrupted before reaching the most promising solution which declares that since God is in Himself 'order' or 'goodness,' He is indeed the ground of the principle in question, but he also 'obeys' it because He acts in accordance with His own nature.

As we have already seen, the debate also brings out the fact that the problem of evil includes the puzzle of God's relationship to time. He is the Creator; but how can He be the source of mutable things while Himself remaining changeless? This was, of course, the main problem to which Aristotle addressed himself, without using the concept of creation, in his notion of the Unmoved Mover. One kind of relationship, at first, seems to present no difficulties. In so far as man, through supra-sensible reasoning, can apprehend the eternal, a direct linkage is established between his intellect and the nature of God. But Augustine points out that such a line of reflection dichotomizes man; it splits him into a soul that can be related to God and a body that cannot; it overlooks the fact that the content of the soul must include items that come via the senses; it ignores the fact that intellecual contemplation of God involves the use of memory, which is obviously connected with temporality. What the argument establishes, therefore, is that when a soul is separated from the body it can share God's immutability; but, literally speaking, this means that the man is dead; we are contemplating the kind of knowledge that is possible for the blessed in heaven. Because of God's omnipresence we must believe that a human soul can remain in the body and be 'with' God simultaneously. But our reasoning has thrown no light on God's relationship to matter and temporality.

God's relationship to error is also puzzling. To hold that error is included in His knowledge seems to attribute imperfection to some of the content of His mind. To hold that it is excluded seems to imply that God's knowledge is limited. Alypius tries to find a solution by means of analogy. He suggests that, so long as a man is engaged in a struggle against error, he has not yet reached wisdom and that therefore error can rightly be excluded from the mind of God. But Augustine points out that if a wise man has lost touch with error entirely, he cannot help a searcher to be released from it. And it would also follow that God cannot help such a searcher. The proper solution is to say that error cannot be a constituent *in* knowledge, because it is irrational, although one can know 'about' it — that is, know it for what it is.[10]

At the end of the dialogue Augustine describes the exacting moral and intellectual discipline which must be followed in

seeking an answer to their problem. They have for their instruction the twofold guidance of authority and reason. 'In point of
time, authority is first; but in the order of reality, reason is
prior.' [11] The former is the safer guide for the uninstructed multitude, but the latter is better suited to the educated. Any individual, as he makes the transition from ignorance to knowledge,
must begin by accepting moral and spiritual precepts on authority; but, gradually, through the exercise of reason, some men at
least can discern the wisdom embodied in these precepts. At one
point Augustine speaks almost contemptuously of those who do
not or cannot use knowledge and a liberal training in trying to
discern the providential ordering of the world; of those who are
'too slothful or preoccupied with other affairs or dull of understanding' he writes: 'let them provide for themselves a stronghold
of faith.' [12] He adds, however, that since rational solutions will
satisfy only a few, philosophy should try to understand the path-
way of faith, so far as possible, instead of spurning it.

The philosophical path that Augustine himself wishes to
follow is clearly modeled upon the Neoplatonic ascent from the
multiplicities of the material world to particular instances of
rationality, thence to a contemplation of Reason itself, and —
beyond all — to a vision of the Source of all. This path is difficult
to follow because man is able to turn in either direction, upward
toward reason or downward toward the objects of sense; and,
once he has started along the latter road toward bestiality and
death, it is hard to turn around. When properly developed, however, the life of reason permeates all the arts of man. It trans-
mutes delight in the senses themselves into delight in the significant import they can convey. It develops language, logic, and
written history as means of intelligible communication between
one man's 'rational center' and another's. In one of its efforts to
ascend from particular instances of beauty to the Beauty which
they symbolize, reason begets poetry. In another aspect of its
quest toward immutable truth it follows mathematics. Thus all
culture might be described as due to the soul's yearning to fly
upward from transitory things that can be seen and heard toward
the Eternal, which can only be thought. Reason's kinship with

the divine 'ordering power' is such that it must grasp universal truth in order to understand itself; reason's ability to discern the unifying principle underlying all things makes it the suitable means for searching after things divine. It finds fulfillment, however, only as its own distinctions open that *via negativa* which approaches God more by learning what He is not than by a direct apprehension of what He is.

The concept Augustine desires to nail down at the conclusion is one which, according to many modern thinkers, is sure to leave the problem of evil unsolved. That is the immutability of God. Augustine acknowledges that his group may still be puzzled as to how God can be purposive when He needs nothing; as to whether the world and evil are co-eternal with Him or began in time; and as to how creation, evil, and the corruptible human soul can be distinct from Him and yet always under His providential control. But he is also convinced that the more they turn toward God's changeless perfection, which evil has no power to affect or trouble, the less shall they be burdened by the dangers and misfortunes belonging to a world that is passing away.

Probably most readers will finish this dialogue with the feeling that it has failed to answer at least two crucial questions. First, why should one turn away from the world of matter and temporality if it has been created by God, and why should one turn away even from evil if it contributes to perfection? Second, how could man's irrational inclination to prefer lesser goods to the Supreme Good ever arise; in other words, how could anything so definite and powerful as sin originate from anything so insubstantial as nonbeing? We should recall, however, that Augustine is engaged in his first, by no means his last, struggle with these problems as a Christian thinker.

IV. The Ground of Knowledge

Our treatment of the *Soliloquies* will be confined to its philosophical contribution, leaving aside its devotional and psychological importance. This little book marks the end of the phase we have been examining, for shortly afterward he returned to Milan to prepare himself for baptism.[13] Despite the title, it preserves a dialogue form by means of discussion between Augustine and 'Reason.'

The superb prayer at the beginning re-echoes the conclusion of *De ordine*. God has created all things from nothing. He does not cause evil; but, because He is able to check and transmute it, the universe, even with its sinister side, is perfect. Hence it is through communion with God that men receive wisdom, blessedness, and eternal life, learning that what they regarded as meaningless afflictions can be turned into benefits. Knowledge of the soul and God is supra-sensible, and we cannot learn what is most important even about another human being by means of the senses. The closest analogy, perhaps, is furnished by mathematics, wherein truths are grasped with certainty by the pure intellect. But actually the Being of God transcends all analogies, inasmuch as knowledge depends upon a ground that unites the knowing and the object.[14] God is this ground. Therefore reason can reach its goal only in *vision;* the soul and God must meet, just as in physical perception there must be a meeting between the 'seeing' and the object.

We have already noted a passage in *De ordine* in which Augustine indicates that faith will gradually be supplanted by reason, so far as possible, as a person matures intellectually and morally. In the *Soliloquies* we encounter a somewhat different emphasis. Faith is assigned a preparatory function in purging the soul from bodily taints before it is in a position to follow rational demonstration; but, since the senses can mislead a man as long as he remains on earth, it is only after death that the vision of God is fully possible and that faith is no longer necessary. Hence Augustine warns himself against being prematurely confident that he is morally ready for what knowledge of God exacts of the soul. In terms of the imagery of Plato's 'Allegory of the Cave,' the eye must first be healed before it can look directly at the sun. By comparison with his earlier condition, Augustine seems to be far along the road to spiritual health. He has given up the desire for riches, honors, and marriage, and only fear of pain, bereavement, and death now stands in his way. But under cross-examination by 'Reason,' he is compelled to admit that his sensual imagination has not been conquered as completely as he would like to think. Chastened, he expresses his willingness to wait patiently and to submit himself wholly to God's guidance.

Despite his shattered self-confidence, he is able to find a starting point that seems to be completely impregnable. Centuries later Descartes adopted the same starting point, with fateful consequences for modern philosophy. As Augustine puts it, he is certain of his own existence because no matter how doubtful he may be concerning other things about himself, he is certain that he thinks.[15] The discovery is of the utmost importance because to grasp a truth that is certain is to be in touch with something eternal. Truth is eternal because, even if the world ceased to exist, it would remain true that the world had ceased to exist. Indeed, one cannot deny the eternity of truth without falling into contradiction; for, if truth perished, one truth would remain — namely, that it had perished.

On this basis 'Reason' attempts to deduce directly that the soul is immortal. The argument is as follows: If the possibility of error is eternal, then the soul by whose mistake error arises must likewise be eternal. On the other hand, if falsity can be removed entirely, then the pure truth which remains can be grasped only by a living soul. Augustine quite properly protests, however, that the possibility of error and the grasping of truth require only that there shall be at least *one* soul alive at any given time. The argument fails to demonstrate that any particular soul is immortal.

Without meeting the objection, 'Reason' begins a new attempt to show that truth and mind (or soul) are in some sense correlative. One of the most interesting things about the *Soliloquies* is the way Augustine anticipates later philosophical positions, and this time we get a foretaste of Berkeleian idealism. 'Reason' argues, in effect, that, since all true judgments about physical objects are dependent upon sense perception, we have no grounds for believing that the physical world exists apart from being perceived. Augustine cannot find a flaw in the argument, but the conclusion seems absurd to him. He still feels that things 'are as they are' and that sense data derive from them, enabling us to

apprehend their qualities more or less adequately. 'Reason' insists, however, that we cannot form a notion of truth without
presupposing a mind that discriminates between truth and falsity; we cannot conceive of an item of knowledge in abstraction
from a knower. As in other passages of this dialogue, the discussion leaves several verbal ambiguities and major philosophical
issues dangling. Augustine remarks at one point that he is content to let his thoughts have free rein because he feels no embarrassment at the prospect of losing to himself in a debate!

Despite inconclusiveness, the *Soliloquies* remains impressive
as an exercise in intellectual honesty. Augustine longs for some
sort of assurance concerning immortality, for he does not see how
earthly life can really be blessed if the soul is destined to die.
Moreover, he cannot relinquish the conviction that *immutability*
somehow furnishes a linkage between God, truth, and the soul.
Harking back to the Socratic doctrine of *anamnesis*,[16] he is impressed by the fact that the mind *possesses* timeless truth before
sensory experience. For example, in mathematics one can apprehend by pure thinking that a sphere can be touched by a plane
at only one point, even though nothing in spatio-temporal existence perfectly fulfills what this pure thinking contemplates.
The empirical world only approximates or imitates what the
mind 'already' knows. Nevertheless, honesty compels Augustine
to demolish arguments which support the conclusion he desires
to reach. He is not convinced by the Platonic thesis that the
soul, since it is the source of life, can never fall under the
'opposite Idea,' death. He sees that although a soul cannot 'be
itself' and at the same time be joined with death, it might nevertheless simply cease to 'be itself.' Finally, he is not entirely satisfied with 'Reason's' reiterated claim that, since eternal truth is
resident in the soul, the latter must similarly be eternal.

V. The Soul

The Immortality of the Soul (*De immortalitate animae*), which
was written after Augustine's return to Milan, is little more than
a series of notes to remind him that his investigation of this theme
needs to be carried further. Considerable attention is paid to

the question of how the soul can remain immutable even though it moves the body. The word 'immutable' is likely to give rise to misleading connotations, however. Augustine of course recognizes that the soul is affected not only by bodily changes consequent upon age, illness, and pain but also by changes 'within itself' that occur when it passes from ignorance to wisdom. His point is that the soul (self) possesses an identity which in some sense transcends time. It can remember the past, promote future ends, retain constancy of purpose, and remain 'the same' soul, despite the changes just referred to. These facts suggest that the 'accidental' changes it undergoes provide no grounds for holding that it could be subject to the 'substantial' change which death would involve.

On the other hand, there are positive grounds for holding that nothing can separate the rational soul from timeless truth. The death of the body cannot, because the relationship between the soul and truth is not corporeal. The soul would not will such a separation, because union with truth fulfills its highest longings. And Truth itself would not withdraw, because it always gives itself bountifully to all to be enjoyed. This type of thinking reflects, of course, the notion of a hierarchical structure of being: God, human souls, matter. Augustine assumes that because the corporeal plane of existence is 'lower' than the soul, it could not force death upon the latter. Underlying the hierarchical structure is the general conviction that Mind, as a guiding principle, can explain the material world, whereas no conceivable arrangement of matter can account for the existence of mind.

Augustine seems to recognize, however, that at one point he has argued too well. For if the soul never separates itself from truth, then error and unwisdom cannot occur. He grants therefore that the soul can fall into defect and thus be led toward death; but he adds that to tend toward nothingness is not the same thing as to reach it. For example, matter is infinitely divisible, at least in thought, but however small the pieces may get they remain 'something' instead of 'nothing.' If matter is indestructible, how much less should we fear the death of the soul, which is more excellent. To be sure, the human body does die, even though its physical constituents are never completely destroyed. But unwisdom cannot literally kill the soul, inasmuch as even the most degraded person does not cease to be a soul. The more Augustine presses such arguments, however, the more he approximates a position that makes the soul self-existent and co-eternal with God.

During the winter of A.D. 387-8, after Monnica had died at Ostia and Augustine had returned to Rome, he wrote another book on the same problems, *On the Measure of the Soul (De quantitate animae)*. In it he tests and elaborates his own views against the somewhat naïve materialism of his friend Evodius. We are already familiar with most of his arguments, but it is interesting to note that he takes for granted that the soul is *created* (and therefore distinct from God) even though it is immortal (and therefore like God). He urges that even men can make things which are distinct from themselves and yet like themselves; but this is a very weak analogy. The soul is not a 'thing,' and if it is eternal there is no temporal interval between the creative act and the created effect. Indeed, the analogy throws no light on how the soul can be distinct from God before and after its association with a human body.

In refuting Evodius, however, Augustine is able to make the following points: First, if the soul is regarded as coterminous with the body, it becomes impossible to understand how the mind can grasp (e.g. through memory) distant places which are not present to bodily perception. Second, although the soul uses the body as its instrument, its power consists primarily not in force but in its capacity to evaluate and to grasp incorporeal truths. Third, it is necessary to postulate a *sensus communis* in order to account for those things which the soul apprehends directly through reason instead of through any one of the five senses. Fourth, even in moments when a man is not engaged in reasoning, he remains a possessor of reason.

Evodius remains puzzled as to how the soul can know what is going on in the body when the soul is not in space, and Augustine himself is baffled by the recollection of an incident which suggests that the soul is divisible. Some of his students cut a centipede in half, then divided the parts, and so on; each part reacted as a new whole. But this biological mystery is not a major obstacle, because Augustine's main point in the dialogue is that man's rational capacities distinguish him from all other creatures in a fashion which materialism cannot explain.

The dialogue culminates in a description of seven 'levels' in order to make clear this distinctiveness: (1) Life. This sort of 'animation' man shares with plants and animals. (2) Sensation and local movement. These are possessed by animals but not by plants. (3) Memory. Science, language, tradition, culture, and attempts to envisage the future are dependent upon it. Though some animals seem to possess a kind of 'sensory' memory, the higher developments are exclusively human. (4) Moral goodness. At this point man has the right to rank himself higher than the entire physical universe. Yet the possession of moral consciousness also subjects man to temptation and to the fear of righteous punishment after death. Therefore the attempt to remove anxiety by eradicating conscience can succeed only at the cost of ceasing to be human. (5) Contemplation of the Truth itself. Here anxiety is effectively conquered. (6) The moment of vision, wherein contemplation reaches its fruition. But if one attempts to attain this goal without the preceding moral purification, the light of truth may be blinding instead of illuminating. (7) 'Vision' as an abiding instead of a momentary state. Here we shall 'see' the truth of things which we must now accept on faith: the resurrection of the body, the Incarnation of the Son of God for our salvation, the Virgin Birth, and other marvels of the Gospel story. If the life of the soul can culminate in such a destiny, then departure from this earthly body, which men so pervasively dread, is actually the highest favor.

It will be seen immediately that this scheme presupposes human freedom, to which we shall presently devote a longer discussion. In this dialogue Augustine maintains that denial of freedom is self-contradictory because if the denial is uttered through automatic compulsion it cannot claim to be true. He also holds that although the gift of freedom is granted by God, its abuse (sin) is due to man and not to any defect in God's creative activity.

VI. The Means of Learning

Before turning once again to these weighty issues, we shall consider a short dialogue *On Teaching* (*De magistro*) between Augustine and his son Adeodatus, written in 389. The little book elaborates Augustine's theory of knowledge in connection with the function of language. The primary characteristic of words is taken to be the fact that they point to 'realities' beyond themselves. A problem arises in connection with *nihil* ('nothing') because it does not point to a reality; but, since men can communicate intelligibly by means of this word, it must signify something, and Augustine suggests that this 'something' must be a thought. The main conclusion reached is that, although all words are signs, not all signs are words; for one can also use gestures, and, in certain instances, meaning can be denoted directly — for example, the reality of 'walking' can be presented by performing the act.

Words can signify: (*a*) themselves, (*b*) other signs, or (*c*) realities that are not signs. Examples under the first category are to be found in such words as 'sign,' 'word,' 'noun,' and so on. Indeed, in one sense all words are nouns because when we think them as words they become items of knowledge and any word, thus considered, can be used as the subject of a sentence. Unless the difference between the word and what it points to is carefully noted, ambiguities easily arise. Augustine jokingly tells Adeodatus that he had better not answer the question: 'Are you a man?' unless he has made sure that the questioner has the reality (a rational animal) instead of merely the word in mind. In general, words are instrumental and we should value the knowledge they convey more highly than the words themselves. Adeodatus brings up the question as to whether we should not shun knowledge of 'filth' far more than we shun the word; but Augustine denies this on the ground that an ethically sound knowledge of filth is superior to knowledge of the word.

The manner in which language may be made to serve precision is illustrated by the fact that, if one tries to convey the reality of 'walking' by performing the act, an observer may identify the concept ('walking') with the particular instance; then he might fail to realize that anyone who was moving more slowly or more swiftly was also walking. Nevertheless, the fact remains that we learn the meaning of words through acquaintance with what they stand for, instead of gaining knowledge of reality simply by being exposed to words. They can help acquaint us with new realities only in so far as we form ideas of what we have never seen on the basis of what we have seen. For example, I can understand a story about three youths in the fiery furnace because I already know what 'three,' 'youths,' 'fiery,' and 'furnace' stand for; but no words can make me acquainted with the individuals involved. Similarly a man born blind can use words about colors to convey intelligible meanings, but only a man who can see can in the full sense know what the words refer to.

The conclusion of the dialogue brings these considerations into connection with the Platonic view of the soul which Augustine has already adopted. In the case of knowledge that depends directly upon rationality instead of upon sense perception, understanding issues from interior enlightenment. No man can endow another with rationality through teaching and the use of words; the gift of intelligence can be bestowed by God alone. Hence, in leading Adeodatus from one insight to another, Augustine has really been eliciting what the boy already in some sense 'knows.' The same point can be put in another way. If the learner must take what the teacher says on faith, then he has not yet reached knowledge; whereas, if he is certain that what the teacher says is true or false, his certainty is independent of the teacher. In any case, unless the pupil apprehends objective realities by means of his own interior understanding, no amount of listening to a teacher can lead him to knowledge. Sometimes the pupil can even reach truth *despite* the teacher, as, for example, when the latter repeats an argument, thinking it is false, and the former discerns that it is valid. The conclusion is that men have no real masters on earth, since God is the Master of all.

Augustine was to write further on the problem of teaching, particularly in his *On Christian Instruction* (*De doctrina Christiana*), which is reviewed by Professor Scott-Craig in Chapter IV.

VII. Free Will

Augustine's *Freedom of the Will* (*De libero arbitrio*) is the most substantial volume to be considered in this essay. Although he began it in Rome during the winter of 387–8, the second and third books were written after his return to Africa, and by the time he finished it (395) he was not only an ordained priest but on the verge of being made a bishop. Hence the work provides a convenient link between his beginnings as a 'Neoplatonic philosopher' and his maturation as a Father of the Church. By studying it we gain insight into the continuity of his development and we are also introduced to problems that occupied a major portion of his attention in later years. The Pelagians claimed that his position in *Freedom of the Will* conforms to their views; but he denied this in his *Retractations* (i. 9). We must examine the dialogue itself before commenting on this dispute.

First Augustine helps Evodius, the other participant, to reach clarity concerning moral values. The basic distinction, which we encountered at the very beginning in *The Happy Life,* is between those who desire temporal goods and those who desire eternal goods. Because human law reflects the former, it is often in contrast with divine law. The one regards killing in self-defense as a lesser evil than being murdered by an aggressor; but the other may imply that being killed cannot rob a man of anything of real value when earthly life is compared with immortality. In any event, moral goodness must not be equated uncritically with what human society sanctions. Obedience to government is right so long as it promotes the common good over private interest; but, when a people and a government become corrupt, rebellion may be ethically obligatory. Civil law is to be understood primarily as an instrument used by Providence to keep evil men in check. Order can be maintained in family, economic, and political affairs only by means of temporal punishments directed against men who set their hearts on temporal goods; unless men were evil, civil law would have no effective penalties at its disposal. On the other hand, a virtuous man will use his temporal possessions in subordination to the Supreme Good, and he will also be prepared at any time to lose them. This division of the human race into two classes receives further elaboration, of course, in Augustine's great work *The City of God.*

Since the argument thus far depends for its cogency upon belief in God, Augustine brings forward rational considerations in support of this belief. His basic 'proof' moves from (*a*) the existence of the self through (*b*) the objectivity of truth to (*c*) the reality of God. Let us examine each of these steps. (*a*) In accordance with the 'Cartesian' formula already encountered in the *Soliloquies,* the existence of the self cannot be undermined, because the activity of doubting entails it. Augustine conceives of the self as including sense perception, the *sensus communis,* and reason. The *sensus communis* must exist because the five senses themselves cannot provide for their own correlation, nor can they make us aware, as we are, of the distinction between the activity of perceiving and the object apprehended. (*b*) The *many* individual selves can know *one* common world. This statement applies not only in connection with physical things but also in connection with mathematical and ethical concepts. In none of these cases is objectivity undermined by the fact that some men may be unable to reach the truth at all or may make mistakes in their thinking. Even in ethics, where conflict of opinion is so notorious that each man seems to be defining 'the good' privately, disagreement cannot be genuine unless we assume that our opponent is making a mistake. (For example, what 'appears' good to him is not 'really' good.) And we can regard him as mistaken only if we assume that valid judgments are possible. Augustine cites examples of valid principles which cannot be undermined by the vagaries of private opinion: less excellent things should be subordinated to more excellent things; honesty is better than its opposite; justice is better than its opposite, and so on.[17] These considerations lead him to the conclusion that objective truth must be superior to our human minds. For, if it were inferior, we would pass judgments on the rules of right thinking in mathematics and ethics, whereas, instead, the quality of our thinking is judged by them. And if it were merely equal, then truth would vary the way our minds do when they see a thing more clearly in one moment than in another. Therefore apprehension of the truth is superior to all temporal delights, and it furnishes the standard whereby other goods are to be judged. Some men are wiser than others because they have turned away more completely from the material world and from particular instances of truth in order to contemplate truth itself. Their enjoyment of freedom and security is noncompetitive because no man can make truth his private property; the more one possesses it the more it remains available to all. (c) The last step of the argument is simple and sudden. Augustine declares that if there is something superior to truth it must be God, and that if nothing is more excellent, then truth itself must be God. In either case, God exists. We may add 'by faith' that Truth or Wisdom is co-equal with the Father. The 'proof' as a whole must be looked upon, of course, as elaborating the structure of an ontology which Augustine has already adopted. On the basis of this ontology he assumes: (1) that the possibility of apprehending objective truth indicates that the structure of Being is rational as a whole and (2) that the grounding of Being in rational order is equivalent to grounding it in 'Goodness.' Anyone who rejects these assumptions is bound to feel that there are gaps in the 'proof.' Indeed, unless one accepts these assumptions, the same arguments which Augustine uses to establish the objective reality of 'good' can be used to establish the objective reality of 'evil.'

He adds another 'proof' which moves from the world to God under three topics — rational order, causation, and value. Roughly speaking, we can say that the first proof has an ontological character because it is based on the nature of thought itself, whereas — again, roughly speaking — the second proof is a posteriori.[18] The latter can be summarized very briefly: (a) The orderliness of the material universe points to a rational ground through which it has been created and by which it is sustained. (*b*) Nothing can form itself, because to do so it would have to precede itself as a cause. Therefore the human soul as well as the physical world, viewed as 'effects,' are dependent upon an immutable, 'uncaused' source. (*c*) All instances of 'good' in inorganic existence, living things, and rational understanding point to the supreme Source of goodness.

Having 'established' the reality and goodness of God, Augustine is then in a position to declare that, if free will is a good, there is no problem in affirming that God has given it. But if he has granted it for the purpose of enabling men to live right, the question arises as to how men can go contrary to this purpose (inasmuch as God is omnipotent). Augustine points out initially that there is a real question as to whether free will can even be *conceived* as something that could never be abused. If men cannot sin, freedom does not exist. He adds that free will, despite its abuses, is such a 'good' that we cannot say it ought not to have been granted. A man can do evil with his hands or eyes; but we would say that the body lacked 'goods' if he were without hands or eyes. And if we praise God for the good gifts of the body, we should praise Him even more for the good gifts of the soul. It is true that God's goodness is more evident in virtues which no one can use wrongly than in lower goods of soul and body which men can misuse; but it is most evident in the order, viewed as a whole, whereby He gives to each thing its proper nature. If providence is not fulfilled positively, through conformity to virtue, then it is fulfilled negatively, through the fact that the proud, selfish, lustful man receives the kind of soul he merits.

Let us grant, for the moment, that, while the possibility of sin is due to God, the actuality is due solely to man. How can man actualize something that goes contrary to the will of God? Basically Augustine's reply is that the soul voluntarily turns to lesser goods when it could have willed the highest good. Since a 'good will' has only to be willed in order to be possessed, the defect from which the wicked man suffers is due to his own fault. In the last analysis, therefore, this wrong movement of the will originates from 'nothing'; but the lack (defect) can occur only because we will in such a way that it does occur. Thus man 'falls' through his own choice; but it does not follow that he can similarly remedy the defect through his own choice. Evodius objects to this explanation on the ground that, in many instances, at least, the soul is driven compulsively by the power of natural instincts instead of making a free choice. But Augustine insists that impulses do not exist apart from the soul; an impulse *is* the soul moving; if an unworthy impulse has become dominant, this is only because the soul has made it its own; no external power can gain mastery except by means of capitulation within the soul.

Evodius points out, however, that if God foresees how man will abuse his freedom, then the actuality as well as the possibility of sin must in some sense be due to Him. Augustine replies that for God to foreknow an event does not imply that He causes it [19]; there is a distinction between events that happen by necessity and those that happen through human willing, and unless God's foreknowledge apprehends this distinction, He is not omniscient. Moreover, since human sin is due to a defect, it does not derive from a *cause* that stands over against God and limits Him; on the contrary, it derives from 'nonbeing,' from a failure to use the will as it could have been used. God can foreknow sin without causing it because in a strict sense sin is not caused; it is due to the absence of rational causation.

To hold that God, foreseeing sin, would have 'done better' to withhold the gift of freedom entirely, is to say that the universe would have been better if men had never existed. But even in the case of a terribly degraded person, we have no right to say that 'it would have been better' if he had never existed; for, even when ruined by sin, he has greater worth and dignity than the lower levels of creation can possess. It is easy, of course, to imagine a world in which men would possess freedom without abusing it so gravely. But, instead of constructing imaginary pictures of a hypothetically perfect world, it is better to deal with every level of actual existence as making some contribution to the fullness of Being. This means that a world in which men can sin, and can be brought back to blessedness through the grace of God, is to be accepted thankfully, instead of suggesting that God ought to have done His work differently. If He paid heed to the various specifications men might draw up for a 'better' world, the result would be chaos. Some would relish a life of worldly delights, free from having to trouble about eternity; others would prefer an existence of contemplation, free from the inconvenience of having to bother with the body and with temporal affairs.

In short, Augustine is prepared to assert that since existence, as such, is good, even a wretched existence is better than non-existence. Most of those who declare that they would prefer extinction keep right on living, even though they could always commit suicide; and if they have not learned to praise God in all things, it is just that they should be unhappy. As for those who do commit suicide, they do not actually desire extinction; what they long for is 'relief,' that is, an *existence* freed from misery.

Does it follow, then, that if all men were to reach beatitude the universe would lack something and thus become defective? And does it follow that since sinning contributes to the perfection of the total scheme men should not be punished for it? Augustine's answer is that human freedom is necessary for the perfection of the universe, but that human sin is not. It is more than doubtful whether this reply is consistent with other aspects of the point of view he is seeking to defend. Apparently he assumes that every level of existence, viewed positively as existence, makes a necessary contribution to the fullness of Being. Sin makes a negative contribution, in the sense that the punishments, unhappiness, and 'diseased' condition of the soul which attend it at the same time manifest the justice and providence of God; but it cannot be said that sin is necessary in order to make God either just, when He punishes, or merciful, when He saves. The difficulty remains, however, that it is impossible to conceive of how the lower levels of existence, which do contribute necessarily and positively to the perfection of the whole, could become 'lower' except through admixture with evil. Moreover, Augustine's insistence that we should talk about the actual world, instead of a hypothetical one, may well be turned against him in this connection. To say that the possibility of sin (freedom) makes a necessary contribution to the perfection of the universe is irrelevant. If we are dealing with the actual world, the possibility of sin cannot be divorced from its actuality.

Toward the end of the book Augustine brings his views of divine goodness and human freedom into connection with the Christian doctrines of Original Sin and of Atonement through Christ. These passages deserve special scrutiny because they incorporate one of his earliest attempts to deal systematically with Biblical (as contrasted with Neoplatonic) concepts. His main concern is to show that, because man is free, he can turn either toward salvation or toward reprobation. In other words, man can choose to come under the control of either God or the devil. The role of Christ as Saviour is set forth in connection with two basic ideas. First, the word comes to us in the *flesh* because men fall into sin through becoming attached to the material world. They are saved by following an example of humility which reaches them in the midst of their bondage and leads them from the visible to the invisible. It should be noticed that this interpretation of the Incarnation puts the stress not on *redeeming* the physical and the temporal but upon leading away from them. In the second place, Christ destroys Satan's 'right' to ruin men who, through abuse of their freedom, have come under his dominion. At this point Augustine adopts an idea that frequently played a role in patristic theories of the Atonement. He holds that when the devil brought about the undeserved death of the sinless Christ, he forfeited his claims over the descendants of Adam as heirs of sin. Thus Christ has paid a debt, on behalf of sinners, which He did not owe; and no obstacle now stands in the way of the salvation of those who consent to follow Him. On the other hand, we reproach those whom the devil can persuade to remain in unbelief and reprobation; and the reproach implies that such men could have used their freedom differently.

This whole interpretation rests on the assumption that a man always 'can' do what he 'ought.' He has no right to claim that God has failed to supply him with sufficient strength to resist temptation, inasmuch as God has given him a free will and nothing can lead him into sin against his will. When the question arises about what causes the will to choose either the right or the wrong, Augustine replies that the question lands in an infinite regress. There is no cause of wrongdoing prior to the action of the will itself [20]; anything that causes human behavior apart from the will results in involuntary action and therefore cannot be the cause of sin.

It is not surprising that he encounters difficulties when he tries to reconcile this conception of freedom with Romans 7:18ff., where Paul vividly describes the condition of *not* being able to do what one ought. Augustine attributes this 'bondage of the will' to an impotence which has resulted from man's failure to use his power aright when he possessed it. Therefore the impotence is a just punishment, and we should not allow the sinner's present condition to blind us to the freedom which he received in accordance with the goodness of creation. The complaint that individuals today are not responsible for Adam's sin and its consequences would be justifiable, Augustine acknowledges, if salvation from the defects we inherit were not available. Moreover, God does not hold us responsible for any aspects of this inherited weakness which we literally cannot help; blame arises, rather, at that point at which men neglect to study what they ought to know and do and fail to heed Him who has the power to heal them. Despite the Fall and Original Sin men can still discriminate between right and wrong, and they can move forward, with God's help, toward truth and virtue. Fallen man is born into ignorance and bondage; but he is not forced to remain in that condition; he can use the consequences of Original Sin as stimuli to moral advancement.

At this point Augustine introduces, more or less parenthetically, a discussion of the origin of the soul. He lists four hypotheses none of which, so far as he knows, is regarded as definitely preferable according to Catholic thinkers: (1) Each soul is directly created by God at the time when the individual is created. (2) Souls are propagated, like bodies. (3) They preexist and are sent by God to dwell in human bodies when the latter appear. (4) They pre-exist and enter bodies through their own choice. Some of his remarks indicate that at this time he favored either the third or the fourth hypothesis, but he recognizes that dogmatism should be avoided because the problem transcends experience and no definite guidance is available from authoritative sources. His main concern is to point out that no matter which theory is adopted, sin remains properly attributable only to voluntary activity. He concludes from this fact that children who die before reaching any kind of moral responsibility will receive something other than either reward or punishment. Other specific questions are also dealt with, such as why animals suffer and how Satan could fall; but they do not pose any difficulties which have not already either been met or evaded.

We come therefore to the question: Were the Pelagians right in contending that *Freedom of the Will* coincides with their position? On the whole, it must be acknowledged that the Pelagians have a strong case. In his *Retractations* Augustine is able to point out that he makes little mention of the grace of God in this book because his primary concern at the time was to affirm human responsibility against a form of necessitarianism which would deny it. He adds that *Freedom of the Will* is devoted largely to a description of the gift which man received from God before the Fall. Clearly, however, the work also describes freedom after the Fall in terms that are incompatible with Augustine's later position; for it states that even after the Fall men are able to turn, through an act of will, either toward Christ or toward Satan; it assumes that even after the Fall men can move toward salvation by making the moral effort involved in following Christ as an example.

Because they are overshadowed by later writings, the books we have just examined are sometimes given scant treatment in discussions of Augustine. Yet it is impossible to understand the respects in which his major works either retain or abandon Greek philosophical premises without approaching the whole problem in the light of his early reflections. As the years pass, he brings his deepening knowledge of the Bible to bear upon such themes as Creation, Original Sin, the interpretation of history, and the doctrine of the Trinity. Yet his theology bears the traces of having been arrived at through Platonism, even where it finally breaks away from Platonism. Apart from the fact that they are indispensable in a study of Augustine's development, these early books are interesting in their own right. There is a freshness, at times a naïveté, about them mixed with penetration. Most of the great themes are here — the problem of knowledge, the nature of selfhood, freedom, immortality, the reality of God, the problem of evil, relations between faith and reason. In some instances Augustine is posing for the first time problems which he pondered throughout his life without reaching an entirely consistent answer. Although the Platonic metaphysics which he has accepted and the Christian conversion which has transformed his life are in the forefront of his consciousness, he realizes that he and his friends must grope toward truth for themselves and in their own fashion. Thus we see in these dialogues the dilemmas of every thinker. How can I enter into the truth genuinely except by an independent use of my own reason and insight? Yet how can I begin without presuppositions? May not the answer which I am seeking already await me in a tradition or a body of doctrine? May not the chief obstacle to my appropriation of truth be moral or spiritual rather than intellectual? How can I be honest, following the argument wherever it leads, and at the same time be faithful to convictions which can be neither established nor undermined by argument because they spring from a deeper level? Even where Augustine seems to be betrayed by his own preconceptions, he may help us to be wary of the respects in which the same sort of thing may be happening to us.

FOR FURTHER READING

V. J. Bourke, *Augustine's Quest of Wisdom* (Milwaukee, 1945), Chap. VI.

John H. S. Burleigh, ed., *Augustine: Earlier Writings,* in the Library of Christian Classics (Philadelphia, 1953).

W. J. Sparrow Simpson, *St. Augustine's Conversion* (New York, 1930). This book contains a brief review of Augustine's early works.

NOTES

1. The probable sequence of these discussions: *Contra Academicos*, November 10–12 and 19–21, A.D. 386; *De beata vita*, November 13–15; *De ordine*, November 16–18; possibly also November 22–23. Note that *Contra Academicos* is interrupted.

2. *Enchiridion*, VII. 20.

3. *Contra Academicos*, III. 19. 42.

4. Ibid. III. 20. 43.

5. This reflects a Socratic-Platonic view of the body and the senses as obstacles to rational knowledge. The idea that the body is a prison or tomb is of Orphic origin.

6. *Contra Academicos*, II. 9. 22.

7. Ibid. III. 10. 23.

8. Ibid. III. 15. 34.

9. It is interesting to note that Spinoza, using substantially the same approach at this point, was led to an opposite conclusion. For him, overcoming anthropocentrism involved recognizing that teleological categories apply only to human activities, not to the universe as a whole.

10. Aristotle protects the perfection of God's knowledge at the cost of His having no cognitive relationship to matter and evil. Aquinas retains the Aristotelian principle that God has knowledge only of the content of His own perfect mind; but in order to safeguard His omniscience, Aquinas then goes on to attribute to God's mind what might be called the 'reduplication' in detail, as well as in universals, of all reality. Thus, according to Aquinas, God can have exhaustive knowledge of evil without evil things themselves being in the mind of God. The issue involved for Aquinas, as for Augustine, is how to steer a middle course between pantheism, which engulfs created existence within the Being of God, and dualism, which attributes an independent existence to whatever falls outside the Being of God.

11. *De ordine* II. 9. 26.

12. Ibid. II. 5. 15.

13. The *Soliloquies* were probably written between December 386 and January 387.

14. This passage may reflect the influence of Socrates' 'Parable of the Sun' in Plato's *Republic* vi. 508ff.

15. Descartes' formula was: *Dubito ergo cogito; cogito ergo sum.* But the *ergo* does not really lead to anything new in the conclusion. This can be seen by writing the latter proposition as Kierkegaard does: 'I am thinking; therefore I am.' In other words, thinking presupposes the existence of the self; it cannot provide a basis for mov-

ing by proof from uncertainty to certainty concerning the existence of the self.

16. Later he repudiates this doctrine in his *Retractationes*.

17. The formal certainty which Augustine illustrates here rests on the logic of definitions which a man might grasp without being morally good in his behavior.

18. Aquinas criticizes the first type of proof on the ground that it cannot really bridge the gap between the order of thought and the order of being. He adopts the second type of proof as suited to our earthly condition because it starts with empirical data, and he covers the three topics mentioned with greater precision than Augustine does.

19. In this connection Augustine appeals to an analogy, pointing out that a man can foreknow events without causing them. But the analogy is weak. (*a*) It may be claimed that men have fore*knowledge* (certainty) only in connection with events that are physically or logically necessitated, even though they do not do the necessitating. (*b*) In any case, God, who creates the world with foreknowledge of how men will employ their freedom, is in a different position from human beings.

20. It might seem to be impossible to reconcile this with his preceding references to the devil; but Augustine holds that the devil cannot *cause* sin in a man unless the man's will first consents. The further question about how a monistic theory of evil can be combined with belief in the devil is one which Augustine does not answer.

V

ON CHRISTIAN INSTRUCTION

T.S.K. Scott-Craig

AUGUSTINE is now commonly regarded as one of the founders of the *Middle* Ages; yet such a perspective could hardly be his own. He did not think of himself as initiating the ages that were in the middle of history. He worked rather as a representative of a new religion inside an old culture. The institutions of that culture were well established and were therefore difficult to transform. Some of them could be regarded as religiously irrelevant, some accepted as religiously neutral. Those that were inextricably interwoven with the old religion had to be excised or at least purged; those that were not so contaminated, and were in themselves useful and profitable, could, however, be adopted with enthusiasm. Moreover, the civilization of his time was under attack from without; the barbarians were at the gates. It seemed wise, therefore, to preserve existing institutions as far as possible rather than to have none at all. Some such general picture was no doubt in Augustine's mind when he discussed the instruction of Christians.

I. The Range and Limits of Culture and of Instruction

One of the major tasks of any culture is to discover and then to communicate fact. From the bewildering sea of data, from the vast ocean of the given, we must fish out the significant. We must make a record; and that selective recording, that statement of fact, must be and remain intelligible. Such a task is natural to man, and with it the impact of the supernatural does not normally interfere. It was a measure of the anguish of Shakespeare's Hamlet that the supernatural commands of the Ghost forced him to cry: 'I'll wipe away all trivial fond *records';* just as it was an index of the demonic depths to which the Witches had led Macbeth that 'till the last syllable of *recorded* time' life seemed a furious surge of non-significant sound.

It is not surprising, therefore, that Augustine devotes the first three books of the *Christian Instruction* to the meaning of records, especially written records or scripture, including sacred Scripture. He limits his treatment of the method of communication to the fourth and last book of the treatise. 'The entire treatment . . . is based on two factors: the method of discovering what we are to understand, and the method of teaching what has been understood.' [1]

Augustine properly spends more time on the more difficult process, on how we keep a record of significant fact, including the Christian fact of faith, hope, and love. The easier problem of communication or the method of teaching could be more succintly dealt with. And since he held in addition that the principles for the communication of supernatural or Christian fact were no different from those for the communication of sublime though natural fact, he had ample reason for the short treatment of communication. Christians must, nevertheless, have instruction in how to record and communicate both general and specifically Christian fact.

Such instruction, just because it is good instruction, knows its own limits. It can give us knowledge *about* things, but not a knowledge *of* things. It enables one to take a look from the outside in; it does not confer that intimate acquaintance which comes from being on the inside and looking out. Through exposure to symbol systems, what Augustine more simply calls signs, we can have knowledge *about* the nature and existence of things; but instruction cannot convey that knowledge *of* things which comes from the habitual possession of the power to avoid, use, or enjoy them. This profound insight into the problem of education came to Augustine in part from the Platonists but chiefly from his religion. For the Platonists recognized the distinction between types of knowledge, but the Christians have that knowledge *of* God which enables them to recognize that He alone is to be enjoyed, and consequently have that knowledge *of* things which enables them to avoid the misuse of things.

From Christian sources comes above all the abiding conviction that the greatest possible misuse of things is the pagan superstition that they can be really enjoyed — which raises them to a false divine status. And since this assigning of things to the place of God is the basis of pagan religion, Christians are better off if they do not, through study, acquire knowledge even *about* pagan religion. That item is therefore omitted from the Augustinian curriculum. The excision is a large one. But it still leaves plenty for Christians to know about — a great area of signs and symbols which are harmless, convenient, or even necessary; and a great area of things — (sensuous, mental, or divine) which should be known about through these symbols.

Augustine's general attitude toward the range and limitations of instruction was sharpened by his own career and conversion. He had studied the competing philosophical and religious movements of his day with anxious care. He had also been a professor of rhetoric for a long time; he was adept at discovering the meaning of literary texts, and was interested in questions of style and communication. And when he eventually discovered what Christianity really was, he knew that he had been taught something revolutionary and that he had to teach others. But even when, in the *Confessions,* Augustine looked back (like Wordsworth in the *Prelude*) and saw that in all his searching he had really been led; even when he knew that he had been called of God, he had to face the fact that he recognized the call when it came. The sounds he had heard possessed meaning; the words he had read told him something. So that for the proper exercise of his work as a teacher of Christianity, he had to know the conditions under which he, too, would be understood.

He expressed himself on the matter chiefly at two of the four main periods of his literary career; quite early, when he had just commenced his activities in the Church but had already composed his philosophic dialogues; and again much later, when his controversial and dogmatic treatises as a teaching bishop were for the most part behind him. In other words, his reflections on instruction are a product of his own attempt to teach, and thereby all the more rewarding. It would also appear that despite the interval between the early and the late pedagogical works there was no major development in his theory or practice. There is no contradiction between the works composed in the last decade of the fourth century (*On Music; Concerning the Teacher; Christian Instruction I–III; First Catechetical Instruction*) and those composed in the second decade of the fifth century (*Faith, Hope, and Charity; Christian Instruction IV*). This is especially clear when we examine the *Christian Instruction,* which was written over a period of twenty years.

Augustine's view that instruction and learning (or knowledge *about* and knowledge *of*) must be sharply distinguished in general was clearly enunciated in the early dialogue *Concerning the Teacher.* Professor Roberts reviews this work in Chapter IV. According to the dialogue, a teacher is concerned with instruction in signs and symbols, which awaken in us knowledge *about* things. Just as the mind uses the senses for the recognition of the external world, so it uses words for the recall of the intelligible world, the world of ideas and values. But, as Augustine says in conclusion, the instructor who converses about wisdom and folly merely recalls a knowledge *of* things which the pupil already possesses.[2]

This sounds just like Platonism, but not if we remember that for Augustine the Christian knowledge of things is revolutionized by the fact that the Platonists did not know that God alone is to be enjoyed. And when Augustine expounds what education in Christianity means, the distinction between instruction and real learning is driven home still more sharply.

As he points out in *The Profit of Believing,* our concrete learning of Christianity, our actual turning away from the love of this world to the love of the only true God, is based on authority. Authority or authoritativeness, when faithfully believed, has its supreme usefulness; it alone moves fools (namely, all of us) to hasten to or love wisdom. In the Incarnation of our Lord, at which time God in true man appeared to men, divine authority was moving toward itself the wandering souls of men. Since the incarnate life proper, time has elapsed; and if we are now seeking to deliver up our souls for cleansing and renewal, without doubt — in the view of Augustine — we must turn to that authoritative body, the Church Catholic. There is the new Israel; there is the organic whole as distinct from any party, sect, or heresy. And so Augustine sets forth how it went with him and how it can go with his reader. He tells how he settled in Italy, deliberating at length with himself about how to find the truth, and concluding that the truth was not so much hidden as was the way to it, the authoritative way. And despite the conflicting claims of various bodies to authoritativeness, he decided to become an adherent in the Church in which he had been raised, until it should become clear either that his experience was the culmination of his search or that the whole enterprise was unnecessary. For him the seeking ended in finding, or in being found; and he advises his reader — if he feels that he has been long enough tossed to and fro — to put an end to such labors. Instruction has done what it can; believing or faith alone will now be of use. The seeker must be immersed in that current 'which hath flowed down from Christ Himself through the Apostles even unto us, and will hereafter flow down to posterity.' [3]

The perhaps overweening importance, in both secular and Christian instruction, of certain stipulated subject matters comes to the forefront throughout Augustine's pedagogical work. In the secular field, for example, a long early work, *On Music*, stresses the educational value of prosody, or the music of poetry, and ends with an almost mystical confidence in the reality of number. And the point is repeated in the *Christian Instruction* itself: 'no one can decide merely because he desires it, that three times three are not nine, or do not form a square.' But we must remember that behind Augustine lies a cultural tradition going back through the Platonists to the Pythagoreans, who wrote figures in geometrical forms — three as a triangle of points and nine as a nine-point square. So that it might well seem to him that numbers were as undeniably real as the visible world, and that the study of enumeration could open a path to self-evident truths.

What seems a little odd in the secular field is not so strange in sacred matters, for all Christians have regarded certain stipulated subject matters as definitive of their specifically religious instruction. Modernists have taught chiefly the kingdom of God. Reformation thinkers stressed justification and the divine sovereignty. Similarly, the more Catholic mind of Augustine concentrated on faith, hope, and charity. Indeed *Faith, Hope, and Charity* was his own title for what others called the *Enchiridion* or *Handbook* of the Christian religion. In and through that formula he expounded, in the light of current misunderstandings, what he regarded as the essence of the Creed and the Lord's Prayer. And when he comes to his magnificent section on the Lord's Resurrection and our risen life in him, we can begin to comprehend, from the sheer mystery of the faith, just why instruction is not enough for Christian learning, and why indeed even knowledge of other things cannot be equated with knowledge of Christian fact. What was wrought upon the Cross of Christ — in his burial, Resurrection, and Ascension — was so wrought as to serve as a transforming model for the life the Christian is to lead on earth; a moving example, not merely a showing forth in words. And the newness of life far transcends anything of which men as men were always and everywhere capable.[4] To Augustine there would therefore be no sense in reducing Christianity to the claim of Kant that Jesus is the grand illustration of the categorical imperative, or of Hegel that He is the exemplar of man's consciousness of the divinity of spirit; and still less could Augustine declare (as Mr. Chaplin did in *The Great Dictator*) that according to the Gospel of Luke the kingdom of *man* is within us!

The 'faith, hope, and love' summary of his Christian subject matter is also used by Augustine in the *Christian Instruction* to expound the central emphasis of the Biblical record. But he there correlates it, as we shall see, with a parallel distinction between enjoyment and use, which embodies his balanced insight into the instruction of the whole, or catholic, Christian man.

In one of his most interesting pedagogical works, the *First Catechetical Instruction,* we find Augustine giving two examples of how to display the Christian religion to inquirers; two addresses, one longer than the other, to people wishing to become adherents of the Church.[5] The addresses do not read like stenographic reports of his own actual teaching, but rather as set compositions for his textbook. And in fact that vitality of imagery and suggestion which springs up spontaneously in the teaching situation is better exemplified in an address contained in the *Christian Instruction,* concerning the One who, although He Himself is our native land, has graciously made Himself also the way to that native land.[6] Nor is the little guidebook, *The Christian Combat* — an aid in identifying and combating heresy, a summary of strange pathways that lead away from our native land, as it were — more than a mediocre example of Augustine's teaching technique. Its elementary rather than elemental character may be due to the fact that Augustine was attempting to reach in Latin a local audience which for the most part thought in Punic.

The *Christian Instruction* is by far Augustine's greatest single work on pedagogy. In it the themes of his other works in the field — the distinction between instruction and learning, between general and Christian fact, between use and enjoyment — are systematically and intricately unfolded; and to it we must now turn.

II. The Discovery and Recording of Fact in General

The treatment of the discovery and recording of fact in the *Christian Instruction* can be conveniently divided into three subdivisions: the nature of signs and things, with the dangers of a superstitious use of signs and records, and the problem of symbolic forms which are unnecessary rather than positively dangerous; (2) a great division of useful signs, of institutions and contrivances which concern the things of the senses and of the body — societal conventions such as the languages, and scientific records of history and nature; and (3) another great division of useful signs which concern the things of the mind — such as the sciences of reasoning and of number, to which is added a footnote on philosophy.

Augustine considered language to be the most useful part of the process through which we discover or unfold significant fact. Language is as it were the envelope of thought:

> Conventional signs are those which living creatures give to one another. They thus indicate, as far as possible, either the operations of their minds or anything perceived by sense or intellect. The only reason we have for indicating by signs is that we may call forth and transfer to another's mind what is in our mind as we give the sign.

Some significant signs are addressed to taste, touch, and smell; the Lord gave a sign by means of the perfume with which His feet were anointed and by the touch of the tassel of His cloak; He made known through taste what He intended in the sacrament of His body and blood. But most signs are addressed to the hearing and the sight. Not all of these signs are words; when we nod we make a significant gesture, as do actors by the motion of their limbs; banners, military standards, and martial music are all suggestive of meaning. But the majority of signs through which men express their thoughts are words, both heard and read. The written word, scripture, is more permanent than speech; hence Augustine's insistence on so much book learning and on the sacred Scriptures whether in the original tongues or in translation. Since 'things are learned by means of signs' training in signs and symbols has priority in instruction.

No *thing* is in itself evil; of that Augustine was sure once he had disposed of Manicheism. All created things can be used, though never enjoyed and sometimes not even loved; but many things tend to be misused, especially through their being *assigned* to evil ends. Worst of all is a superstitious pagan search for signs in things. Augustine roundly condemns all books of soothsayers and diviners, all amulets and charms. He pours scorn on wearing lucky rings made of ostrich bone, on telling a person with hiccups to hold the left thumb in the right hand, and on retiring to bed if you sneeze when putting on your shoes. Today he would condemn seances in which people seek a sign from the alleged spirits of the departed; fortunetelling by cards or tea leaves; or seeing a sign of impending evil in lighting three cigarettes from one match or in walking under a ladder. And he relates the apposite tale of a superstitious man who was worried because his shoes had been gnawed by those uncanny little creatures, mice; and who was advised by the rational, even though not Christian, Cato to begin worrying when the shoes had eaten the mice!

One kind of signs and symbolic forms is for Augustine not so much dangerous as unnecessary. The creative arts of painting, and of storytelling are dismissed as not worthy of study or use. Paintings and statues are among the unnecessary constructions of men; imagined fables and stories are charming but untrue.

A great division of signs and symbols which a Christian should learn and use has a physical or bodily reference. It is conditioned by the fact that we are living beings in a living society.

Thus fashions in dress are important to recognize and note, in so far as they distinguish the reverend old from the undignified young, or set off the male from the female: useful, too, are the weights, measures, and coinages of the nations. A Christian should not 'shun this whole division of human institutions which are helpful for the necessary intercourse of life. Instead, he should even give a sufficient degree of attention to them and remember them.' But above all the Christian must not neglect the useful institution of language; he must learn his own language and if possible other languages — if he is to live significantly in a physical universe. Each of us learns his own language by hearing it from childhood; other languages are acquired either by hearing or by instruction. Real understanding of the Scriptures requires Hebrew and Greek; but even if the Scriptures exist in one's own tongue, such as Latin, one has to learn their particular idioms or turns of speech. We cannot expect to receive communications from the Lord except through a physical medium; we must go physically to church and physically listen to the words of the Gospel and of its readers and preachers. The language must therefore be taught.

The physical side of existence involves placing things before and after not only in space but also in time, a subject that fascinated Augustine. He was as interested as we are in the irreversibility of time; and he was also interested, as we tend not to be, in the distinction between the created world of spaced and timed things and the eternal world of the Creator. It is therefore not surprising that much of Augustine's justification of instruction in the arts is founded on the view that they indicate the nature of things temporal and also mark them off from things eternal. His view of time as irreversible leads him to approve most highly of historical writing; for history by its records instructs us in the inescapable order of events in time past. History is not a mere invention, but (when valid) it is the record of an irreversible process, of 'things which have now passed away and cannot be revoked.' So that historical writing is perhaps the most important of all symbolic records for educational study.

He also endorses the writing of geography, natural history, and astronomy, though less enthusiastically. By these records we can be taught the location and properties of animate and inanimate bodies in the present, and even calculate something of their movements in the past and the future, especially the courses of the stars. The interests of Augustine were hardly those of a Newton or a Darwin.

The approved practical arts are brought, with a little strain, under the category of being signs of the times. It is the enduring effect of a laborer's work, 'such as a house, a bench, a dish, or anything else of this nature,' that justifies it. And instruction in the professional skills of medicine, agriculture, and government can be justified on the ground that doctors, farmers, and rulers 'display a sort of assistance to God in His works'; in some measure they contribute in time to the high designs of Eternal Providence for time. Even dancing, running, and wrestling can be studied if it is remembered that no skilled worker in the arts 'moves his limbs in any operation without uniting the remembrance of past events to his hopes for future ones.'

'There are left, now, those institutions which concern not the senses of the body but the intellect, where the sciences of reasoning and of numbers have the mastery.' Augustine sees clearly the weakness in the life of reason and intellect of formal syllogistic logic apart from material logic; of what use is a correct conclusion based on false premises? Of what significance is it to deduce the fact that Socrates is mortal unless I know that all men are mortal and that Socrates is a man? But even formal logic has a temporal value; the nature of logical conclusions is not a fiction but 'perpetual in the order of things.' And the preparatory discipline of 'definition, division, and partition,' or the right construction of sentences and propositions, is also 'discovered in the reason of things.' In other words, the whole structure of language in some measure reflects the structure of reality; a noun is rightly the name of a thing. Even the principles of rhetorical persuasion are in the very nature of created temporal existence: 'Men did not ordain that a demonstration of regard would win over a listener, nor that a brief and intelligible narration easily makes the impression at which it aims, and that its variety holds its listeners without any tedium.' Logic and rhetoric are thus useful parts of instruction; but they must not supplant that knowledge of first principles which it is not in the province of instruction to provide. The developing life of the mind and spirit is like learning to walk, in which instruction is a little silly:

> For instance, some one is desirous of giving rules for walking. He admonishes you not to raise the foot behind until you have put down the other foot. Then he explains in detail how you ought to move the sockets of your knee-joints. The facts he is telling you are true, and you cannot walk in any other way. Men walk more easily, however, by doing these things than they notice them as they are doing them, or understand the directions they hear.[7]

Finally, it is clear that mathematics, the science of numbers, 'was not ordained by men but rather investigated and learned by them.' As we saw above, some confusion existed in Augustine's mind because of the Pythagorean tradition of drawing numbers. But even in our era of symbolic logic it is still true that 'whether numbers are regarded in themselves or in their application to the principles of figures, sounds or other movements, they have unchangeable rules . . . not ordained by men.'

After his summing up of recommended and permissible studies, Augustine adds a footnote on philosophy, suggesting that instruction in some philosophies, especially that of the Platonists, is not wholly unprofitable. 'Even some truths about the service of the one God Himself are discovered among them,' and 'very useful principles about morals.' Augustine never quite forgot that he had been a Neoplatonist. But the passage is interesting chiefly for its more generous and enthusiastic elaboration, at the Renaissance, by St. Thomas More in his famous letter of 1518 to the University of Oxford.[8] As More argues, from the testimony of Augustine himself, the chief value of studying Greek is the discovery of philosophy. Not only are Christians entitled, like Moses, to rob the Egyptians; we can build a path to Theology through Philosophy and the Liberal Arts, and thus adorn Theology as the Queen of Heaven with those spoils of the Egyptians.

But Augustine's outlook was more astringent:

> It seems to me, therefore, that it would be advantageous to instruct eager and talented young men, who fear God and strive for a happy life, that they should not rashly presume to study any sciences taught outside the Church of Christ in order to seize upon a happy life. They should rather decide upon them prudently and cautiously. Some sciences . . . they should completely repudiate and abhor, especially if their authors . . . have also formed any alliance with demons . . . through agreements about signs. They should also discard the study of the unnecessary and excessive creations of men. However, because of the necessity of this life,

they should not disregard those human institutions which
are of value for intercourse with their fellow men . . .
the history of either past or present events . . . matters
which concern the bodily senses . . . mechanical arts . . .
reasoning . . . numbers. [But] in all these we must maintain the principle: 'Nothing in excess.' [9]

Perhaps it is noteworthy that Augustine's restrictive principle
— nothing in excess — is itself a piece of traditional Hellenic
wisdom.

III. The Discovery and Recording of Christian Fact.

All signs and symbols may be either proper or figurative. They
are proper, or literal, when they are employed to signify those
things for which they were instituted. When in Latin we say *bos,*
we mean literally that bovine creature the ox, as Augustine remarks. But when the literal Old Testament command not to
muzzle the ox that treads out the grain is referred by St. Paul to
the treatment of teachers of the Gospel, 'it is clear that Holy
Scripture itself intimates that somehow we must recognize a
figurative use of the sign "Ox." ' The figurative use of signs is,
of course, not confined to elevated or to written records. 'For,
who does not say: "So may you flourish"?'; yet we do not expect
the recipient of the greeting to burst into flower. And anybody
knows that in conversational Latin one can call a swimming
pool a fish pond (*piscina*), even though it contains no members
of the piscine tribe and was not even made for fish to swim in.

The difficulties of figurative discourse are, perhaps, in Augustine's view, the central problem in the discovery of Christian
fact. For what do the records of Scripture refer to? (Incidentally,
it is pleasant to note that Augustine never dismissed the serious
views of those from whom he radically differed; his doctrine of
evil always kept in mind the counterdoctrine of the Manichees
and of the Pelagians. And twice he actively borrowed from a
Donatist, Tychonius — once in the matter of the celestial and
terrestrial cities, and again in this difficulty of the figurative
character of Scripture.)

In records as a whole, but especially in sacred Scripture, the fact that some expression is used figuratively rather than properly may be hidden by ignorance of secular things. If we do not know that a serpent exposes its whole body, rather than its head, to those attacking it, what can we make of the figurative command to be wise as serpents? If we do not know that the olive tree is everlastingly in leaf, how can we comprehend that the olive branch brought by the dove to Noah's ark is a symbol of *everlasting* peace? If we did not know that the unpretentious hyssop plant is potent in purifying the lungs, how could we grasp the psalmist's desire to be sprinkled with it?

But even the informed mind may miss the inherent ambiguity in any transferred or figurative sign. 'The obscurities of figurative words . . . require extraordinary attention and persistence.' It is a wretched but understandable slavery of soul if when one hears about the Sabbath one thinks only of its being the seventh day; or if when one hears of sacrifices one thinks only of the animals and fruits that are sacrificed. On the other hand it would be absurd (perhaps Augustine is distinguishing his position from that of the too Platonizing Clement and Origen) to interpret a literal expression as if it were figurative. 'If the passage is didactic, either condemning vice or crime, or prescribing utility or kindness, it is not figurative.'

Nor must one suppose that, because a thing has a figurative meaning in one place, it has the same figurative significance in all places. The Lord used leaven or yeast at various times in various ways to illustrate his meaning. He singled out its fermenting and corrupting quality to indicate the dangers of pharisaism: 'Beware of the leaven of the Pharisees.' But its power of penetrating all of the dough is emphasized on another occasion to suggest the surprising power of God's sovereign rule: 'The kingdom of heaven is like a woman who hid leaven in three measures of flour, until all of it was leavened.'

Whether a term is to be taken properly or figuratively — and the determination of the analogy which is actually being drawn — is in the long run decided by the nature of the thing being talked about and the possibility of communicating it to men. Christians are above all concerned, as we have seen Augustine reiterate in several treatises, with faith, hope, and love. If one envisages the whole matter of figurative utterance in Christianity as an aid to the discovery of faith and hope and love, then one will not go astray. And Augustine gives an excellent example:

> The Lord said: 'Unless you eat the flesh of the Son of Man, and drink His blood, you shall not have life in you.' This seems to prescribe a crime or a vice; therefore, it is a figure of speech directing that we are to participate in the Lord's passion and treasure up in grateful and salutary remembrance the fact that His flesh was crucified and wounded for us. Scripture says: 'If thy enemy is hungry, give him food; if he is thirsty, give him drink.' This undoubtedly prescribes a kindness, but the part that follows — 'For by so doing thou wilt heap coals of fire upon his head,' — you might suppose was commanding a crime of malevolence. So, do not doubt that it is a figurative expression.[10]

When the primary Scriptural reference to faith, hope, and love — which is also joy — has been apprehended, then the secondary reference to utility can be duly emphasized. 'There are some things which are to be enjoyed, others which are to be used.' The only proper object of our love and enjoyment is the eternal Triune God, that Reality to which alone we may cling 'with affection for its own sake.' If we attempt to enjoy anything else, anything meant merely for use, our life is frustrated and we become incapable of enjoyment. We are indeed commanded to love our neighbor as ourselves, but not to enjoy him; he is loved for God's sake, not his own; and one cannot be rightly said to enjoy *oneself*. We enjoy God, He enjoys Himself; but not even God can enjoy us; He uses us, in His own way, though not just as we use those things that are to be used. Thus the discovery of specifically Christian fact in the sacred record allows for instruction in useful fact in general and in secular and useful records.

All this may seem very far from the scientific studies of the Bible to which we are accustomed, the so-called lower and higher criticism, the search for a pure primeval text and for the historical situation in which the Biblical writers existed. No one would today (or, one hopes, tomorrow) deny the usefulness of such studies. But even in secular studies such a search can be overdone. It is interesting and important to establish, for example, the best possible text of *Hamlet* from a careful consideration of the merits of the various quartos and folios; and to know how far it was Shakespeare who really wrote *Hamlet,* and what the play meant to an Elizabethan audience. But Hamlet is, in addition, a great work of literature, to be read as such by us. It is an image of human life, and, as Miss Spurgeon has reminded us, we must be deeply aware of the range and levels of imagery in this play, in all Shakespeare's plays, and in the works of other poets, if we are to discover the meaning. Shakespeare's imagery is the clue to Shakespeare. And if the Bible through its imagery and figures is meant to suggest that Divine Joy which is the source of our faith and our hope and our charity, then something like the Augustinian approach to Scriptural discovery would seem to have a permanent validity.

IV. The Communication of Fact

Augustine quotes with approval the central tenet of Ciceronian rhetoric that, 'He will be eloquent . . . who can speak about trivial subjects in a subdued style, ordinary subjects in a moderate style, and noble subjects in a grand style.' Thereby the speaker or writer will not only teach but communicate, will both please and persuade. He will be able to teach people trivial subjects, interest them in ordinary matters, and win their favor for sublime things. The problem of Christian communication from the point of view of instruction is complicated by the fact that the Christian teacher is, of course, teaching and communicating not trivial or ordinary things but noble things, or at least all things in the light of sublime things. Yet it would be absurd and inappropriate to say that the Christian teacher must teach in the grand style. The rhetoric of Christian communication, for the teacher or instructor at least, must be primarily the subdued or plain style. For he is a teacher.

The nature of this plain teaching style is illustrated from

Scripture and the earlier Fathers. Yet it is noteworthy that for Augustine this style does not mean anything like what has been regarded as a plain style for the past three hundred years. Any advocate of the plain style in English since the days of Dryden and Swift would regard the Augustinian style as ornate; 'metaphysical' in the manner of Cowley and Donne; as far removed from simplicity as possible. It does not avoid metaphor, or allusion of a complex, or even contorted suggestiveness. It has continuous overtones and undertones. It is plain only as Eliot and Joyce and Stein are plain. It is difficult.

Precisely that fourth chapter in St. Paul's Galatians, for example, with which commentators have always had to wrestle, is chosen by Augustine as his leading example of style at its plainest, communication at its most communicative. In order to explain and communicate the nature of the new dispensation as compared with the old, the distinction between Judaism and Christianity, St. Paul had evoked a complex image in which the reader must hold in mind a very intricate interpretation of the life of Abraham. He must remember that Abraham's first wife, Hagar, was a slave and his second wife, Sarah, a free-woman; that Ishmael, the son of the slave, mocked at Isaac, the son of the free-woman, and was cast out. The reader must remember that Hagar was also allegedly an alternative name for Mt. Sinai, associated with the giving of the Commandments to Moses, with the burdensome law as distinct from the life of promise and faith announced to Abraham and republished effectively in Christ. 'Hagar-Sinai' religion is now practiced in the Judaism of Jerusalem; Judaism is a form of religious slavery; the slave woman and her son must as of old be cast out; then 'Sarah or promise' religion will be realized; then the true Jerusalem, the Jerusalem on high, which is free, will be realized; for she is our true mother.

Not only sacred Scripture but the writings of the earlier Fathers exemplify this plain style, and naturally. For if, as Augustine claims, the Fathers made progress in the knowledge of divine and salutary truths through their reading of Scripture, it was not unlikely that they would catch something of the manner and style of Scripture and employ it in their presentation of that knowledge to the Church. And the prime example of patristic plain style which Augustine cites, from a letter by Cyprian on the sacrament of the chalice, shows in fact both the Biblical source and the complex character of patristic rhetoric. Cyprian is explaining that in offering the chalice nothing must be done which is different from what the Lord did first for us. Consequently the chalice which is offered in commemoration of Him is to be offered filled not with water but with wine. And to convey his meaning with more penetrating power, Cyprian proceeds to evoke the image of Noah drinking wine in his tent to the point of intoxication and abandon.

Such a style seemed natural to St. Paul, and St. Cyprian, and St. Augustine himself, however artificial it may appear to us. And our difficulty in appreciating it is not due only to the fact that time has marched on, education decayed, and religious illiteracy become rampant. Do we not experience a similar sense of discomfort in recent poetry and in recent painting? It may well be that in each case something is being communicated to the audience which a simpler and plainer style would merely traduce. Augustine's rhetoric of communication in teaching has a validity parallel to that of his use of symbolism in discovery.

The delight and bane of all interpreters of a Christianity that is in any sense Scriptural has always been the Song of Songs. Is that canticle literal, and if so what does it signify? Is it figurative, and if so what then does it signify? Somehow Augustine manages to convey, through his figurative comment on one of its stanzas, both the heart of his Christian faith, hope, and love and the relation of those things to the problem of their discovery and communication:

> Those who read indiscreetly are deceived by numerous and varied instances of obscurity and vagueness, supposing one meaning instead of another . . . I am convinced that this whole situation was ordained by God to overcome pride . . . There are holy and perfect men by whose lives and example the Church of Christ rids those who come to

her of superstition and incorporates them with herself through the imitation of these good men. These good and faithful servants of God, ridding themselves of worldly cares, have come to the holy laver of baptism, and arising from it, produce by the infusion of the Holy Ghost, the fruit of a two-fold charity: a love of God and of their neighbor. Why is it, then, I ask, that when anyone asserts these facts, he affords less charm to his listener than when he explains with the same interpretation that text from the Canticle of Canticles where the Church is alluded to as a beautiful woman who is being praised: 'Thy teeth are as flocks of sheep, that are shorn, which come up from the washing, all with twins, and there is none barren among them'? Does one learn anything more than when he hears the same thought phrased in the simplest words, without the aid of this simile? But, somehow or other, I find more delight in considering the saints when I regard them as the teeth of the Church. They bite off men from their heresies and carry them over to the body of the Church, when their hardness of heart has been softened as if by being bitten off and chewed. With very great delight I look upon them also as shorn sheep that have put aside worldly cares, as if they were fleece. Coming up from the washing, that is, the baptismal font, all bear twins, that is, the two precepts of love, and I see no one destitute of that holy fruit.[11]

The views of St. Augustine on the instruction of Christians are inseparable from his views on all the great topics to which he turned a mind both richly diversified and singularly unified. We can understand and evaluate the *Christian Instruction* much better for being familiar not only with his other pedagogical essays but with the heart of what he has to say on the City of God and the Blessed Trinity, on man and on grace. For the distinctions between fact in general and Christian fact, between recording discoveries and communicating them, between instruction and learning, are all patterns in that intricate and fascinating intellectual tapestry which is Augustinianism. Moreover,

Augustinianism cannot be fully comprehended from any mere statement of its essence; for Augustinian pedagogy like Augustinian theology is on the whole existentialist rather than essentialist. As Augustine himself indicates at the conclusion of the theoretical portion of *First Catechetical Instruction:*

> As we are now treating of instructing . . . I can testify to you from my own experience that I am differently stirred according as he whom I see before me waiting for instruction is cultivated or a dullard, a fellow citizen or a stranger, a rich man or a poor man, a private citizen or a man honored by a public office, a man having some official authority, a person of this or that family, of this or that age or sex, coming to us from this or that school of philosophy, or from this or that popular error; and in keeping with my own varying feelings my discourse itself opens, proceeds, and closes . . . Wherefore, if anything in us has so pleased you that you want to hear from us some plan to be observed by you . . . you would learn this better by watching us and listening to us when actually engaged in the work itself than by reading what we dictate.[12]

FOR FURTHER READING

J. J. Gavigan, tr., *Christian Instruction,* in *The Fathers of the Church: Augustine,* vol. IV (New York, 1947).

V. J. Bourke, *Augustine's Quest of Wisdom* (Milwaukee, 1945).

T. Sullivan, *S. Aureli Augustini . . . De Doctrina Christiana Liber Quartus, A Commentary* (Washington, D.C., 1930).

NOTES

1. *Christian Instruction (De Doctrina Christiana),* IV, sec. 1, tr. J. J. Gavigan, *The Fathers of the Church* (New York, 1947) in the fourth of the volumes devoted to the *Writings of Saint Augustine.*
2. *Concerning the Teacher (De Magistro),* sec. 40, tr. G. C. Leckie in *Philosophy Source-Books* (New York, 1938). Other translations of the dialogue include F. E. Tourscher, *The Philosophy of Teaching* (Villanova College, 1924) and J. M. Colleran, *The Teacher* in *Ancient Christian Writers* (Westminster, Md., 1950).

3. *The Profit of Believing (De Utilitate Credendi)*, secs. 34, 19, 20, tr. C. L. Cornish in *Select Library of the Nicene and Post-Nicene Fathers* (Buffalo, 1887).

4. *Faith, Hope and Charity (Enchiridion)*, sec. 53, tr. B. M. Peebles, in the volume cited in footnote 1; also tr. by L. A. Arand in *Ancient Christian Writers* (Westminster, Md., 1947) and by A. C. Outler in *The Library of Christian Classics*, vol. VII (Philadelphia, 1955).

5. *The First Catechetical Instruction (De Catechizandis Rudibus)*, secs. 24–49, 51–5, tr. J. P. Christopher in *Ancient Christian Writers* (Westminster, Md., 1946).

6. *Christian Instruction*, I, sec. 11.

7. Ibid. II, sec. 55.

8. Tr. T. S. K. Scott-Craig in *The Thought and Culture of the English Renaissance*, ed. E. Nugent (New York, 1954).

9. *Christian Instruction*, II, sec. 58.

10. Ibid. III, sec. 24.

11. Ibid. II, sec. 7.

12. *The First Catechetical Instruction*, sec. 23.

VI

THE ANTI-MANICHEAN
WRITINGS

Stanley Romaine Hopper

MANICHEISM was one of the three great religious systems of southern Europe, Africa, and eastern Asia at the close of the third century. The other two were Neoplatonism and Catholicism. There were Manichean sects in southern France even as late as the Crusades; and everyone knows how St. Thomas Aquinas had still to bring 'his huge fist' down 'like a club of stone' on the table of King Louis IX exclaiming (to the consternation of all save the King), 'And *that* will settle the Manichees!'

All of which is long since a matter of history — a history largely forgotten in recent times through our generally low estimate of the historical. Nevertheless M. Jacques Maritain continues to protest against 'a kind of Manicheism' in the works of André Gide and François Mauriac,[1] and describes the modern mind as being both Rousseauist and Manichean, as both adoring nature and hating it. We all know something of the 'natural goodness of man' and the adoration of nature after the pattern of Rousseau and the romanticists; but the term 'Manichean' means considerably less to us. Indeed a considerable effort of the imagination is required to recover sympathetically a religious point of view which seems to us, at least at first sight, so manifestly fantastic and extravagant. Yet if we are to understand the fascination which this system held for the younger Augustine, and to recognize its significance and bearing upon his thought, we must try to put ourselves in possession of its characteristic features and the most prominent aspects of its thought.

I. The Manichean System

The religious system of the Manichees was founded by Mani, a Persian, who lived in the third century. He was born about A.D. 216. He was persuaded quite early in his life that he was the recipient of divine revelations and that he was called to preach a new faith. He gained several disciples, enjoyed the patronage of the king's brother, journeyed extensively in central Asia, India, and China, wrote several books, and acquired fame as a painter. Spengler, with his gift for impressive generalization, credits Mani with having knit together 'the whole mass of Magian religions in one of the most powerful theological creations of all times — for which in 276 the Mazdaist priesthood crucified him.' [2] Other sources say that he was flayed alive, and that his skin was subsequently stuffed with straw and hung up, by order of the king, at the gate of the city of Gundē-Shāpūr — a gate afterward known as the Mani-gate. In any case it appears that his execution was due to the hostility of the Zoroastrian priesthood.

Mani's teaching was evidently compounded of varied Oriental teachings, with elements from Zoroastrianism and the old Babylonian religion (of the Ophitic type) predominating. It contains large accretions from Buddhism, and it is probable also that many of the Gnostic sects of the second century were absorbed into it.[3] Despite the general agreement of scholars on this somewhat synthetic character of the teaching, it is neverthe-

less held that Mani 'displayed a boldness and originality of conception which entitle him to be regarded as a genius of the first
order. To represent his system as a mere patchwork of older
beliefs is therefore a total perversion of the facts.' [4] Certainly
Mani himself had little doubt as to the nature of his commission:

> Wisdom and deeds have always from time to time been
> brought to mankind by the messengers of God. So in one
> age they have been brought by the messenger called Buddha
> to India, in another by Zaradusht [Zoroaster] to Persia, in
> another by Jesus to the West. Thereupon this revelation has
> come down, this prophecy in this last age, through me,
> Mani, the messenger of the God of truth to Babylonia. [5]

As for the teaching itself, allowance must certainly be made
for its imaginative and poetical character. At the same time one
may not go so far as Bevan, who holds that Mani's dualism — the
fundamental characteristic of the system — was imaginative and
poetical, but 'not of the philosophical kind.' [6] Though its ultimate perspective consists in the dramatic opposition of darkness
and light, the problems that emerge are dualistic and they are
philosophical. One must agree with Harnack in holding that
the system is based upon a fundamental dualism — 'radical,
essential, eternal . . . a consistent, uncompromising dualism in
the form of a fantastic philosophy of nature.' [7]

This dualism, and the kind of naturalism that informs it, is
clearly set forth in the *Fihrist,* or 'Catalogue,' generally regarded
as the most important Oriental source of Manichean writings
available [8]:

> Mani teaches: Two substances form the beginning of the
> world, the one light the other darkness; the two are sepa-
> rated from each other. The light is the most glorious being,
> limited by no number, God himself, the King of the Paradise
> of Light . . . The other being in the darkness . . . Mani
> teaches: that the light subsistence borders immediately on
> the dark subsistence, without a dividing wall between
> them; the light touches with its lowest side the darkness,

while upwards to the right and left it is unbounded. Even
so the darkness is endless downwards and to the right and
left.

This is a clear-cut starting point. The two kingdoms are co-
eternal and hostile. Mani co-ordinates good with light and evil
with darkness, and, as Harnack insists, 'this is no mere figure of
speech, but light is actually the only good, and darkness the
only evil.' [9] Spirit is identified with light, and matter (or *Hyle*)
with darkness.

In the dramatic expansion of these two principles, however,
matter comes into existence through conflict between the two
kingdoms. The Princes of Darkness became enamored of the
light and launched an attack upon the realm of Spirit. To meet
this attack God sent forth an emanation of Himself, called
Primary Man (*Primus Homo*), to do battle with the demons. But
Primary Man was at first overwhelmed by Eblis, the leader of
the demons, and a part of his panoply (the five pure elements)
was taken from him. Then the God of Light Himself, with the
assistance of some new aeons, rescued Primary Man. But Primordial Man had already lost to Eblis his five 'finer elements'
(the Gentle Breeze, the Wind, the Light, the Water, the Fire).
Five elements of darkness (Smoke, Burning, Darkness, Hot Wind,
and Cloud) had become mixed with these, and so the finer
elements were trapped. To liberate these finer elements, the God
of Light then created the visible world from these mingled elements, and this creative act was the beginning of the liberation
of the imprisoned elements. Reservoirs were next established for
the liberated light — ten heavens and eight earths upheld by
angels, plus the sun and the moon. The twelve constellations of
the zodiac were then formed, and placed in such a way as to
form a great wheel with buckets. The light being liberated from
the world was then caught in these buckets, wheeled upward into
the heavens, and poured into the sun and the moon — the moon
collecting the light for the first half of the month and then
pouring it into the sun during the second half. Now the sun was
the abode of the Primordial Man. When the sun had received

151

all the light that could possibly be liberated in this way, a fire would be kindled on the earth to burn for 1468 years, when no light would be left; then the King of Darkness and his demons would withdraw into the pit prepared for them beneath their kingdom of darkness.

To the Western mind (and certainly to the modern consciousness) this account will seem far more fantastic than spectacular. What stands out quite markedly is that Mani's real starting point is the contradictory character of the visible world — the presence in it of good and evil, the finite and the infinite, the mutable and transcendent principles, darkness and light. His account of the creation of man ties in with this. For Primordial Man was not earthly man. The formation of the world was the work of the King of Light in order to bring about the deliverance of light; but the formation of man was the work of Satan, a counter gambit, as it were, designed to secure his hold even more firmly upon the imprisoned light. Thus Adam was engendered by Satan in conjunction with Avarice, Lust, and Sin, and the several portions of captured light were secreted in him. Eve, who was similarly engendered (but with only a small spark of light!), was given to Adam as a companion representing seductive sensuousness — Satan's aim being to imprison as much light as possible in man through the propagation of the race, thus hindering the bucket lift of light to the sun and the moon. Therefore man is a discordant being, created in the image of Satan, but compounded with the principle of light.

But the heavenly conflict did not end here. This action called forth a further riposte from the side of heaven. Aeons were sent down to man to reveal to him a true knowledge, or *gnosis,* of his real condition, whereby he might be forewarned against the flesh and so be liberated from the power of the demons. Among these revealers or prophets Mani appears to have included Adam, Noah, Abraham, perhaps Zoroaster and Buddha, and Jesus. This was not the historical Jesus, however. He was regarded as the devilish Messiah of the Jews. This was a *Jesus impatibilis,* 'a contemporaneous phantom Jesus, who neither suffered nor died.' This view of Christ was completely docetic; the representations of Jesus as God manifest in the flesh were, to Mani, both Jewish and abominable. Moreover, Mani had set himself forth as the last and greatest of the prophets, not only going beyond *Jesus impatibilis* and Paul but being the first to bring full knowledge. Therefore he was the 'leader,' the 'ambassador of light,' and the 'Paraclete.'

The *ethical outcome* of this teaching is easy to see. Ethics is naturalized from the beginning with the identification of good with light and evil with darkness, or matter. The way of the true gnosis is an ascetic way: it is to get free of the entanglement with matter through abstention from sensuous enjoyment. Here appears the doctrine of the three 'seals' — the seals of the mouth, the hand, and the bosom. The first forbids the enjoyment of unclean foods (flesh and wine); the second forbids the use of any unclean elements; and the third forbids all sexual community. On this point Augustine is explicit: 'When I name the mouth, I mean all the senses that are in the head; when I name the hand I mean every operation; when I name the bosom I mean every seminal lust.' [10] A double morality resulted. The full severity of these requirements was laid upon the 'elect'; the 'auditores,' or lower members of the community, had only to abstain from the coarser offenses (idolatry, magic, fornication, lying, and so on). Kessler has held that Mani made use of Buddhism in elaborating this ethic; but he has also shown that the ancient Babylonian religion — the original source of all the gnosis systems of western Asia — is the real base of the Manichean system. Manicheism is 'the most complete gnosis, the richest, most consequent, and most artistic system formed on the basis of the ancient Babylonian religion.' [11]

What, then, are the essential characteristics of Manicheism? It would appear that, *theologically,* its framework is Zoroastrian, with the principles of light and darkness (Ormazd and Ahriman) pushed into a thoroughgoing dualism. Its *cosmogony* is Gnostic, deriving from the ancient Babylonian source. Its *soteriology,* or plan of salvation, is also Gnostic, not Christian. It is misleading to say that 'Mani's system may be divided into two great periods — one of involution, or mingling of spirit and matter, adopted from

Zoroastrian sources; and the second of evolution, or the separating of spirit and matter, borrowed chiefly from the Christian faith.' [12] Christ's purpose and work are here represented in a radically different way. Here he is a teacher of right gnosis, showing the way of release to a spirit already groping upward, instead of being mediator between God and man. And finally, its *morality* is a compound of the foregoing, with Buddhist ethics possibly predominating, which gives it an aspect, it may be added, similar in many respects to that of Neoplatonism.[13]

The reader may well wonder how a religion so compounded, and so fantastically decked out with syzygies, aeons, and cosmic battle, could have dominated the early Christian centuries as much as it did, to say nothing of its incalculable influence upon the mind of Augustine. Harnack suggests that this may be explained by the fact that Mani offered spiritual benefits — revelation, salvation, moral virtue — on the basis of a religion of nature. Also Manicheism offered 'a simple, apparently profound and yet convenient solution of the problem of good and evil.' [14] And in its Christian guise, as in Augustine's time, by dispensing with the Old Testament and the Incarnation, and by presenting Mani as the supreme prophet of God, it could easily appeal to the 'cultured' and the 'sophisticated,' who, while seeking for a religion that would be more 'rational' and at the same time somewhat Christian, are nevertheless easily duped by any religious pretension that claims to be 'superior' or more 'enlightened.' Especially is this true in a disrupted age, such as our own, where, since no single view unites the whole, every view rises up to claim it. Mani also supplied an elaborate mythology wherewith to unify the amorphous spiritual sensibilities of the religiously untethered; and while it is true that mythology is ofttimes a true 'Serbonian bog where armies whole have sunk,' and while we are sometimes tempted to think of Mani himself as 'half mad, between metaphysics, mountains, lakes, love unextinguishable, thoughts unutterable, [in] the nightmare of [his] own delinquencies,' nevertheless it is true in all ages that in place of a received myth the religious consciousness will contrive one of its own, compounded usually, like the abstracted dragons of logic, from the myth projections of ancient religions eclectically and/or theosophically blended.[15] The 'modern mind,' especially the 'intellectuals,' is prey to this sort of thing, preferring always something more 'rational' than orthodoxy. And Mani himself may in this connection be taken as a type of himself. He wore, it is reported, high-soled shoes, one red, the other green, and a mantle of azure blue, which changed color as he moved; he carried an ebony staff in his right hand and a Babylonish book under his left arm. Thus his system is dualistic at its base; but, compounded of Babylonian cosmogonic mysteries with partial support from Christian teachings, his theology shifts uncertainly in the eristic azure of the dualist's inevitable dilemmas. As Augustine learned to his subsequent dismay, 'any errors whatever might be dressed up in this fashion, so as under cover of a showy exterior to steal in unawares into the minds of the ignorant.' [16]

II. Augustine and the Manichees

For nine years Augustine adhered to the Manichees. The story has been sketched in Chapter II; we must here review it in greater detail.

Following his first intellectual awakening via the *Hortensius* of Cicero, he was easily caught in the 'bird-lime' of the Manichean teaching.[17] With youthful arrogance he felt a contempt for the simplicity of the Scriptures: he 'shunned their style,' not having learned that Scripture was 'honeyed with heaven's honey and luminous with its light.' He 'scorned to be a little one,' and, 'swollen with pride,' looked upon himself 'as a great one.' Thus he 'fell among men proudly raving, very carnal, and voluble . . .' [18]

Two things especially, he says, influenced him in that 'unwary age': one was association and familiarity with the Manichees of Carthage, where the sect was very strong; the other was the sense of ego-satisfaction which came to him from his easy victories in religious debate, 'in arguing with ignorant Christians' not sufficiently informed to defend the faith. His 'ardor in disputations' increased daily, and with it, his affection for the Manichees; so that he was flattered into approving whatever they held, 'not because I knew it to be true, but because I wished it to be.' Thus, for a very long time he 'followed men that preferred a sleek straw to a living soul.' [19]

A third reason for this adherence must be assigned, however. The Manichees were insistent on getting at 'the Truth.' 'The Church,' they held, '*imposes* truth upon you instead of teaching it, and the truth which it offers is composed to a great extent of anile fables, which cannot be supported by the reason. The Church demands faith before reason, and terrifies you into submission by superstitious threats. We, on the other hand, only invite you to accept truths which we have first explained, and which you can perfectly understand.' [20] This appeal to reason may strike the reader as odd after the fabulous extremes to which Mani had gone to frame his bellicose cosmos; but, as Augustine later complained, the Manichees had 'two tricks for catching the unwary' [21] — the one, finding fault with the Scriptures and elaborating the contradictions to be found there; the other, laying claim to a superior moral regimen as over against the moral requirements of other religions. The former of these allowed for much negative reasoning, and effectually established Reason as the criterion for judging the Scriptures.[22]

But the positive side of this rationalism is revealed by Augustine in his *Confessions*. He says that he did not, in these years, 'perceive the hinge' on which the whole matter turned. His mind 'ranged through corporeal forms — lineaments, colours, bulky magnitudes'; and in his experience of division and discord in the nature of things he 'imagined there was I know not what substance of irrational life.' [23] Thus evil was for him a substance-not-rooted-in-God. More bluntly, his thinking was materialistic, and the possibility of a spiritual metaphysic of the Neoplatonic sort had not yet dawned on him. He believed evil to be a substance. He 'conceived two masses, the one opposed to the other, both infinite . . . though on that side where the mass of evil was in opposition to Thee I was compelled to confess Thee finite . . .' [24] — which would suggest that, philosophcally, he matured late.

Morally, the reflex of these opinions was simple. 'It still seemed to me "that it was not we that sin, but that I know not what other nature sinned in us." And it gratified my pride to be free from blame.' [25] *Theologically* it seemed clear that God was opposed by some thwarting power and 'erred of constraint.' [26]

Several factors led to his break away from the Manichees. One was the solicitude of Monnica, his mother, already noted in Chapter II.[27] The death of an unnamed friend who was converted to Christianity shortly before his death also shook Augustine considerably. His studies in science, together with the arguments of friends, led him to distrust astrology, and thus to recognize the scientific incongruities in Mani's heavenly scheme. He was also gradually disillusioned in regard to the moral purity of the Manichean 'electi.' In his book *On the Morals of the Manicheans* numerous instances of moral and religious defection are cited. The appearance of Helpidius in Carthage was impressive, too, for here was one Christian who was equal to the Scriptural bickerings of the Manichees. Meanwhile, Augustine was contriving questions of his own, for which no local answers were forthcoming. He was told to await patiently the coming of Faustus, a celebrated expounder of the Manichean doctrines, and all would be made clear. Faustus arrived in Augustine's twenty-ninth year. He was an eloquent and graceful speaker — 'a great snare of the devil,' as Augustine reports it, by whom many were entangled 'through the allurement of his smooth speech.' 'But of what profit to me was the elegance of my cup-bearer, since he offered me not the more precious draught for which I thirsted?' [28] Faustus 'was undoubtedly the acutest, most determined and most unscrupulous opponent of orthodox Christianity in the age of Augustine.' [29] His failure to meet Augustine's questions 'now began to loosen the snare' in which Augustine had been taken. And when, in 393, Augustine engaged in public disputation with Fortunatus, a Manichean priest, and so outpointed him that he left the city never to return, Augustine's release from those Manichean 'fictions of his misery' was fairly complete. He lapsed for a time into skepticism, 'doubting everything and fluctuating between all.' But not long thereafter he came under the influence of Bishop Ambrose at Milan, and under the influence also of Neoplatonism by way of the translations of Victorinus.

Augustine's own account of his experience with the Manichees is to be found, of course, in his *Confessions*. But prior to his ordination he wrote five anti-Manichean works which Paulinus called his 'anti-Manichean Pentateuch.' These included the *De Libero Arbitrio, De Genesi contra Manichaeos, De Moribus Ecclesiae Catholicae, De Moribus Manichaeorum,* and *De Vera Religione.* After his ordination he published (391) his *De Utilitate Credendi* and then the *De Duabus Animabus, contra Manichaeos.* The year after came the *Acta seu Disputatio contra Fortunatum Manichaeum;* and then, at intervals, *Contra Adimantum, Contra Epistolam Manichaei quam vocant Fundamenti, Contra Faustum Manichaeum, Disputatio contra Felicem, De Natura Boni contra Manichaeos,* and *Contra Secundinum.* Among Augustine's letters, the 79th and 236th are the most relevant; also the homily on the 140th Psalm, and Sermons 1, 2, 12, 50, 153, 182, and 237. The *De Agone Christiano* and the *De Continentia* among his moral treatises complete the list of principal sources.

III. Augustine's Refutation

As the Manichean religious system derived from a basic dualism, so the refutations of Augustine are directed at this problem and at the series of dilemmas that emerge from it. These difficulties are *theological, cosmological, psychological,* and *moral:* the nature of God and his relation to the world, the nature of the world, the nature of man, and the problem of good and evil. Augustine's method is one of raising irreconcilable either/ors for his opponents, and of establishing his own doctrine by way of the Neoplatonic theses learned from his reading of the 'Platonists.' For, in the following passages, the truth of Dean Inge's contention is unavoidable: to wit, 'Plotinus read in a Latin translation was the schoolmaster who brought Augustine to Christ.'

His initial argument against the Manichean system, however, he learned from his friend, Nebridius, and he did not hesitate to employ it on every occasion. It turns upon the question whether God be corruptible or incorruptible, and clarifies the dilemma presented by the belief in two eternal principles. 'What could that reputed nation of darkness,' Nebridius' argument ran, 'have done unto Thee hadst Thou objected to fight with it? For had it been answered, "It would have done Thee some injury," then shouldst Thou be subject to violence and corruption; but if the reply were: "It could do Thee no injury," then was no cause assigned for Thy fighting with it . . . So that should they affirm Thee . . . to be incorruptible, then were all these assertions false and execrable; but if corruptible, then that were false, and at the first utterance to be abhorred.' [30]

Augustine employed this argument to good advantage in his disputation with Fortunatus. Fortunatus held God to be incorruptible: 'In the substance of light . . . God is to be held incorruptible; but there was a contrary nature of darkness' standing over against him from which evil arose. 'My argument,' said Augustine, 'is brief, and as I suppose, perfectly clear to anyone. If God could have suffered nothing from the race of darkness because he is inviolable, [then] without cause he sent us hither that we might suffer distress. But if anything can suffer, it is not inviolable, and you deceive those to whom you say that God is inviolable.' [31] The same argument occurs, with variations, in his book *On the Morals of the Manicheans,* and in his *Nature of the Good, against the Manicheans.*[32] Similarly, in his letter to the Manichean teacher, Felix, he demands that Felix 'answer, if he is able, the question which baffled your predecessor, Fortunatus.' [33] Augustine evidently regarded the argument as decisive. And indeed, it proves so, not so much on its own account as in terms of its corollaries: for it is a wedge which may be driven *cosmologically, anthropologically,* and *morally,* reducing to the absurd the Manichean doctrines that touch upon these areas.

The moment this question is applied, for example, to the Manichean view of God in His relation to the world, the notion of God is forthwith finitized and materialized. The attempt of the Manichees to limit him in extension 'on one side' (that bordering on the region of darkness) and to leave him unbounded on the others is ridiculed by Augustine in his book *Against the Epistle of Manicheus Called Fundamental.* 'How could you be so blinded in mind as to say that only the region of darkness was material, and that the so-called region of light was immaterial and spiritual? . . . two regions cannot be joined at their sides unless both are material.' [34] In like manner, when Faustus 'glibly defends himself' by saying he speaks not of two Gods, but of God and *Hyle,* Augustine shows how absurd it is to deny the name of God to that which has the power of God (the power of forming bodies). 'You ascribe the act of God to a being you are ashamed to call god.' And in the conflict between the two, *Hyle* is the poison, which nonetheless proved nutritious for earthly life, while God is the antidote, 'who could condemn his own members, but could not restore them.' 'In reality it is as absurd to call the one *Hyle,* as it is to call the other God'; indeed, we may well ask 'who has got the victory!' [35] And when it comes to the mingling of these principles and to the devious devices whereby the light is to secure its release once more from the darkness, Augustine sets forth innumerable absurdities that arise. He belatedly bemoans the fact that he could himself have been led to believe in 'such follies, as to credit that a fig-tree wept when it was plucked, and that the mother-tree shed milky tears. Which fig notwithstanding, plucked not by its own but another's wickedness, and by some "saint" eaten and mingled with his entrails, he should breathe out of it angels; yea, in his prayers he shall assuredly groan and sigh forth particles of God, which particles of the most high and true God should have remained bound in that fig unless they had been set free by the teeth and belly of some "elect saint!" ' [36]

Similar difficulties appeared when the Manichees asserted the existence of two kinds of souls, attributing to these souls properties so distinct that 'they wished one to be regarded as of the very substance of God, but were not willing that God should be accepted as the author of the other.' [37] On the one hand they hold that we are 'temples of God' and particles of His nature. At the same time flesh is unclean because of the mixture with the regions of darkness. 'But this would make not only flesh unclean,' Augustine protests, 'but your God himself, in that part which he sent to become subject to absorption and contamination, in order that the enemy might be conquered and taken captive.' [38] This does not comport well with the inviolability of God, which they also maintain. If the soul is a particle of God, why should He have placed it in mortal bodies belonging to the devil? The confusion, moreover, which results from the presence in us of two wills deliberating between two alternatives, or among three, or four, or five, or six, all equally desirable, becomes attenuated and absurd.[39]

Finally, in the field of morals, the dualist position moves toward a contradictory asceticism and perfectionism. The Manichees looked pale and gaunt.[40] The term 'Manichean' became a by-word for any one who failed to appreciate the enjoyments of good living. Marriage, for example, was necessarily sinful through the propagation of sin, leading to the birth of souls caught in the mesh of the flesh; begetting children was a greater sin than cohabitation.[41] 'By such assertions they cut themselves off not only from Christians, but from mankind.' [42] In Christianity the inward man is renewed day by day that it may press on toward perfection; but 'you wish to begin with perfection!' [43] Meanwhile, the actual practices of the Manichees failed to bear out their moral claims. 'This is the end of your notable precepts, in which there is nothing sure, nothing steadfast, nothing consistent, nothing irreproachable, but all doubtful . . . contradictory, abominable, absurd.' [44]

So much for Augustine's negative argument. *Positively*, Augustine's argument is simple and consistent. The 'hinge' of the problem, for him, was in the recognition that God is not corporeal, and that He is supreme. 'God is not corporeal, no part of Him can be perceived by corporeal eyes, nothing of His Substance or Nature can any way suffer violence or change, or is compounded or formed; and if you grant me these (for we may not think otherwise concerning God), all their devices [the Manichees] are overthrown.' [45] This being granted, God is the sole cause of the world, evil is an unsubstantial negation, and sin arises solely in the weakness of human wills.

The basic structure of Augustine's argument here is Neoplatonic.[46] The transcendental monism he expounds, his doctrines on the soul, on evil as the negation of the good, and on freedom are all derived from this source. But his argument is also intellectualistic, and attention should be called to this. 'After many centuries and much contention,' he writes, 'a philosophy has finally been evolved which, in my opinion, is entirely true. It is not limited to this world — it reveals another, the Intelligible world.' [47]

The first motion of his argument is *epistemological.* Just as he had employed the premise of self-deception of the skeptics as the point of departure from skepticism — 'If I deceive myself, I am' — so now, by an analysis of the sensible understanding, he employs the Manichean sensualism as a point of departure from Manicheist materialism. Our senses, held the Manichees, perceive only extended bodies. But behind this corporeal perception Augustine recognizes another light which is the active cause of the perception.[48] The first is the light that we sense by the eyes; the second is that by which the eyes themselves are capable of sensing, namely, the soul. But, Augustine continues, 'if the mind . . . is perceived to be without any local or material extension, and to have a vigor of action which surmounts these material conditions, what must we think or conclude of God Himself, who remains superior to all intelligent beings in His freedom from perturbation and from change . . . ?' [49] The conclusion is that God must be regarded as the principle of all understanding, the principle of all existence, and the principle of all good. 'God is the author of all natures.' [50] As the soul is seen to be without extension in space, yet present to each part of the body, so God is not extended, yet is everywhere perfect, everywhere present.[51] And He is the source of all good. 'The highest good is that than which there is nothing higher. But God is good, and than Him nothing can be higher. God therefore is the highest good.' [52]

Two qualifications on behalf of Christian teaching must at this point be interjected, the first having to do with Augustine's *doctrine of creation,* and the second with his view of *the soul.* To account for creation was a difficulty. The question of how there might be a relation between the infinite and the finite was part of the Manichean puzzle, the puzzle posited by dualism. Hence the importance of Augustine's rejection of materialism. For him any substantial connection between the two became unthinkable. The alternative was a relation of causality. For Plotinus, the finite was a shadow, an image, an accident, an emanation from God Himself; matter participated in Being so little as almost to slip entirely away into nonbeing. Whatever is, is by virtue of its participation in and absolute dependance upon God. God's power permeates all. But Augustine specifies the creation of the world as God's act, *creatio ex nihilo*. He had himself regarded God, at one time, as an immense and glowing body, and himself as a part thereof. He saw now that the world had either of two origins: either God created it from nothing, or He formed it from His own substance. To admit the latter would be to admit that a part of the divine substance could become mutable and finite and subject to corruption. So also with the individual soul. We are not fragments of the divine, as the Manichees held, imprisoned in the flesh. In his disputation with Fortunatus, Augustine exclaims: 'make this reply concerning the soul: that it is not God; that God is one thing, the soul another . . . For if the soul is the substance of God, the substance of God errs, the substance of God is corrupted, the substance of God is violated, the substance of God is deceived; which it is impious to say.'[53]

This is the point of transition to Augustine's resolution of *the problem of evil,* which on the one side is entirely Neoplatonic, and on the other quite centrally Christian. This is also the crucial point of the Manichean controversy. 'There is no way of solving the religious question of good and evil,' he holds, 'unless whatever is, as far as it is, is from God; while as far as it falls away from being it is not God, and yet is always ordered by Divine Providence in agreement with the whole system.'[54] Evil is not nature, but is contrary to nature. It is 'that which falls away from essence and tends to non-existence.'[55] Evil is thus a corruption of the good. It does not exist of itself, 'but in some substance which it corrupts.'[56] 'Whatever is corrupted is deprived of some good . . . but the deprivation implies the previous possession of the good they are deprived of; and if they possessed this good, they were not the perfection of evil, and consequently all the Manichean story is a falsehood.'[57] Evil is thus 'naught but a privation of the good'[58] which Augustine had been so long a time discovering.

This was the Neoplatonic side to Augustine's solution of the difficulty. But with equal clarity and with equal tenacity he held that sin was from the human will. 'Sinning takes place only by exercise of the will . . . no one compelling . . .' [59] 'Sin is the will to retain and follow after what justice forbids, and from which it is free to abstain.' [60] 'God is not the progenitor of things evil . . . Evils have their being by the voluntary sin of the soul to which God gave free will . . . There is no sin where there is not free exercise of will.' [61] 'I say it is not sin, if it be not committed by one's own will.' [62] For Augustine this condemns 'the whole heresy of the Manichaeans.' 'For to speak of souls, and that they are evil, and that they do not sin, is full of madness; but to say that they sin without will, is great craziness, and to hold anyone guilty of sin for not doing what he could not do, belongs to the heighth of inquity and insanity. Wherefore whatever these souls do, if they do it by nature not by will, that is, if they are wanting in a movement of mind free both for doing and not doing, if finally no power of abstaining from their work is conceded to them; we cannot hold that the sin is theirs.' [63] Augustine wishes to fix the fact of personal responsibility. Far from evils arising from two minds, it 'was I who willed, I who was unwilling. It was I, even I myself . . . Therefore was I at war with myself, and destroyed by myself.' [64] 'And I inquired what iniquity was, and ascertained it not to be a substance, but a perversion of the will, bent aside from Thee, O God, the Supreme Substance, towards these lower things . . .' [65]

IV. Conclusions

A conclusion from Augustine's anti-Manichean writings is perhaps inadmissable: even the more tentative term 'conclusions' will be premature if viewed from the standpoint of his later writings. The anti-Manichean writings are polemical and do not respond to the demands of systematic thinking. Something of the arrow's flight may be plotted, however, if a segment of its trajectory is given: though it is possible that 'the arrow endures the string, to become, in the gathering out-leap, something more than itself.' [66]

The one clear-cut conclusion that may be drawn is a negative one: the rejection of the dualistic world view with its materialistic presuppositions. The argument of Nebridius, employed so skillfully by Augustine, is substantially that used by Irenaeus two hundred years earlier against the Valentinian Gnostics: 'If God permitted the creation of such things [defects, evils], because powerless to prevent them, He were not omnipotent; but if He had the power to prevent and did not, He were a deceiver and hypocrite, the slave of necessity.' [67] This is but another phrasing of the dilemma postulated by Lactantius' Epicurean.

Pierre Bayle, in his eighteenth-century *Dictionnaire historique et critique,* puts this succinctly. 'Either God is willing to remove evils, and not able; or able and not willing, or neither able nor willing, or both able and willing. If he be willing and not able, he is impotent, which cannot be applied to the Deity. If he be able and not willing, he is envious, which is generally inconsistent with the nature of God. If he be neither willing nor able, he is both envious and impotent, and consequently no God. If he be both willing and able, which is the only thing that answers to the Notion of a God, from whence come evils? Or why does he not remove them?' Lactantius' answer to this dilemma was that God 'brings forth evil, for otherwise he could not make us know the wisdom, nor the virtue, nor the feeling of goodness.' [68]

Bayle does not approve this answer, regarding it as weak and heretical. It is no better than Jurieu's absurdity, that 'God permitted sin in order to disclose his glory and his wonderful providence . . . The creatures over against him are a mere nothing; he loves his glory more than all his creatures, for he has created all only for his glory.' Which is no better than Theodore Beza's claim: 'Man had to be created that he might be a vehicle for God's compassion.' Except for man's sin 'God would have had no opportunity to show his compassion or his justice.'

But all of this activity of God *ad majorem Dei gloriam* is self-contradictory. For Bayle there is no point in toning down evil. Yet the more seriously we take it the greater are the contradictions to be resolved unless we accept dualism — recognize, that is, a principle somehow acting over against God and 'thwarting' God's will in the world. Bayle's answer is simple. Do not argue with the Manichee. If you match reason against reason you will lose. You must oppose reason with God's word, and leave it there. Why did God permit men to sin? you ask me; and I answer you: I can't say at all, I only believe He had reasons for doing it, reasons worthy of His infinite wisdom, but past my understanding.[69]

This answer might satisfy Tertullian's classic formula, *credo quia absurdum!* But it would not satisfy a man such as Leopardi: 'All is evil. That is, all which exists, is evil; that all things exist, is an evil . . .'[70] Nor would it satisfy the accusing bitterness of James Thomson:

> *Who is most wretched in this dolorous place?*
> *I think myself; yet I would rather be*
> *My miserable self than He, than He*
> *Who formed such creatures to His own disgrace.*
>
> *The vilest thing must be less vile than Thou*
> *From whom it had its being, God and Lord!*
> *Creator of all woe and sin! abhorred,*
> *Malignant and implacable! I vow*
>
> *That not for all Thy power furled and unfurled,*
> *For all thy temples to Thy glory built,*
> *Would I assume the ignominious guilt*
> *Of having made such men in such a world.*

That is strong talk; but it serves to point up the problem. That this problem persists into our own time will be evident from two citations, the first from William James and the second from Paul Elmer More.

God himself . . . may draw vital strength and increase of very being from our fidelity. For my part, I do not know what the sweat and blood and tragedy of this life mean, if they mean anything short of this. If this life be not a real fight, in which something is eternally gained for the universe by success, it is no better than a game of private theatricals from which one may withdraw at will. But it *feels* like a real fight — as if there were something really wild in the universe which we, with all our idealities and faithfulness, are needed to redeem . . .[71]

So far the pragmatist; now the Christian Platonist:

> . . . we must think of God . . . as of one who achieves His end through some obstacle, or condition, or limitation . . . I must believe that God is good and wills good, and I must attribute the evil of the world to some other obscurely guessed factor that thwarts the full working of His will . . . everything about me, the very meaning of the word 'purpose' as drawn from intuition of my own nature, tells me that there is something in the sum of existence besides the will of God, and beyond that patent fact I deem it folly to conjecture.[72]

The central problem of the Manichean world view may be refined to this when the cluttering husks of its cosmology and mythology are stripped away; and precisely on this account its attraction to believers throughout the ages must not be disesteemed. Yet the dilemma of Lactantius' Epicurean, upon which the dualistic view is built, is precisely the dilemma turned by both Irenaeus and Augustine against those who would conserve the inviolability of God by introducing a second cosmic principle in order to account for evil: for, as Irenaeus held, 'that which limits is greater than that which it limits, and must be the real God.'[73]

Constructively, however, there is a difference between Irenaeus' view of sin as apostasy and Augustine's view of evil as defect, or privation. Nowhere does Augustine's use of the Neoplatonic world view appear more sharply than in his refutation of the Manichees. It is true that, as Monsieur de Saci remarked to Pascal regarding the skepticism of Montaigne, 'it was by this same doubt of the academicians that Saint Augustine renounced the Manichean heresy.'[74] Augustine himself confirms this, but in a negative way: 'after the manner of the Academics . . . doubting of everything and fluctuating between all, I decided that the Manicheans were to be abandoned.' [75] His conversion to 'Neoplatonism and good habits' at just this point in his development is to some extent crucial for the history of Christian thought. 'Neoplatonism is a school he does not leave; even as a Christian he never breaks with it. All his life he remains a Neoplatonic Christian . . .' [76] No doubt this claim is excessive, as it does not take into account sufficiently the psychological or existential focus on the will which accompanies this Neoplatonic development, and which he steadily matured throughout his later works toward the primacy of the Biblical categories. This we shall note below. At this stage it remains trapped, as it were, within the framework of substantialist metaphysics: 'I inquired what iniquity was, and ascertained it not to be a substance, but a perversion of the will, bent aside from Thee, O God, the Supreme Substance, towards these lower things . . .' [77] Evil as privation is still dominant. The same view is retained by Thomas Aquinas: evil as privation is that means whereby 'is refuted the error of the Manichees who held that there are certain things evil by their very nature.' [78] The derivation of this view from Aristotle's metaphysics is clear, and it is quite possibly true, as Harnack supposed, that Augustine's study of Aristotle (he mastered the *Categories* at the age of twenty) was a most potent factor in bringing about his change of mind. [79]

Augustine's failure at this point resides, as Brunner has indicated, not in his Neoplatonic and unscriptural identification of being with the good, but in his failure to distinguish between privation of the good 'as an ontological, and the *privatio boni* as an ethical or existential statement'; in his failure, that is, to distinguish between 'defect' as the nonbeing of something and the *defectio* as an act (or, as Irenaeus says, an apostasy). As a result nature (ontology) is ranked higher than personality, and Kierkegaard's insight that 'sin is not a negation but a position' is lost.

This naturalizing, or ontologizing, of the contents of moral action results in an ethic of denial of the world and asceticism, bearing striking resemblances both to Manicheism and to Gnosticism. Harnack and Eucken are probably wrong, however, in attributing Augustine's ethic to the retention of Manichean influence [80]; Hall's observation is more accurate: 'He wished to avoid Manicheism by denying that sin was a "substance," but in fact he identifies it with the body and its natural impulses as such.' [81] The real point is that *the Neoplatonic world view also produces a dualistic ethic.* Concerning which, two observations are to be made: (1) that dualism leads necessarily to an intellectualistic conception of religion, or to an intellectualistic or transcendental mysticism (vision of God, ecstasy, union with God, contemplation) [82]; and (2) that in the 'naturalizing' of the ethical 'the heathen root of the whole theory of Gnosticism comes most decidedly to light.' [83] Schweitzer has shown how German idealism is related generically to Greco-Oriental Gnosticism. [84] The question may now be raised whether Augustine, through failure to subordinate sufficiently the aesthetico-metaphysical appropriation from Neoplatonism to the categories of Scriptural revelation, subtly introduced into Christian history a concealed *Gnosis* (the mystical knowledge of God, and Christ as revealer of the Way) which obtains until the Reformation.

As over against this view, Gilson has held that 'every ontological interpretation of Saint Augustine pre-supposes a more or less complete misunderstanding of his radical empiricism.' [85] This radical empiricism (elsewhere called his *psychological* empiricism) refers to Augustine's exploration of his own soul. [86] We have seen above how, in the anti-Manichean writings, this turn inward upon the mind takes an intellectualistic form, anticipating Descartes and subsequent idealisms. Harnack held that, epistemologically, there was for Augustine a metaphysical continuity between God and the soul discoverable in the deepest inwardness of the soul as such; 'The *Gnothi seauton* became for him the way to God.' [87] But nowhere in Augustine do we find the claim that whoso knows the soul knows God. On the contrary, the highest achievement of the self-knowledge of the soul is a negative disclosure of its own deficiency, a deficiency which only *faith* in God can compensate. Or, as Pascal put it, 'All your light can only reach the knowledge that not in yourselves will you find truth or good.' [88] This is the true *Gnothi seauton.* In short, the proper orientation of Augustine's 'intellectualism' — his psychological empiricism — is toward Pascal, not Descartes: it is not I think, therefore I am, but I believe, therefore I know.

It is in this latter context that Augustine's real refutation of the Manichees lies. For it is here that his Christian notions preside: the primacy of will over intellect ('we are nothing but wills' [89]); the existentializing of sin ('the wicked walk in a circle' [90]); the organic view of the self before God; the belief in the embodied logos as opposed to the disembodied logos of the classical idealists; his turning from the *ratio scientiae* of Greek intellectualism to the *ratio sapientiae* — the love of wisdom — with its Christian corollary of the primacy of faith; and his elaboration of the Trinitarian formula — all of which lie beyond the scope of this paper. But in these writings the arrow points either toward subordination of Christ to Neoplatonic Gnosis (or toward intellectualism), or toward psychological empiricism with its corollaries: the primacy of will and the primacy of faith. The refutation of the Manichees was a necessary part of his soul's elaborate transition, in which, as he says, 'Thou wert with me, but I was not with Thee . . . I tasted, and do hunger and thirst. Thou didst touch me, and I burned for Thy peace.' [91]

NOTES

1. *Art and Scholasticism*, 212; *Art and Poetry*, 65.
2. *The Decline of the West*, II, 251.
3. The dependence of Mani upon Buddhism has been claimed by F. C. Baur (*Das Manichäische Religionssystem*, 433ff.) and Neander (*Church History*, I, 480ff.) notably. Kessler (*Untersuchung zur Genesis des manich. Religionssystems*) holds to Babylonian origins, but admits the use of Buddhism in Mani's ethics. Cf. also Paul Elmer More's argument for Buddhist sources in his fine essay on 'Saint Augustine,' in the *Shelburne Essays*, vol. VI.
4. A. A. Bevan in the *Encylopedia of Religion and Ethics*, VIII, 400b.
5. Quoted by al-Bīrūnī, from the *Shāpūragān;* cited in *ERE*, VIII, 397a.
6. Ibid. 397b.
7. *Encyclopedia Britannica*, 9th ed., XV, 483a.
8. The *Fihrist* (c.980), ed. by G. Flügel and published after his death at Leipzig, 1871-2. The section dealing with Manicheism was published separately by Flügel in 1862 under the title, *Mani, seine Lehre und seine Schriften*. Sources for study fall into four main

groups: Oriental Christian, Zoroastrian, Western, and Muhammadan. Most of these are listed in the *ERE*, the *Encyc. Brit.*, or in A. Newman's introductory essay, 'The Manichaean Heresy,' in *The Nicene and Post-Nicene Fathers* (Nicene Library), first series, IV, 5f.

9. *Encyc. Brit.*, 9th ed., xv, 483a.
10. *De Moribus Manichaeorum* (On the Morals of the Manicheans), 10. 19.
11. Harnack, *Encyc. Brit.*, op. cit. 486a.
12. P. E. More, *Shelburne Essays*, VI, 76, 79.
13. But compare with More, Neander's claim, op. cit. p. 482: 'Mani adopted the Zoroastrian dualism in all cases where he represented his ideas in images of sense: but he introduced into these symbols Buddhist *notions*.' And concerning Neoplatonism the argument of Plotinus 'Against the Gnostics,' or, more properly, 'Against those that affirm the Creator of the Cosmos and the Cosmos Itself to be Evil' (Enneads II, ix), ought not to be overlooked. Nevertheless Plotinus scorned the flesh stubbornly and systematically, refusing, for example, to permit his disciples to celebrate his birthday because of the implicit concession to the flesh.
14. Harnack, op. cit. 486a.
15. Cf. the elaborate theosophical spiritualism of William Butler Yeats: 'I had made a new religion, almost an infallible church of poetic tradition, of a fardel of stories, and personages, and emotions . . . passed on from generation to generation by poets and painters with some help from philosophers and theologians'—Plotinus, Swedenborg, Boehme, Buddhism, et cetera. Also see Charles Baudouin, *Le Myth du moderne,* for an impressive examination of contemporary susceptibility to uncritical myths.
16. *Contra Ep. Man. quam voc. Fund.* (Against the Epistle of Manichaeus called Fundamental), 11. 12.
17. *Confessions,* III. 6. 10; *De Utilitate Credendi* (On the Profit of Believing), 2.
18. *Conf.,* III. 5. 9.
19. *De Duabus Animabus, contra Manichaeos* (On Two Souls, against the Manicheans), 9.
20. Farrar, *Lives of the Fathers,* II, 309.
21. *De Moribus Ecclesiae Catholicae* (On the Morals of the Catholic Church), 1.
22. Cf. Faustus' argument, *Contra Faustum Manichaeum* (Reply to Faustus the Manichean), XVIII. 3.
23. *Conf.,* IV. 15. 24.
24. *Conf.,* V. 10. 20.
25. *Conf.,* V. 10. 18.
26. *Conf.,* IV. 15. 26.

27. See pages 26–7, 32 above.

28. *Conf.*, v. 6. 10.

29. A. M. Newman, Introduction to *Reply to Faustus, Augustine's Anti-Manichean Wrtings,* Nicene Library, iv, 154.

30. *Conf.*, vii. 2. 3.

31. *Disputatio contra Fortunatum Manichaeum* (Disputation against Fortunatus the Manichean), i. 18; i. 7.

32. *De Mor. Man.,* 12; *De Natura Boni* (Concerning the Nature of the Good), 42.

33. Letters, lxxix.

34. Chaps. 21, 22; cf. also Alfaric, *L'Evolution intellectuelle de Saint Augustin,* 279–86.

35. *Con. Faustus Man.,* xxi. 4, 16. The following limerick is apropos:

God's plan made a hopeful beginning.
But man spoiled his chances by sinning.
We trust that the story
Will end in God's glory,
But, at present, the other side's winning.

36. *Conf.,* iii. 10. 18; cf. *De Mor. Man.,* 15. 36; 16. 39, 50, 53.

37. *De Dua. An.,* 1. 1.

38. *Con. Faustus,* vi. 8; cf. Alfaric, op. cit. 292f.

39. Cf. *Conf.,* viii. 10. 22–4.

40. Jerome remarks of a certain class of women, 'quam viderint pallen-tem atque tristem Miseram, Monacham, et Manichaean vocant.' *(De Custod. Virg. Ep.,* 18; Pref. to 'Aug. Writings against the Mani-chees,' Nicene Library, iv, p. 36, note 1.)

41. *De Mor. Man.,* 18. 65.

42. *De Mor. Cath.,* 28. 57.

43. Ibid. 35. 80.

44. *De Mor. Man.,* 19. 67.

45. *De Utilitate Credendi,* 36.

46. Cf. Boyer, *Christianisme et neoplatonisme dans la formation de Saint Augustin;* Boyer, *L'Idée de vérité dans la philosophie de Saint Augustin;* L. Grandgeorge, *Saint Augustin et le neo-platonisme;* Alfaric, op. cit.

47. *Contra Academicos* (Against the Academics), iii. 19. 42.

48. Cf. E. Gilson, *Introduction à l'étude de Saint Augustin,* 85; cf. also *De Dua. An.,* chaps. 3 and 5.

49. *Con. Ep. Man. q. voc. Fund.,* 19. 21.

50. Ibid. 33. 36; cf. *Conf.,* vii. 17. 23, for Augustine's use of the Plotinian chain of being, wherein, beginning with the mind, he passes 'by degrees' to 'that which is.' Also xiii. 32. 47, in which the Imago Dei is defined as 'the power of reason and understanding.'

51. *Con. Ep. Man.,* 16; 15. 20.

52. *De Dua. An.*, 8; also *De Mor. Man.*, 11. 24; 37. 42.
53. *Disp. con. Fort. Man.*, I. 11; also *De Mor. Man.*, 11. 21: 'You say that the soul is God, or a part of God. I do not see how it can be part of God without being God . . . A part of light can be nothing but light.' Cf. *De Civ. Dei*, XI. 22.
54. *De Mor. Man.*, 7. 10.
55. Ibid. 2. 2.
56. Ibid. 5. 7.
57. *Con. Ep. Man. q. voc. Fund.*, 35. 40.
58. *Conf.*, III. 7. 12; VII. 12. 18.
59. *De Dua. An.*, 10. 14.
60. Ibid. 11. 15
61. *Disp. con. Fort. Man.*, II. 20.
62. Ibid. II. 21.
63. *De Dua. An.*, 12. 16, 17. In his *Retractations* Augustine transfers this entire argument from the actual condition of man to the primitive Adamic condition.
64. *Conf.*, VIII. 10. 22.
65. Ibid. VII. 16. 22.
66. Rainer Maria Rilke, *Duino Elegies*, I, 11. 51–2.
67. *Adv. Haer.*, II. v. 2.
68. Lactantius, *De Ira Dei*, 12; Bayle, *Dict.*, III, 625b: article on the Manicheans.
69. Ibid. 634b.
70. *Zibaldone*, VII, 104b.
71. *The Will To Believe*, 61.
72. *The Sceptical Approach to Religion*, 163; cf. also *The Religion of Plato*, 237.
73. *Adv. Haer.*, II. i. 1.
74. Pascal's Conversation with Monsieur de Saci on Epictetus and Montaigne, *Great Shorter Works of Pascal* (Philadelphia, The Westminster Press, 1948, tr. by Emile Cailliet and John C. Blankenagel), 128.
75. *Conf.*, V. 14. 25.
76. A. Nygren, *Agape and Eros*, II. ii. 240; also Boyer, Grandgeorge, et cetera (see note 46).
77. *Conf.*, VII. 16. 22.
78. *Summa Contra Gentiles*, III. 7.
79. *Augustin's Konfessionem*, 20.
80. Harnack, *History of Dogma*, V, 102, 211n.; Euken, *The Problem of Human Life*, 229.
81. T. C. Hall, *History of Ethics within Organized Christianity*, 240.
82. Hermann Mandel, *System der Ethik als Grundlegung der Religion*, I, 138.

83. C. E. Luthardt, *History of Christian Ethics*, I, 158.
84. *Civilization and Ethics*, 125.
85. *A Monument to Saint Augustine*, 306.
86. *Soliloquies*, I. 7: 'deum et animam scire cupio. Nihilne plus? Nihil omnino.'
87. Quoted by O. Zänker, *Der Primat des Willens vor dem Intellekt bei Augustin,* 36.
88. *Pensées*, 430; also 434 (Brunschvig).
89. *Retractations*, I. 8, 3.
90. *De Civ. Dei*, XII. 13; cf. XIV. 24.
91. *Conf.*, X. 27. 38.

VII

THE ANTI–DONATIST

WRITINGS

Frederick W. Dillistone

R<small>ARELY</small> in history can the circumstances that led to the writing of the anti-Donatist works have been so closely paralleled as in the mid-period of the twentieth century. As, through these writings, the reader becomes familiar with conditions in North Africa in the fourth century, he is irresistibly reminded of the happenings in Germany after Hitler's rise to power, the 'quisling' movements in occupied countries during World War II, the conditions in the Church in Japan after V-J day, the struggle of the Church in China since the communist occupation, the new uprisings of nationalist sentiment in the Church in Africa, the behavior of certain sectarian extremists on the North American continent, and last, but not least, the problems of reunion that are exercising the minds of so many Christians today. Of special interest are the parallels between the temper and outlook of important sections of the North African

Church in Augustine's time and those of groups in both East African and West African Churches today. Thus a study of these writings, far from being a piece of purely academic research, should result in much practical guidance for those who are confronted with perplexities similar to those that troubled Augustine's mind for more than thirty years. His own attempts to strengthen the faithful and to refute the schismatics are of particular importance to modern Church leaders in that they throw much light on the doctrines of the Church and the Sacraments, doctrines that have taken a new interest since the desire for reunion began to be felt so strongly within the Church of the twentieth century.

Only recently has a full-scale treatment of the anti-Donatist writings appeared in English. In 1950, S.P.C.K. published in London a book entitled *Saint Augustine and the Donatist Controversy* by Geoffrey Grimshaw Willis. This book gives an admirable historical background and provides a careful tabulation in chronological order of the various writings of Augustine dealing with the controversy. It then takes up the doctrine of the Church, the theory of the relations of Church and State, and the doctrine of the Ministration of the Sacraments, showing how these may be formulated on the basis of principles laid down by Augustine. The author's final conclusion is that in dealing with these subjects Augustine shows himself astonishingly modern. 'For in him we see the transition from primitive to later notions on all these subjects. Truly he was a theological pioneer, and the history of Christian doctrine could never have been quite the same had he not been raised up to bear his witness to the faith at such a critical period as the turn of the fourth century.' [1] The brief historical account of the Donatist movement which we now propose to give may easily be supplemented by reference to Mr. Willis's more exhaustive survey.

I. The Historical Background of the Writing

The blood of the martyrs may be the seed of the Church: the zeal of martyrs can easily prove to be the disruption of the Church. Nothing is clearer from the records of the Church of

North Africa in the fourth century than that it was constantly being harassed by the misguided zeal of fanatics and extremists. To say this is not to depreciate in any way the heroism of those who in times of persecution were faithful unto death. But in a strange way, a willingness to die for a just cause can easily be perverted into what Monsignor Knox has called 'the lust for martyrdom.' And when wild enthusiasm is given a religious sanction, there seem to be no limits to the excesses and cruelties which men will perpetrate.

Back of the fanaticism and violence of the Donatists there was a long period during which the Church had suffered violence. First the Decian persecution, then the persecution under Diocletian had caused divisions within the Church. Some Christians stood rock-like and invited martyrdom. Some submitted to the demands of the persecuting power. Some, however, sought to discover ways and means whereby the final penalty of resistance might be averted and some temporary accommodation made until the tyranny should be past. It is the third group that has always been the principal target of criticism in such circumstances. The first may sometimes be criticized for its intransigence, the second for its pusillanimity. But the third is attacked from both sides as being traitorous to its true principles or as being half-hearted in its acceptance of the inevitable. Generally speaking it was this third position which those who remained faithful to the Catholic Church sought to maintain in Africa during the fourth century.

The point on which everything was made to turn may seem at first to be of minor importance. It was the question of whether a man had or had not been a *traditor,* that is to say, one who under pressure delivered up copies of the Christian sacred books to the persecuting authority. Apparently Diocletian believed that if he could confiscate and destroy the Scriptures he would go far toward exterminating the Christian religion. The case of those who openly complied with the order was simple. But what of those about whom there was real doubt? Or what of those who had sought perhaps to gain respite by handing over books which their persecutors ignorantly thought to be the Scriptures when in fact they were not? These doubtful cases proved to be the source of unending suspicion and bitterness and controversy. The rigorists were unbending, to the extent that they were ready to separate themselves from any who might be under suspicion as *traditores* and to claim that even sacraments performed by *traditores* were invalid. Such an attitude was bound to lead to schism; and soon after the Diocletian persecution had ended, a separate Church was in existence in North Africa, with bishops, priests, and deacons, basilicas, and the full discipline which belonged to the Catholic Church. Not being willing to recognize the validity of sacraments contaminated in any way by a minister who was a *traditor,* they insisted on the necessity of a second baptism for those who desired to be admitted to their fellowship, if, that is, they had previously been baptized within the Catholic Church.

The actual occasion for the founding of a schismatic Church was the vacancy of the see of Carthage in A.D. 312. The Archdeacon of Carthage, one Caecilianus, was elected by the people and duly consecrated, but the rigorist group in the city was opposed to him and soon trouble was brewing. The dissenters appealed to the bishops of Numidia for help, and the final outcome was that a rival bishop was consecrated and African Christianity was divided into two camps. Appeals and counterappeals were directed first to the Emperor, then to the bishop of Rome. In each case Caecilianus was vindicated, but this did not check the zeal of the schismatic party and their numbers rapidly increased. Their first noted leader was one Donatus, from whom the name Donatist was taken. He held his position as schismatic bishop of Carthage for some forty years and was responsible not only for the growth of the Church in Africa but also for its expansion overseas. Not that the Donatists ever made substantial advances in other countries. From first to last it was an *African* movement and its members were determined to assert their own independence, not only of the Catholic Church but also, in more subtle ways, of the power of imperial Rome.

Soon after the middle of the fourth century Donatism became increasingly wild and fanatical. This appears to have been due

partly to an attempt by the imperial authority to restore order
and unity within the African Church, an attempt that was sav-
agely resisted. For the first time we hear of the infamous Circumcellions, bands of armed marauders who have been aptly
termed by Monsignor Knox the 'shock troops' of Donatism.
Most of them were peasants, speaking only the native Punic, and
they armed themselves with the crudest of weapons, having religious scruples about the use of the sword. Nothing could quench
their blind fanaticism. They committed suicide by throwing
themselves over cliffs, they devastated peaceful villages by sudden
attacks, they murdered or demanded death for themselves indifferently. At times the Donatist leaders seem to have been
embarrassed by their activities, but in general these Circumcellions came to be regarded as the heroes and martyrs of the
indigenous African Church.

Politically the movement had its ups and downs. Under Julian
the Apostate it enjoyed remarkable toleration, even support;
under his successor, toleration was withdrawn and punitive measures were enforced. Yet whatever its status might be in relation
to the imperial authority, it continued to grow, and before the
end of the century was as strong as, if not stronger than, the
Catholic Church in the province. Particularly was this true in
the country districts. As has often happened in history, the cities
were more cosmopolitan and more willing to be associated with
the wider world in matters political and religious. In the rural
areas, however, the Donatist Church was essentially the Church
of the African people and this meant that it was often more
distinctively African than Christian. In part this constituted its
strength but it led ultimately to a serious weakness. Ere long
these self-contained Donatist dioceses began to show signs of
dissensions and threatened schisms even within their own bor-
ders. Having turned away from the ideal of unity they were the
more open to the possibilities of internal division and to the
weaknesses ensuing therefrom. Thus it has been suggested that
by the time of Augustine the movement had passed its zenith [2]
but it was still formidable enough to cause him constant trouble.
As we shall see, from the beginning to the end of his career as a

Christian minister, Augustine felt compelled to take account of the activities of the schismatics, especially in the diocese of Hippo, and to do everything in his power to expose the inconsistencies and irregularities of their position while also doing everything possible to attract them back to the Catholic fold from which they had broken away.

During the time that he was still a presbyter (391–5) Augustine wrote a popular psalm to enable the simplest people within the Catholic Church to understand the origins and chief errors of Donatism: it is notable for the tolerant spirit that animates it and for the fervent appeal to return to Mother Church with which it concludes. Three years after he became bishop, Augustine wrote his first extensive controversial work against the schismatics in the form of a treatise answering a letter which the former Donatist bishop of Carthage, Parmenianus, had written against a fellow Donatist, Tyconius. But it was in or around the year 400 that Augustine produced what was probably his most significant work in the whole course of the controversy. It was entitled *De Baptismo contra Donatistas* and consisted of seven books, of which the first four are the most important. Book I is concerned to show that whereas the grace of baptism can certainly be conferred outside the Catholic communion, yet it does not profit the recipient until he returns to the unity of the true fold. In Book II Augustine comes to grips with the teaching of Cyprian, a writer venerated by both sides in the controversy. He admits that Cyprian had been in favor of repeating baptism but believes that this was because the question had not been completely worked out in his day. Augustine is certain that on this particular point Cyprian went contrary to the general teaching of the Church and therefore his authority is not to be invoked in support of a novel practice. Let attention rather be given to Cyprian's earnest desire to preserve unity at all costs. Books III–V continue the discussion of the writings of Cyprian, and Books VI–VII contain a detailed account of the opinions of bishops expressed at the Council of Carthage (A.D. 256), together with Augustine's own comments on them.

The next important work dealing with the schism comes from

approximately the same year. It consists of three books written in response to letters sent by Petilianus, the Donatist bishop of Cirta, to his own clergy and to Augustine himself. The first of these books is designed to instruct Augustine's own flock concerning the points at issue, but the second and third take up Petilianus' statements and answer them point by point. These two books tend to be tedious and unhelpful, often consisting in little more than an attempt to destroy the force of one text of Scripture by quoting another against it.

Other works dealing with the controversy are the *De Unitate Ecclesiae,* a pastoral addressed to Augustine's own flock; a letter in four books replying to a Donatist layman, Cresconius, who had come to the defense of Petilianus; a letter in eleven chapters to Boniface, who was Tribune and afterward Count in Africa; and numerous letters and sermons scattered throughout Augustine's episcopate. Many of these documents tend to repeat the same arguments and to revert to the same Biblical images and proof-texts. We are left in no doubt about Augustine's own position concerning the issues at stake, and the documents are of special value in enabling us to gain a comprehensive view of his doctrine of the Church and the Sacraments. They also throw a good deal of light on the conditions existing within the ecclesiastical life of North Africa at the beginning of the fifth century. Our main task, however, is to draw out the leading elements in Augustine's teaching and to attempt some estimate of its enduring value.

II. The Main Issues in the Conflict

The Seat of Authority. The question of the seat of proper authority has recurred again and again in the history of the Church. When a dispute has arisen concerning matters of belief or practice, each side in the discussion has attempted to appeal to some earlier decision or direction or precedent or custom to support his claim. If there has been some clear guidance from Scripture, that has normally been regarded as carrying final authority; but in many cases there has either been no reference to the matter in the canonical writings or there has been doubt about the correct interpretation of whatever relevant material there is to be found.

On the matter of the rebaptism of heretics little was to be found in the New Testament. But the Donatists seemed to have a clear court of appeal. No less an authority than the great Cyprian, bishop of Carthage, was on their side; and if this was not enough, the Council of Carthage (A.D. 256), with eighty-seven African bishops present, had declared in favor of rebaptizing schismatics and heretics who had been baptized already outside the communion of the Church. Yet Augustine will not allow that this settles the matter once and for all. He quotes Cyprian's own words to the effect that every bishop has the right of forming his own judgment and is not to be excluded from communion if he differs from the rest. But beyond that he goes on to define his own conception of the transmission of authority:

Who can fail to be aware that the sacred canon of Scripture, both of the Old and New Testament, is confined within its own limits, and that it stands so absolutely in a superior position to all later letters of the bishops, that about it we can hold no manner of doubt or disputation whether what is confessedly contained in it is right and true; but that all the letters of bishops which have been written, or are being written, since the closing of the canon, are liable to be refuted if there be anything contained in them which strays from the truth, either by the discourse of some one who happens to be wiser in the matter than themselves, or by the weightier authority and more learned experience of other bishops, or by the authority of Councils; and further, that the Councils themselves, which are held in the several districts and provinces must yield, beyond all possibility of doubt, to the authority of universal Councils which are formed for the whole Christian world; and that even of the universal Councils, the earlier are often corrected by those which follow them when by some actual experiment, things are brought to light which were before concealed, and that is known which previously lay hid, and this without any whirlwind of sacrilegious pride, without any puffing of the neck through arrogance, without any strife of envious hatred, simply with holy humility, catholic peace and Christian charity.[3]

At a later point Augustine sums up his own position in a still more pointed way: 'What the custom of the Church has always held, what this argument [i.e. of the Donatists] has failed to prove false, and what a general Council has confirmed, this we follow! To this we may add that it may also be said, after a careful inquiry into the reasoning on both sides of the discussion and into the evidence of Scripture, "What truth has declared, that we follow." ' [4]

From these quotations and from the accompanying discussions we may infer that Augustine had a much more complex and dynamic view of authority than his opponents. He refused to be satisfied by a mere appeal to one of the great Fathers or even to one of the Church Councils. He demanded to be allowed to examine any question in the light of (a) the testimony of Scripture, (b) the generally accepted custom of the Church, (c) the decision of a widely representative Council, (d) the arguments that might be put forward either in support of or in opposition to any proposed change of practice or belief. Obviously the canonical Scriptures occupied the place of supreme authority: their 'truth' was inviolable. But beyond them the process of weighing variant authorities was far from easy. Of greatest weight for Augustine was undoubtedly the decision of a general or universal Council. When 'very many men of the same religion and communion, all endowed with great talent and abundant learning,' were gathered together, their decision could not be lightly set aside. Yet even it could not be regarded as finally determining the issue. Augustine insists upon the right of free inquiry, so long as it is carried on in the spirit of humility and charity and with the desire to promote unity in the bond of peace.

In the particular matter of the rebaptism of heretics, Augustine believes that the custom handed down from the time of the apostles and bearing their approval was that of recognizing as valid any baptism in the triune name, even though it had been performed outside the communion of the Catholic Church. Yet history recorded that at the Council of Carthage held in A.D. 215 Bishop Agrippinus had proposed to amend this custom and his proposal had been accepted. When later in the century Cyprian had to grapple with the same problem he finally fell back upon the decision of the earlier Council, and his decision likewise was accepted by the bishops gathered with him. But, as Augustine points out, a General Council in the fourth century reaffirmed the original custom derived from apostolic tradition.[5] Hence the refusal to rebaptize heretics carries the greater conciliar authority; and in addition it conforms, he believes, to the testimony of Scripture and to the logic of reasonable argument. Although the particular method by which Augustine made his appeal to Scriptures has had to be revised by later generations, his attempt to approach the question of authority by a weighing of evidence derived from Scripture, from decisions of Church councils, from the works of individual leaders of the Church, from the free inquiry of honest minds — this attempt was of the utmost value in his own day, and we may hold that it established a pattern which can still be of value in a day when the question of the proper seat of authority has not ceased to vex the Church. So long as the Church is willing to listen for the Word of God in the Scriptures, to study the history of the developments of thought in its own tradition, to recognize the importance of the general consensus of widely representative councils, and to carry on its own inquiries in the spirit of humility and charity, it is not likely to go far astray.

The Nature of the Church. One of the most famous and possibly one of the most determinative sayings about the Church recorded in Christian history is that only those have God for their Father who acknowledge the Church as their Mother. The thought occurs in the writings of Tertullian, it is stated explicitly by Cyprian, it is referred to by Augustine ('You are safe, who have God for your Father and His Church for your Mother'[6]), and it is taken up centuries later by Calvin. The vision of the Church as the enduring and all-embracing mother clearly made a deep appeal to Augustine. 'The same mother which brought forth Abel and Enoch and Noah and Abraham, brought forth also Moses and the prophets who succeeded him till the coming of our Lord; and the mother which gave birth to them gave birth also to our apostles and martyrs and all good Christians.' All these have been brought forth of the seed of the bridegroom, they have been generated by the sacrament of either the old or the new covenant. Some, alas, of those brought forth from the womb of the true mother show ultimately that they do not belong to the true seed: some of those brought forth from the womb of Hagar, a bondwoman (the reference is to a heretical church) receive the inheritance belonging to the true seed when they return to the embrace of the true mother.[7] 'She it is alone who holds as her privilege the whole power of her Bridegroom and Lord; by virtue of which power as bride, she can bring forth sons even of handmaids. And these, if they be not high-minded, shall be called into the lot of the inheritance; but if they be high-minded, they shall remain outside.' [8]

Another symbol frequently used by Augustine in his references to the Church is that of the dove. He takes it from an Old Testament reference in Song of Solomon 6:9 'My dove is but one; she is the only one of her mother.' The Church resembles the dove in her unity, her chasteness, her gentleness, her perfection — without spot or wrinkle — her compassion in her lamentation over her children through the prayers of the saints. 'He is loosed who has made peace with the dove, and he is bound who is not at peace with the dove, whether he is openly without, or appears to be within.' [9] Those who live contrary to Christ 'are not in the Church of which it is said "My dove is but one; she is the only one of her mother"; for she herself is without spot or wrinkle.' [10] The dove, the bride, the mother — these are the images Augustine loves to employ in speaking of the Church. It is not unlikely that his relation to his own mother influenced him in this choice of terms. The purity, the tenderness, the yearning, the beauty, the fecundity of his mother in the flesh were transferred to the institution which he acknowledged as his mother in the spirit, and something of the emotional attachment he felt for the one was doubtless transferred to the other. It was beyond comprehension to him that men should deliberately cut themselves off from the peace and the unity of the great Mother of all.

With these images in mind we can now proceed to examine Augustine's treatment of the four traditional notes of the Church.

(a) UNITY. Two passages from the Pauline Epistles seem to have been constantly in his mind. One was the thirteenth chapter of I Corinthians. To have the gift of prophecy, to possess the sacraments, to distribute to the poor, to offer the body for burning under stress of persecution — all these are of no avail if charity is lacking; and what is charity save remaining within the bond of the unity of the Catholic Church? 'In these apostolic words which commend the excellence of charity, we are wont to show to you how profitless it is to man that he should be in possession of faith or of the sacraments, when he has not charity, that, when you come to Catholic unity, you may understand what it is that is conferred on you, and how great a thing it is of which you were at least to some extent in want; for Christian charity cannot be preserved except in the unity of the Church and that so you may see that without it you are nothing, even though you may be in possession of baptism and faith, and through this latter may be able even to move mountains.' [11] The other passage continually in his mind was the opening verses of the fourth chapter of Ephesians, where the apostle beseeches the members of the one body to preserve the unity of the Spirit in the bond of peace. In Augustine's view, charity and unity and peace were inseparably bound together; and outside the unity of the one Catholic Church deeds of charity could not avail nor could true peace be found.

(b) CATHOLICITY. The note of catholicity was so closely associated with that of unity in Augustine's mind that we shall consider it next. What did he mean by the *Catholic* Church to which he so often referred? In a word it was the Church whose extension was world-wide. In a letter to the Donatists,[12] he pleads with them: 'Why have you severed yourselves, by the heinous impiety of schism, from the unity of the whole world?' He quotes Psalm

2, Genesis 22:18, Psalm 22:27-8, Luke 24:44-7, all in order to show that God's promises and blessings are for all nations, for the whole world. 'Lift up the eyes of your souls, and see how in the whole world all nations are blessed in Abraham's seed . . . Wherefore will you be guilty of dividing the garments of the Lord, and not hold in common with the whole world that coat of charity, woven from above throughout, which even His executioners did not rend?' In his letter to Boniface concerning the correction of the Donatists, he returns to the same passages of Scripture and concludes that as the Lord Christ is made manifest in all of them, 'so is His Church made manifest, not in Africa alone . . . but spread abroad throughout the world.' [13]

Throughout these writings Augustine shows little understanding of nationalist aspirations or of the possibility that the Donatists might have discovered a truth that was being neglected or even denied by the Catholic Church. For him it was a fundamental principle that 'the whole is always, with good reason, looked upon as superior to the parts.' [14] 'Catholic,' he recognizes, is derived from two Greek words meaning 'according to the whole,' and the Catholic Church is that which has extended into the uttermost part of the earth (Acts 1:8). Therefore those who do not belong to the communion which is spread throughout the whole earth are not members of the Catholic Church. It is, in his view, ridiculous for any schismatic Church in Africa to set itself up against the world-wide whole, for the whole must be superior to any of its parts.

(c) HOLY. The difference between Augustine and the Donatists concerning the holiness of the Church was essentially the same as that which has arisen again and again between liberals and rigorists in the history of the Church. Is it right for any group within the Church which believes that the wider whole has been contaminated by the condoning of some flagrant and obvious sin to withdraw and form a 'perfectionist' Church of its own from which this particular sin is rigorously excluded? As we have seen, the bitter dispute in Africa raged around the treatment of the *traditores*. All were agreed that the actual offense, if definitely proved, must be condemned. But the Donatists wished to go beyond this. They desired to institute investigations, to withdraw from all fellowship with those proved guilty (and often with those only suspect of being guilty), and even to separate themselves from those known to have had contact in any ecclesiastical way with *traditores*. In other words every 'quisling,' every collaborator, everyone tainted with pro-*traditor* sympathies must be ruthlessly exposed and excluded from membership or office in the Church. In reading the story of the Church in the fourth century it is impossible to avoid making certain comparisons with more modern times.

Midst all the tumult of voices and the cries of those demanding extreme measures, Augustine kept his head. We quote one of his most vivid passages, which reveals clearly the principles by which he set his course:

> If you cling most firmly to what I urge on you . . . then you will in no wise desert the threshing-floor of the Lord on account of the chaff which either is now being dispersed beneath the blast of the wind of pride, or will be separated by the final winnowing; nor will you fly from the great house on account of the vessels made to dishonor; nor will you quit the net through the breaches made in it because of the bad fish which are to be separated on the shore; nor will you leave the good pastures of unity, because of the goats which are to be placed on the left when the Good Shepherd shall divide the flock; nor will you separate yourselves by an impious secession, because of the mixture of the tares, from the society of that good wheat whose source is that grain that dies and is multiplied thereby, and that grows together throughout the world until the harvest. For the field is the world — not only Africa; and the harvest is the end of the world — not the era of Donatus.[15]

In few points were the Donatists more open to criticism than in their doctrine of the holiness of the Church. It is clear that they laid an altogether disproportionate emphasis upon the one issue of the *traditores*. Holiness could not possibly be identified with a spotless record on that one issue. Moreover the energies of the Church could not possibly be devoted solely or even mainly to the scenting out of this particular failing. And to claim that the assistance of one *traditor* in a consecration could muddy the whole stream of Catholic ministry was absurd. Augustine's wider and more patient view of the nature of the Church's holiness, never condoning sin yet recognizing that *men* could not act as final judges, has commended itself to the conscience of the vast majority in the Church of subsequent generations.

(d) APOSTOLICITY. The fourth note of the Church receives less treatment in the controversy than is given the other three. In general it is interpreted simply in terms of succession within an apostolic see. Rome in particular, being able to trace an unbroken succession of bishops back to St. Peter himself, is undoubtedly an apostolic see. In its long line of bishops there has never been a Donatist. Hence it is useless for the Donatists to seek an apostolic sanction for their doctrines. True apostolicity is that which maintains the truth of the Gospel as it has been handed down by the successors of the apostles in the sees that they founded.

One final element in Augustine's doctrine of the Church as it appears in these writings deserves to be mentioned, for it was to play a considerable part in later discussions of the subject. This is the distinction he makes between those who truly belong to the Body of Christ and those who, though formally included within its membership, do not belong to the true seed. Let us consider, for example, the following passage:

It is therefore possible that some who have been baptized without may be considered, through the foreknowledge of God, to have been really baptized within, because within the water begins to be profitable to them unto salvation . . . And again, some who seemed to have been baptized within may be considered, through the same foreknowledge of God, more truly to have been baptized without, since by making a bad use of baptism, they die by water . . . Certainly it is clear that, when we speak of within and without in relation to the Church, it is the position of the heart that we must consider, not that of the body, since all who are within in heart are saved in the unity of the ark through the same water, through which all who are in heart without, whether they are also in body without or not, die as enemies of unity.[16]

Or we may look at some of his more pithy and epigrammatic sayings: 'This much, however, I think I may say without rashness, if no one outside can have anything which is of Christ, neither can anyone within have anything which is of the devil.' [17] 'As therefore what is of the devil within the fold must be convicted, so what is of Christ without must be recognized.' 'If those only are to be called tares who remain in perverse error to the end, there are many ears of corn outside, and many tares within.' [18] And finally the oft-quoted saying: 'In that unspeakable foreknowledge of God, many who seem to be without are in reality within, and many who seem to be within yet really are without.' [19]

Taking these passages in conjunction with a careful summing-up toward the end of Book VII of the *De Baptismo*, we may define Augustine's position as follows. He recognized first the central core of those within the Catholic Church who were either already spiritual or were making progress with earnestness of heart toward that end: these certainly belonged to the true house of God. Then there were those within the Catholic Church whose conduct was a constant affliction to the hearts of the saints and whose character was so perverse that they could be regarded only as vessels of dishonor doomed to final destruction: they could not be regarded as belonging to the *substance* of the house of God, though formally they were to be found within it. Thirdly there were those who through delight in heresy and schism had finally 'burst the meshes of the net' and were living openly in separation from the true Church: their doom was certain. But finally, even within the schismatic bodies, there were those who had received baptism and were destined in due time to be received into the Catholic Church: already through baptism they had been brought into the ark but their baptism could begin to be profitable to them for salvation only when they became united to the true fold.

Though he approaches the question in a variety of ways, Augustine never attempts to give a final test whereby those who are chaff *within* the Church may be separated from those who are grain *without* the Church. The final judgment is in God's hands. His deepest concern — the concern of a pastor's heart — is that those already within the Church shall live worthy of their vocation and that those who have been baptized into a schismatic body shall be joined to the unity of the Catholic Church without delay. Through all that he writes on the subject there breathes a spirit of charity and liberality which is in sharp contrast to the fanatical and intolerant attitudes of his Donatist adversaries.

The Policy toward Schismatics. Possibly no passage in the anti-Donatist writings has gained such notoriety as that in which Augustine interprets the injunction from our Lord's parable, 'Compel them to come in,' in the sense that the Church is justified in invoking the aid of the secular arm in seeking to bring her wayward sons back to their true obedience. The passage occurs in Chapter 7 of the letter to Boniface. Taking the Lord's saying as it is given in Luke 14:22, 23, Augustine comments: 'In those who were first brought in with gentleness, the former obedience is fulfilled: but in those who were compelled the disobedience is avenged. For what else is the meaning of "Compel them to come in"?' It could not be compulsion by the terrifying power of miracles, for many miracles were actually being wrought. Rather, he says, 'if the power which the Church has received by divine appointment in its due season, through the religious character and the faith of kings, be the instrument by which those who are found in the highways and hedges — that is, in heresies and schisms — are compelled to come in, then let them not find fault with being compelled, but consider whether they be so compelled.' [20]

Clearly Augustine desired always to go to the limit in using powers of persuasion to draw schismatics back to the Catholic Church. 'It is indeed better,' he writes, 'that men should be led to worship God by teaching than that they should be driven to it by fear of punishment or pain.' [21] To train the young by shame or dread of meanness, to guide by love, this is assuredly the better way. But Augustine does not believe that it will succeed always, not even in the majority of cases. More are corrected by fear than won by love. He turns to the Book of Proverbs, with its advice not to spare the rod; he appeals to the violent measures taken to halt the steps of the persecutor Saul of Tarsus; he takes up the analogy of sheep who have strayed from the fold and need forcibly to be brought back; and finally he comes to the Parable of the Great Supper. All these confirm him in his conviction that the use of force may be necessary, especially if the end for which it is being used is right and good.

As far as the Donatists themselves were concerned, their own case was weakened by the fact that in the beginning of the controversy they had themselves appealed to Constantine for redress. Moreover, if they could find a sympathetic ruler and it suited their purposes, they would not be averse to gaining secular support at any time. Still further, their own records abounded with examples of violence and cruelty. The Circumcellions were notorious for their unprovoked attacks and for their use of any and every weapon save the sword.

In an interesting passage in the *Answer to Petilian,* Augustine considers at length whether the Church has the right to appeal to 'the kings of this world.' Petilianus had tried to show that in the record of Scripture, kings were constantly depicted in the role of persecutor and murderer; and in more recent days a succession of Roman emperors had persecuted the Christians. To all this Augustine replies that the Donatists have little right to speak, since they themselves had invoked the aid of Julian, the apostate and enemy of the name of Christ. In any case, however, he proceeds to show that the Scripture record also bears witness to many kings who were the friends and supporters of the people of God. Moreover the Roman emperors, of whom Petilian had spoken, had persecuted the whole body of Christians, not the Donatists in particular. And if Scripture is examined more closely, it shows that in the Second Psalm, for example, kings are bidden to perform a duty which no private individual could undertake. Thus 'kings, in the very fact that they are kings, have a service which they can render to the Lord in a manner which is impossible for any who have not the power of kings.' [22]

In this part of the controversy Augustine's arguments, whether from Scripture or from history, do not impress. There is something to be said for an appeal by the Church to the secular power to maintain order and to save its Christian citizens from the wild attacks of fanatical extremists. But there is little or nothing to be said for any attempt to bring men into the Catholic Church with the aid of the instruments of fear and compulsion. Both sides were at fault in the controversy, but unfortunately the prestige of Augustine meant that his principles on this matter carried weight for future generations. All that can be said to offset his willingness to use coercion toward the schismatics is that he showed a remarkable spirit of leniency and tolerance toward those who were ready to return. He steadfastly refused to demand that heretics or schismatics should be rebaptized, and he even insisted that those who had been ordained before their secession and then had returned to the Catholic Church should not be ordained again. 'Either they again exercise their former ministry, if the interests of the Church require it, or if they do not exercise it, at any rate they retain the sacrament of their ordination.' [23] At all times his principle was that those in separation were sick and wounded and needing healing — not that they were perverse and rebellious and needed condemnation. His earnest desire was that what was sound in them might function healthily — and that, he believed, could happen only within the charity of the Catholic Church. In a noble appeal to the schismatics he cries: 'Bring those whom you have wounded [a reference to rebaptism] to be healed by the medicine of peace; bring those whom you have slain to be brought to life again by the life of charity. Brotherly union has great power in propitiating God. "If two of you," says our Lord, "shall agree on earth as touching anything that they shall ask, it shall be done for them." If for two men who agree, how much more for two communities? Let us throw ourselves together on our knees before the Lord. Do you share with us our unity; let us share with you your contrition; and let charity cover the multitude of sins?' [24]

The Significance of Baptism. We have discussed a number of the underlying principles at stake in the controversy but there was one simple outward test that came to distinguish one side from the other. The Donatists required that any Catholics who desired to join their Church should first be rebaptized; Augustine on his part refused to rebaptize any who had been baptized already in the Donatist Church. The baptism of Christ, he held, was one, whether administered within the Catholic Church or within a schismatic body. The all-important thing was that it could not avail for the salvation of those who deliberately remained outside the fold of the true Church.

It was no easy task for Augustine to vindicate his position, since the authority of the great Cyprian seemed to be against him. Yet because he is in effect arguing his point with Cyprian as well as with the Donatists we find that to this particular issue some of his most careful thought is given. We shall endeavor to set out in order some of his main contentions.

(a) The source and origin of baptism is not man or even the Church but God Himself. Comparing the case of a vicious Catholic with that of an upright heretic, where each has received baptism, Augustine asks, 'Why do we recognize in one of them the sacrament of Christ, and not in the other, as though it belonged to this or that man, whilst really it is the same in both and belongs to God alone?' [25] Again in his *Answer to Petilian* he reverts constantly to the theme that Christ is the origin, Christ the root, Christ the head of the baptized person. It matters not whether the water is Petilian's or Augustine's. 'We are neither made fouler by our washing, nor cleaner by yours. But when the water of baptism is given to anyone in the name of the Father and of the Son and of the Holy Ghost, it is neither ours nor yours, but His of whom it was said to John, "Upon whom thou shalt see the Spirit descending, and remaining on Him, the same is He which baptizeth with the Holy Ghost." ' [26] Baptism is from God through Christ — this is the first principle on which Augustine builds his case.

(b) Baptism is an integral part of the Gospel and may be

compared with it in its operations and effects. The exact relation of baptism to the Gospel is not altogether clear in Augustine's thought. He seems to give primacy to the Gospel by asserting that the seed by which we are born again is the Gospel; by magnifying Paul, whose main task was to preach the Gospel rather than to baptize; and by pointing out that Paul claimed to have begotten his converts through the Gospel. Yet he affirms that baptism 'belongs to the gospel in such wise, that without it no one can reach the kingdom of heaven,' [27] and that in one respect baptism seems to be superior to the Gospel, for whereas Paul speaks of 'my gospel,' no one ever spoke of 'my baptism.' Baptism belongs to Christ alone.

Whatever the exact relation may have been in Augustine's mind, it is evident that he regarded the two as parallel in their operation. Those who are astray sometimes employ the words of the Gospel: that does not make the Gospel false. Similarly heretics may administer the sacrament of baptism: that does not make their baptism 'adulterous.' Baptism can be common to Catholics and heretics just as the Gospel can be common to both.[28] The Gospel is Christ's, baptism is Christ's. 'Neither one without the other leads to the kingdom of heaven.' [29]

(c) The *gift* of baptism and the profitable *use* of it are to be carefully distinguished. It would be difficult to overstress the importance of this principle in Augustine's thinking. On the one hand it enabled him to adopt an attitude of generosity to the schismatics and to say: 'You have already received the gift of baptism: you need not be re-baptized.' On the other hand it justified him in adopting an attitude of urgency in saying: 'You cannot profit by that which you have received until you return to the fold of unity. It is one thing not to have, another to have so as to be of use. He who has not must be baptized that he may have; but he who has to no avail must be corrected, that what he has may profit him.' [30]

In seeking to define his own position as against that of Cyprian and other eminent Christians, Augustine claims that their departure from the ancient custom of the Church 'simply arose from their not distinguishing the sacrament from the effect or use of the sacrament; and because its effect and use was not found among heretics in freeing them from their sins and setting their hearts right, the sacrament itself was also thought to be wanting among them.' [31] But Augustine will not allow that this is so. Sheep wandering outside had received the mark of the Lord; seeking the salvation of Christian unity they had returned to the fold; this did not mean that their mark of identification must be rejected; rather it was to be retained while they now went forward to attain the truth and freedom to which their mark entitled them. This doctrine may involve many difficulties, but that it held a determinative place in Augustine's thought is scarcely open to doubt.

(d) Baptism does not depend for its validity upon the place where it is received or upon the character or associations of him who administers it or upon the adequacy of the faith of the recipient. Toward the end of the *De Baptismo,* when Augustine was obviously weighing his words with great care, he writes, 'If any one were to press me to declare what my own opinion was . . . I should have no hesitation in saying that all men possess baptism who have received it in any place, from any sort of men, provided that it were consecrated in the words of the gospel, and received without deceit on their part with some degree of faith; although it would be of no profit to them for the salvation of their souls if they were without charity, by which they might be grafted into the Catholic Church.' [32] What the position would be if the whole ceremony were performed in jest or as a farce, without desire or faith on the part of any, Augustine does not feel able to judge.

The main point at issue with the Donatists had been the qualifications of the minister of baptism. They insisted that the man must neither be a *traditor* nor have been ordained by a bishop in any way associated with the *traditores.* They urged that he must be a man of such clean conscience that the recipient's conscience would be cleansed through his. This latter plea Augustine deals with firmly and even scathingly in his *Answer to Petilian.* How can the recipient of baptism be sure that the conscience of him who baptizes him is clean from all stain? He has little difficulty in showing that to make the validity of baptism depend upon the character of the ministrant quickly leads to an intolerable position. So the principle was deduced that even if a murderer were baptizing, the gift of the Holy Spirit would still be secure, for 'it is God . . . that gives the Holy Spirit even when a man of this kind is baptizing.' [33]

III. Appreciation and Criticism

In a brief appraisal of Augustine's contribution to Christian thought in and through the anti-Donatist writings, let us consider first their *form*. In many ways they closely resemble the writings of St. Paul. They consist of letters written to groups or to individuals and they deal with living situations. The most systematic treatise (corresponding perhaps to St. Paul's Epistle to the Romans) is the *De Baptismo* but even that is taken up to a large extent with objections raised by those who differed from him. He writes with vigor, often with passion, and shows himself a master of the art of dialectic. It is a considerable feat to take up the opinions of the successive bishops who had spoken at the Council of Carthage and deal with them so clearly and convincingly.

The writings are full of Scriptural references, and after the pattern of his own day Augustine uses texts in controversy without much regard for their context or their original meaning. Yet there is a sense of continuity through the Scripture record and a recognition of the close connection that exists between the old and the new covenants. He is well-informed on the history of the fourth century and his writing gains in power by his frequent references to incidents in the long-drawn-out conflict. But perhaps the most notable feature of his writing so far as style is concerned is his constant appeal to images and parables that had left a deep impression on his mind. His favorites are the wheat and the tares, the dragnet, the sheep and the goats, the good tree and the corrupt tree, the house with some vessels for honor, some for dishonor; to these he returns again and again. They are excellently suited for his purpose, for each illustrates in some way the inevitable admixture of good and bad and the disastrous folly of seeking to distinguish at too early a stage between the worthy and the unworthy. Augustine rarely becomes theoretical or dull. By the use of vivid images and metaphors he sustains interest and establishes his main positions, though he sometimes allows himself to press a point too far and to pile up his illustrative material beyond what is needed for his purpose.

Turning to the *contents* of the writings we shall confine our attention to two points. Is Augustine's doctrine of the Church, as found in these writings, satisfactory? Is his view of the effectiveness of baptism satisfactory?

(a) It would not be unfair to say that the notes of the Church ever before Augustine's mind were its unity and its catholicity. The one Church scattered throughout the known world with all its parts in communion with one another — that to Augustine was a precious reality. The only place where the unity was seriously broken was in Africa. What right had this group of extreme, illogical, and impatient men to set themselves up against the judgment of the whole Church? To Augustine, who had been trained in the classical tradition and had imbibed much of the spirit of imperial Rome, the rebellion of a small fraction against the accumulated wisdom and tradition of the whole seemed madness. Why would these men not see the folly of their ways and return to the place of true peace and health?

Everything Augustine read in Scripture confirmed him in his view. Was there not one Dove, one Bride, one Body? Was not the Church the one Mother of those who acknowledged God as their Father? Did not charity imply the preservation of unity? How then could those imagine that they possessed charity who refused to return to unity? But what his head told him was reinforced by his heart. He longed to see a united Church of peace and brotherhood. He was willing to go to the limit in making it easy for the Donatists to return. He would receive them without rebaptism, he would have their bishops come and minister in the Catholic churches. This man with great heart and wide-ranging mind, himself devoted to the Church as his true Mother, was willing to consider even the application of force to bring men back into what he believed to be the only home of charity and peace.

We recognize the nobility of his spirit and the sincerity of his desire. Yet there was one thing, it seems, that Augustine was quite incapable of understanding. This was the intensity of the longing in men's hearts at certain times for independence, for self-expression, for intimate personal loyalties, for a group dynamic. Such a longing may burst out in strange ways. It may lead to revolt against existing institutions or to dissatisfaction with the accepted pattern of social custom or to a fierce self-assertion coupled with condemnation of others. Especially will this be the case when people have lived in hard and primitive conditions, when they have had constantly to struggle for their own existence, and when there has been the pressure of some superior power weighing down upon their souls. Revolution or schism seems for a while to be inevitable. All then depends upon the attitude of the larger body, the long-established institution. Will it condemn, oppose, scold, discipline the offending group? Will it condone the revolt? Its position is exceedingly delicate, for it cannot be indifferent to the challenge of the separatists, while at the same time it cannot afford to close the door to the possibility of reconciliation. We doubt if Augustine was wise to insist so much upon the breach of unity and the lack of charity on the part of the Donatists. We question whether his arguments and exhortations made much impression upon the schismatics. At the same time we must recognize the magnitude of his achievement in being willing to break through the sterner rigidity of Cyprian's attitude in order to open a door, to make an accommodation, for the sake of the greater peace and charity of Christ's Church. He set an example that has helped to save the Church from pursuing so completely rigorist and legalistic a policy as to make reunion with schismatic bodies quite impossible.

(b) Our second question concerns his view of baptism. It is intriguingly simple. Baptism is *God's* gift, or, to put it in another way, it is *Christ's* baptism. If its source is divine, it matters not where or by whom it is performed. If the given divine words are used, if the given divine action is performed, that is all that matters. The context of the ministration, the character of the ministrant are irrelevant, at least so far as the validity of the sacrament is concerned. God's gift has been bestowed *ex opere operato* (Augustine does not use this phrase) and this is one part of the process necessary for any man's salvation.

This is Augustine's starting point. But there is another part necessary in the process. It is conversion, the attainment of righteousness, growth in grace. For this part the context matters a great deal. Only within the Catholic Church can there be advance toward salvation. The minister, too, is important. He alone can give guidance in the way of righteousness. Thus baptism wherever given is valid but it becomes truly effective only within the unity of the Church. 'What then,' the imaginary schismatic asks, 'do we receive with you when we come over to your side?' To which Augustine answers, 'you do not indeed receive baptism which was able to exist in you outside the framework of the body of Christ, although it could not profit you; but you receive the unity of the Spirit in the bond of peace, without which no one can see God; and you receive charity, which, as it is written, "shall cover the multitude of sins." ' [34]

But is this not too simple? Are God's gifts given in this impersonal and quasi-mechanical way? A water rite accompanied by the recitation of the triune name — does this alone constitute baptism? It is true that Augustine seems to regard any such valid baptism as being in reality a baptism within the general context of the Catholic Church, even though its immediate context is that of schism. But this would still mean that the personal attitude of the ministrant and the presence of a body of the faithful are irrelevancies so far as the gift itself is concerned. Moreover the distinction between *gift* and *use* seems to imply that in no circumstances can baptism profit an individual outside the formal unity of the Catholic Church.

Granted that this was a more liberal view than that held in many quarters in the Church of the fourth century, it still seems too rigid to win final acceptance. If it be held that God in His dealing with those capable of personal existence acts always in personal ways, then in the administration of baptism place must be found for at least some context of personal relationships if the act is to be distinguished from a purely mechanical operation. Moreover, if within some group that is not formally united to the Churches standing within the 'Catholic' tradition a person is baptized with water in the name of the Trinity and is nurtured with Christian devotion by those personally related to him, it is impossible to believe that no advance is made in the life of sanctification. These are large questions which are still causing perplexity within the councils of the Church. We may be thankful for Augustine's positive and charitable approach to the subject even though we may not accept his solution as final. At least we may believe that he would have us at all times continue to inquire and confer in the spirit of his noble words in the *Answer to Petilian:*

> These things, brethren, I would have you retain as the basis of your action and preaching with untiring gentleness: love men, while you destroy errors; take of the truth without pride; strive for the truth without cruelty. Pray for those whom you refute and convince of error . . . May ye live and persevere in Christ, and be multiplied, and abound in the love of God, and in love towards one another, and towards all man, brethren well beloved.[35]

FOR FURTHER READING

G. G. Willis, *Saint Augustine and the Donatist Controversy* (London, 1950).

W. J. Sparrow-Simpson, *The Letters of St. Augustine* (London, 1919), Chapter IV.

Ronald Knox, *Enthusiasm* (Oxford University Press, 1950), Chapter IV. This chapter gives a vivid picture of the Donatists.

NOTES

1. Willis, p. 187.
2. R. A. Knox, *Enthusiasm* (New York, 1950), p. 58.
3. *De Bapt.*, II. 4.

4. Ibid. IV. 9.
5. It is uncertain whether the General Council to which Augustine refers was that of Arles (A.D. 314) or of Nicaea (A.D. 325).
6. *C. Litteras Petiliani Donatistae* (Answer to Petilian), III. 10.
7. See *De Bapt.*, I. 10, 15-16.
8. Ibid. IV. 1.
9. Ibid. III. 23.
10. Ibid. III. 4.
11. *Answer*, II. 172.
12. *Epis.*, 76.
13. I. 3.
14. *De Bapt.*, II. 14.
15. *Answer*, III. 3.
16. *De Bapt.*, V. 39.
17. Ibid. IV. 10.
18. Ibid. IV. 13–14.
19. Ibid. V. 38.
20. *Epis. 185 ad Bonifacium*, VII. 24.
21. Ibid. VI. 21.
22. *Answer*, II. 210.
23. *De Bapt.*, I. 2.
24. Ibid. II. 18.
25. Ibid. IV. 27.
26. *Answer*, II. 5.
27. Ibid. III. 67.
28. *De Bapt.*, IV. 24.
29. *Answer*, III. 68.
30. *De Bapt.*, IV. 24.
31. Ibid. VI. 1.
32. Ibid. VII. 102.
33. Ibid. V. 28.
34. *Letter to Boniface*, X. 43.
35. *Answer*, I. 31.

VIII

THE ANTI–PELAGIAN

WRITINGS

Paul Lehmann

Τ HE FIFTH century had scarcely turned its first decade when the energies and thoughts of Augustine were forcibly drawn into a long and lively controversy with Pelagius.[1] The issues of this argument are still present with us. Indeed, they have been in the center of theological discussion during the last quarter century. The burning question then, as now, concerned the truth and the relevance of the Christian view of man.

I. The Course of the Controversy

Pelagius' name is supposed to be the Greek version of the Welsh name of 'Morgan,' originally, a 'man of the sea' (Marigena; in Greek, πελάγιυς). This supposition has led to the conjecture that Pelagius was a native of Wales and attached to a monastery at Bangor. The sole item of this conjecture to have stood the test of investigation is that Pelagius was a monk. That means that he was a Christian. And the controversy shows that howsoever he may have differed from Augustine, the frame of reference of his thought was dependent on the Bible.

From Pelagius' own writings, it appears that he was at work in Rome before the fall of the city in 410.[2] He was then at the height of his creative powers, a man of culture and character, sensitive to the moral corruption of his times and seeking both reform and the propagation of Christianity. His efforts were early rewarded by his conversion of the gifted lawyer, Coelestius, to monastic life and to his views. Owing to Coelestius' zeal and superior intellectual powers, he drew much of the fire of the controversy upon himself. An even more learned and brilliant controversialist was Julian, bishop of Eclanum, near Capua in Campania. Owing to Julian's power as a systematic thinker, Augustine was compelled to write against him in detail. The longest single treatises of the anti-Pelagian corpus are directed against Julian.[3]

Probably in order to avoid falling into the hands of Alaric, the Gothic conqueror of Rome, Pelagius and Coelestius went to North Africa in 410 or 411. They passed through Hippo, intending to visit Augustine, only to find that the Bishop had gone to Carthage on business pertaining to the Donatists. As it turned out, Augustine and Pelagius, whose names have ever since been ranged against each other in the history of the Church and of ideas, never met.

Pelagius continued his travels to Palestine. Coelestius tarried at Carthage, where his application for ordination as a presbyter of the Church brought on a long and bitter dispute which shook the Church from Jerusalem to Rome. Augustine presided at a council of the North African Church at Carthage in 412, at which Coelestius was accused of false teaching and excluded from the fellowship of the Church. Thereupon Coelestius went to Ephesus, where he was welcomed into the Church and ordained a presbyter.

Two years after the council at Carthage, the dispute over Pelagius' views flared up in Palestine. The occasion was a letter which Pelagius had written to the nun Demetria. The Eastern

Church, under the considerable influence of the theology of Origen, had never felt so strongly about the issue raised by Pelagius as had the Western Church. Consequently, the letter to Demetria might have passed unnoticed except for the simultaneous presence in Palestine of two influential western theologians, Jerome and Orosius.

At a diocesan synod called by Bishop John of Jerusalem in June 415, Orosius appeared against Pelagius and reported among other things what the council at Carthage had done about Coelestius. It was decided to lay the matter before Innocent, bishop of Rome. Meanwhile, a second council was held in December of 415 at Diospolis, or Lydda, under the presidency of the bishop of Caesarea. Pelagius had been accused again, this time touching the teachings of Coelestius. But by admitting that Coelestius had been rather more indiscreet than heretical, Pelagius again escaped condemnation.

The fate of Pelagius was now to be determined in the West. Innocent understood the issues of the debate and was inclined to agree with the condemnation of Pelagius and Coelestius by two North African synods in 416. But before Innocent could be called upon for an official ruling, he died and was succeeded by Zosimus. Zosimus was indifferent to theological issues. He accused the North Africans of thinking they knew more than was proclaimed by the Holy Scriptures, and emphasized the orthodoxy of Pelagius and Coelestius. But the North Africans were not to be put aside. In a General Council at Carthage in 418, over two hundred bishops defined their opposition to the errors of Pelagianism. This impressive display of strength brought Zosimus to terms. He issued an encylical upholding the decision at Carthage and condemning Pelagius and Coelestius, who had meanwhile left Rome. Eighteen bishops in Italy refused to subscribe to the encyclical and were deposed. Among those who stubbornly refused to recant was Julian of Eclanum. He, together with Coelestius and others, perhaps also Pelagius, took up exile in Constantinople in 429, where they were hospitably received by the Patriarch Nestorius. Nestorius vainly interceded for them with Pope Celestine at Rome.

What happened to Pelagius and Coelestius after this is not known. Julian is said to have died in Sicily about A.D. 450, after having sacrificed all his property to the poor during a famine. It is unlikely that Pelagius and Coelestius were present at the ecumenical council of Ephesus in 431, the year after the death of Augustine. At this council, they were condemned in the course of an explicit rejection of Nestorius, rather than for their own views. But the ideas they had put forward continued, in a modified form known as Semi-Pelagianism, to stir the Church to intermittent though waning controversy for another century. It remained for the Council of Orange (Arausio) in 539 explicitly to condemn the Semi-Pelagian system and to approve, without the doctrine of absolute predestination, the position on sin and grace which had been so sharply and so unyieldingly formulated by Augustine.

II. The General Character of the Anti-Pelagian Writings

Augustine tells us that he 'first became acquainted with Pelagius' name at a distance, and when he was living at Rome.' Reports had come to the Bishop at Hippo, full of 'much commendation and respect.' But later Augustine heard that Pelagius 'was a frequent disputant against the grace of God.' It became apparent that

> the doctrines connected with his name were warmly maintained, and passed from mouth to mouth, among his reputed followers . . . We thought it would be a better way of proceeding against them, if, without mentioning any names of individuals, the errors themselves were met and refuted . . . And so both by books and by popular discussions we ceased not to oppose the evil doctrines in question.[4]

How closely Augustine adhered to this resolve may be debated. On the whole, the writings against Pelagius disclose a studied effort on the part of Augustine to be both objective in his analysis and charitable in his judgments. There are, to be sure, occasional biting passages. But only in the last treatises is the reader permitted to sense the full measure of their author's indignation. And even here, the wrath of Augustine is directed more against the followers of Pelagius, notably Coelestius, than against Pelagius himself.[5] Augustine may have cast a shadow over his cause by deviating from his initial desire of 'ascertaining information on the matter either from [Pelagius] himself or from some treatise of his,'[6] in the relentless pursuit of 'the wild thickets of this heresy.' If so, Pelagius can scarcely have done less, since he 'anathematized all who help the opinions in question not indeed as heretics, but as simpletons.'[7]

The question of whose behavior was the more exemplary, that of Augustine or that of Pelagius, has never really been settled. It is a misfortune that in the extant and readily available texts Pelagius' position comes to view exclusively through the selective exposition and polemics of his opponent. Nevertheless, Augustine seems to be at special pains in every treatise to make full use of Pelagius' own words, with their rhetorical vividness and power. Not infrequently the debate rises to memorable heights of eloquence and cogency, of wit and innuendo.[8]

The principal anti-Pelagian writings of Augustine are fifteen in number. Most of them bear titles that do not disclose the fundamental issue over which the controversy raged. They were not planned by Augustine as a careful and thorough exposition of the truth and relevance of the Christian view of man. Instead, they were pressed from him, as it were, by the accelerating tempo at which the Pelagian position was infecting the faith of the devout, and by the correspondence that poured into his episcopal residence from various sections of the Church and from persons in various walks of life, seeking his guidance with regard to the Catholic truth. What the corpus lacks in systematic form it gains in vitality.

The theological and Biblical orientation both of Pelagius and of Augustine gives to these treatises a distinct and somewhat obtrusive coloring. Long passages are not infrequently devoted to debates over the meaning of the Bible, particularly the letters of Paul. The reader gets the impression of having suddenly been led off the main track of an exciting and comprehensible argument into a cul-de-sac where he is exposed to inconsequential

Biblical word-play. If he can restrain the impulse to jump the barrier, he will often be rewarded with an epigrammatic or ironical gem. In the last resort, Pelagius and Augustine were required to confound each other out of the Scriptures. There was no other ultimate authentication of their rival claims. It is for this reason that Augustine can begin by arguing that the will of man is free because the Scriptures declare and assume it to be so. And it is for this reason that Pelagius goes out of his way to insist over and over again that he is far from denying the assisting grace of God and the saving work of Christ. Indeed, if Augustine can finally be said to have the better of the argument, the triumph rests upon his consummate knowledge of the Scriptures and his skill in adapting to that knowledge his classical rhetorical training. Quite aside from the truth or falsity of the issue, any judge of forensics would, I think, award the Bishop the victory.

III. The Main Issue and the Claims of Pelagius

Pelagius had written a book which he called *Defense of the Freedom of the Will.* In this work, he had declared that

> we have implanted in us by God a possibility for acting in both directions. It resembles, as I may say, a root which is most abundant in its produce of fruit. It yields and produces diversely according to man's will; and is capable, at the cultivator's own choice, of either shedding a beautiful bloom of virtues, or of bristling with the thorny thicket of vices.[9] . . . But that we really do a good thing, or speak a good word, or think a good thought, proceeds from our own selves.[10] . . . Nothing good, and nothing evil, on account of which we are deemed either laudable or blameworthy, is born with us, but is done by us: for we are born not fully developed, but with a capacity for either conduct; we are formed naturally without either virtue or vice; and previous to the action of our own proper will, the only thing in man is what God has formed in him.[11]

The concluding phrase of this passage certainly does not link Pelagius with those who, in the name of human freedom, deny the divine activity. Augustine knows this; and he tries, therefore, to discuss the issue on Pelagius' terms. The point is not that of deciding between the free will of man and the activity of God. Instead, the matter to be clarified is how the free will of man and the activity of God are related. Pelagius constantly claimed in his book that he was not concerned to prove that a completely good life had ever been lived. His was the more modest though no less important contention that such a perfect life was possible because man was, by the very nature which God had given him, free to pursue the good and to avoid the evil:

> The fact [he wrote] that we have the possibility of accomplishing every good thing by action, speech and thought, comes from Him who has endowed us with this possibility, and who also assists it . . . Man's praise therefore consists in his willing and doing a good work, or rather, this praise belongs both to the human being and to God, who has bestowed on him the possibility of exercising his very will and work.[12]

As a careful reader of Pelagius' book, Augustine noticed that this acknowledgment of God's activity was explicitly made in what may be called the theoretical statement of Pelagius' position. But when it came to the illustrations, that is, to the actual application of his view, Pelagius failed to include his references to God and laid all stress upon human volition.

> Now what is the reason [Augustine inquires] why he did not remember this admission when giving his examples . . . For, when wishing to point out what lies within our own competency, he says: 'Because we are also able to turn all these actions into evil.' This, then, was the reason why he was afraid to admit that such an action proceeds *both from ourselves and from God,* lest it should be objected to him in reply: If· the fact of our doing anything good by action, speech or thought is owing both to ourselves and to God, on the ground that He has endowed us with such a power, then it follows — and God forbid that we should admit any such

—that just as God is associated with ourselves in the praise of good actions, so must He share with us the blame of evil actions. For that 'possibility' with which He has endowed us makes us capable of both good and evil ones.[13]

There you have it. The real interest of a man like Pelagius is in the freedom of the will as the only basis for authentic moral experience and endeavor. He draws back, however, from the ultimate consequence of this contention, namely, that man is the author of his own existence and of the existence of the world in which the moral life is lived. Instead, he makes a place for God as the Author of freedom but not as the Author of that character which is the fruit of freedom. And he justifies his analysis by suggesting that his real concern is not for the integrity of man but rather for the reputation of God.

Plainly, whether in the fifth century or in the twentieth, the problem of the nature and function of the will is crucial for man's understanding of himself, of his place in the world, and of the question whether man can or cannot get on without God. It was inevitable that somewhere in the course of human reflection this problem should arise with particular controversial vitality. It was also inevitable, I think, that the problem should arise in the context of the vigorous claims of the Christian faith. The redemptive significance of the life and death and resurrection of Jesus of Nazareth and the overwhelming testimony of Holy Scripture required that the whole range of issues and phenomena dealing with the relation of human volition to freedom, on the one hand, and to God, on the other hand, should be rethought and recast. The Pelagian controversy served this occasion.

It is, therefore, only in a general and non-technical sense that the fundamental issue of the Pelagian controversy can be defined in terms of the proper correlation of human volition and divine activity. The actual terms of the dispute werè narrower. The real argument had to do with the nature and power of the will in view of the fact that Christ had died to deliver man from sin and so to prepare him to enter into that eternal kingdom of perfection and glory which God had established and reserved for all the redeemed.

Pelagius put forward three claims in support of his position on this issue. In the first place, he contended that the nature of willing had to do with the power and the possibility of choice. The will had, so to say, been set into the nature of man by God the Creator. It followed that the possibility of exercising the will so as to act in conformity with the Creator's purpose (perfection) was open to man. So also was the contrary exercise of the will. Otherwise, human volition was emptied of significance. And worse, if good and evil were not of man's choice and doing, then they must be ascribed to God. A God who was the Author of evil was intolerable and unthinkable; certainly vastly more intolerable and unthinkable than a God who assisted man to avoid the evil and acknowledged the meritorious good of man's proper choices. It did not matter that no man ever lived up to this possibility. The decisive point was that the possibility of so living must be regarded as real.

Secondly, there was no denial of the grace of God and the saving grace of Christ in this view of the freedom of the will. The creation of man with this kind of volitional function was itself an act of grace. Further provisions of grace were available in the commandments and the teaching of the Church.[14] These were especially designed to assist in indicating the way around evil and in fortifying the choice of the good. As for the saving grace of Christ, there was no Scriptural warrant for claiming an original and inherited taint of sin in human nature in order, as it were, to guarantee Christ's saving work against irrelevance. There were enough willfully committed sins to be redeemed. More than that, there was something positive about the work of Christ. He had not come to negate the effect of a dubious involuntary human corruption. He had come to call men to the kingdom of God and to admit them by baptism to its blessings. Pelagius was fond of quoting John 3:3ff., 'Except a man be born again . . . of water and the Spirit, he cannot enter into the kingdom of God.' The baptismal formularies of the Church made sense if infant nature was morally neutral and volitionally free.

It was contrary to the most obvious experience with infants and to the moral experience of adults to focus the whole human and religious problem upon a biologically transmitted predisposition to sin. Such a contention not only undermined the theory and practice of infant baptism but called in question the institution of marriage as well. Certainly the Scriptures were unmistakable in their high praise of marriage. And just as certainly, the Scriptures were in error if the fruit of marriage was declared to be innately spoiled. In such a case, God could not possibly ordain and sanctify marriage without also incurring the responsibility for its evil issue.

Pelagius' third argument was that only on his position could the ways of God with men be comprehended. He did not disallow the mystery of the divine nature and activity. But if the relation of God's activity to human choices were such that man could never of his own and natural freedom choose to do God's will, then the mystery of God's being and of His redemptive purpose was reduced to arbitrariness. And this would mean that God was ultimately incalculable and could not be depended upon at all.

It is not strange that these views of Pelagius should have commended themselves. They are so persuasively human; and they make God so appealing. Under the direct propagation of Pelagius, they could be kept within the limits of cogency. But let a bolder and rasher man, such as Coelestius, take up the debate,[15] or let a scheming and ambitious man, such as Julian, circulate letters in a whispering campaign,[16] and the result is plain. The proportion of truth to error in the original position is profoundly dislocated and dangerously defaced. At all events, when the Pelagian views came to Augustine's attention, he elected to defend the Catholic faith by beginning at the hottest, if not at the central, point.

IV. The Principal Lines of Augustine's Argument

An extract from the *Retractations* sets the stage:

A necessity arose which compelled me to write against the new heresy of Pelagius. Our previous opposition to it was confined to sermons and conversations, as occasion suggested, and according to our respective abilities and duties; but it had not yet assumed the shape of a controversy in writing. Certain questions were then submitted to me . . . at Carthage, to which I was to send . . . back answers in writing. To begin with, I wrote three books under the title, *On the Merits and Forgiveness of Sins,* in which I mainly discussed the baptism of infants because of original sin, and the grace of God by which we are justified, that is made righteous . . . It is in direct opposition to these principles that they have devised their new heresy.[17]

There was a certain tactical wisdom, as well as honesty and courage, on the part of the Pelagians in beginning their defense of human dignity by an oblique thrust at the practice in the Church of baptizing infants. They were not advocating the abolition of the practice. They were appealing rather for a fresh consideration of the grounds for it. To the Pelagians, it seemed contrary both to nature and to Scripture to argue that infants must be baptized for the remission of sins and for deliverance from eternal death because Adam had sinned and been punished with death. The Pelagians interpreted the divine prohibition against eating from the tree of the knowledge of good and evil as referring to the death not of the body but of the soul. Augustine regarded this as tantamount to saying that

> Adam was so formed that he would even without any demerit of sin have died, not as the penalty of sin, but from the necessity of his being . . . If he had happened to live on here longer in his natural body, he would have been oppressed with old age, and have gradually, by reason of senility, arrived at death.[18]

Reading this today, we readily tend to agree with Pelagius. Is not death the most inevitable and biological of facts? And is religion not an affair of the soul rather than of the body, a manifestation of the inner and spiritual rather than of the external and physical life? It seems grotesque that Augustine should find it possible to remark that if God granted to the clothes and the shoes of the Israelites that 'they waxed not old' during forty years, what wonder if for obedience it had been by the power of the same [God] allowed to man, that his natural and mortal body should have in it a certain condition, in which he might grow full of years without decrepitude, and, whenever God pleased, pass from mortality to immortality without the medium of death. For even as this very flesh of ours is not therefore invulnerable, because there happens to be no occasion on which it receives a wound; so also was it not therefore immortal, because there arose no necessity of dying.[19]

The passage is striking as an instance of Augustine's matter-of-fact use of the Bible and of his rhetorical skill in the use of analogy. The point about the wound, however, is a neat logical turn against the Pelagian position and contains a phrase that we, with our naturalistic habit of mind, are too likely to pass over. Death is certainly an inexorability of nature: so much is obvious; it was obvious also to Augustine. But what about 'the necessity of dying'? It should be obvious that *that* is not so obvious. For what is the actual experience of death? Is it not that man dies *naturally,* without finding death *natural?* If death is simply necessary, why is it so difficult to come to peace with it? Augustine's answer may not be the best one, but it is good enough not to be ignored.

Now previous to the change into the incorruptible state which is promised in the resurrection of the saints, the body may have been *mortal,* although not likely to die; just as our body in its present state may, so to speak, be capable of sickness, although not likely to suffer sickness. For whose is the flesh which is incapable of sickness, even if from some accident it die before it ever experienced an illness? In like manner was man's body then mortal, but this mortality was to have been superseded by an eternal incorruption, if man had persevered in righteousness, that it so say, obedience.[20]

Man's failure to persevere in righteousness is no slight defection. And in so far as the Church's theology and practice of baptism proceed from the attempt to deal seriously with human corruption, they are on ground more solid than that taken by Pelagius.

Augustine is perfectly clear about why infants are baptized in the Church.

> Take then the case of any infant you please: If he is already in Christ, why baptize him? If, however, as the Truth puts the case, he is baptized for the express purpose of being with Christ, it certainly follows that he who is not baptized is not with Christ; and if he is not 'with' Christ, he is 'against' Christ . . . And how can *he* be 'against' Christ, if not owing to sin?, for it cannot possibly be from his soul or his body, both of these being the creation of God. Now if it be owing to sin, what sin can be found at such an age, except the ancient and original sin? [21]

On this point the Bishop was so explicit that he became an innovator in the history of the Church. The definitive theology of infant baptism in Roman Catholicism as well as in the Protestant Reformation was formulated by Augustine in the anti-Pelagian writings.[22] The logic is this: the Church administers the sacrament of baptism; the sacrament bestows upon the infant the grace of Christ for the remission of sins; this grace is superfluous unless infants are corrupted by sin; infant corruption is a corruption antecedent to volitional wrongdoing; this antecedent corruption is inherited at birth from parents involved in the natural taint received through the first parents of the race. The true course of the argument runs from the sacramental grace of baptism to original sin, and not conversely, as Pelagius was endeavoring to state it.[23]

It must be admitted that the force of Augustine's argument was such that he laid himself open to the charge of making a wholesale condemnation of the human race for the sake of validating ecclesiastical sacramental theory and practice. A careful study of the anti-Pelagian writings shows, however, that Augustine's true concern lay elsewhere. He chose to meet the

Pelagians on ground they themselves had selected, and he labored to move as quickly as possible beyond the discussion of the validity of infant baptism to the underlying issues. These issues are two. In the order of their importance for Augustine, they are the fact and the nature of the grace of God in Christ, and the fact and the role of the will in the attainment by man of moral excellence. In the order of discussion, although these two foci of Augustine's argument are always interrelated, he devotes the major portion of his refutation of Pelagius to the disposal of the human problem, reserving for the last treatises the concentrated elaboration of the divine initiative and purpose.

The Fact and the Role of the Will. Augustine insisted that the Pelagians were expounding an erroneous view both of the freedom of the will and of how the grace of God was related to it.

> They, however, must be resisted with the utmost alacrity and vigor who suppose that the mere power of the human will in itself, without God's help, can either perfect right-eousness or advance towards it in an even tenor; and when they begin to be hard pressed about their presumption in asserting that this result can be reached without divine assistance, they check themselves . . . They allege that such attainments are not possible without God's help seeing that God created man with the free choice of his will, and by giving him His commandments, teaches man, Himself, how he ought to live; and indeed assists him, in that he takes away his ignorance by instructing him in the knowledge of what he ought to avoid and to desire in his actions . . .[24]

Here was the fifth-century form of the doctrine of salvation by education. Augustine was quick to see that there were two diffi-culties in such a doctrine. For one thing, it assumed that the will had the power to keep the law and that the failure to do so could be remedied by renewing the effort. In the second place, the divine assistance was restricted to God's work in creation and made no real place for the redemptive work of Christ.

Augustine, on the contrary, sets the free grace of God in

Christ in direct relation to the impotence — not the capacity — of the human will.

> Now we shall see this question more easily if we first ex-
> amine with some care what 'our own power' means. There
> are then two faculties, — the exercise of the will and the
> exercise of power, — and not every one that has the will has
> therefore the power also, nor has every one that possesses
> the power got the will in immediate control; for as we some-
> times will what we cannot do, so also we sometimes can do
> what we do not will.[25]

This distinction between the willing of the will and the ability
to do what is willed is the crux of Augustine's analysis of human
volition. Pelagius never faces it. Consequently, he keeps on insisting that the nature of the will is the power to choose and that
the grace of God has no enabling function. Augustine, on the
other hand, can include the free exercise of volitional choice
within the enabling function of grace, because for him the real
exercise of the will's freedom lies not in the capacity to choose
but in the capacity to fulfill. That is why he can say, as he does
in a famous epigram in *The Spirit and the Letter,* 'not that by
nature grace is denied, but rather by grace nature is repaired.' [26]

The gulf between Pelagius and Augustine regarding the impotence of the will is rooted in a basic disagreement on the context within which the will operates. Pelagius called this context
'nature'; Augustine called it 'grace.' It is not surprising, therefore, that when they talked about 'nature' and about 'grace,'
they understood these terms in different senses. The treatise on
Nature and Grace addresses itself to the problems involved and
reveals the extent to which the two disputants were by-passing
each other. According to Pelagius, 'nature' was the 'necessity'
ordering all things. Such an order of causes and effects contradicts the self-determination of the will. Grace, on the other
hand, was primarily the act and intention of the Creator in making the world, including the will. The exercise of the will in
making choices is its freedom, and this is the way the will was

made. Freedom is thus consonant with the grace of creation but not with 'nature.' Augustine quotes Pelagius as affirming that

> whatever is bound by natural necessity is deprived of all freedom of will and deliberate choice . . . We may perceive . . . that to hear, and to smell, and to see is our own, while the capacity to hear, and to smell, and to see is not our own, but lies in natural necessity . . . The actual capability of not sinning lies not so much in the power of man's will as in the necessity of his nature. Now, whatever is placed in the necessity of nature undoubtedly appertains to the Author of that nature, that is, God. How then . . . can that be regarded as done without the grace of God which is shown to belong in an especial manner to God? [27]

Over against this view, Augustine uses 'nature' to refer not to the order of causes and effects but to the human constitution. There is a 'necessity' about this, too. But the 'necessity' of human 'nature' is the necessity imposed upon the will by the will itself. It is the sinful condition that determines not the capacity to will but the incapacity of the will *to do* what it wills. And 'grace' corresponds to the impotence of the will. Grace is the gift, in Christ, of the power of the will to do what it wills. With vivid and typical subtlety, Augustine turns Pelagius' argument against himself:

> Either I do not understand what he means, or he does not himself . . . As to his remarks . . . concerning our sense of smell, does he not display no little carelessness when he says, 'that it is not in our own power to be able or to be unable to smell, but that it is in our own power . . . to smell or not to smell'? For let us suppose some one to place us, with our hands firmly tied, but yet without any injury to our olfactory organs, among some bad and noxious smells; in such a case we altogether lose the power, however strong may be our wish not to smell, because every time we are obliged to draw breath, we also inhale the smell which we dislike . . . Man's nature, indeed, was created at first

faultless and without any sin . . . But the flaw which darkens and weakens all those natural goods, it has not contracted from its blameless Creator . . . but from that original sin, which it committed of its own free-will . . . This grace, however, of Christ, without which neither infants nor adults can be saved, is not bestowed for any merits, but is given *freely*, on account of which it is also called, *grace*.[28]

The only common element in this discussion of nature and grace is that Augustine and Pelagius both see that the nature and freedom of the will are profoundly involved. For the rest, they are poles apart. Since Pelagius refuses to face the impotence of the will, he cannot resolve the dilemma between a natural necessity which cancels the capacity of the will to choose and grace which can give the will its being and guide its operation but cannot govern and empower the will when it weakens and fails. Augustine also knows a natural necessity in Pelagius' sense. But he sees that this has nothing to do with the real problem of the will. The freedom of the will lies deeper than the power of choice. It is the power to achieve; and this is the gift of grace. Having arrived at this insight, Augustine is able to regard the order of causes and effects as an order not of bondage but of providence. Augustine recognizes that between himself and Pelagius there can be no meeting of minds. For Pelagius 'has not assumed . . . any such position as we wish to have understood by *grace* . . . for this is a topic which is concerned about the *restitution,* not the *constitution* of natural functions.'[29]

The treatises *On the Grace of Christ, On Original Sin,* and *On Marriage and Concupiscence* show Augustine still trying to convince the Pelagians that the human will was free though impotent, and impotent though free. At the same time, he is preparing the way for his own full-orbed view of grace.

Pelagius' constant insistence that he, too, was a believer in the grace of God did not conceal from Augustine the fact that 'it is by no means clear . . . what grace he means, or to what extent he supposes our nature to be assisted by it.'[30] The distinction between the power to will and the power to choose was being refined as the heresy spread. Pelagius was now differentiating 'possibility,' 'volition,' and 'action' (posse, velle, esse), as three faculties by which the law and doctrine of God were fulfilled. The first of these faculties he assigned to the grace of the Creator. The other two 'he asserts to be our own' and contends that 'they proceed simply from ourselves.'[31] Augustine elaborately shows that this position is untenable. Such a differentiation of volitional functions does not come to terms with the grace of Christ, or with the impotence that permeates the will entire.

> Let them therefore read and understand, observe and acknowledge, that it is not by law and doctrine uttering their lessons from without, but by a secret, wonderful, and ineffable power operating within, that God works in men's hearts not only revelations of the truth, but also good dispositions of the will . . . By such grace is it effected, not only that we discover what ought to be done, but also that we do what we have discovered, — not only that we believe, too, what ought to be loved, but also that we love what we have believed.[32]

In a significant passage toward the end of this work, Augustine makes a final attempt to break through the ambiguities in Pelagius' use of grace and in his analysis of the will. He states the terms on which the whole debate could be ended.

> If, I repeat, he thus consents to hold with us, that even the will and the action are assisted by God, and so assisted that we can neither will nor do any good thing without such help; if, too, he believes that this is that very grace of God through our Lord Jesus Christ which makes us righteous through His righteousness, and not our own . . . then, so far as I can judge, there will remain no further controversy between us concerning the assistance we have from the grace of God.[33]

It may seem strange to the casual reader that Augustine's views on marriage should find their place in the corpus of writings primarily concerned with the nature and function of the will. The reason is that the marriage relationship provides Augustine both with the most telling proof of the impotence of the will and with the explanation of its hereditary transmission. The treatise *On Marriage and Concupiscence* has exercised a decisive influence quite apart from the Pelagian controversy. It is at once the basis for and the most succinct statement of the ethical teachings of the Roman Catholic Church concerning sex. If one wants to know why the Roman Catholic Church holds that the chief and decisive end of marriage is procreation, that divorce and birth control are inadmissible, and that continence is the ideal of sexual self-discipline, the reasons are all given by the bishop of Hippo in his discussion of marriage. From our perspective, reinforced by medical and psychological sexual research, Augustine seems to be at his worst in this treatise. A man who can say that 'the weakness of incontinence is hindered from falling into the ruin of profligacy by the honorable estate of matrimony' [34] stirs up an immediate and strong resentment in the modern mind. No wonder Pelagius found Augustine's whole argument a perverse libel upon human nature and a virtual blasphemy against the divine ordination of marriage so plainly taught in Scripture. For further discussion on this point, the reader will want to refer to Chapter XIV in this volume.

It must be admitted that Augustine goes to extravagant lengths in depicting the ravages of lust upon the institution of marriage. But when this work is taken together with the writing *On Original Sin,* as Augustine intended, it appears that the Bishop is intensely preoccupied with the demolition of Pelagius' position on the will. The treatise *On Original Sin* is notable for what is perhaps the sharpest outburst against the heresy (see chapter 25) and for an explicit formulation of the well-known Augustinian doctrine of the *massa perdita*. This doctrine affirms that the will is thoroughly vitiated because of the solidarity of the human race with the sin of Adam.

On what account, therefore, is an infant rightly punished with such ruin, if it be not because he belongs to the ruined mass, and is properly regarded as born of Adam, condemned under the bond of the ancient debt [of original sin], unless he has been released from the bond — not indeed by any merit of his own, but by grace? [35]

Those who are inclined to find in this question more evidence of Augustine's excessive reliance upon Scripture than of a valid defense of social sin will want to reflect on the treatise as a whole. For the doctrine of the *massa perdita* is Augustine's way not only of establishing the impotence of the will but also of refuting the doctrine of transmigration. Let those who are quick to identify the problem of human freedom with the power of the will to choose look to it how they will deal with the intricate and infinite complexity of evil in the world. Is the 'spiritual' solution which ascribes the tenacity of evil to a previous existence of the soul really any more satisfactory than the 'fleshly' solution which ascribes it to a seminally transmitted vitiation of the will? Neither solution may, of course, be true. But when Augustine, in the treatise on marriage, identifies the corruption of the will with concupiscence and shows how concupiscence despoiled the original relation of the parents of the race to God and to each other, he is nearer to our true condition. For how can a man ignore the behavior of his parents whom he does see in favor of speculation about souls which he has not seen? [36] Certainly if we look at our parents and then at ourselves, we can appreciate the profound penetration into the recesses of human motivation in Augustine's oft-repeated insistence upon the connection between the secrecy that surrounds our sexual life and the impotence of the will. It is not too much to say that the fact of concupiscence is the final proof that the will of man is free to will but powerless to do what it wills. Augustine notes that marriage

is itself 'in honor among all' . . . yet, whenever it comes to the actual process of generation, the very embrace which is honorable and permitted cannot be effected without the ardor of concupiscence, in order that that may be accomplished which appertains to the use of reason and not of lust. Now, this ardor, whether following or preceding the action of the will, does somehow, by a power of its own, move the members which cannot be moved simply by the will, and in this manner it shows itself not to be the servant of a will which commands it, but rather to be the punishment of a will which disobeys it. It shows, moreover, that it must be excited, not by a natural and willing choice, but by a certain seductive stimulus, and that on this very account it produces shame. This is the carnal concupiscence, which . . . in no case happens to nature except from sin . . . Now from this concupiscence whatever comes into being by natural birth is tied and bound by original sin, unless, indeed, it be born again in Him whom the Virgin conceived without this concupiscence.[37]

The Fact and the Nature of the Grace of God in Christ. Already in the work on *Nature and Grace,* Augustine had recognized that the Pelagian heresy emanated from a defective view of what it means to be 'born again in Him whom the Virgin conceived without this concupiscence.' 'The inquiry,' he says, 'did not concern that grace of God by which man was created, but only that whereby he is saved through Jesus Christ our Lord.' [38] Although Augustine's connection of the Virgin Birth of Christ with the problem of concupiscence points to a profound aspect of the Church's doctrine concerning the Nativity, he accepted the fact of the Virgin Birth on the basis of the Bible. His real concern, however, was with 'Jesus Christ our Lord'; and he would be the first to assert that the Lordship of Christ is manifest in His saving power rather than in His Virgin Birth. It is with the fact of this saving power, and with its bearing both upon the freedom of the will and upon the mystery and faithfulness of the divine will and purpose, that the last four treatises in the anti-Pelagian corpus are concerned.

The *Retractations* tell us that in the monastery at Adrumetum, the Pelagian heresy had broken out with acute divisiveness. 'There are some persons who suppose that the freedom of the will is denied whenever God's grace is maintained, and who on their side defend their liberty of will so peremptorily as to deny the grace of God.' [39] In order to deal with these opinions, Augustine composed the work *On Grace and Free-Will*. His aim is to show that they do not exclude each other. Scripture declares both that the will is free and that the grace of God is a fact. On any other view, the plain sense of the Bible is obscured, nature and grace are confused, and Christ died in vain. With these arguments we are already familiar. But Augustine makes the additional point that his contention is also true to human experience. 'No man, therefore, when he sins, can in his heart blame God for it, but every man must impute the fault to himself. Nor does it detract at all from a man's own freedom of will when he performs any act in accordance with the will of God.' [40]

Next to Augustine's distinction between capacity and power in the operation of the will, this division of responsibility between God and man as regards what the will actually does is indispensable to the proper understanding of the anti-Pelagian position. The first distinction is, as we have seen, the crux of Augustine's argument about the will; the second is the crux of his argument about the fact and the nature of grace. This distinction is that man is responsible for the evil which he both chooses and does, whereas God is responsible for whatever good man chooses and does. Augustine is perfectly frank about the fact that the second distinction is the fruit of faith, just as the first is the fruit of sin. But the significance of the second distinction is that it puts the whole problem of grace and free will on a new and higher level. Faith is defined as 'the disposition and will of the man who believes.' [41] And faith provides an entirely new perspective upon God's activity and its relation to human choices.

For one thing, in the light of faith the troublesome term 'co-operation' is clearly and properly defined. In short, it is not we who by virtue of the freedom of our wills co-operate with God, but God who by virtue of the gift of grace *co-operates* with us.

He who wishes to keep God's commandment, but is unable to do so, already possesses a good will, but as yet a small and weak one; he will, however, become able when he shall have acquired a great and robust will . . . And who was it that had begun to give him his love, however small, but He who prepares the human will, and perfects by His co-operation what He initiates by His operation? Forasmuch as He begins his influence by working in us that we may have the will, and completes it by working with us when we have the will.[42]

Another result of the perspective of faith is that it disposes of the notion that human effort is meaningless and futile if God gets the credit for the good that man does whereas man must take credit for the evil. The form of this problem in the Pelagian debate was the high-sounding one about rebuke. Why should one man rebuke another for an evil course of action, or try by rebuke to lead him in the godly way, if everything depends upon the work of grace? To this question Augustine devotes the treatise *On Rebuke and Grace,* and answers:

Whoever you are that do not the commandments of God that are already known to you, and do not wish to be rebuked, you must be rebuked even for that very reason that you do not wish to be rebuked. For you do not wish that your faults should be shown to you; you do not wish that they should be touched, and that such a salutary pain should be caused you that you may seek the Physician . . . Let men then suffer themselves to be rebuked when they sin, and not conclude against grace from the rebuke itself, nor from grace against rebuke; because both the righteous penalty of sin is due, and righteous rebuke pertains to it, if it is medicinally applied, even although the salvation of the ailing man is uncertain . . . Under that very uncertainty, therefore, it must of charity be applied . . . and prayer must be made on his behalf to whom it is applied, that he may be healed. But when men either come or return into the way of righteousness by means of rebuke, who is it that worketh salvation in their hearts but that God . . . whom no man's will resists when He wills to give salvation? For to will or not to will is in the power of Him who willeth or willeth not, so that it hinders not the divine will nor overcomes the divine power.[43]

In the context of this discussion, Augustine draws his celebrated line between man's inability to sin (*non posse peccare*) and his ability not to sin (*posse non peccare*). As often in such an analysis, it helps to start at the beginning; so Augustine goes back to Adam. He points out that Adam's advantage was not that he could choose the good and avoid the evil. These choices belong to our wills also. Nor was Adam's advantage the kind of a will that could choose only the good. Adam's real advantage was the possibility of merit. That is, he had not only a good will but also the power to continue to will the good and receive the reward of full and certain blessings for such perseverance. But the graces conferred upon Adam, while not to be despised, are scarcely to be preferred to the grace bestowed in Christ. With subtle vividness, the Bishop bids the believer to focus attention upon his advantages over Adam rather than upon Adam's advantages over him:

At that time, therefore, God had given to man a good will,* because in that will He had made him, since He had made him upright. He had given help without which he could not continue therein if he would; but that he should will, He left in his free choice. He could therefore . . . perseveringly hold fast the good which he would. But that he willed not to continue is absolutely the fault of him whose merit it would have been if he had willed to continue . . . to wit, such a fulness of blessing that by it [he] might have the fullest certainty of always abiding in it . . . Now, however, to those to whom such assistance is wanting, it is the penalty of sin; but to those to whom it is given, it is given of grace, not of debt . . . Because by this grace of God there is caused in us, in the reception of good and in the persevering hold of it, not only to be able to do what we will, but even to will to do what we are able. But this was not the case in the first man; for the one of these things was in him, but

226

the other was not. For he was not without the grace to receive good, because he had not yet lost it; but he was without the aid of grace to continue in it . . . and he had received the ability if he would but he had not the will to exercise the ability; for if he had possessed it, he would have persevered. For he could persevere if he would . . . For what shall be more free than free-will, when it shall not be able to serve sin? But now that good deserving has been lost by sin in those who are delivered, that has become the gift of grace which would have been the reward of deserving.

On which account we must consider with diligence and attention in what respect those two things differ from one another, — to be able not to sin [posse non peccare], and not to be able to sin [non posse peccare]; to be able not to die, and not to be able to die; to be able not to forsake good, and not to be able to forsake good. For the first man was able not to sin [posse non peccare], was able not to die, was able not to forsake good . . . Therefore, the first liberty of the will was to be able not to sin [posse non peccare], the last was much greater, not to be able to sin [non posse peccare]; the first immortality was to be able not to die, the last was much greater, not to be able to die; the first was the power of perseverance, to be able not to forsake good — the last was the felicity of perseverance, not to be able to forsake good.[44]

The third and final result of the perspective of faith is that it opens up the mystery of grace. The mystery of grace is a twofold mystery. It concerns, on the one hand, the question of why some people seem to have the perspective of faith and other people do not. On the other, it has to do with the question why some people persevere in doing the will of God and other people fall away. How closely the two problems are interrelated is shown by the fact that the two treatises on *The Predestination of the Saints* and on *The Gift of Perseverance* are regarded by Augustine as the first and second books of a common work. As the titles to these books suggest, the grace of predestination refers to the mystery of faith; the grace of perseverance, to the mystery of righteousness.

'This is the predestination of the saints, nothing else; to wit, the foreknowledge and the preparation of God's kindnesses, whereby they are most certainly delivered, whoever they are that are delivered.' [45] Already in the treatise on *Grace and Free-Will* (Chapter 43), Augustine had been forced by the course of his argument to refer the gift of faith to the secret counsels of God. In the work on predestination, he confesses that he had not always espoused so consistent a view.

> For I did not think that faith was prevented by God's grace, so that by its means would be given to us what we might profitably ask, except that we could not believe if the proclamation of the truth did not precede; but that we should consent when the gospel was preached to us I thought was our own doing, and came from ourselves. And this my error is sufficiently indicated in some small works of mine written before my episcopate . . . I discovered little concerning the calling itself, which is according to God's purpose; for not such is the calling of all that are called, but only of the elect . . . But that even the merit itself of faith was God's gift, I neither thought of inquiring into, nor did I say.[46]

Increasingly, however, Augustine was driven to recognize that the alternative was unavoidable. Either a man does not 'see why the whole should not be attributed to man, — as he who could originate for himself what he had not previously, can himself increase what he had originated,' or a man sees that 'it is impossible to withstand the most manifest divine testimony, by which faith . . . is shown also to be the gift of God.' [47] Over and over again, the Bishop returns to the Scriptural claim that 'our sufficiency is of God' (2 Corinthians 3:5). But what impresses him with equal persuasiveness are the facts of life. These facts are conspicuous in the case of infants and in the weirdly diverse fortunes of adults, as well as in the perseverance of the faithful. A sober consideration of these facts may not lead one to regard the will of God as their ground, but it certainly disposes decisively of the notion of merit, of the attempt to interpret the facts of life in terms of the free choices of the human will. Augustine simply thinks that it is more realistic to refer these exigencies to the purposive mystery of grace than to the capricious mystery of chance.

> Some infants not regenerated [are taken] from this life to eternal death, and others, regenerated, to eternal life; and those themselves that are regenerated, some going hence, persevering even to the end and others kept in this life even until they fall, who certainly would not have fallen, if they had departed hence before their lapse; and again some falling, but not departing from this life until they return, who certainly would have perished if they had departed before their return . . . From all which it is shown with sufficient clearness that the grace of God, which both begins a man's faith and which enables it to persevere unto the end, is not given in respect of our merit, but is given according to His own most secret and at the same time most righteous, wise, and beneficent will; since those whom He predestinated, them He also called . . .[48]

The fruit of such faith can never be pride. For the believer can never be sure that he is among the elect. He knows only that the number of the elect is determined according to the divine will and purpose. Instead, the fruit of such faith is the confident assurance that the sinful impotence of the will has been overcome and its true freedom restored. The true freedom of the will is the power to do what is willed in a world in which all one's choices are meaningfully related to the purposes of God.

FOR FURTHER READING

Philip Schaff, *History of the Christian Church,* vol. II (New York, 1876), 783–870.

The author, sometime professor of Church History in the Union Theological Seminary, New York, deals with the Pelagian controversy: its general character and external course; its structure of ideas; its influence upon the development of Christian thought; the condemnation of Pelagianism and the triumph of a modified Augustinianism. The strong convictions of the author, who writes in the tradition of the Reformation, emerge from time to time.

B. B. Warfield, *Studies in Tertullian and Augustine* (New York, 1930), chapter v.

An eminent and judicious scholar, who was professor of Theology in Princeton Theological Seminary, offers here a clear and brief introduction to the Pelagian controversy and its importance.

N. P. Williams, *The Grace of God* (New York, 1930).

The author, Lady Margaret Professor of Divinity in the University of Oxford, thinks that grace can be more fruitfully understood, and the problem of its relation to free will more adequately solved, if we abandon the 'metaphysical' orientation of the past in favor of a 'psychological' understanding. The discussion is organized around historical periods, with a chapter on Augustine.

Oscar Hardman, *The Christian Doctrine of Grace* (London, 1937).

The author has been professor of Pastoral and Liturgical Theology in the University of London. After an initial chapter on the formulation of the doctrine of grace, the discussion proceeds by the method of theological exposition. The important ways of defining grace and distinguishing between its various forms are examined, with considerable attention to the contribution of Augustine.

NOTES

1. My essay and its references are based upon the Latin text of the anti-Pelagian writings, as found in the Benedictine edition of the works of Saint Augustine, Paris, 1836-9, eleven volumes. Volume x, which contains the treatises against Pelagius, is in two parts, which appeared in 1838.

    The standard English translation is by Peter Holmes, edited by the Reverend Marcus Dods, published in Edinburgh by T. & T. Clark, 3 volumes, 1872, 1874, 1876. Where I have modified the translation in favor of the original, the same has been indicated; otherwise the passages cited are to be found in the Dods edition.

    The fifteen primary treatises which make up the anti-Pelagian corpus are listed below. Volume x, part II, of the Benedictine text has also an appendix containing smaller and sporadic discussions of the controversy. According to Volume xi (index) of the Benedictine text, there are also the following discussions of the controversy: Volume II, Letters 191, 193, 194, and two letters to the Presbyter Sixtus; Volume v, Sermon 294, a Treatise on Infant Baptism in 21 chapters. The primary treatises: (1) *On the Merits and Forgiveness* of Sins, 3 books, A.D. 412; (2) *On the Spirit and the Letter,* at the end of the year A.D. 412; (3) *On Nature and Grace,* A.D. 415; (4) *On Man's Perfections in Righteousness,* toward the end of A.D. 415; (5) *On the Proceedings of Pelagius,* at the beginning of A.D. 417; (6) *On the Grace of Christ and on Original Sin,* 2 books, A.D. 418; (7) *On Marriage and Concupiscence,* 2 books, A.D. 419, 420; (8) *On the Soul and Its Origin,* 4 books A.D. 419; (9) *Against Two Letters of the Pelagians,* written to Boniface, 4 books, A.D. 420 (in the Dods translation this treatise appears last, and out of chronological order). (10) *Against Julian,* 6 books, A.D. 420 or 421; (11) *On Grace and Free Will,* A.D. 426 or 427; (12) *On Rebuke and Grace,* A.D. 426 or 427; (13) *On the Predestination of the Saints,* A.D. 428 or 429; (14) *On the Gift of Perseverance,* A.D. 428 or 429; (15) *Against the Second Reply of Julian,* an unfinished work, 6 books being completed, A.D. 430.

2. Pelagius had written, before 410, a *Commentary on the Letters of St. Paul;* a *Letter to Demetria,* in 30 chapters, A.D. 413; a *Brief Treatise on the Faith* (Libellus fidei), 417. These three works have been preserved complete, as supposed works of Jerome (Opera, XI, ed. of Vallarsius). See Philip Schaff, *History of the Christian Church* (New York, 1876), II. 783.

3. Toward the end of 420 or early in 421, Augustine wrote against Julian in six books. Ten years later, he was writing against Julian again, which work was interrupted by Augustine's death. Nevertheless, six books had been completed. The substance of these treatises is not discussed in the essay, since the argument is a detailed refutation of Julian's views and adds nothing to the position elsewhere and more systematically taken by Augustine.

4. *On the Proceedings of Pelagius,* 46.

5. Augustine first mentions Pelagius by name in Book III. 1, of his treatise *On the Forgiveness of Sins and Baptism.* See also the four books, *Against Two Letters of the Pelagians.* Since these books do not really add anything to the argument already developed in earlier treatises, they may best be regarded as Augustine's attempt, under particularly captious provocation, to state once more the position he has maintained, and to apply it in specific rebuttal of minor points that were being made by his opponents.

6. *On the Proceedings of Pelagius,* 46.

7. Ibid. 65.

8. Cf. *On the Forgiveness of Sins and Baptism,* 30; *On Nature and Grace,* 8, 12; *On Marriage and Concupiscence,* 10, 44; *On the Grace of Christ,* 26; *On Original Sin,* 25; *On the Predestination of the Saints,* 5.

9. *On the Grace of Christ and on Original Sin,* I. 19.

10. Ibid. I. 17.

11. Ibid. II. 14. In the interest of clarity, I have departed from the English translation which reads: 'at the planter's own choice.' The ambiguity is due to the rendering of *cultoris*. The noun *cultor* may mean 'planter.' But it may also mean, 'the one who plants'; hence the alteration adopted here.

12. Ibid. I. 17.

13. Ibid. I. 17, 18.

14. Pelagius characteristically speaks of 'law' and 'doctrine.' Usually the two are distinguished and conjoined, although sometimes one gets the impression that 'law' and 'doctrine' refer to the Decalogue, and then again to the Pentateuch.

15. Augustine tells us that 'Coelestius found his way before an ecclesiastical tribunal, and developed opinions well-suited to his perverse character.' *On the Proceedings of Pelagius,* 46.

16. 'Julian is said to have sent [a letter] to Rome, that by its means, as I believe, he might find or make as many allies as he could; and . . . eighteen so-called bishops, sharers in his error, dared to write to Thessalonica, not to any body in general, but to the bishop of that very place, with a view of tempting him by his craftiness and bringing him over, if it could be done, to his views . . .' *Against Two Letters of the Pelagians,* I. 3.

17. *Retractations,* II. 23. Quoted in the English translation of the *Anti-Pelagian Writings,* I. 1. For stylistic reasons, and in accordance with the original, the translation of the fourth sentence has been slightly altered.

18. *On the Merits and Forgiveness of Sins,* I. 2–3. In accordance with the original, the definite article which in the English translation precedes 'senility' has been omitted.

19. Ibid. I. 3. The Biblical allusion is to Deut. 29:5. In the Holmes translation, the first sentence is interrogative. It has been quoted here to fit the context as indicative, without changing the sense.

20. Ibid. 5. The original contains an effective play on words in the distinction between *mortale* (capable of dying) and *moriturus* (likely to die). The anti-Pelagian writings are replete with this kind of argument.

21. Ibid. 55. The stress upon 'with' and 'against' in this passage arises from Augustine's use of Mt. 12:30: 'He that is not with me is against me.'

22. The so-called 'Free Churches' are an exception to this generalization. They are Protestant churches. But there are some groups among them, such as the Baptists, which reject infant baptism. It is interesting that the question of infant baptism is today being debated afresh in Europe, although the issue is different. The present

discussion has to do with the relation of faith to baptism; the Pelagian debate focused upon the relation between baptism and sin.

23. Cf. especially, *On the Merits and Forgiveness of Sins*, II. 44–7.

24. *On the Spirit and the Letter*, 4.

25. Ibid. 53.

26. Ibid. 47: 'non quod per naturam negata sit gratia, sed potius per gratiam reparata natura.'

27. *On Nature and Grace*, 54, 55, 59. Cf. *On the Grace of Christ and Original Sin*, I. 17, where the same argument is applied to speaking. The point is repeated, *On Nature and Grace*, 53.

28. Ibid. 55. 3, 4. The italicized words are, in the original, a word play on *gratis* and *gratia*.

29. Ibid. 12. Literally, 'about the making healthy, not the setting up of, natural functions' (*ubi de sanandis, non de instituendis naturis agitur*). I have departed here from the English translation.

30. *On the Grace of Christ and Original Sin*, I. 8.

31. Ibid. I. 4.

32. Ibid. I. 13, 25.

33. Ibid. I. 52.

34. *On Marriage and Concupiscence*, I. 18.

35. *On the Grace of Christ and Original Sin*, II. 36; cf. also *On Nature and Grace*. 5. The bracketed phrase has been supplied by the translator.

36. To such speculation, Augustine himself devoted the four books *On the Soul and Its Origin*. They need not concern us here, except to note that the problem of the soul, like that of marriage, arose during the controversy because of Augustine's insistence upon the corruption and impotence of the will. The treatise is notable, moreover, because it shows that Augustine was open on the question of traducianism. Traducianism is the position that souls are generated by natural descent as bodies are. It is opposed to the view that God gives to each body a soul at birth. Augustine is willing to try to meet the points raised by his correspondent. But he refuses to do so by the kind of speculation that forsakes the area of experience for one about which a man knows nothing. See the vivid passage, I. 26.

37. *On Marriage and Concupiscence*, I. 27. The quoted phrase is Hebrews 13:4. I have adopted the phrase as it stands in the RSV, rather than as it appears in the Dods edition.

38. *On Nature and Grace*, 62.

39. *Retractations*, II. 66. Quoted in the English translation of the anti-Pelagian writings, III. 1. Adrumetum was a maritime city of Africa and the capital of the province of Byzacium.

40. *On Grace and Free-Will*, 4.

41. Ibid. 28.
42. Ibid. 33.
43. *On Rebuke and Grace,* 7, 43.
44. Ibid. 32–3. The asterisk indicates that some manuscripts read: 'a free will.' In order to emphasize the force of Augustine's distinctions, I have inserted into the translation, in brackets, the Latin infinitive forms.
45. *On the Gift of Perseverance,* 35.
46. *On the Predestination of the Saints,* 7.
47. Ibid. 6.
48. *On the Gift of Perseverance,* 32–3. The allusion in the last sentence is to Romans 8:30.

THE ENIGMA OF THE

TRINITY

Cyril C. Richardson

N O DOCTRINE is so fundamental to the Christian faith and yet so difficult of interpretation as that of the Trinity. It has been observed that by denying it one may be in danger of losing one's soul, while by trying to understand it one may be in danger of losing one's wits. 'I am compelled,' says Augustine, embarking on his large inquiry into this topic, 'to pick my way through a hard and obscure subject' (1. 3. 6). [1] Yet the study of the Trinity is basic to Christian theology. 'In no other subject is error more dangerous, or inquiry more laborious, or discovery of truth more profitable' (1. 2. 5).

Augustine's treatise on the Trinity ranks as one of his foremost works, and indeed as one of the ablest presentations of the doctrine in Christian literature. Few have wrestled with its discouraging problems or penetrated its mysteries so successfully as Augustine. He brought to the task a keen philosophic mind and a theological grasp which have seldom been rivaled. Moreover, his treatise was the fruit of his maturity, and of long reflection. It was written over a period of some twenty years. Begun when he was in his prime, about the age of forty-five, it was finally published around A.D. 419, and then only with reluctance and under the pressure of circumstances. These he recounts in his *Retractations* (2. 15) and in a covering letter to Bishop Aurelius of Carthage, which he prefixed as a sort of prologue to the treatise. He tells us how the early manuscript was stolen from him and surreptitiously published before he could complete it. The first five books with a part of the twelfth thus gained a premature circulation. Augustine first intended to make his complaint on this matter public in another work, and so to warn his readers against the incomplete nature of his treatise. Responding, however, to the insistence of friends and in particular of Aurelius, he corrected and finished the work, though he was far from pleased with its final state.

Augustine recognized that only a few of his readers would understand and follow the *De Trinitate*.[2] He definitely wrote for the learned, and his work demands considerable concentration if one would conquer it. His restless mind continually poses to itself difficult questions. Sometimes these will remain altogether unanswered; at other times he will propound a question, wrestle with it a while, but defer its solution to a later book. In consequence, the argument does not flow easily or with careful organization. 'Set me free, O God, from the multitude of speech which I suffer inwardly in my soul,' he cries in the prayer with which he ends his work. It is a typical confession. His fertile and inquiring mind passes from one problem to another without a due sense of proportion or order. While brilliantly sententious, his style is nonetheless difficult. It is repetitious and prolix, with many irrelevancies and excursions into unallied topics. Part of this is to be explained by the fact that the canons of rhetoric in which Augustine was trained varied widely from our conceptions of good writing. It was considered inept to treat arguments in too consecutive a manner. Excursions were intended to rest the mind and to add variety to a treatise. Or again, if two or three points were propounded for discussion, it was viewed as boorish to treat them all with equal length or in a similar way. Yet these rules of rhetoric, while they doubtless enhanced the treatment of less exacting subjects, surely make the reading of Augustine unduly laborious. A more direct and a better-organized style would have lightened the cares of his readers.

I. The Cappadocian Trinity

Augustine wrote at a time when the main lines of the doctrine of the Trinity had been settled. The Council of Constantinople in A.D. 381 had witnessed the final triumph of the Nicene cause — a triumph that had been made possible by the rise of the Cappadocian theology, and the careful distinction between the terms *hypostasis* and *ousia*. Moreover, the Council of Constantinople had settled not only the question of the deity of Christ but also that of the deity of the Holy Spirit. Three *hypostaseis* and one *ousia* in the Godhead was the definition finally accepted. What was the meaning of this formula? It is not needful here to enter the large debate on this issue or to refute the misunderstanding that gained currency largely through Harnack, whereby the Cappadocians were charged with being Homoeans and abandoning the essential Athanasian position.[3] Suffice it to say that the Cappadocians began their consideration of the threefold life of the Divine from the point of view of a plurality rooted in the unity of the divine essence. They looked at the matter Platonically: the one essence or *ousia* of the Godhead expressed itself in three *modes of being,* to which they applied the term *hypostaseis.* They found an analogy in three men: Peter, James, and John, for instance, were three individuals; yet by sharing in the common essence of manhood, they should strictly be referred to as 'three man.' But lest the analogy should be pressed too far, with the dangerous result of tritheism, they were most careful to point out that the distinctions we observe in men are altogether inapplicable to the Godhead. For what distinguishes Peter, James, and John is their *individual circumscription,* something which is quite foreign to the Persons of the Trinity. An individual actor or orator goes about his business in his own special way, dependent on his particular environment and talent. But what characterizes the Persons of the Godhead is their mutual interrelationship. 'No activity is distinguished in the Persons of the Trinity as if it were brought to completion individually by each of them or separately apart from their joint supervision.' [4] The life that comes from God is not three separate things from three Life-Givers. The only distinctions in the Trinity are those of causation. The Father is uncaused, the Son and Spirit are caused, the Spirit being caused from the Father through the mediation of the Son. Thus the *hypostaseis* are not particular instances of a 'universal,' the divine *ousia:* that would imply tritheism. The Cappadocian idea is more subtle. The nature of the Godhead more nearly corresponds in their thought to Aristotle's idea of a particular concrete existence (*prōtē ousia*), not to the *deutera ousia* which members of a species have in common. The *ousia* in the Godhead is *identical* in each Person, while with men the manhood is *generic*.

In short, the formula, 'three *hypostaseis* and one *ousia*,' means that the one divine essence expresses itself in three *modes of being,* which are differentiated in terms of causality.

Such was the doctrine of which Augustine was the inheritor. Unfortunately he was not able to read Greek with sufficient fluency for him to grasp the full implications of the Cappadocian theology (3 Pref.). He never penetrated what they meant by *hypostasis* (see 5. 8. 10), or appreciated that their use of the term to distinguish differences between things enjoying the same *ousia* went back to Plotinus. Moreover, the fact that the precise Latin equivalent of *hypostasis* was *substantia* made the Greek use of the terms particularly unintelligible to Augustine. Yet the essence of the Cappadocian view is clear in those statements of the Catholic Faith with which his work opens, and which form the authoritative foundation for his own reflections. He speaks, for instance, of the fact that there are 'not three Gods but one God,' that Father, Son, and Spirit form 'a divine unity of one and the same substance in an indivisible equality,' and that 'in the Trinity what is said of each is also said of all, on account of the indivisible working of the one and the same substance' (1. 4. 7; 1. 12. 25).

The fact that Augustine was ignorant of the Greek Fathers and had as his only guide the treatise of Hilary on the Trinity,[5] on which he comments in 6. 10. 11–12, is a remarkable testimony to his own originality and penetration. While his approach to the subject, as we shall see, differs quite markedly from that of the Greeks, he arrived at their central idea of the divine co-inherence quite independently, and, indeed, worked it out with even more clarity and depth than they.

II. The Necessity of the Trinity

Before turning to the main lines of argument which Augustine develops, it may perhaps be helpful to pose the question, Why is the doctrine of the Trinity necessary? Augustine does not raise the issue in this ultimate sense at all. He is content to expound and to seek to penetrate the established Catholic doctrine on the subject. But one will appreciate his treatment more when one sees the necessity of the dogma.

It is needful, in the first place, in order to give a metaphysical ground to the threefold experience of God which the Christian enjoys. He knows Him as the source of Being in the Father, as Redeemer in Christ, and as Sanctifier in the Spirit. How are these three related and interrelated?

But more important still, it is necessary to distinguish modes of being in God, in order that He may be conceived as independent of His creation. The divine life must be thought of as complete in Itself, and not as needing the created world as a necessity of Its existence and fulfillment. Augustine's analogy of Lover, Beloved, and the uniting bond of Love is particularly helpful as a means for understanding the plenitude of the divine life apart from the created universe. If God is only the One, then it is scarcely possible to think of Him as independent of the created order. Ultimate reality cannot be conceived as loneliness, and so there is an inner necessity to derive the world from God by emanation, and not to do justice to the Christian view of *creatio ex nihilo*.

Finally, the distinctions in the Godhead are needful in order that the principles of God both *in* relations and *beyond* relations may be maintained. To sacrifice either, as it is necessary to do in any form of Unitarianism, is to land ourselves in difficulties. Either we are forced to say (as did Arius) that God did not enter human life in the Incarnation, and so, by stressing the divine transcendence, we deny the principle of God *in* relations. Or else we must abandon the principle of transcendence and say with the Sabellians that the Father suffered (Patripassianism). In either case we fail to do justice to one of two essential truths.

It is for these reasons that the Trinity is necessary, and by bearing them in mind we shall find Augustine's exposition of the doctrine peculiarly fruitful.

III. De Trinitate: The Doctrine and the Scriptures

Characteristically, Augustine begins with the authority of revelation. First, something must be believed. Then it is the duty of reason to penetrate it, and to try to understand it. In a way, authority is for Augustine a short cut to truth. It gives, as it were, the answers which reason *might* be able by itself to discover. But reason has three defects. For one thing it operates so slowly that a lifetime would never suffice to reach the right conclusion. Then again, it is darkened by sin and cannot exercise itself in divine matters as it ought to. But its special defect in the issue before us is that it is only by *contemplation* that the Divine can be known and enjoyed with certitude (15. 24. 45). Discursive reason by inquiry can establish much; but God will be known as He truly is only in the after-life, when we are freed from the limitations of our present mortal existence. Reason needs as a starting point the experience either of the senses or of the intellect. But God's nature is directly accessible to neither of these.[6] Moreover, while we may enjoy some experience of contemplation in this life (as Augustine did when he leaned from the window with his mother at Ostia), the weakness of our love prevents its being either enduring or complete.

It is necessary, therefore, to start with truth as it is revealed. Unaided reason falls into three errors about the Divine. It thinks of Him as material, as if He were red or white, or else as human, as one who forgets and then remembers in the way we do; or else it thinks of Him as so transcendent that all analogies become impossible (1. 1. 1). Hence we need the guide of the Catholic Faith and the Scriptures to assist our inquiry.

The first part of the *De Trinitate* (roughly Books I–VIII) is concerned with defining the Faith in the Trinity, and in examining those passages of Scripture which elucidate it, and particularly those which appear to contradict it. The last part of the work is the most original. It develops, with a wealth of psychological detail, a long series of analogies in terms of which we get hints of the nature of the Trinity. The argument is based upon the fact that man is created in the image of God, that is, of the Trinity, and hence his nature must in some way disclose the divine impress. The problem, however, is to discover which aspect of man's nature most clearly reveals this and so gives us an indication of the kind of Trinity God is.

Having defined the Catholic Faith in the Trinity (1. 4. 7), Augustine plunges into a defense of the deity of the Son and gives close consideration to those texts of Scripture which the Arians had used to deny His equality with the Father. He lays it down as a principle that we are to distinguish in the Scriptures 'what relates to the form of God, in which he is equal to the Father, and what to the form of a servant, which he took, and in which he is less than the Father' (1. 11. 22). Such a saying, therefore, as 'My Father is greater than I' (John 14:28) does not contradict the verse, 'I and the Father are one' (John 10:30). The first of these refers not to the essential nature of the Son but to His Incarnation. In this connection an interesting exegesis of Mark 13:32 emerges. Augustine is unwilling to admit that even in His incarnate state the Son had limited knowledge and was unaware of the day and hour of the Parousia. Consequently he has to twist the verse to mean that Christ, even as man, was not really ignorant, but is called ignorant in the sense that He made others ignorant, by hiding truths they were not ready to grasp. 'For a man is said not to know what he hides,' just as we call a ditch that is hidden 'blind' (1. 12. 23).

He continues by dealing with a third type of text concerning the Son, namely that which refers to Him neither as less than the Father nor as equal to the Father, but intimates only that He is of the Father (2. 1. 2–3). This leads Augustine into a consideration of the birth of the Son from the Father and the sense in which the Son is 'sent' (e.g. John 14:26). The first of these points is dealt with in a later book (5. 3. 4–5. 5. 6). On the second, he shows that being 'sent' does not imply the subordination of the Son to the Father, as the Arians claimed, but that 'sending' is an operation in which the three Persons of the Trinity are all involved, and which entails 'making visible,' exhibiting and presenting to mortal eyes (2. 5. 9–10). This is true of the Incarnation and of the appearance of the Holy Spirit at the baptism; and it is essential to understand 'sending' in this way, because the Son and Spirit are omnipresent by their deity and can be sent only where they already are (2. 5. 8). And yet the Father is not said to be 'sent,' although He, too, appeared in theophanies. This constitutes a difficulty for Augustine (2. 7. 12), and he returns to it in 4. 20. 28, contending that for the Father such an expression would be inappropriate since it would imply derivation, and the Father 'has no one of Whom to be or from Whom to proceed.'[7]

There follows a lengthy discussion of the Old Testament theophanies, the importance of which is very great. One of the fundamental Arian claims was that it was the Logos, and not the Father, who appeared to the patriarchs. This had, indeed, been the early Christian exegesis of these stories. The Apologists, especially Novatian, had referred the theophanies to the Son, thinking of the Logos as the Mediator between the One and the Many. The Arians pressed the point to the logical conclusion that the Son was therefore inferior to the Father and *visible by nature* (2. 9. 15). It is for this reason that Augustine seeks to establish that the Father was visible in the Old Testament theophanies; for he is thus able to rob the word 'sent' of any tinge of subordination, and to show the mutual co-operation of the Trinity in the works of God. Thus he argues that the three men who appeared to Abraham in Genesis 18 'visibly intimated by the visible creature, the equality of the Trinity and one and the same substance in the three Persons' (2. 11. 20). Similarly he interprets Daniel 7:9–11 to mean that the Father gives, while the Son receives, an eternal kingdom (2. 18. 33).

Moreover, the theophanies do not imply that God manifests Himself 'as He properly is, but by intimations such as suited the causes and times of the several circumstances' (2. 17. 32). God's nature cannot be seen by men; but by means of 'the creature made subject to Him,' He gives 'intimations of Himself to mortal senses by a corporeal form and likeness' (2. 18. 35). Exactly how this takes place Augustine does not fully answer. He proposes that the theophanies occurred through the agency of angels, since God in His substance is unchangeable (3. 11. 21–2). But whether the angels assumed something from the bodily elements to effect a theophany, or whether they transformed their own bodies into whatever form was necessary, he leaves unanswered (3. 1. 5).

The discussion, however, provokes an important consideration of miracles, for it is under this category that Augustine understands the theophanies. Miracles differ from natural events in this way: When things happen 'in a continuous kind of river of ever-flowing succession . . . by a regular and beaten track,' they are called 'natural.' But when 'for the admonition of men they are thrust in by an unusual changeableness,' they are called 'miracles' (3. 3. 6). The difference, however, is not between an inflexible chain of causation and a divine intervention in this chain; but rather is it between God's usual and unusual operation (3. 5. 11). God being 'the first and highest cause of all corporeal appearances and motions' (3. 4. 9), there can be no such inflexible chain of causation. Rather does Augustine think of the world as pregnant with the relative causes of all things that are born, and both miracle and magic make use of these inherent powers (3. 9. 16). Just as the Egyptian magicians were able to make frogs and serpents, so the angels can even more easily draw out the proximate causes of things than can men, who lack their subtlety of perception and bodily motion (3. 9. 17). Thus what the angels do appears marvelous, though the proximate causes of their actions are inherent in creation, and the final cause is the will of God, who directs what they do. A study of these proximate causes (what we should call 'science') Augustine rates far from highly. The knowledge of the Self is superior to that of the stars (4 Pref.), for the former and not the latter leads to true beatitude. Hence for Augustine the issue of miracles is merely one of God's different modes of operation. There can in principle be no conflict between religion and science, not only because the latter is quite unimportant but also because God is the cause of all.

From this excursion into miracles Augustine further wanders from his topic to discuss the Incarnation and redemption (4. 1. 2–4. 18. 24), and the perfection of the number six (4. 4. 7; 4. 6. 10). The mathematics of symbols, in which he here indulges, may strike us as rather fanciful, though that type of mystical interpretation is gaining some prominence today. Numbers are important for Augustine, however, since they show the capacity of the mind to grasp eternal truths. Since two times two will always equal four, the immutable character of numbers and mathematical relations gives us some knowledge of God, who is unchangeable and eternal Being. Here, then, the mind is able to rise above its own transitory and changeable nature, to apprehend reality. In consequence the symbolic meaning of numbers has religious importance.

Returning again to his central theme, Augustine now seeks to establish the co-equality of the Persons of the Trinity (4. 20. 27-end). Having shown that the sending of the Son refers not to His eternal relation to the Father but to His being made visible to mortal eyes, Augustine is able to maintain that the begetting of the Son does not imply subordination. The Son is 'the brightness of eternal light,' an emanation (*manatio*) from the Omnipotent, and hence Himself omnipotent (4. 20. 27). Similarly the Holy Spirit, as proceeding from the Father and the Son, enjoys the same essential nature as they. The relations between the Persons of the Trinity are not those of degree or order but of causality. 'The Father is the beginning of the whole divinity, or if it is better so expressed, of the deity. He therefore who proceeds from the Father and the Son is referred back to Him from whom the Son was born' (4. 20. 29). Here we get, too, an indication of a theme which will be more fully developed later in the analogies, and which is one of Augustine's major contributions to the doctrine of the Trinity — namely, that the Spirit is the unifying principle in the Godhead. He is 'a certain unutterable communion of Father and Son,' and so called 'Holy' and 'Spirit' — terms which apply equally to Father and Son, but which are especially used for the third Person to indicate this communion (5. 11. 12). It is this idea that leads Augustine so to stress the double procession of the Spirit, from *both* Father and Son (4. 20. 29). This is a point on which Western theology markedly differs from the Greek, and which provoked the controversy over the *filioque* in the Creed. This phrase was an addition that occurred in the sixth century and became widespread in the West by the ninth. To the Greeks it seemed as if the Westerners implied two principles of causality in the Godhead. To the West the double procession was a way of expressing the equality of Father and Son (the *filioque* was first defended in Spain in opposition to Arianism), and in particular the bond of union that united Father and Son.

The co-equality of the three Persons is evident in the fact that every theophany is a work of the Trinity. But this is not immediately apparent, since divine manifestations often appear to refer to only one of the Persons. Yet this is due to the limitation of the 'bodily creature' necessary for a theophany. It is incapable of portraying the indivisible nature of the Trinity. This is clear from one's inability to say the words Father, Son, and Spirit simultaneously and without an interval. But this limitation does not deny the truth that 'the Trinity together wrought both the voice of the Father, and the flesh of the Son, and the dove of the Holy Spirit' (4. 21. 30). Indeed, we have an intimation of this indivisible nature of the Trinity in the separate utterance of the words 'memory,' 'intellect,' and 'will.' For each separate word actually implies all three, since each is uttered by all three at once, i.e. by the unity of the soul which combines memory, intellect, and will (4. 21. 30). This idea of the co-inherence of the Trinity is expressed later by Augustine thus: 'So both each are in each, and all in each, and each in all, and all in all, and all are one' (6. 10. 12).

But how are we to speak of the distinctions in the Godhead? Augustine, as we have already observed, never grasped the Cappadocian sense of *hypostasis*. 'They intend to put a difference I know not what between *ousia* and *hypostasis*' (5. 8. 10). He translates *hypostasis* by 'substance,' and then proceeds to show how inadequate it is. For the distinctions in the Godhead are relative. They express relations, not essence, and 'substance' cannot be used in this sense. It is an absolute term. Furthermore, it is not really right to say God 'subsists,' for this would imply that 'God is a subject in relation to His own goodness.' But with God He is Himself His own goodness. In any case, if we do use the word 'substance' of God, we must say there is *one* substance in the Trinity, not three; for with God, to be is the same thing as to subsist (7. 5. 10).

The word with which Augustine was familiar to express the distinctions in the Godhead was Person (*persona*); but he saw how inadequate even this was for the purpose. It was a generic name, and included men (7. 4. 7), and was hence misleading. 'The super-eminence of the Godhead surpasses the power of customary speech,' and in consequence no term is adequate to describe what is ineffable (7. 4. 7). But we have to use some term lest the poverty of language should leave us inarticulate (5. 9. 10). Hence we say three Persons. Yet it would be more accurate to say *one* Person (7. 4. 8), for the word 'person' does not properly refer to relations but to essence. To call the Father a 'Person,' therefore, does not denominate His relation to the Son or to the Spirit, but says something of His essence. 'For with God it is not one thing to be, and another to be a person, but it is absolutely the same thing' (7. 6. 11). And since there can be only one essence in the Trinity, there should be only one Person.

Another difficulty with the term is that it might lead us to think that Father, Son, and Spirit were three species of the genus essence. But a single essence has no species, just as a single animal can have no species. Hence the terms cannot be used according to genus and species. Nor can they be used in the same sense in which we speak of three statues being made out of the same gold. 'For there it is one thing to be gold, another to be statues.' But the Persons of the Trinity cannot be so distinguished since they have an *identity* of essence. They are not made *out of* the same essence (7. 6. 11). We have to say 'three somethings' (*tria quaedam*) in order not to fall into the error of Sabellius and do away with the distinctions; and we cannot say three essences, for this would imply a difference in the absolute equality of the Trinity (7. 4. 9). The only thing we can fitly say is that God is one according to essence, and three according to relation (7. 6. 12). And by using 'Person' to denominate these relations, we do so in order not to be reduced to silence.

One may comment that Augustine has well expressed the truth that the Persons of the Trinity have an identical and not a generic essence. Thus he avoided the danger which beset the Cappadocian theology and to which Basil of Caesarea was particularly open in defining *ousia* and *hypostasis* as what is common and what is particular.[8] Yet it may well be that Augustine has not done justice to the term 'Person.' By regarding it as appropriate to essence rather than to relation, so that we should strictly speak of one Person in the Trinity, he comes close to robbing the Trinitarian formula of an important element. If the Cappadocians were sometimes in danger of tritheism, Augustine's danger lies in the opposite direction. The very fact that all his analogies are taken from the internal relations *within* a single person, as we shall see in a moment, reflects the strong Neoplatonic element in his thought, with its concern for the One, and gives his treatment of the Trinity a tinge of Unitarianism, or at least of Sabellianism. Of course he does not fall into those errors, and is, indeed, aware of them (see 15. 22. 42). But the tendency remains.

When we draw analogies with the Trinity, we must say that the distinctions of the Persons are both *less* than and *different* from those between the component faculties within *a* person. Thus the Godhead means *more* than *a* person and less than *three* persons when we speak analogically in terms of human personality. The Cappadocian tendency to think in terms of plurality needs to be balanced by the Augustinian emphasis on the unity, while Augustine's approach equally needs the corrective of the Cappadocian.

IV. De Trinitate: The Psychological Analogies

At the end of the eighth book Augustine proposes that the key to knowing God and the Trinity is to be found in love. The mind knows love within itself, and in consequence knows God, for God is love. But how does this help us to discover the Trinity? Precisely because love implies a trinity — 'he that loves, and that which is loved, and love' itself (8. 10. 14).

Thus begins the long series of analogies which Augustine develops in his search for the nature of the Trinity. They are based on the fact that man is created in the image of God, that is, of the Trinity, and by looking into the depths of his own being he can discern the impress of the Divine. In Genesis 1:26, God says, 'Let *us* make man after our image and likeness,' and this implies man is made in the image not of one of the Persons of the Trinity but of all three. It implies also that the image is inadequate. Man is not fully the image of God, but *'after* the image.' 'He is not made equal by parity, but approaches to Him by a sort of likeness' (7. 6. 12; cf. 9. 2. 2; 12. 6. 6). Thus every analogy is in the last resort unsatisfactory, for it can only hint at a truth it does not embody. Not only by his very nature is man unlike as well as like the Trinity, but by sin, by his own fault, he has changed for the worse what likeness he had (15. 20. 39). Hence we can never rise to the knowledge of God as He actually is. We can only get hints and intimations, as we ascend from the world of the senses to those higher aspects of man's being which more nearly reflect the Divine (15. 1. 3). The Trinity, as we have entitled this chapter, remains an 'enigma.' By this Augustine intends an obscure image. Commenting on I Corinthians 13:12, he takes the apostle to mean that by looking, as it were, in a mirror, we *do* see the image, but only in a darkened fashion — 'in an enigma' (*in aenigmate,* 15. 9. 16). The mind, man's highest faculty, which most nearly reflects the divine impress, is still an 'inadequate image,' although it is an image in some degree (10. 12. 19).

In the fifteenth book, where Augustine summarizes the analogies of the preceding six books, he emphasizes that his method has been to ascend from the world of the senses to the contemplation by the mind of eternal realities, and at each stage to find indications of the Trinity, which grow clearer as the ascent progresses (15. 3. 4). For every aspect of creation has some likeness to God 'in proportion to its kind and measure, seeing that God made all things very good' (11. 5. 8).

Owing, however, to the fact that the different books were written at different times, this scheme was not entirely followed. As we have observed, the first trinity which Augustine introduces is that of love, and this leads to a discussion of the mind's love of itself. For it would seem that when the mind loves itself, no trinity is evident. There is only the mind and love. But closer examination reveals that the mind cannot love itself without knowing itself, and so we find these three, 'the mind itself, the love of it, and the knowledge of it' (9. 4. 4). In four ways this trinity reflects the nature of the divine Trinity. There is equality, because were the knowledge and love not equal, were the mind to love itself *more* than it actually is, the love would be imperfect. Then again, there is identity of essence, for when the mind knows and loves itself, the *whole* mind is involved. No separation or division is possible. Different substances are not involved: for while love is a 'substance' in its own right (compare 6. 5. 7) in Augustine's thinking, that is, a reality, this substance is not something different from the mind (9. 4. 6–7). Then again, they are mutually *all in all,* and while severally a substance they are together one substance and essence (9. 5. 8). Finally, they provide an indication of the begetting of the Word and the procession of the Spirit (9. 7. 12-end). For when true knowledge arises in the mind a 'word' (a concept) is begotten within us, and this word is on a par with and equal to the mind. The mind does not know itself as less or more than it actually is. But the love cannot be said to be begotten. For, in a way, it precedes the begetting of the word, since love is implied in the very desire or will (*appe-*

249

titus, voluntas) of seeking, which finally issues in knowing. Thus love proceeds from the mind in the act of searching for knowledge. We may note, in passing, that this equivalence of love and will runs through Augustine's analogies, and the terms interchange.

These last points are further developed in the fifteenth book. The 'word' begotten by the mind is an internal word — an idea, which exists before it is actually phrased in words or language. When, however, it is spoken it can be compared to the Incarnation of the Word, which does not imply that the Son is changed *into* flesh, any more than that the inherent idea is changed *into* language and outward sound. Moreover, this word begotten in the heart is the first step toward our creating anything, just as the Word begotten by the Father is Creator (15. 10. 19; 15. 11. 20).

Similarly the procession of the Spirit is developed in 15. 27. 50. The Spirit, like the love which combines the memory with its begotten word, as parent to offspring, is 'a kind of consubstantial communion of Father and Son,' and proceeds from both; and the procession differs from birth or begetting in this, that 'to behold by thought is not the same as to desire.'

Here, it will be noticed, 'memory' has been substituted for 'mind,' and this leads us to consider Augustine's second trinity — memory, understanding, and will (10. 11. 17–18). Here again we have three things which in essence are one. Each is life, mind, and substance in respect to itself, and only *relatively* to the others is it memory, will, or understanding. Thus the identity of essence and the distinctions of relation in the Trinity are intimated. Moreover, they are equal to each other and each to all, or else they could not mutually contain each other. 'For I remember I have memory, will, and understanding; and I understand that I understand and will and remember; and I will that I will and remember and understand; and I remember together my whole memory and understanding and will' (10. 11. 18).

In this analogy and in others we shall be considering, it may be well to bear in mind the arbitrary aspect of Augustine's analysis. The faculties of memory, understanding, and will do not exhaust a description of the mind. We have the power of imagination and other capacities which do not adequately fall under the categories he has chosen.

Augustine now turns to consider a trinity in connection with the 'outer man': that of the object we see, our vision or act of seeing, and the attention of our mind (11. 2. 2). Here the substances are different, since we can distinguish the object from the act of seeing, yet they sufficiently coalesce into a unity in the mind that they give a hint of the Trinity (11. 2. 5). But since the soul lives in a degenerate fashion when living according to the world of sense, a better trinity is to be discerned in this: the memory of the object, internal vision, and the will which unites both in conception (11. 3. 6). Here the diversity of substance is overcome, and we have a more fitting analogy.

The twelfth book sets out to refute the view that the Trinity is evident in the human family of father, wife, and son. This gives Augustine an opportunity to discuss the meaning of masculine and feminine. The analogy of father, wife, and son he finds unfitting because Adam by himself was created in God's image; and even if one were to contend that wife and son were already implied in him, I Cor. 11:7 shows that every male is the image of God (12. 7. 9). Augustine's objection to viewing the Trinity as reflected 'in three human beings' (12. 6. 8), in the way of the Cappadocians, runs very deep. Starting as he did from the conception of God as one Mind, the analogy of the family seemed to endanger the divine unity; and, as we have already observed, this prevented him from doing full justice to the concept of the three Persons in the Godhead. Thus, he insists that the Trinity is to be found in the unity of the human mind, which comprehends in 'a rational wedlock' both contemplation and action (12. 12. 19). The masculine part of the mind symbolizes the contemplation of eternal truth, while the feminine part symbolizes that aspect of it which is concerned with handling and directing inferior and corporeal things (12. 13. 21). The former is 'wisdom,' the latter is 'knowledge.' Thus the family which reflects the Trinity is the mind with its masculine and feminine principles.

This plunges Augustine into the most disheartening of the books (13), from the point of view of the reader who is concerned with the main thread of the argument. It is a book which he himself confesses is unduly 'prolix.' Yet it is full of important things, despite their irrelevance to his topic. It is concerned with distinguishing wisdom and knowledge in terms of contemplation and action (13. 1. 1; 13. 19. 24; 13. 20. 25), and it contains a long digression on blessedness, discussing the problem, though never really answering it, of how men can be said to will to be blessed when we can only will what we know and most men do not know in what true blessedness consists (13. 3. 6; 13. 6. 9). There is, too, a significant consideration of the Incarnation and Atonement, and the fact that the devil was overcome by God's righteousness rather than by His power (13. 10. 13; 13. 14. 18). The questions of concupiscence and the virginity of Mary are also discussed (13. 18. 23). The book concludes with three trinities which illustrate the principle of ascent from the corporeal world to the noetic, in the quest for the most fitting analogies to the Divine (13. 20. 26). We have first a trinity of sounds which are not understood, being in a foreign tongue, but remaining in the memory, of the mental vision of them in recollection, and of the will by which these are remembered and which unites the sounds with their recollection. But because this trinity involves images of corporeal things, it cannot mirror a Trinity which is eternal. Yet by ascending to one in which the sounds are understood, we come closer to the Trinity, though not much closer, for even here there is a defect if the sounds are not believed to be true. So we ascend higher to a trinity in which the sounds are both understood and believed, belief introducing the principle of love. But we are still far from the eternal Trinity, since a temporal and corporeal element is implicit in the sounds.

Hence the fourteenth book returns to Augustine's original trinity in which the mind remembers, understands, and loves itself (14. 6. 8–9). Here the corporeal element is overcome, for the soul by its nature is immortal (14. 4. 7). When, moreover, the mind contemplates itself, not only is it free from all adventitious subject matter and even from temporal faith, but it is *always* contemplating itself. Thus we have stumbled upon something eternal. For even when it is not actually thinking of itself, the mind always knows and contemplates itself, just as we say a musician knows music, although he may not be actually thinking about it (14. 7. 9–14. 8. 11). Moreover, the mind's activity implies simultaneity, so that time itself is overcome. The mind does not see itself in memory by recollection *subsequently* to knowing itself, as though it had not been already there before it knew itself (14. 10. 13). Nor does memory apply only to things past. It applies, too, to things present. Did not Virgil say of Ulysses that he 'did not forget himself'? And does not this imply that he remembered himself, and being present to himself, he remembered something present (14. 11. 14)?

But we must go one step higher in our ascent. The Trinity is not to be found in the fact that the mind remembers, understands, and loves *itself*. For this would imply a defect in love. It is only when the mind loves God that it loves itself rightly. And so the image of God is to be found in this: that the mind remembers, understands, and loves God (14. 12. 15; 14. 14. 18). Only by so doing does the mind discover true wisdom and understand itself.

Yet in the final analysis all these trinities we have considered are inadequate. Man's chief part, his mind, may mirror the Trinity, but only 'in an enigma.' The image is obscure. For one thing, these trinities are *in* man; whereas the Trinity is not *in* God, but God *is* the Trinity. Then again, the three Persons are of one essence, in a different way from which an individual man is one person (15. 7. 11). Once more, memory, will, and understanding inadequately reflect the Trinity, since we remember only by memory, and understand only by understanding. But the Father does not understand only by the Son, or love only by the Holy Spirit. The Father *is* His own understanding, memory, and love; and the same applies to the Son and the Spirit. For to God to *be* is the same thing as to be wise. Essence is identical with wisdom (15. 7. 12). Again, my memory, understanding, and love are not *their own,* but *mine.* A single person *has* these three:

253

he is *not* these three. Moreover, they are *in one* person, while God *is three* Persons (15. 22. 42–3). Here we may observe that Augustine rectifies to some degree the implicit tendency in all his analogies, and on which we have already remarked, to think of God as a single Mind.

Augustine concludes his work with a further discussion of the begetting of the Son and the procession of the Spirit. We have already dealt with these questions and may merely mention one or two further factors. On the first point he stresses the unlikeness between God's begetting of the Word and our begetting of a word. For one thing, God's knowledge is not dependent upon anything but Himself, whereas ours is. He does not know His creatures because they are: they are because he knows them (15. 13. 22). Then again, His Word is eternal, while we are not always thinking even of eternal truths, such as the fact that we exist. Furthermore, our word is formable before formed, while His was so in the form of God as not to be formable before formed (15. 15. 25). Once more, our word is a thought which can be revolved and forgotten, while His is not (15. 16. 25).

The discussion on the Spirit establishes that He is love. Augustine admits that had Scripture directly said this no small part of his inquiry would have been unnecessary. As love He is the gift of God, but not less than God because given, 'for He Himself also gives Himself as being God' (15. 19. 36). He is not created by the Father and Son who give Him, nor do they rule over Him. Rather is He 'the concord of the given and the givers.' And so He is especially called 'love' and 'Spirit,' because these the Father and the Son are by substance and have in common. Thus the Spirit is the bond of union between Father and Son (15. 19. 37) — 'a kind of consubstantial communion of Father and Son' (15. 27. 50).

And so Augustine reaches the end of his long and difficult inquiry. He is well aware of its defects, and of the fact that the nature of the Trinity cannot be discerned in this mortal life. Only when we are fully rescued from the limitations of our present bodies and of discursive reasoning will we fully know the truth. Then we 'shall discern by a mind that contemplates, why the Holy Spirit is not a Son, although He proceeds from the

Father' and so on (15. 24. 45). Conscious of the deficiencies of his work, he characteristically ends it with a prayer, 'which is better than an argument': 'I have sought Thee, and have desired to see with my understanding what I believed; and I have argued and laboured much . . . O Lord, the one God, God the Trinity, whatever I have said in these books that is of Thine, may they acknowledge who are thine; if anything of my own, may it be pardoned both by Thee and by those who are Thine.'

On the merits and defects of Augustine's treatise we have commented throughout our chapter. We may conclude by the observation that his work is one of the foremost treatments of the Trinity in Christian theology. While it may lack the precision of thought to be found in St. Thomas, and is deficient in its treatment of the term 'Person,' it laid the foundations for the classical formulations in the West; and in its psychological penetration, its perception of the co-inherence of the Trinity, and its grasp of the Spirit as the bond of union between Father and Son, it remains unsurpassed.

FOR FURTHER READING

The history of the doctrine of the Trinity can be conveniently studied in I. A. Dorner, *History of the Development of the Doctrine of the Person of Christ,* Eng. tr., 5 vols., Edinburgh, 1890–97, and in the volume edited by A. E. J. Rawlinson, *Essays on the Trinity and the Incarnation,* New York, 1933 (particularly Chap. 5 by F. W. Green, which does not, however, do full justice to the Cappadocians). There are two important German works on Augustine's view of the Trinity: M. Schmaus, *Die psychologische Trinitätslehre des hl. Augustinus,* Münster, 1927, and M. Grabmann, *Die Grundgedanken des hl. Augustinus über Seele und Gott,* 2nd ed., Köln, 1929. M. Schmaus has also translated the *De Trinitate* into German, with a useful introduction and elaborate bibliography, in the *Bibliothek der Kirchenväter,* 2nd Series, vols. 13–14, Munich, 1935–6. In French there is the valuable study by I. Chevalier, *S. Augustin et la pensée grecque: Les relations Trinitaires,* Fribourg en Suisse, 1940. Of the many articles on this subject, mention may be made of J. Lebreton, 'S. Augustin théologien de la Trinité. Son exégèse des théophanies,' in *Miscellenea Agostiniana,* vol. 2, pp. 821–36, Rome, 1931; and F. Cavallera, 'La doctrine de S. Augustin sur l' Esprit Saint à propos du De Trinitate,' in *Recherches de théologie ancienne et médiévale,* 1930, pp. 365–87; ed. 1931, pp. 5–19.

NOTES

1. References to the *De Trinitate* are taken from the translation by A. W. Haddan and W. G. T. Shedd in the *Nicene and Post-Nicene Fathers*, Series I, vol. 3. Occasionally I have made a change in the renderings after consulting the Latin. The Latin text, reprinted from that of the Benedictines of St. Maur (1679–1700), will be found in Migne, *P.L.*, vol. 42, cols. 819–1098.

2. *Ep.* 169. 1.

3. This has been fully answered by J. F. Bethune-Baker in his study in *Texts and Studies*, vol. 7, Cambridge, 1901. 'The Meaning of Homo-ousios in the "Constantinopolitan" Creed.'

4. Gregory of Nyssa, *On 'Not Three Gods.'*

5. The doctrine of Hilary, Bishop of Poitiers, has been studied with equal care and clarity by Pierre Smulders in his work *La Doctrine trinitaire de S. Hilaire de Poitiers*, Rome, 1944. Hilary's great work on the Trinity has been rendered into English by E. W. Watson and L. Pullan in the *Nicene and Post-Nicene Fathers*, Series II, vol. 9, New York, 1899, and more recently into German with a useful introduction by Anton Antweiler, vols. 5 and 6 of the second series of *Bibliothek der Kirchenväter*, Munich, 1933–4. The treatise was written during his exile in Asia Minor (A.D. 356–9), and is remarkable for its defense of the Nicene faith and for paving the way for the final reconciliation of conservative Homoeans with the defenders of the *homoousios*. A notable theme which he develops is that of the *circuminsessio,* the mutual co-inherence of the Father and Son by virtue of their identity of substance. It is this theme which Augustine enlarged upon with no little originality, intimately relating it (as Hilary had not done) to the doctrine of the Holy Spirit.

6. Enchiridion, IV.

7. It may be remarked that Augustine's argument here is not consistent. First he tries to rob the expression 'sent' of all subordination by applying it not to the eternal begetting of the Son but to 'making visible.' But he now applies it to eternal relations in the Godhead, since the Father cannot be 'sent,' as being unoriginated. Later on he treats the Holy Spirit as 'sent,' in the sense that He proceeds from Father and Son (4. 20. 29).

8. See *Ep.* 214. 4.

– X –

THE CITY OF GOD

Edward R. Hardy, Jr.

T HE EMPEROR Charlemagne was accustomed to have serious
books read to him at dinner. His biographer tells us that
he enjoyed listening to the writings of St. Augustine, especially
the books entitled *De Civitate Dei*.[1] Historians have seen in
this an indication that he found in St. Augustine's *City of God*
an inspiration for the Christian Empire he hoped to revive in
the changed world of the eighth–ninth century. As the Middle
Ages wore on, St. Augustine's phrases and ideas were quoted on
both sides of the great dispute within that Empire. Both parties
agreed on the political and social ideal of an organically unified
Church-State, a Christian Commonwealth in which civil and
religious authorities would work together for the common good.
But was Pope or Emperor, prelate or king, to be the dominating
and controlling authority? Conclusions drawn from St. Augustine could be and were used on either side of this great argument.
When we turn to his own words we find that he is describing a
human conflict rather than propounding a political program.

He sees mankind as occupying a battleground between two loyalties, heavenly and earthly, the self-denying love of God and the God-denying love of self. Every area of human life is a spiritual field of battle. Yet we are all striving toward achieving harmony and concord in some form or other.

In modern times the unification of nations and the re-formation and division of the Church have produced a number of new forms of this ancient struggle. Tempting but ultimately futile was the effort to avoid it by dividing human life between a strictly secular state and a strictly other-worldly Church. In the naïve or cynical words of the historian Taine, there need be no conflict between Church and State, since they are concerned with distinct objectives, the State aiming at the safety of property, the Church at the eternal salvation of the soul.[2] Neither could accept such a division. The State must aim at the general welfare; the Church cannot deny that its concern for man has something to do with his life here and now. In America, at least, separation of Church and State has never meant a denial of this field of common interest. But perhaps our national temptation in this connection is a new form of the imperial ideal in which the civic idealism of the 'American dream' replaces the religious vision of brotherhood in God. If St. Augustine heard a modern American school or congregation singing with devout fervor:

> *O beautiful for patriot dream*
> *That sees beyond the years*
> *Thine alabaster cities gleam*
> *Undimmed by human tears!*

he would assume that these words referred to our true fatherland, the heavenly city which can be reached only after the sin and sorrow of this earthly pilgrimage are ended. And we should have to tell him that for many of those present there was no truer heaven than the future United States of America. Some would suggest that our national church is the public-school system, as in St. Augustine's time schoolmasters rather than priests passed on from generation to generation a more than secular loyalty to the great traditions of Rome.

Some of these broader implications of St. Augustine's ideas were doubtless in old Kaiser Karl's head as he listened to the reader in his hall at Aachen. But probably the books of the *City of God* — which the biographer quite properly refers to in the plural, as a series rather than a unit — provided the monarch with amusement as well as instruction at mealtime. In these *XXII Books of St. Aurelius Augustine the Bishop on the City of God against the Pagans* one is charmed and sometimes confused by finding notes on almost every subject of human interest. The extracts from them which appear in the pages of the *Breviarium Romanum* for the devotional reading of the clergy do not deal with political theory but with the Second Temple, the names of the Prophet Hosea's children, and the miracles of St. Stephen. Some other items to be found in the *City of God* are a sketch of the Assyrian Empire, attacks on the absurdities of paganism, discussions on the nature of time, the eucharistic sacrifice, and the main principles of social ethics, and a rhetorical passage on the wonders of nature. One never knows quite what is coming next, and doubtless Charlemagne, like many other readers since, found this one of the attractions of the work. It has the fascination of a book about everything.

Yet though variegated in detail, the *City of God* has a real and intense unity. It arose out of a particular occasion, and its structure follows a definite line of thought. The occasion was the sack of Rome by Alaric the Goth in 410, the event that gave the ancient world the shock which modern writers might expect to have been felt at that obscure and elusive crisis, the fall of the Roman Empire. 'The whole world perished in one city,' wrote St. Jerome, who in his monastery at Bethlehem did not cease to be the Roman and the rhetorician.[3] Rome, the center of secular faith and loyalty for centuries, was not invulnerable. History recorded no such calamity since the Gallic invasion in the days of Rome's youth, eight hundred years before. Refugees turned up in Sicily, in North Africa, even in Palestine, presenting problems like some of those of our own day. The first reaction of horror and distress was succeeded in the minds of many by the thought, 'So this is what Christianity, this new religion, has brought us to!' In reply to that attack the bishop of Hippo took pen in hand. The earthly city had fallen, or might fall. Was this what really mattered? How stood it with the heavenly city, if there be one?

Fifteen years later Augustine's task was finished, after many interruptions. The questions raised by the siege of Rome had led to ten books in defense of the faith, in which the exposition of the claims of the true religion included incidentally a formulation of principles of political judgment. Twelve books followed on the history of the two cities, or two Commonwealths, of the servants of God and the children of the world, the two kingdoms of love and pride. What began with the sack of Rome ends with the Last Judgment and the eternal Sabbath, and not without relief the Bishop writes: 'It seems to me that I have accomplished, by God's help, the responsibility of this vast work.' [4]

It seems probable indeed that the *De Civitate Dei* was not originally planned by St. Augustine as the magnificent structure he finally produced. Book I starts with informal comments on current events, such as in modern times would have appeared as a series of magazine articles or a short book. Then he realized that this was leading him into broader questions of apologetics and historical interpretation, and when the *apologia* grew into nine books it was necessary to construct the positive section on a similar scale. The remaining twelve books, which fall into groups of four, were then probably planned and constructed as a whole. We must be grateful for this expansion of what began as an occasional, almost journalistic, piece of writing, since not only the treatment of central topics but the *obiter dicta* have turned out to be of great importance in the history of Christian thought.

I. Rome's History

The first ten books of the *City of God* take up three related questions: (1) Was Christianity responsible for the fall of Rome, paganism for its rise? (2) If not paganism, what spiritual power had presided over the rise of Rome? (3) Has any pagan system a serious claim against Christianity as the true spiritual religion? These are problems of universal significance, although St. Augustine's discussion is naturally related to the particular form in which they presented themselves in his time. The answers interlock to some extent, though they may conveniently be discussed separately.

Book I begins with the immediate problems raised by the sack of Rome by the Goths. Critics are requested to remember that Christianity had mitigated, not aggravated, the horrors of war.[5] The modern reader may pause to reflect that such consolation as that thought provides is still available. The argument then proceeds another step: it is true that in this life material good and ill happen to the good and the bad alike; what matters is the use we make of these things. No Christian, whose treasure is in heaven, can admit that spoliation, death, or deprivation of burial is an ultimate loss. It seems that St. Augustine is here writing for the refugees and their friends rather than against the pagans. So also with the following chapters, which deal with the problem of moral theology raised by the fate of the Christian maidens of Rome. Involuntary unchastity, it is argued, is no sin, since it involves no consent of the will. Though tragic, it should not be avoided at the cost of the sinful act of suicide. To pagan critics Augustine answers, for the moment, that the degeneracy of the Romans was enough to bring on the fate of the city.[6] The eternal City of God still remains — the home of the righteous, whose pilgrim life on earth is interwoven with that of the earthly city. Even some who now attack the City of God are destined for her eternal fellowship, and some of those who now share her sacraments will fall away, for 'these two cities are indeed intertwined and mixed in this world, until they be separated by the final judgment.'[7] It does indeed seem as if this interesting preliminary discussion had a separate existence before the rest of the book grew out of it.

Book II argues that a religion which was preposterous when it was not indecent could not have been the source of divine blessings. As a matter of fact, the Roman heroes were much better than their gods. Book III surveys the wars and disasters which the pagan Romans had suffered. St. Augustine's pupil Orosius later expanded this hint into a universal history written 'against the pagans.' The argument has now excluded the pagan religion as a cause of Roman prosperity, and a further section disposes of the explanation that the fate of Rome was written in the stars. It was due to intelligible causes, including human wills, acting under the providence and foreknowledge of God.[8] On the immense questions raised by this combination of freedom and providence St. Augustine says little more here than to assert the reality of both.

To what specific cause, then, is the rise of empires due? One must first note that empire as such is not necessarily good. Indeed, what are empires without justice but robber bands on a large scale (*magna latrocinia*)? The rule of good men may be beneficial for their subjects, but the extension of empires comes either by the lust for conquest, as with the Assyrians, or as a result of the repulse of unjust aggression. The Romans might well have added *Iniquitas Aliena* to *Victoria* among their divinities, since just victory depended on the previous wickedness of others. The world would probably be better off with a number of small states in friendly relations with each other.[9] These anti-imperialist sentiments of St. Augustine's were theoretical, since the Roman Empire was for him an established fact. If called on to make the comparison he would probably, with Gibbon and others, have preferred the *pax Romana* to most of the systems that have followed it. Yet it is significant that such ideas occurred to him, and that he can be quoted in favor of international co-operation. It was probably this passage that encouraged Mgr. Marius Besson, the learned bishop of Fribourg, to declare in a sermon at Geneva during a session of the League of Nations that the League was an expression of the ideals of St. Augustine.[10]

It may be that all we can say is that God gives kingdoms to the just and the unjust alike for reasons known to Him alone, thus teaching us that these matters are no part of true happiness.[11]

St. Augustine, however, was enough of a Roman not to be satisfied with this explanation of Roman good fortune. Although they were aliens to the truest and highest good, the Romans rose by real merit and for providential purposes. St. Augustine had learned in school Virgil's lines about the Roman mission 'to spare the humble and war down the proud,' and they still meant something to him. Even the love of glory, though a vice, restrained other more harmful vices. The Empire was won by men who sacrificed themselves for the good of the state as they saw it; and in the long run the provincials were the gainers by the gift of Roman laws and letters and final equality with their conquerors. A Roman by sentiment, St. Augustine was also a provincial, born in the conquered province of Africa, perhaps by ancestry partly Carthaginian. But his patriotism is mainly Roman, and it is natural for him to argue that the sacrifices made by the Romans of old for the sake of liberty and glory should be an inspiration to Christians when they are called upon to make their sacrifices, often lesser ones, for true freedom and the love of God. But we must remember, he adds, that they did it for an earthly crown and 'have received their reward.' Our prospects are eternal.[12] The context of the phrase here quoted from the Gospels is scarcely complimentary, referring to the Pharisees who did their righteous acts in public for the praise of men. Still less complimentary is St. Augustine's epigrammatic variation on it elsewhere — *receperunt mercedem suam, vani vanam.*[13] Nothing but vanity? One is moved to quote from a modern commentator of unquestioned orthodoxy:

> St. Augustine . . . saw no hope of any sort of happiness awaiting pagans in the life to come. And in this view many have concurred. I should not be so ready to pronounce sentence on so large a portion of mankind, God's creatures, after all, human beings for whom Christ died. If we are unable to formulate any definite scheme of hope for them, then we had better fall back on our ignorance, avowing with Newman that 'we do not understand the dispensation of

paganism' (*University Sermons*, pp. 21, 23). And has not the Supreme Judge himself warned us not to forestall his sentence? *Judge not* (Matt. 7:1).[14]

Finally St. Augustine closes this section with some recent examples. God's judgments have been shown in the destruction of the pagan Goth Radagaisus, who would have been much worse than Alaric. Seeing today the rise and fall of tyrants, we can realize the force of such an argument in the fifth century. Augustine offers at the same time the fine examples of some, at least, of the Christian Emperors. Here he remarks that we do not call Christian rulers happy because of long life or victory, but only if they remember to rule justly, if they use their power to spread the true religion, if they see through the deception of flattery, 'if they have greater love for that kingdom where they need not fear to have colleagues,' if they use punishment for the public welfare and exercise the power of pardon to encourage reform, if they prefer to rule themselves rather than their realms, if they do not neglect to offer the true sacrifice of prayer to God.[15] This section, interesting both for what it contains and for what it omits, has been well called the Mirror of Princes. More than any other passage in St. Augustine's writings it puts his hope for a Christian public order in that dream of many Christian centuries, the godly prince.

II. Rome's Religion

From the mainly political section we turn to the primarily religious in Books VI–X. Two books of not very laborious argument are sufficient to show that popular paganism had no claim to be a satisfactory spiritual religion. This section is of interest chiefly for the curious facts it preserves about the ancient gods, largely from the writings of the antiquarian Varro. Has philosophy anything more to offer? Certainly it has, since those who loved wisdom did to some real extent find it, even in the things of God. In Socrates, St. Augustine sees the same quest to which his own life was given, the desire to find unity both in the ultimate cause of things and in the goal of human life. Among the disciples of Socrates, Plato comes nearest to Christian truth. 'If, then, Plato spoke of the wise man as the imitator, knower, and lover of God, by fellowship with whom one may be blessed, why need we bother with the others?' [16] In metaphysics, logic, and ethics, says St. Augustine, the Platonists excel all other philosophers. He has indeed no quarrel with them, as far as they go.

The vexed question of St. Augustine's relation to Neoplatonism does not belong primarily to the study of the *De Civitate*. One may notice, however, that in these books, written some thirty years after his baptism, he still holds and uses the philosophy he had accepted some years before that event. The distinction between Platonist and Neoplatonist is of course a modern one, though St. Augustine was familiar enough with the difference between the religious interpretation and development of Plato's thought, which he learned from those whom he called Platonists and we call Neoplatonists, and the skeptical interpretation, supported by those whom he knew as Academics. Substantially what he learned from the Neoplatonists was an interpretation of Plato, together with information about him. St. Augustine's direct knowledge of the philosopher was apparently slight, but his Platonism seems to be a case of one great mind speaking to another through and over the heads of lesser interpreters.

The greater part of Books VIII–X, however, is devoted not to St. Augustine's Platonism but to his disagreements with the Neoplatonists — in fact on first reading one is in danger of missing the central but brief statement of agreement. From the point of view of practical religion the most conspicuous difference between the pagan and the Christian Platonist was the willingness of the former to include popular paganism in his system, on the ground that the pagan gods, though of course not God, were still *daimones* of considerable power. (The term for these spirits must remain in Greek, since they are morally neutral supernatural beings, neither the evil demons of common English usage nor the ambiguous demonic powers of some modern speculation.) In some cases, conspicuously in the circle of Julian the Apostate in the middle of the fourth century, new developments of the occult arts were thus associated with a lofty philosophy. St.

Augustine naturally attacks this worship of wandering spirits, or perhaps of dead men, and distinguishes from it something externally similar — the cult of the martyrs, the most striking form of popular Christian piety in his day:

> for who ever heard a priest of the faithful standing at the altar, even at one erected over the holy body of a martyr for the honor and worship of God, saying in his prayer 'I offer sacrifice to thee, Peter or Paul or Cyprian' when oblation is made at their shrines to God (who made them both men and martyrs and joined them with his angels in heavenly honor) that by this solemnity we may both give thanks to God for their victories and stir up ourselves by renewing their memories to the imitation of their crowns and palms [that is, to follow the martyrs in their struggle and triumph], calling upon God for aid? [17]

What the Platonists seek for in vain in their *daimones* is mediation between God and man. This Christians have in the true mediator of God and man, the man Christ Jesus (I Timothy 2:5), 'of whose divinity, by which he is always equal to the Father, and of whose humanity, by which he was made like unto us, this is not the place to speak as much as we might.' [18] To God alone, and not to any lesser power, must sacrifice be offered; and the only acceptable sacrifice is the dedication of human life to the Father, an offering which we are able to make in our lives because it has been perfectly made by Christ:

> so that the whole redeemed City, that is the congregation and society of the saints, might be offered to God as a universal sacrifice by the great High Priest, who offered himself when he suffered for us in the form of a servant, that we might become the body of so great a head.

In the Sacrament of the Altar the Church observes this divine sacrifice, making oblation of herself in and with Christ to God.[19] St. Augustine does not deny that God has used the ministry of holy angels to bring men to Him, but contrasts them with the *daimones,* who maliciously demand divine honors for themselves — a point suggestive of the current use of 'demonic' for intermediate objects of loyalty (such as the State) which become evil when claiming to be ultimate. At the end of Book x St. Augustine almost plaintively addresses the Neoplatonist Porphyry, in whose works he had read of God's Word and Spirit and of the need for redemption by union with God. On the authority of Bishop Simplicianus, St. Ambrose's successor at Milan, St. Augustine quotes the story of a Platonist who said that the opening words of the Gospel of John deserved to be inscribed in letters of gold in all churches. Why did pride keep such men from acknowledging the humility of the Word who 'was made flesh and dwelt among us'? [20]

III. History as the Story of Two Cities

The glorious City of God has so far been in the background of this work written in its defense. St. Augustine is now at last ready to begin the positive section of his work, and quotes testimonies from the Psalms to the glories of the Holy City. The rise, history, and end of the two cities is the great theme on which he will now embark. Our knowledge of this depends on faith, since the mind as well as the heart and soul is injured by sin and needs purification by the one Mediator.[21] In effect these chapters are the beginning of a Christian epic, in which Christ rather than the classical Muse is invoked. Parallels with Milton's opening invocation to the 'heavenly Muse' naturally come to mind.

We begin our story with Creation, by which the universe and time began together, and reflect on the nature of the Trinity, the one simple and unchanging good. Then comes the Fall of the angels, which St. Augustine thinks may be referred to in the separation of light from darkness in Genesis 1:4, or at least it may legitimately be associated with that text. The two angelic societies have been, not without reason, compared to the kingdoms of light and darkness in which St. Augustine had believed in his Manichean days.[22] Certainly the emotional effect is similar, as is the principle that good and evil were already striving in the universe when man was created. But St. Augustine is careful to make the reservations he had urged in his anti-Manichean writings: since there can be no such thing as absolute evil, we must describe one of these societies as good by nature and will, the other as good by nature and perverse in will, yet restrained by God's supreme providence.[23]

The concept of the primal Fall is perhaps a more intelligible idea today than it would have been to many of us a few years ago. That some grave defect was present in the world before the making of man seems to be the only hypothesis that will explain the facts of the universe. As to how this happened we can only speculate; such speculation may lead the pious mind to observe that knowledge of this topic is evidently not required to enable us to do our duty and attain salvation, or it would have been revealed.[24] Great as was the authority they gathered from his name, St. Augustine's speculations remain no more than that.

The Creation and Fall of man, and many related topics, follow in Books XII–XIV. A central principle is that all evil of the will, human or angelic, is a perversion of the power to love which our Creator shared with us, and is an inordinate desire for something good — which, so desired out of due order, becomes in effect evil.[25] In dealing with Creation St. Augustine has occasion to defend the reality of history. The world does not revolve in eternal cycles but moves onward to a divine goal. When God made man He was not ignorant of the evil which men would work, fighting among themselves more fiercely than the naturally wild creatures. Man was created in an earthly Paradise; we are to understand this as a historical place and event, although it also beautifully symbolizes the life of the righteous guided by the four virtues, or the Church nourished by the four Gospels.[26] From this, however, man fell by disobedience, thus becoming subject to the death of the body and the more fatal death of the soul. Turning from God he was abandoned to himself, and his desires were corrupted. The nature of man is to desire things, and St. Augustine emphasizes that in his Latin Bible there was no distinction between the words used for desire, whether good or evil. *Amor, dilectio,* and even *caritas* may be employed indifferently. Goodness or badness is first of all in the direction of the will, not in the nature, still less in the flesh, of man as opposed to man's spirit.[27]

God, planning and beginning the work of redemption, now initiates the restoration of mankind, and thereby the foundation of the two cities, or rather of their earthly colonies, is completed. St. Augustine pauses to summarize:

So two loves have constituted two cities — the earthly is formed by love of self even to contempt of God, the heavenly by love of God even to contempt of self. For the one glories in herself, the other in the Lord. The one seeks glory from man; for the other God, the witness of the conscience, is the greatest glory. The one lifts up her head to her own glory; the other says to her God, 'My glory and the lifter up of my head.' In the one the lust for power prevails, both in her own rulers and in the nations she subdues; in the other all serve each other in charity, governors by taking thought for all and subjects by obeying.[28]

A sketch of the history of the two cities occupies four books, from Cain and Abel down to the time of Christ. On the one side there is the history of God's people, as recorded in the Old Testament; on the other there are the nations of the world, foreshadowed in the city built by Cain in the land of Nod. St. Augustine employed the best Biblical and historical scholarship available to him. At times, indeed, he engages in historical criticism; thus, in spite of his belief in the inspiration of the Septuagint Greek version, he settles the problem of the discrepancy between the Hebrew and Greek figures for the ages of the patriarchs by assuming textual corruption in the manuscripts from which the Greek was translated.[29] Interesting as these books are, however, for the glimpse they give us of the state of Biblical and historical studies in the fifth century, the intention rather than the performance is of permanent significance. The historical work must be done freshly as the state of our knowledge changes. Yet the Christian interpreter will always share St. Augustine's conviction that the Old Testament is both a real historical story and also the record of a promise that finds its fulfillment only in Christ. In this sense, for instance, what is said of Jerusalem in the Psalms and elsewhere may be interpreted as pointing to the eternal city. St. Augustine is aware, too, that others who were not of Israel belonged to God in ancient days, although he assumes that this must have been made possible by some special and unrecorded revelation.[30] But this topic, of more interest to us than to him, is not pursued any further. With the coming of Christ history reaches its climax and in a sense its end. No further development in principle is to be expected, although the earthly pilgrimage of the Catholic Church is not without incident. Spreading throughout the world, suffering from persecutions without and the attacks of false brethren within, she continues to serve God in hope from generation to generation.

IV. Ethics in History

At the end of Book XVIII St. Augustine has arrived at his own time. The following book is in a practical sense the climax of his work, since it deals with the principles of personal and social conduct relevant to the present age. Before entering upon it he pauses to summarize his main idea:

> We may now conclude this book, having discussed and sufficiently expounded the temporal careers of these two cities, which are mixed together from the beginning to the end. One of these, the earthly, has made for herself false gods as she chose, from anywhere or even out of man, to serve by sacrifices; but the other, the heavenly, a stranger and pilgrim on earth, makes no false gods but herself is made by the true God, whose true sacrifice she herself is. Both alike enjoy temporal goods or suffer temporal ills, but differ in faith, in hope, in love, until they be separated by the final judgment and each receive its end, of which there is no end. Of the ends of the two it is now for us to discourse.[31]

St. Augustine is here playing on the two related senses of *finis,* as the goal aimed at and the terminus finally reached. The con-

nection is more than purely verbal, since it is part of his eschatology that the justice of God's judgment consists in giving men
(in the long run of eternity) what they want. If they want God
and long to love they attain to God's love, which is heaven; if
their desires are proud and selfish they are abandoned to the
lord of pride and find themselves in hell. But of that more later.
The present discussion is on the end desired, or what man really
wants, and with that topic Book xix opens.

We all want to be happy; here as elsewhere Augustinian
ethics begins on this firm eudaemonistic basis. Where is this
happiness to be found? For his present purpose St. Augustine
finds an adequate answer in the popular eclectic philosophy of
Varro: the good life is to be found in the rounded development
of body and soul, the life of social harmony with one's family,
with one's fellow citizens, with mankind, and indeed with the
higher powers of the universe, whom Varro calls the gods and
St. Augustine is willing to call angels. As between action and
contemplation he decides in favor of neither in isolation, but of
the mixed life which gives due place to both.[32]

How beautiful is this picture of human happiness; and how
different from life as we know it. St. Augustine points out how
at every point what is attainable here and now falls short of
this ideal. Our bodies and minds are threatened by disease; if we
escape this ourselves we are distressed to see it in others — and
don't let the Stoics persuade you that these are not real evils.
Furthermore, the life of society, essential to happiness, surrounds
us with snares and pitfalls; our friends and relatives may deceive
us — at best they bring us worries as well as joys. And in larger
areas of the social order we find evil integrated into its very
structure. St. Augustine takes a startling example from the customs of his own time. The judge is compelled by duty to take
his place on the bench, but in order to decide criminal cases he
must employ torture, which is more likely to punish the innocent
defendant (not to mention witnesses) than to discover the guilty.[33]
The modern reader is somewhat startled to find the saint accepting this institution as unavoidable, and is relieved to be
assured by writers on the subject that St. Augustine did in fact

use his influence on occasion toward mitigating the horrors of the law of his time.[34] But no judicial system has entirely escaped the kind of situation that he contemplates here. Certainly it would not be hard to find in modern life illustrations of the basic principle that we may have to take part in the working of necessary institutions in spite of the evils connected with their administration.

From local affairs St. Augustine passes to reflect on international divisions, of which the distinction of languages is the external sign. The latter had been much reduced by the spread of the imperial tongue, but at the cost of much war and bloodshed. If there are no foreign wars, there are civil conflicts. By one or the other 'the human race is thrown into distress, either when fighting in the hope of some repose, or fearing that conflicts may again break out' — a description as applicable to 1954 as to 420. The wise man will fight only justified wars. This, I believe, is always the meaning of *justa bella*, from St. Augustine to the Thirty-nine Articles. Yet granting that this rule can be followed (and even St. Augustine is not too confident), the wise man is doubly distressed, by the war itself and by the wickedness that made it justifiable.

When our thoughts pass on from earth to heaven, we reflect that at least the friendship of angels is secure. But those who present themselves as gods or angels may in fact be evil *daimones* taking advantage of our noblest moments. For St. Augustine this principle accounts for the indecencies connected with pagan worship. Might we not suggest that it helps explain also, in our own age, the perversion of love and patriotism, for instance? We have seen youth by the millions immolating themselves for causes worthless or worse. In a more than merely figurative sense demons have been masquerading as angels. As a contemporary writer has noted, the struggle that St. Augustine described is still with us in various forms.

If we read for the pagan gods of the fifth century the gadget gods of the twentieth, the slogan gods, the scientific gods and the thousand superstitions of rationalism, the struggle is not foreign to us: only the terms in which it is couched.[35]

But to summarize: in comparison with the perfect harmony that we can conceive, this life is one of unhappiness. We are said to be happy here 'when we possess such peace as can be possessed in the good life; but this happiness, compared with that which we call final, may rather be considered misery.' [36] Such a judgment springs not from a depreciation of the goods of this mortal life but rather from a profound and sensitive appreciation of them. We must sometimes contrast the humanist and the ascetic in St. Augustine, but in this connection one grows out of the other. Heaven is longed for not because the apparent goods of earth are bad but because they are not good enough. God has given us a desire for perfect happiness and in this world the experience of a happiness that is imperfect. While pursuing the good life here (whether it take the form of enjoying before God the blessings of the temporal order or of holding firm to the course of duty amid misfortune, either of which is likely to happen) we naturally long for its consummation in the land of eternal peace.

Peace is for St. Augustine much more than the absence of hostilities. It is the state of harmony that makes possible the full functioning of any creature or of any society. In fact — and here, as in speaking of happiness, St. Augustine pushes his thought to its logical extreme — the worst of men can pursue his destructive course only for the sake of some kind of peace, even though it be the perverted peace of domination. For an example St. Augustine cites Cacus, a murderous giant in the *Aeneid,* who still desired peaceful possession of his cave. An ultimate example is the devil, whose own nature is not evil, but only his perversity. But let us turn to the general statement:

So the peace of the body is an ordered harmony of its parts. The peace of the irrational soul is an ordered satisfaction of its desires; the peace of the rational soul is an ordered agreement of thought and action. The peace of body and soul is the ordered life and health of the living being. The peace of mortal man and God is an ordered obedience in faith under the eternal law. The peace of men is ordered harmony; the peace of a household is an ordered harmony of those who dwell together, in commanding and obeying; the peace of a commonwealth is a similar ordered harmony of its citizens. The peace of the heavenly city is a most ordered and most harmonious fellowship in enjoying God and one another in God. The peace of all things is the tranquillity of order.[37]

In this statement we have reached the central proposition of Book XIX, and of Augustinian social theory.

The principle of ordered harmony, which finds its perfection and model in the mutual society of believers in God, is St. Augustine's form of the great problem of Plato's *Republic* — how to apply the simple rule of justice, giving 'to each his due.' Plato was obliged to construct an imaginary city to display justice in action, and was led to improvise a myth of immortality to affirm it. In the *City of God* faith in the Resurrection and in the actual existence of the heavenly commonwealth takes the place of these magnificent hypotheses, but the basic mold of thought is not dissimilar. Any detailed social theory, however, though it may be Augustinian, cannot claim to be St. Augustine's. His application of his social principles was critical rather than constructive, and though the applications are brilliant they are not systematic. The conditions of the early fifth century did not stimulate St. Augustine or anyone else to undertake a work of social construction. Even so, some detailed applications of the principle of harmony in the common life appear in St. Augustine's directions for monastic communities, which are one of the sources of the classical Rule of St. Benedict a century later. If he had worked out his principles in more detail they would probably have lacked the stimulating quality that has made them influential in every subsequent age.

In Book XIX, however, several important applications are

indicated. The Christian family, St. Augustine believes, will exemplify the heavenly peace. He speaks with some conviction of the possibility of Christian families; never, in the same way, of larger units. On a large scale, the primary expression of the heavenly city and its peace on earth is the Church. Unlike the Empire, it welcomes the diversity of nations and languages, rejoicing that the variety of earthly customs is no hindrance to divine unity. The mark of its rulers is the will to serve, as shown by the etymology of the word *episkopos,* which refers to responsibility rather than to authority — 'he who loves to govern rather than to do good is no bishop.' But the earthly peace, though imperfect, is still necessary. The citizens of the heavenly city will therefore gladly co-operate in promoting it as long as they live in this land of their pilgrimage. Yet they must challenge the laws of the earthly city whenever these laws infringe on their own supreme loyalty to God. Since the worship of false gods is harmful to the worshipers, disloyalty to the earthly commonwealth when it commands idolatry is in fact a service to it, and so by no means breaks the unity of the two great commandments of love to God and man by which the life of the Christian is regulated.[38]

At this point a question of some importance comes up incidentally. Was the Roman state ever a true commonwealth, a *res publica?* Cicero had defined the latter in terms of a definition of the *populus* as a body of men united by justice and common interests. In this sense the title could not be given to the Romans because (to inquire no further than the first objection) they violated justice by not giving God his due. So St. Augustine offers another definition: 'A people is an assemblage of rational beings united by a common object of love.' By this definition not only the Romans but also the Greek cities and the Oriental empires could claim the status of peoples and *res publicae.*[39] St. Augustine has, surprisingly, been criticized for this distinction, as removing the element of justice from the definition of a state.[40] Yet he rather deserves credit for providing a basis for Christian criticism of the State by defining it objectively, and recognizing that between perfection and nonexistence (in this case between the ideal State which would deserve unreserved loyalty and the wholly corrupt one which would deserve none) there are many degrees. He at once exemplifies this principle by contrasting the early integrity of the Roman Republic with its later corruption — thus evidently recognizing that error in religion is not the only possible defect of a State.

Many Christian observers in recent years have confused their judgments of non-Christian states one way or another. To some the treatment of religion, especially of the organized church, has been almost the only consideration; while others have acted as if it were improper to criticize the anti-religious policy of a country which one believed to be promoting justice in secular affairs. Surely St. Augustine was on sounder Christian ground in remembering that piety toward God is a form of justice. Its absence is an unjust condition, but one may still raise the question of the presence or absence of justice in other respects. It is also to be noticed that St. Augustine defines the nature of a people in terms of a common love, that is, a common goal or ideal, rather than, for instance, a common origin. This seems to correspond to the facts: nationality is a spiritual conviction more than anything else. This approach is also a good example of an important element in St. Augustine's thought. For him love (perfect or imperfect, human or divine) is the essential quality of a spiritual being, and therefore occupies a central place in his deepest thoughts about the nature of human life.

V. History and Eschatology

St. Augustine's survey of the two cities has passed the present and now looks into the future. The last three books contain his eschatology. Though often neglected in modern study of the *De Civitate Dei,* this has had no small influence on the traditional thought of Western Christendom. We may note that the 'four last things' of pious meditation each receive a book in the *City of God.* Book XIII has dealt mainly with death, and the topics of the last three books are judgment, hell, and heaven respectively. Following older African commentators, St. Augustine does not interpret the thousand years when Satan is bound according to Revelation 20 as a future millennium, but as the present age. Between the Resurrection and the Judgment the Church Militant, which 'even now is the Kingdom of Christ and Kingdom of Heaven,' represents God on earth. The saints, living and departed, already reign with Christ, though not in the manner to be hoped for hereafter.[41] When the last day comes the wicked and the righteous will finally be separated, though some of the latter may still need to be purged by fire.[42]

For the impenitent, eternal punishment cannot be avoided. St. Augustine criticizes no fewer than six attempts to extend the prospect of ultimate salvation outside the circle of those to whom he was willing to assure it, that of righteous and orthodox baptized believers. All modern theologians offer more hope than this and so belong in some respect to those whom St. Augustine smilingly calls 'our kind-hearted brothers,' *misericordes nostri*,[43] though few follow Origen in being concerned about the ultimate salvation of the devil. Even the modern Christian, however, will surely agree with St. Augustine that right and wrong will never be confused, nor will the sinner ever attain salvation except by abandoning his sins and turning to God and man in love.

The pleasanter topic of heaven, the consummation of the City of God, is reserved for the final book. But first we are reminded that faith in the resurrection has spread through the world by divine power. It is confirmed today, writes St. Augustine, by the numerous miracles accomplished by the power of Christ, often through the prayers or with the aid of the relics of the martyrs. Of these he narrates a long series, mainly healings, a number connected with the relics of St. Stephen which he had recently had brought to Hippo.[44] When we are raised from the dead we shall no longer face the sorrows of this life, which St. Augustine enumerates at length, and our bliss will surpass its joys and beauties, which he enumerates in still greater detail. Above all we shall see the Lord in perfect freedom, felicity, and peace, lost forever in love and praise. What St. Augustine wrote in prose the medieval poets who wrote of heaven turned into verse, singing of the social joys which we long for in our earthly Sion and hope to attain in the heavenly Jerusalem:

> *And now we watch and struggle,*
> *And now we live in hope,*
> *And Sion in her anguish*
> *With Babylon must cope.*

> *But he whom now we trust in*
> *Shall then be seen and known,*
> *And they that know and see him*
> *Shall have him for their own.*[45]

So the pilgrimage of thought that began amid the debris of Rome ends at the gates of Paradise. In a few years St. Augustine would lie on his deathbed, with the penitential Psalms written on the walls of his sickroom, and the Vandals at the gates of the city. None of the vast legacy of writings which he left behind him were to be more influential than the *De Civitate Dei*. In part this is because it is one of his most varied works — 'this brilliant but uneven book,' as a modern monk has perhaps too candidly called it [46] — mingling some of the deepest topics of his thought with long sections of a quite practical or specific character. Its main theme continues to be of general interest. Not everyone, or even every Christian, is concerned with the definition of the divine nature, the doctrine of grace, or the problem of knowledge. But as citizens and churchmen we are all concerned with our life in Church and State, and legitimately interested in the background of these institutions. For centuries St. Augustine's work offered the best available information on these points, and the grand outline of his view still appeals to all for whom the Christian is a citizen of two worlds, earthly society and the Kingdom of God. Anyone who has read carefully Book XIX of the *City of God* cannot but pause when he hears a clergyman say, as many have been heard to do, 'Let us pray for the peace of the world.' Before we make the *pax terrena* an object of prayer, we shall want to consider its relation to the *pax Dei*.

Then we may hope and pray that we may bring into our earthly commonwealth as much of the peace of Jerusalem as God permits.

VI. Augustine's Ambiguities

In reading the *City of God* we are in contact with the scholarship and philosophy of St. Augustine, but even more with his practical convictions and his complex personality. The book is not to be separated from the man. In this connection there are two aspects of ambiguity, even perhaps of indecision, in the Augustine of the *City of God,* ambiguities that make this a greater and more comprehensive work than the neater work of a lesser man would have been. The first is that St. Augustine's analysis of human society is formally twofold, but often practically threefold. The Kingdom of God is opposed by the Kingdom of Satan, but not quite in the same way by the kingdoms of men. The Roman Empire, for all its defects, is not considered diabolical. St. Augustine contemplates the possibility of Christian Emperors, if not of a thoroughly Christian government; and one of his letters at least touches on the possibility of a Christian city which might be considered part of the City of God.[47] Only the categories of his contrasts are absolute. In contrast with perfect bliss earthly happiness is misery; in contrast with the Kingdom of Heaven the kingdoms of earth are wicked. Still, they are not hellish. I venture to think that St. Augustine would have done more justice to his own thought if he had formally described the State, like our earthly life generally, as a battleground of good and evil. The earthly representative of the Kingdom of God is the Church, that visible body of believers which is also the mystical fellowship of all the righteous. Some of those destined to be its citizens in eternity are not at the moment externally united with it; still the Catholic Church is the true home of all who love.[48] But the State, and human society generally, is not a similar representative of the lower powers. It is rather the corporate expression of natural humanity, wounded by the Fall yet still by nature a creature of God — capable of horrible perversity, yet also capable of much good. The thinkers and statesmen who have developed and applied the ideas of the *City of God* have modified St. Augustine's thought on this point. Apart from some stern words from Pope Gregory VII, few of those inspired by St. Augustine's social principles have spoken of civil authority and human society with the harshness that his categories seem to suggest. This world may be Babylon, but if so we are all in some sense Babylonians. And it seems not unfair to claim St. Augustine's authority for the search after various expressions of the principle of ordered harmony which he saw in the heavens, in the souls of the righteous, in the Catholic Church, and, although on a lower level, in the Roman Empire.

The second Augustinian ambiguity is one of personal attitude. Does St. Augustine in the last resort look on this world with a friendly eye, or is he anxious only to escape from it? I think it must be answered that both attitudes are equally present:

> In Augustine there were struggling two men, like Esau and Jacob in the womb of Rebecca. There was Augustine of Thagaste, of Madaura, of Carthage, of Rome, of Milan, the brilliant boy, the splendid and expansive youthful leader, 'skilled in all the wisdom of the Egyptians,' possessed of the antique culture, rhetorical, dialectic, Roman — the man of the world, the developed humanist with enough tincture of Platonism to gild the humanism; and there is the Augustine of the 'Confessions,' of the 'Sermons,' of the 'De Civitate,' the monk, the ascetic, the other-worldly preacher, the biblical expositor, the mortified priest.[49]

One predominated in his early life, the other in the priest and bishop, but both Augustines are represented in the *De Civitate*. Even when attacking the world or the philosophers he does so with a pure joy and a delightful skill in the arts of expression and argument. Even in the section on the last things there is the magnificent passage on the joys of life, though it be introduced to indicate how the joys of heaven must be beyond all description.[50] Somewhat earlier, when a number of the wonders of nature are mentioned for the somewhat macabre purpose of arguing that if these things exist eternal fire could exist too —

even there the pleasure of the description outruns the immediate purpose of the argument, and we forget for a while the sufferings of the damned as we listen to a series of striking stories like that of the magnet which Bishop Severus of Milevis was shown when dining with Bathanarius, former Count of Africa.[51] In other words, the *De Civitate Dei* is not only a book on history, theology, and ethics, three very important subjects. It is also the reflection of a great man's mind and practically a world in itself. And I think we can understand why Charlemagne enjoyed it.

FOR FURTHER READING

The best guides to the *City of God* are the small but masterly books of Joseph Rickaby (*St. Augustine's City of God, A View of the Contents*, London, 1925), and J. N. Figgis (*The Political Aspects of St. Augustine's 'City of God,'* London, 1921). The best edition is J. E. C. Welldon's (*S. Aurelii Augustini Episcopi Hipponensis De Civitate Dei*, 2 vols., London, 1924), with a useful introduction. A valuable essay by Ernest Barker is prefixed to the Everyman's Library edition of the seventeenth-century translation by John Healey (2 vols., London and New York, 1945), and one by E. Gilson to the version by D. B. Zema and G. G. Walsh (*Fathers of the Church*, vols. VIII, XIV, and XXIV, New York, 1950–54). These are the best translations; that by Marcus Dods and others in the *Nicene and Post-Nicene Fathers* (series I, vol. II, Buffalo, 1887), several times reprinted, is dependable but pedestrian. The non-Latinist will do well to consult more than one version; and the best approach to the study of the *City of God* is to read Books I, X, and XIX of the work itself.

NOTES

1. Einhard, *Vita Caroli*, 24.
2. H. A. Taine, *The Revolution,* Book II (New York, 1878), p. 176.
3. Preface to *Commentary on Ezechiel*, Book I.
4. XXII. 30 (references are to the *De Civitate Dei* unless otherwise stated; translations mine).
5. I. 1–7.
6. I. 8–33.
7. I. 1 and 34.
8. V. 1–10.
9. IV. 4–6, 14–15.
10. A. Keller, *Christian Europe Today* (New York, 1942), p. 203.
11. IV. 33.

12. V. 12–18; *Aeneid* VI. 853.
13. Matthew 6:2; *Enarrationes in Psalmos*, on Psalm 118:2.
14. Joseph Rickaby, S.J., *St. Augustine's City of God* (London, 1925), p. 23.
15. V. 23–6.
16. VIII. 5.
17. VIII. 27.
18. IX. 17.
19. X. 6; cf. 19–20.
20. X. 29.
21. XI. 1–2.
22. F. C. Burkitt, *The Religion of the Manichees* (Cambridge, 1925), pp. 102–4.
23. XI. 33.
24. Cf. such speculations in our own time as those of N. P. Williams, *The Doctrines of the Fall and Original Sin* (London, 1932).
25. XII. 8.
26. XII. 17–22; XIII. 21.
27. XIV. 5–7.
28. XIV. 28.
29. XV. 10–14.
30. XVIII. 47.
31. XVIII. 54.
32. XIX. 3.
33. XIX. 4–6; cf. the rather similar discussion of the place of the executioner in the social order, *De Ordine*, II. 12.
34. Cf. G. Combes, *La Doctrine politique de Saint Augustin* (Paris, 1927), pp. 192–5; and *Epistles*, 133.
35. XIX. 7–9; C. V. Wedgwood, 'The City of God,' *Velvet Studies* (London, 1946), pp. 74–9.
36. XIX. 10.
37. XIX. 12–13; *Aeneid* VIII. 175–279.
38. XIX. 14–19; note comparison of Christians in the world to the Jews in Babylon, praying for the peace of the land of their exile, XIX. 26.
39. XIX. 21, 24.
40. A. J. Carlyle, *A History of Mediaeval Political Thought in the West*, I (Edinburgh, 1903), pp. 164–9; 'St. Augustine and the City of God' in F. J. C. Hearnshaw, ed., *The Social and Political Ideas of Some Great Mediaeval Thinkers* (London, 1923), pp. 49–51.
41. XX. 9.
42. XX. 25; cf. XXI. 26.
43. XXI. 17.
44. XXII. 7–9.

45. From Bernard of Cluny, *De Contemptu Mundi*, tr. J. M. Neale —
the source of several hymns, of which the best known is 'Jerusalem
the Golden' (cf. *The Hymnal 1940 Companion*, New York, 1949,
nos. 595–8).

46. Gregory Dix, *The Shape of the Liturgy* (London, 1945), p. 386.

47. *Epistles,* 91; and cf. 138, where he speaks of what a Christian Empire
might be.

48. Cf. passages on the Church referred to above; and note in I. 34, the
case of the just who are still outside the visible Church; and in
De vera religione, VI. 10–11, the still more delicate case of those who
have been unjustly expelled from it but still belong to it in reality;
St. Augustine does not contemplate the possibility of any citizens
of the heavenly city who are not at some time members of the
visible church.

49. J. N. Figgis, *The Political Aspects of St. Augustine's City of God*
(London, 1921), p. 114.

50. XXII. 24.

51. XXI. 4.

Part Three

SPECIAL ASPECTS OF

ST. AUGUSTINE'S THOUGHT

FAITH AND REASON

Robert E. Cushman

I. The Priority of Faith

CHRISTIANITY boldly asserted that the eternal Logos had been manifested in the personal history of Jesus called Christ. Once this claim began to receive wide acceptance, the older ways of philosophizing characteristic of the classical ages were shaken. On the one hand, Christians affirmed positively that God had drawn nigh, disclosing himself in history to those who believed. On the other hand, they held that, apart from reliance upon this divine disclosure, the efforts of scientific reason to apprehend God were pitifully inadequate and perverse.

From the beginning St. Paul had confronted the 'wisdom of the world' with the 'foolishness of the preaching.' He did not scruple to declare openly the contradiction — asserting, nevertheless, that 'the foolishness of God is wiser than men.' It remained for Augustine to make clear exactly how this was so and why. He declared that 'faith precedes reason' because *nisi credideritis, non intelligetis,* unless you believe, you will not understand.[1] He thus opposed Tertullian's view that faith recommends itself in proportion to its absurdity. The priority of *fides,* faith, he regarded as eminently reasonable. In showing how this was so, Augustine laid a new and definitive foundation for Christian philosophy.

For Augustine the Incarnation gave meaning to history, which it could not possess for those classical thinkers to whom history was, along with nature, the realm of the insubstantial and the changing. But the doctrine of the God-man signified henceforth that ultimate reality could be apprehended rightly only through a particular history in time, namely, Jesus Christ. Augustine perceived the offense of this view to the classical mind. Even the Platonists, whose point of view came nearest to that of Christianity in the opinion of Augustine, could make nothing of the Incarnation.[2] Augustine approved much of what was contained in their books; 'But that the Word was made flesh and dwelt among us,' he observed, 'did I not read there.' [3] Yet this which, together with the Cross of wood, was the rock of offense and the stone of stumbling to the philosophic mind, Augustine did not waver in regarding as the very core of Catholic Christianity.

It was because Augustine, with singular clarity of mind, located this cleft of conviction and disparity of standpoint between Christian and classical approaches to knowledge of reality that he in particular was forced to make some settlement. What was a burning personal problem for Augustine was at the same time a prime intellectual problem of the Christian religion. The time was overdue, if Christianity was to be responsibly related to culture, for some elucidation from the Christian side of the antagonism between the standpoint of Christian faith on the one hand and autonomous reason on the other. Here was a contest whether faith or reason provided the most illuminating interpretation of the totality of human experience. The contest was the same between history and metaphysics, nature and grace, and the particular as opposed to the universal.

Augustine unflinchingly rejected any accommodation of the faith-standpoint to that of reason and culture. In his apologetic he undertook to exhibit the faith-factor in all knowledge. His apologetic also recommended the particular suitability of sub-mission to Christ, the historical particular, as the indispensable corrective of a reason disabled by sinful pride. We are privileged to believe that the greatness of the Augustinian solution in no small part depends on the fact that it did not repudiate reason, philosophy, nature, or the universal while, nevertheless, it pre-served to faith, history, grace, and the particular a certain pri-macy. Augustine's undeviating conviction was that *fides* is the gateway to understanding — the way to the Kingdom which none enters except as a little child. This, according to Augustine, is the Gospel wisdom, *sapientia,* which must replace the proud sufficiency of classical knowledge or *scientia.*[4] Faith is the lowly door by which the 'heart,' bowing to enter, is cleansed in order that at length the whole mind may apprehend the universal abiding Truth — may see God. The faithful shall at last see God by the instrument of reason; but reason cannot attain the vision of God uncorrected and unguided by faith. 'For con-templation is the recompense of faith, for which recompense our hearts are purified by faith.'[5]

This general point of view is not a pious opinion or an apology for Augustine's own tardy but eventual flight into Catholic Christianity. It is an expression in keeping with the principle most basic to his revolutionary conception of the knowledge process. The principle is the foundation stone of Augustinian theology. It is responsible for the first full-fledged Christian philosophy. Although it has periodically been influential, it has also frequently been lost to the sight of Christian philosophers; and, beginning with the ascendancy of Aristotelianism in the thirteenth century, was too largely obscured.

The principle may be stated simply. It is the doctrine of the primacy of the will in all knowledge. What is known cannot be divorced from what is loved. At the very minimum, all cognition is directly dependent on interest, and nothing is fully known to which the consent of the will has not been given. Yet there may be awareness of reality without completed cognition of that reality. The completion of cognition lies with affection. Thus full cognition is *re-cognition.* The possibility of so-called 'objectivity' in knowledge is given in the fact that there may be *cognitio* without *agnitio*, acknowledgment. This is possible with respect to God. That is to say, God may be known while not being acknowledged. This is actually the center and depth of the plight of man. Therefore the issue of man's destiny lies with the will. Faith is what moves the will, or, better, it is a certain movement of the will.

It is in this manner that faith serves reason. It does not supplant it. Harnack's opinion that 'Augustine was never clear about the relation of faith and knowledge' and that 'he handed over this problem to the future' [6] clearly indicates Harnack's failure to understand the essentials of the Augustinian epistemology. Augustine held that in knowledge the cognitive faculty (*ratio*) 'takes in,' according to its power, reality both eternal and temporal, but that being primarily passive or neutral it is directed to 'recognize' what it *does* recognize in virtue of the will or dominant affection of the mind. Therefore, what is not effectually known is precisely what is not adequately loved. Man knows God not knowing that he knows God. The double knowledge, which is re-cognition or acknowledgment, is at the mercy of the will. In Augustine it is the will, hardly the reason, which is corrupt; and faith is the means of cleansing the will.

II. The Powers of Reason

In accordance with his conviction that God is altogether good and the author only of good, Plato sought to formulate a rational theology, to moralize the inherited Greek religious world view. This involved the extrusion of the debased but more concrete mythological and historical elements in favor of the universal and rational.[7] Augustine clearly understood the preference of the philosophers for 'natural theology' and their conviction of its superior truth-value to that of either 'civil' or 'mythological' theology.[8] He concurred with the estimate; but this only intensified his problem. He was obliged to relate the particular saving history in Jesus Christ to a manner of approaching God which, relying on mere reason, had eschewed all dependence on history.

Furthermore, while Augustine had no doubt that reason availed for apprehension of God's existence or that natural theology afforded knowledge, he was nevertheless convinced that, unguided by faith, it did equally afford mis-knowledge. He was not so much troubled that the ancient world doubted. It believed too much — a menagerie of error. Even the Platonists did not rise above polytheism to monolatry,[9] while so distinguished a philosopher as Porphyry toyed with theurgy and demonolatry [10]; and everywhere men looked to 'curious and illicit arts' or to astrology rather than to the divine grace.[11] Perversely, men preferred the mediatorship of demons to that of Christ. Accordingly, Augustine declared in *The City of God* that he had not undertaken to refute 'those who either deny that there is any divine power, or contend that it does not interfere with human affairs, but those who prefer their own god to our God.' [12]

Withal, Augustine accepted with thanks what he regarded as the overwhelming weight of the Platonic theistic tradition founded upon reason. 'It is evident,' he said, 'that none come nearer to us than the Platonists.' [13] Their 'gold and silver was dug out of the mines of God's providence which are everywhere scattered abroad.' Such truth as the Platonists possess Christians ought to take away and 'devote to their proper use in the preaching of the gospel.' [14] Of the Platonists, Plato himself is to be preferred 'to all the other philosophers of the gentiles'; for he entertained 'such an idea of God as to admit that in Him are to be found the cause of existence, the ultimate reason for the understanding, and the end in reference to which the whole life is to be regulated.' [15] While admittedly this tripartite division of the conception of God does not expressly offer the doctrine of a trinity, yet Augustine allows that it does suggest the Christian Trinity. For Plato discerned 'that God alone could be the author of nature, the bestower of intelligence, and the kindler of love by which life becomes good and blessed.' [16] Augustine regarded this as defining essentially the several works of the Persons of the Trinity.

Augustine reads Plato as teaching that the 'supreme God visits the mind of the wise with an intelligible and ineffable presence.' [17] He agrees that the 'higher light, by which the human mind is enlightened, is God' — God the Son.[18] This is Christ who already was in the world before He was sent.[19] The Platonists, says Augustine in *The Confessions*, teach that in the beginning was the Word and the Word was God, and that it is the Word which 'lighteth every man coming into the world,' by participation in which men are made wise.[20] Among the Platonists, therefore, reason approaches to the threshold of the Christian faith, yet does not enter in. It refuses to recognize 'the grace of God in Jesus Christ our Lord, and that very incarnation of His.' [21] It accepts the universal but not the universal in the particular — the discarnate not the Incarnate Word.

Notwithstanding, Augustine retains a high estimate of *ratio naturalis,* natural reason, for this reason is never fully 'natural' or to be taken in isolation from the illuminating activity of God. Even reason wholly occupied with creatures and directed away from the Creator by the power of the will is yet empowered by divine illumination to apprehend the creatures which enthrall its interest. Reason in man is pre-eminently to be esteemed.[22] Reason is that in which our nature as man is fulfilled.[23] It is what constitutes man an image of God and thereby capable of being partaker of the Divine Nature.[24] By it God has left a witness to Himself among the gentiles. For even in man's fallen condition, his reason is exalted by the divine *informing,* so that God is the light by which are known whatsoever things are known, temporal or eternal.[25] The Platonists are right: 'the light of our understanding, by which all things are learned by us, they have affirmed to be that self-same God by whom all things were made.' [26]

We may illustrate this general conception of knowledge by observing how Augustine employs it in the areas of science, aesthetics, and moral values. As the sun is the condition of sensible intuition, so God, the inward 'Illuminator,' is the cause of 'all the certainties of the sciences.' [27] They presuppose the *informing* of our minds by the Truth apprehended *a priori*. The invariability of the propositions of the sciences cannot derive from the variability of sensuous experience. Mathematical propositions are valid because they are derived *a priori,* not *a posteriori.*[28] Man's memory contains 'the reasons and innumerable laws of numbers and dimensions,' none of which has been imprinted on the memory by any sense of the body.[29] Moreover, the foundational categories of all science, *esse, quid, quale* 'we suck [*haurimus*] not in any images by our senses, but perceive them within by themselves.' They were, says Augustine, 'in my heart even before I learned them.' [30] Inasmuch as the *forms* constitute things *what* they are, and yet are found only imperfectly in things, the Platonists are correct that their apprehension cannot be from experience; rather, their apprehension is the precondition of experience.[31] It is because these *intelligibili* are 'at hand to the glance of the mind' that science is possible:

> It is part of the higher reason to judge of these corporeal things according to incorporeal and eternal reasons; which unless they were above the human mind, would certainly not be unchangeable; and, yet, unless something of our own were subjoined to them, we should not be able to employ them as our measure by which to judge corporeal things. But we judge of corporeal things from the rule of dimensions and figures, which the mind knows to remain unchangeably.[32]

Even physical knowledge, then, is available only by virtue of the omnipresence of the eternal Word. This is in a manner the prevenience of divine grace.[33] Yet there is a vast gulf between being enlightened by God and acknowledging the light by which we are enlightened. Both nature and the knowing mind are *informed* by God. Yet the knowledge of nature does not necessarily disclose but may in fact obscure God. It is true that St. Paul taught that the gentiles have a 'natural' knowledge of God in holding 'that what is known of God he manifested to them when His invisible things were seen by them, being understood by those things which have been made.' [34] But Augustine does not interpret St. Paul as teaching that a knowledge of God may be had by a direct inspection of the outward world. Rather, he understands St. Paul to mean that reflection upon nature has theological value only for those 'who compare that voice received from without by the senses, with Truth which is within.' [35] Only because God, the eternal Word, is present within can His handiwork be discovered in nature without. The eye of the soul is blind which goes not within but dwells 'out of doors' while searching for God.[36]

As the Divine visitation is the precondition of scientific knowledge, it is also the unchanging ground of all judgments of value. Aesthetic judgment upon corporeal beauty would be impossible 'had there not existed in the mind itself a superior form of these things, without bulk, without noise of voice, without space and time.' [37] In the aesthetic realm Augustine observed that he made judgments of worth in distinction from judgments of fact. He declared that some things *ought to be* irrespective of time or limiting conditions. He sought for a timeless principle as the sufficient ground for such value judgments. He could find no sufficient ground except the eternal and unchangeable truth and beauty which is above the mind and is God. Augustine therefore concluded that the mind necessarily has conversance with God.[38] With reference to moral worth, God likewise *informs* our minds with a rule of judgment which 'rests firmly upon the utterly indestructible rules of its own right; and if it is covered as it were by cloudiness or corporeal images, yet it is not wrapt up and confounded in them.' [39] This is a Word within us which does not depart from us when we are born.[40] By the discarnate Word we know what goodness or righteousness is; and, by means of it *a priori,* we love and approve a particular righteous man *a posteriori.*[41]

To summarize: God abides in the reason of man or in that more comprehensive vessel, his heart. God is, so to speak, used by many but known or recognized by none except those who go within to themselves. Except a man turn inward to God within, he will not discover the Author of the world by observing the things that are without. He sees without 'that they are, and within that they are good.' [42] Whether by *ratio* or by *fides,* it is the Son of God, either as the eternal Word or as the Incarnate Word, who enlightens and gives understanding of the Father.

The Word made flesh is the same eternal Word that enlightens the reason of the gentiles and every man coming into the world. He comes unto His own. He comes whither He already was, but His own [the philosophers] receive Him not.

III. Reason in Need of Faith

Great, then, are the powers of the natural reason as illuminated by the discarnate Son, the eternal Word of God. To be sure, since there is a continuous divine illumination of the mind, the *ratio* is not in Augustine's thought ever 'unaided' in its learning of God, as it can be in the thought of Thomas Aquinas. But, now, given a reason divinely sustained and empowered, what need is there of faith? Or, again, if the Platonists acknowledge all that Augustine has attributed to them concerning reason,[43] what need is there to force upon them what he calls 'the right rule of faith,' namely, that 'we begin in faith, and are made perfect in sight'? [44]

The answer is that in spite of all he has said to exalt the role of reason, Augustine's pervasive insistence is that Jesus Christ, the eternal Word *incognito,* disguised in the flesh, is the *principium* or the beginning point of knowledge.[45] Along with the Platonists, Augustine taught, to be sure, a certain primacy of *ratio.* We comprehend something of this primacy in Augustine's claim that the divine *informing* by the eternal Word is the precondition of all *scientia.* But how shall we understand this insistence upon a deeper wisdom: that knowledge must necessarily begin with faith and its object — the historical and particular, the Word made flesh?

Clearly, Augustine had not shown that the 'natural' or 'fallen' man is entirely devoid of grace: though he has turned himself from the light, the light still surrounds him.[46] Blindness is never complete while a man has life.[47] Some residuum, some trace of awareness of God, must remain in man though man recognize it not. This is essential for the renewal of knowledge.[48] God cannot be recollected if absolutely forgotten: 'If I now find thee not in my memory, then am I unmindful of thee; and how shall I find thee, if I do not remember thee?' [49]

295

In other words, the *imago Dei* may be obscured or defaced, but it never ceases to be: the defacing 'does not extend to taking away its being an image.'[50] Quite apart from the grace which is in Christ there is a vestigial love of the Truth, for there is a *modicum lumen* not altogether extinguished, and by it men have a desire after the Truth which is God.[51]

But reasons are to be found for Augustine's insistence against the rationalist that reason must begin with the Mediator and be 'nourished by faith in the temporal history.'[52] We are not glibly to suppose that this is required simply as an antidote to a lingering skepticism of Augustine's which must needs lean upon authority. It is true that, in the Scriptures and the Catholic faith, Augustine found a haven of calm after a stormy voyage in quest of certainty.[53] But the appeal to the primacy of faith is not to be identified simply and immediately with an appeal to authority. The fact is that the authoritativeness of both Church and Scripture wait upon the consent of a converted heart and will. The latter is faith and is the work of the Mediator.

If we are to understand Augustine's insistence upon the priority of faith, we must not assume that he was urging upon the pagan reason a sort of blind acquiescence to authority as the condition of understanding. Of course it is to be admitted that for Augustine, the churchman and apologist, the Scriptures offered infallible truth. He regarded Scripture as possessing 'the highest, even the heavenly, pinnacle of authority.'[54] And, in the debates with the Manicheans, Augustine was evidently driven by the logic of circumstances to espouse a view elicited by the exigencies of apologetic: 'I should not believe the Gospel except as moved by the authority of the Catholic Church.'[55] The battle of wits with heretics, if not with pagans, permitted no appeal against the misappropriation of Scripture except that lodged in the continuity of succession and the ubiquity of Catholic tradition.

It must, however, be affirmed that this utterance, which is solitary and conditioned by the immediate issues of the debate, cannot be regarded as exhibiting either the ground or the profound nature of *fides* in Augustine's thought. Augustine's own experience stood surety for the conviction that, although faith cannot do without authority, authority is impotent unless preceded by a redirection of the will through the operation of Grace.

The function of authority is not primarily that of providing an impregnable ground of certainty for the doubting intellect. Nor is it that of propounding a datum which, because *ex hypothesi* it is unamenable to comprehension, must therefore command uncomprehending acquiescence of the mind. It is not that I must believe because reason is inherently incompetent. It is rather that my reason is incompetent in virtue of the perversion of my will, so that I cannot understand until my pride and sinful will to independence is submissive to the Mediator — the eternal Word in the form of the Servant. The Word is, by historical circumstance, necessarily afforded me in a continuous tradition. This is the Church and the Scriptures in the keeping of the Church. The doctrine of the Church is what I believe. But I believe the Church because the grace of God in the Mediator has brought my will low even unto Christ's lowliness. Thus the Scriptures will not be authoritative to the uncleansed will.[56] Likewise, subjectively considered, the Church can be authority only to the heart that has become thankful rather than unthankful, that is, to the heart that has faith.[57]

No one knew better than Augustine, when not on polemical and apologetical business, that neither antiquity, nor continuity of apostolic succession, nor ubiquity[58] was of itself able to confirm the minds of men in the truth of Catholic Christianity. First of all men's minds had to be brought to self-knowledge and contrition. Thus, in his concluding word to Faustus, Augustine admonishes: 'If you ask for demonstration, consider first *what you are*, how unfit for comprehending the nature of your own soul, not to speak of God.'[59] The fact is that in the contest with heretics it became patent to Augustine — as it has become evident in history — that the appeal to either Scripture or Church as authority is convincing only to the warmed hearts of the faithful. As the perorations of Augustine's polemics against Donatist, Manichean, or Pelagian show, his final resort is a warning against perversity in the heart of the unbeliever and a call to repentance. Error, as well as truth, lodges with the state of the will. Augustine was resigned to the conviction that the mind is inclined toward the truth only by 'the first elements of faith,' which works *by love* — a love evoked only by Christ the Mediator.[60]

It comes to this, therefore: I do not believe *on authority*. Rather I have an authority in the Church because, through Grace, my will has been made submissive to what the Church proffers. In addition (*versus* heretics) I cannot believe rightly apart from authority. This, then, is the dialectical truth about faith and authority. In the order of living experience, faith makes authority. In the order of historical actuality, the Church constitutes the persisting historical continuum mediating faith.

The indispensability of tradition was clear, moreover, to Augustine by virtue of his conception of the source of knowledge. Respecting this matter he declared that reason 'must have its starting-point either in the bodily sense or in the intuitions of the mind.' [61] Faith, however, has to do with the Incarnation, which is an event in time but in a time now vanished. As a past historical reality, it is, as Augustine designates it, a datum 'adventitious' to the mind. That is, it does not qualify either as an object for the senses or for the 'intuitions of the mind.' In respect to the latter, the Incarnation is, therefore, not a universal truth accessible to rational reflection or deduction. In respect to sensible experience, nothing is clearer than that the temporal history of the Mediator is forever withdrawn from possible present inspection. Therefore the events done in time on our behalf *can only be transmitted to us* and offered as redemptive facts by Church and Scripture embodying a continuous historical tradition grounded in the testimony of witnesses. Christianity is indefeasibly grounded in a 'particular,' not in a 'universal.' While, therefore, the grace which is in Christ is operative so as to be independent of time, yet the specific saving character of Grace can be apprehended only in association with the original saving transaction in time. And this requires the maintenance of a historical mediation in the midst of temporality.

The indispensability of authority, nevertheless, does not avail to clarify the deeper meaning of the primacy of faith in the epistemology of Augustine. Faith must precede *ratio,* not because reason is intrinsically incompetent but because reason, in a man whose will has not submitted to the Grace of the Mediator, is an untrustworthy reason.

The primacy of faith in the process of knowledge rests on Augustine's conviction that there is a dependency of reason and knowledge upon the character of the will, whereas every actual will is corrupted. It is an extension of the Socratic insight which Augustine clearly noted and openly stated: that God can and will be known only by a purified mind. Socrates

was unwilling that minds defiled by earthly desires should essay to raise themselves upward to divine things. For he saw that the causes of things were sought for by them, — which causes he believed to be ultimately reducible to nothing else than the will of the one true and supreme God, — *and on this account they could only be comprehended by a purified mind;* and therefore that all diligence ought to be given to the purification of the life by good morals, in order that the mind, delivered from the depressing weight of lusts, might raise itself upward by its native vigor to eternal things, and might, with purified understanding, contemplate that nature which is incorporeal and unchangeable light.[62]

With acuteness Augustine rightly construed the Socratic point of view that right knowledge is dependent upon right love rather than right love dependent upon right knowledge. Therefore faith, which was first of all thankfulness, was the token of an unfeigning mind, a mind shorn of *superbia,* pride.[63] This accorded with the word of Scripture, urged constantly by Augustine: 'Blessed are the pure in heart, for they shall see God.' [64]

Will you be able to lift up your heart unto God? Must it not first be healed, in order that thou mayest see? Do you not show your pride, when you say, First let me see, and then I will be healed? [65]

Inescapable it is, then, that 'faith is in some way the starting point of knowledge.' [66] The philosophic search even for God partakes of pride — a puffed-up and vain science.[67] Thus 'if you believe not, you will not understand.' Wherefore it behooves all men.

> to return and begin from faith in due order: perceiving at length how healthful a medicine has been provided for the faithful in the holy church, whereby a heedful piety, healing the feebleness of the mind, may render it able to perceive the unchangeable truth, and hinder it from falling headlong through disorderly rashness, into pestilent and false opinion.[68]

To be sure this is a generalization from Augustine's own experience; for he confesses 'by believing might I have been cured, so that the eyesight of my soul being cleared, might some way or other have been directed toward thy truth . . . which could no ways be healed but by believing.' [69] Therefore, everywhere Augustine's admonition is heard: we begin in faith and are made perfect in sight. Though, with Anselm of Canterbury, faith has acquired somewhat different denotations, the order is the same, *credo ut intelligam,* I believe in order to understand. It is, in Augustine's view, not that we begin with faith *and* go on to understanding. We begin in faith *in order* to go on to understanding. To obscure this distinction is to pass over the working principle of the Augustinian epistemology, for it is to ignore the determinative function of the will in knowledge. According to this conception, then, the Incarnate Christ, who moves the will, becomes the true first *principium* of knowledge, and the adequate starting point for the interpretation of the totality of human experience.[70]

IV. The Function of the Will in Knowledge

The rational approach to God dispenses with the step of faith. Porphyry, that great light among the Platonists, scorns to accept 'the flesh of the mediator.' The Manicheans deride Christian credulity which begins with faith.[71] Augustine's reply to the detractors is that they wish to know God without acknowledging God, to have a God without trusting God. But there is no having or knowing God without having Him in the will. Men want God in the mind, not in the heart, for if God is had merely in the mind He is held tentatively, and the will is free to be its own master.

Augustine perceived in the merely rational approach to God an internal contradiction: it cannot reach God because it does not want to have God. It withholds commitment until it has sight; but it cannot achieve sight until it yields commitment. The rational approach to God does not perceive that it founders upon the original sinfulness of the human heart. The Platonists do not perceive that man does not know God because he does not love God. These best of philosophers do not comprehend the plight of man.[72]

Augustine is not content with the easy diagnosis that a corruptible body 'presseth down the soul' in the pursuit of divine knowledge.[73] It does so in virtue of a deeper disease, namely, that while God continually visits the mind of man with His light, men turn their backs to the light, preferring to pursue their own will among the creatures. Nor can we pass this off by holding that the mind is directed with greater ease toward things temporal. Augustine admits that we 'handle things visible more easily . . . than things intelligible,' and that this becomes habitual.[74] But the cause is found not in defective talent but in a certain ingratitude born of pride. Out of love of dominion, men employ the divine light for *scientia* or science whereby to exploit the creatures, rather than return thanks to the Light.[75]

Similarly it may be said of the philosophers that 'knowing God, they glorified Him not as God; neither were thankful, but became vain in their imaginations . . . Professing themselves wise, they became fools, and changed the glory of the incorruptible God into the likeness of corruptible men.'[76] Even in the case of the Platonists Augustine believed this indictment was warranted, for they did not avoid idolatry but paid divine honors to many gods.[77] Nor was this idolatry attributable to anything else, in Augustine's opinion, than to awareness of God which failed to pass over into submission or commitment to God. The cause of this insubordination St. Paul had again rightly diagnosed: they 'held down' or distorted the truth out of unrighteousness or perverted wills.[78] In place of submission to the inward Illuminator, the philosophers turn outward to the order of nature in an ostensible quest for God. It is a vain pursuit; and Augustine has a shrewd reply to the question why men go forth 'and run to the heights of the heavens and the lowest parts of the earth, seeking Him who is within, if they wish to be with Him?'[79] The answer is widely explored in the *Confessions*. It is because we will, but do not fully will, to be with God. Our dominant preference is to be with ourselves.[80] Therefore we go abroad among the creatures to use them while pretending to seek God through them. In the case of God, as in the instance of all other cognition, full knowledge waits upon desire or love. It is appetition, love, or will which turns diffused awareness into true cognition. The crucial words of Augustine are these: 'the bringing forth of the mind is preceded by some desire, by which through seeking and finding what we wish to know, the offspring, *viz.*, knowledge, itself is born.'[81]

In this manner Augustine founds a Christian theory of knowledge in opposition to Aristotelian intellectualism, in which Being has primacy over the Good and the 'theoretical' has primacy over 'the practical mind.'[82] For while it is true, as Aristotle says, that appetite or desire (ὄρεξις) will be found in each of the parts of the Soul including the mind — in the reasoning faculty as purpose or wish — yet this desire is always there as a consequent and in no sense as either the effectual or even subsidiary determinant of knowledge.[83] For Aristotle this is as it ought to be; for the ideal of objectivity is served if all preferences regarding good or evil do not in the least direct but rather are derived from antecedent cognition of Being. Thus all desire or appetition follows upon sensation, opinion, or thought.[84] Aristotle safeguards 'pure truth' by rendering its acquisition independent of 'practical considerations.'

This is the ground of the subordination of the practical to the theoretical reason in Aristotle and generally in Western thought.

It makes room for the idea of pure 'objective' knowledge and the ideal of knowledge as pure contemplation of Being. For it is Aristotle's view that 'the speculative mind thinks nothing practical [axiological] and does not comment on what is to be avoided or pursued.' [85] It offers objects to the practical mind (ὁ πρακτικὸς νοῦς) which, inspired by appetency, calculates 'with an end in view.' [86]

The will is in all cases subservient to the intellect — the practical to the theoretical reason. Here is the triumph of the intellectual value — of the true over the good, of Being over value. In contrast, Augustine held that the noetic function of *nous* or reason is dependent for its direction and operation on the practical or valuative reason. The theoretical reason as well as the sensible nature has its predisposing affections.[87] Thus Augustine rendered explicit the integral association of the practical and theoretical functions that was implicit in Plato's *Symposium* and *Phaedrus*. The intellectualism of Aristotle, divorcing these two functions, destroyed therewith the Socratic-Platonic concept of *sophia*. This, Thomas Aquinas, laboring diligently, was unable to revive. Eventually, he himself conduced to the ascendency of science over wisdom in modern times.

With Aristotle belief (ὑπόληψις) involves an act of will or consent. It is not so with knowledge or even with opinion.[88] In knowledge, Being is apprehended (or not apprehended), and there is no place for preference or consent of the will. When there is knowledge or true opinion, it is because Being *prescribes itself* necessarily. On the contrary, Augustine regards knowledge as well as belief as involving a movement of the will or consent. Therefore, of the totality of divine and creaturely Being given for apprehension, what a man knows or acknowledges will depend on what portion of the continuum of Being a man most loves. With reference to God, as to anything else, this means that man's universal awareness of God cannot pass to knowledge without *appetitus* or desire or consent of the will.[89] Thus the merely rational or contemplative approach to God is self-contradicted. It requires the consent of the will, but it is Augustine's immovable conviction that the will is perverse. Socrates and the

Gospel are right, only the pure in heart shall see God; for 'the more ardently we love God, the more certainly and the more calmly do we see Him.' [90]

To man's awareness all reality is given, the temporal and the eternal. But in virtue of his fallen condition man is turned from the Light to the creatures made luminous by the Light. The turned back is symbolic of the perverted love (Original Sin). Therefore the order of creatures becomes the dominant object of knowledge in virtue of the coercive inclination of man's will.[91] What else is love (*caritas*) except will, asks Augustine.[92] When this will is directed toward the creatures, the inclination toward God and, therefore, the awareness of God diminish. They decline in proportion to the liveliness of a man's concupiscence toward the world of the senses. The immoderate love of the things of sense is derivative, however, and rests upon a foundational defection, namely, self-love or pride. It is through pride that man consents to the affections of the senses. 'Pride is the beginning of all sin; and the beginning of man's sin is a falling away from God.' [93] The first evil will, which preceded all man's evil acts, 'was rather a kind of falling away from the work of God to its own work than any positive work. And therefore the acts resulting were evil, not having God, but the will itself for their end.' [94] Thus man is the victim of an ambivalent will. His awareness of God and his *appetitus* toward God, with the attendant desire to be like God, are transformed into a desire to be independent of God.[95] Thus the philosophic quest for God may be only a pretense, a disguise by which the seeker hides, even from himself, his fleeing. Paradoxically, man would not flee from God if he were not secretly aware and did not secretly love God; but he fears to acknowledge or commit his will to God lest he lose his autonomy. He does not know that he who would save his life shall lose it. Thus man is, in some way, touched by God even when turned away from him.[96]

V. The Mediator, the Way to Knowledge

It is inevitable that even the Platonists should participate in the failure of the classical approach to God. The being of God

is not altogether obscured from their vision, but the way to God
— the way of the Mediator — they do not acknowledge.

> You proclaim the Father and His Son, whom you call the
> Father's intellect or mind, and between these a third, by
> whom we suppose you mean the Holy Spirit, and in your
> own fashion you call these three Gods. In this, though your
> expressions are inaccurate, you do in some sort as through
> a veil, see what we should strive towards; but the Incarna-
> tion of the unchangeable Son of God, whereby we are saved,
> and are enabled to reach the things we believe, or in part
> understand, this is what you refuse to recognize. *You see in a*
> *fashion, although at a distance, the country in which we*
> *should abide; but the way to it you do not.*[97]

As Augustine will have it, men are born blind in Adam and
need Christ to awaken them. But this is only a shorthand of his
real meaning. Knowledge of God waits upon *re-cognition* of
God. It is not that reason is impotent or that it is inherently corrupted, but that it is perverted by the will. To know, *cognoscere,*
is to acknowledge, *agnoscere.* Thereby real cognition of God is at
the same time the dissolution of the bondage of the will to self-
love. The intellectualists among the philosophers failed to perceive that unless knowledge of the good involved acknowledgment, the consent of the will, right action would not necessarily
follow upon right knowledge. Thus the contemplative conception of knowledge could no more solve the problem of ethics
than it could the theological problem.

Out of soul travail and acute inward reflection, Augustine discovered in the will the key which at one time unlocked both the
problem of theological knowledge and the problem of ethics.
The same volition which turns awareness of God into recognition of God is the death of self-love which hitherto was the chain
binding all benevolence tending beyond expediency. To the
mind of Augustine, therefore, the conception of an axiological
or non-value-directed knowledge not only did not suffice to solve
the problem of ethical motivation but was false of the cognitive
process. It can explain neither ignorance nor knowledge. If Plato

wrestled to account for the ignorance of the sophist and the materialist, neither was he altogether successful in explaining why any of the Cave dwellers emerged into the light. As Augustine conceived the matter, men are in the Cave and willingly committed to Cave-knowledge.

The will is the problem. The solution was the divine Visitant and the divine Emancipator. The Word made flesh, the Mediator, so moves the will that man is enabled to love the good of which he has been aware without acknowledgment, without *caritas*. As mover of the will, Christ becomes 'the *Principium* by whose Incarnation we are purified.' [98] Purified, that is, humbled, the will consents to the intimations of the Truth and the Good which had always been present to reason, and thus reason is made ready for eventual sight. This Christ is the wisdom of God. He is the 'reason of wisdom' to which the 'reason of knowledge' must yield.[99] The latter, which clings tenaciously to the ideal of objective apprehension, usually contenting itself with the investigation of nature, has been shown by Augustine to rest upon a prior commitment of the will, namely, 'the sensuous movement of the soul.' [100]

The products of this movement belong to *scientia* or science as distinguished from *sapientia* or wisdom, that is, to 'the cognition of things temporal and changeable.' [101] They are moreover legitimate and necessary for the management of the affairs of this life.[102] But in so far as the sensuous movement of the will becomes exclusive and directs the reason away from the eternal and unchangeable objects of wisdom or from the Word made flesh, it is the seduction of the serpent, who is the satanic mediator of the Fall of man.[103]

Man is fallen, through pride, into an obsessive love and preoccupation with the creatures, acquiring thereby the false opinion of their unconditional reality. It is *fides*, which alone apprehends the eternal within the historical, that is the correction of man's perversity. Man can be extricated from his unholy marriage to the creatures by God's appearance in the midst of the creatures. The sinner's submission to God as God appears in the form of the Servant, which is *fides*, is the precise antidote for the perverse love of the creatures. Only a new love can expel the old perverse love and make way for the renewed understanding. Thus men are healed only 'by means of the lowliness of the faith of the history, which was transacted in time.' [104] Nowhere is the principle more succinctly stated than in the following:

> Then set I myself a means of gaining so much strength as should be sufficient to enjoy thee; *but I could not find it, until I embraced that Mediator betwixt God and man,* the man Jesus Christ; who is over all, God blessed for ever-more, then calling unto me and saying: I am the Way, the Truth, and the Life: who mingled the food which I was unable to take [his own flesh] unto our flesh. For the Word was made flesh, that by thy wisdom, by which thou createdst all things, he might suckle our infancy. [105]

History becomes the medium of revelation and instrumental to the fulfillment of knowledge. Time and change become, by the Incarnation, the vehicle of the Eternal; whereas, in Platonism, the temporal tended to bind *nous* in ignorance. Augustine has at length, through reflection upon the Incarnation, succeeded in showing what Plato wrestled to make plausible, namely, how, from the knowledge of the particulars, the mind could mount up to the intuition of divine Reality. It is because, in a singular instance, the universal unfolds itself without deficiency in the particular.

The Mediator comes to us in time, seeking us out where we are in bondage to things temporal from which 'contraction of love' we must needs be cleansed.

> But cleansed we could not be, so as to be tempered together with things eternal except it were through things temporal, wherewith we were already tempered together and held fast . . . We then, now, put faith in things done in time on our account, and by that faith itself we are cleansed; in order that when we have come to sight as truth follows faith, so eternity may follow upon mortality. [106]

God was humbled in time, says Augustine. As such, He became the *principium* of knowledge, the wisdom of God.

> It was therefore truly said that man is cleansed only by a *principium*, although the Platonists erred in speaking in the plural of *principles* . . . The *principium* is neither the flesh nor the human soul in Christ, but the Word by which all things were made. The flesh, therefore, does not by its own virtue purify, but by virtue of the Word by which it was assumed when 'the Word became flesh and dwelt among us' . . . The *principium*, therefore, having assumed a human soul and flesh, cleanses the soul and flesh of believers.[107]

But the work of the *principium* as the Mediator between man and God, who comes in 'the form of the servant' and therefore veiled,[108] is not exhausted in exhibiting the condescension of God but in humbling man's pride in that condescension. Christ 'by the drum' of his cross hath opened the hearts of mortal men.'[109] This is Christ the 'troubler' who disquiets the ambivalent will of man until it turns in despair for healing.[110] As men had cast themselves down by pride, so there was no way to return but by humility: 'because pride has wounded us, humility maketh us whole. God came humbly that from such great wound of pride, He might heal men.'[111] In this manner the Mediator converts the will in order that a man may know, remember, the God of whom he had always been aware. Such was the great astonishment of Augustine grounded in his own experience: 'I fell off into those material things, and became bedarkened: but yet even thence, even thence, I came to love thee. I went astray and I remembered thee.'[112]

Even of the *Confessions*, it is incautious and ill-considered to accentuate the 'theo-centrism' of Augustine's form of piety. The Mediator is the indispensable instrument through whom confession is educed and without whom there could be none. Confession is by means of and through Jesus Christ our Lord 'by whom Thou sought us, who sought not for Thee; yet didst Thou seek us, that we might seek Thee.'[113]

What is *fides*? It is acknowledgment (*agnitio*) of the Word in the form of the Servant. Pre-eminently, it is love awakened by the lowly form of the historical. It is fundamentally 'a motion of the heart.' [114] It is the conversion of the will through the crumpling of pride. Whereas faith is elicited by an object in time 'adventitious to the mind,' its eventual object is the Son — not in the form of the Servant — but in the form of God.[115] As Augustine says: 'Our milk is Christ in his humility; our meat, the self-same Christ equal with the Father.' [116] For the present, this latter Christ, who shall be the object of sight and understanding in the world to come, is now an object of belief (*creditum*) rather than of faith. It is most important to note Augustine's distinction in this matter, best summarized in his own words: 'For *fides* is not that which is believed (*creditur*), but that by which it is believed; and the former is believed, the latter is seen.' [117] It is the Servant seen who, abasing man's pride, evokes the *caritas* which, in its turn, requires belief that, in the flesh, the eternal Word is *incognito*. And by faith we shall at length arrive at sight of Him we have believed 'whom, however, we shall never see unless now already we love.' [118]

But, in the understanding of Augustine's thought, never should it be forgotten that no love could be evoked or faith implanted unless, in the Servant, a man *re-cognize*, recall, remember the divine Goodness from which, although always furtively aware, he has turned away to his own will. Nevertheless, not even the Word made flesh could induce faith and love to God had not the eternal Word already visited the reason of man. Of this visitation the heart retains vestiges. Were it not so, the eternal could not be discerned in the historical — wounding man's pride. Neither could the historical recall the heart to the eternal. Thus, of the mind, Augustine says '. . . unless the good remain in it from which it turns away, it cannot again turn itself back thither, if it should wish to amend.' [119] Yet again: 'And because our soul was troubled within us, we remembered thee.' [120] The troubler, He who evokes crisis, is the Mediator. Confession is the will's consent to what was present to reason but was unacknowledged. Faith and reason are required one of the other. They are co-implicates; and it is error, in

Augustine's view, to divorce them. Faith presupposes reason; reason urgently requires the correction of faith.

A final word about confession: it is the valid form of realized or completed knowledge of God. Confession, which is occasioned by the Mediator, signalizes the passage from God's being present to the mind to God's being penitently and therefore willingly entertained by the mind. The mind, that is, the willing-thinking-man, has become an eager host to God whereas before he was inhospitable toward Him. It is confession, therefore, on the part of the converted mind, that betokens the dispersal of that sinful perversity of man in which he denies or distorts his knowledge of God's presence by turning from God in presumption.

The passage, therefore, from knowledge to acknowledgment, from philosophy to Christianity, is the transition, as Augustine so often declares, from 'presumption' to 'confession.' But because of so great misunderstanding, it must be kept firmly in view that this is not a simple passage away from reason to credulity. It is a movement away from the standpoint of autonomous reason, as yet unhumbled by the Mediator, to a willing recognition of God in which reason is operative but at length, being cleansed, unambivalently and vigorously lays hold of God, not as an object but in eager and living conversation. This is what Augustine's *Confessions* is — a penitent conversation with Him whom Augustine at length has come to know through acknowledgment. So does it become clear that sin is the cause and occasion of ignorance, and the ground of the aberrations of 'natural' reason. Therefore, except a man have faith, he shall in no wise understand.

FOR FURTHER READING

Charles N. Cochrane, *Christianity and Classical Culture,* London, 1944, Pt. III, Ch. XI.

Anton C. Pegis, 'The Mind of St. Augustine,' *Medieval Studies,* VI (1944), 8–29; 37–53.

C. C. J. Webb, *Studies in the History of Natural Theology,* Oxford, 1915, pp. 84–136.

NOTES

1. *Ench.*, v. Except for the *Confessions*, references to the literature of Augustine and quoted matter are from the *Nicene and Post-Nicene Fathers*, ed. by Philip Schaff, New York, 1900. The Loeb edition of the *Confessions* is constantly employed: *St. Augustine's Confessions*, London, 1931, 2 vols. For a Latin text I have depended on Perrone, *Œuvres complètes de St. Augustin*, Paris, 1872.
2. *De Civ. Dei*, VIII. 5; X. 29.
3. *Conf.*, VII. 9; cf. *Epist.*, LXXXII. 13.
4. *De Trin.*, XII. 14. 21, 25; cf. *Ench.*, II; *In Joann. Evang.*, XCVII. 7; *De Trin.*, XII. 11. 16; 13. 20.
5. *De Trin.*, I. 8. 17; cf. *Enarr. in Psalm.*, XL. 20; *De Trin.*, I. 2. 4.
6. It is difficult to understand what Harnack meant [*History of Dogma*, trans. by N. Buchanan, Boston, 1899, V, 126] by saying that Augustine 'never advanced to history.' It is true that, unlike the neo-Kantians, Augustine never regarded history as the sole source of divine revelation, *viz.*, Ritschlianism; but it is beyond dispute that the revelatory value of history is precisely that which he regards as distinguishing him from the Platonists. Cf. C. N. Cochrane, *Christianity and Classical Culture*, New York, 1944, p. 416.
7. C. C. J. Webb, *Studies in the History of Natural Theology*, Oxford, 1915, pp. 30, 136.
8. See *De Civ. Dei*, VI; VII; VIII.
9. *De Civ. Dei*, VIII. 10 and 12.
10. Ibid. X. 6.
11. *Conf.*, IV. 3. 4.
12. *De Civ. Dei*, X. 18.
13. Ibid. VIII. 5.
14. *De Doct. Christ.*, II. 40. 60.
15. *De Civ. Dei*, VIII. 4; cf. VIII. 1 and 9.
16. Ibid. XI. 25.
17. Ibid. IX. 16.
18. *In Joann. Evang.*, XV. 19.
19. *De Trin.*, II. 5. 8.
20. *Conf.*, VII. 9. 13; cf. *De Civ. Dei*, VIII. 5.
21. *De Civ. Dei*, X. 28 and 29; cf. *Conf.*, VII. 9. 14; 21, 27.
22. *Soliloq.*, I. 7; cf. *De Lib. Arbit.*, II. 6. 13; *De Trin.*, III. 3. 8.
23. *De Lib. Arbit.*, II. 4. 13; cf. *De Trin.*, XII. 7. 10.
24. *De Trin.*, XIV. 8. 11; XI. 5. 8; XIV. 12. 15.
25. *De Civ. Dei*, VIII. 9.
26. Ibid. VIII. 7.
27. *Soliloq.*, I. 12.
28. *De Lib. Arbit.*, II. 12. 34.

29. *Conf.*, X. 12. 19.
30. Ibid. X. 10. 7. A variant rendering to Wm. Watt's graphic translation of *haurimus* is we 'draw in' or 'drink in.'
31. *De Civ. Dei*, VIII. 6; *De Trin.*, XII. 14. 22; XI. 8. 14; XII. 14. 23.
32. *De Trin.*, XII. 2. 2.
33. Cf. *Conf.*, X. 6. 9; *In Joann. Evang.*, XIII. 5; XV. 19; *De Trin.*, IV. 2. 3; XI. 8. 14.
34. *De Civ. Dei*, VIII. 6; X. 14; *Conf.*, VII. 17. 24; X. 6. 10.
35. *Conf.*, X. 6. 9.
36. Ibid. III. 6. 10; cf. *In Joann. Evang.*, XV. 25.
37. *De Civ. Dei*, VIII. 6; cf. *Conf.*, XI. 5. 13; *De Trin.*, VIII. 3. 4.
38. *Conf.*, VII. 17. 23; cf. *De Trin.*, VIII. 6. 9.
39. *De Trin.*, IX. 6. 10; cf. *In Joann. Evang.*, I. 7.
40. Ibid. IX. 7. 12; cf. *De Civ. Dei*, VII. 6; IX. 16; X. 2.
41. See *De Trin.*, VIII. 6. 9; 9. 13; IX. 6. 9; XV. 4. 6.
42. *Conf.*, XIII. 38. 53.
43. Ibid. VII. 9. 13.
44. *Ench.*, V; cf. *De Trin.*, I. 1. 1; 2. 4; IV. 3. 5.
45. *De Trin.*, V. 11. 12.
46. *In Joann. Evang.*, III. 5.
47. *Enarr. in Psalm.*, VI. 8.
48. *Conf.*, VII. 9. 14; X. 24. 35 sqq.
49. Ibid. X. 17. 26; cf. *De Trin.*, XIV. 12. 16.
50. *De Trin.*, XIV. 4. 6; cf. XIV. 8. 11.
51. *Conf.*, X. 23. 33.
52. *Enarr. in Psalm.*, VIII. 5.
53. *Conf.*, VI. 4. 5 and 5. 7.
54. *Epist.*, LXXXII. 5. In this instructive correspondence with Jerome, Augustine's concern is lest Jerome's form of 'higher criticism' of *Gal.* 2–4 impugn the reliability and infallibility of Scripture.
55. *Contra Epist. Manich. Fundam.*, V. 6.
56. *Contra Faust. Manich.*, XXXIII. 6. 9; cf. *De Util. Cred.*, XIII.
57. *De Spirit. et Litt.*, XI. 18.
58. For this mode of argument see *De Util. Cred.*, XXXI–XXXII; *Contra Epist. Manich. Fundam.*, IV. 5.
59. *Contra Faust. Manich.*, XXXIII. 9.
60. *Ench.*, V; cf. *De Doct. Christ.*, I. 14. 13.
61. *Ench.*, IV.
62. *De Civ. Dei*, VIII. 3; cf. *De Trin.*, I. 2. 4.
63. *De Util. Cred.*, XXIII.
64. *De Doct. Christ.*, II. 7. 11; *De Fide et Symb.*, IX. 20; *Enarr. in Psalm.*, XXXVI. 13; XLIII. 4; LXXXVI. 20; XC. 15; *In Joann. Evang.*, I. 8; I. 19; III. 18; XIX. 16; XX. 11; CXI. 3.
65. *Enarr. in Psalm.*, XL. 20.

66. *De Trin.*, IX. 1. 1.
67. *De Civ. Dei*, X. 28.
68. *De Trin.*, I. 2. 4.
69. *Conf.*, VI. 4. 6.
70. *De Trin.*, VIII. 10. 14.
71. *De Util. Cred.*, I and II.
72. *Conf.*, VII. 21. 27.
73. *De Trin.*, III. 4. 10.
74. Ibid. XI. 1. 1.
75. Ibid. XI. 3. 6; XI. 5. 8.
76. *De Civ. Dei*, VIII. 10.
77. Ibid.
78. *De Civ. Dei*, XIV. 13.
79. *De Trin.*, VIII. 7. 11.
80. *Conf.*, VIII. 10. 22; cf. VII. 16. 22; VIII. 7. 17; X. 6. 8.
81. *De Trin.*, IX. 12. 18.
82. Cf. John Burnet, 'Aristotle,' *Proceedings of the British Academy*, XI, London, 1924, 15–16.
83. *De Anima*, 432b 7 sqq.
84. See *De An.*, 431a 11 and *Met.*, 1072a 30.
85. *De An.*, 433b 28; cf. 434a 17.
86. Ibid. 433a 15 sqq.
87. *In Joann. Evang.*, XXVI. 4.
88. *De An.*, 427b 17 sqq.
89. *De Trin.*, IX. 12. 18.
90. Ibid. VIII. 9. 13.
91. Ibid. XV. 27. 50; cf. *De Civ. Dei*, XIV. 7 where Augustine defines a right will and a wrong will as *bonus amor* and *malus amor* respectively.
92. *De Trin.*, XV. 20. 38.
93. *In Joann. Evang.*, XXV. 15.
94. *De Civ. Dei*, XIV. 11.
95. *De Trin.*, XII. 11. 16.
96. Ibid. XIV. 15. 21.
97. *De Civ. Dei*, X. 29; cf. X. 32; *Conf.*, V. 3. 4; *In Joann. Evang.*, XXXIV. 9; *De Trin.*, IV. 15. 20; XIII. 19. 24.
98. *De Civ. Dei*, X. 24. The italics are mine.
99. *De Trin.*, XII. 12. 17.
100. Ibid. Cf. XII. 11. 16.
101. Ibid.
102. Ibid.
103. Ibid. Cf. *De Trin.*, XII. 12. 17.
104. *Enarr. in Psalm.*, VIII. 8.
105. *Conf.*, VII. 18. 24.

106. *De Trin.*, IV. 18. 24; cf. *In Epist. Joann.*, III. 1.
107. *De Civ. Dei,* X. 24.
108. See *De Trin.*, I. 6. 11; II. 17. 28. *In Joann. Evang.*, XIII. 3; XIV. 12; XVII. 3; XXXIV. 6; LXXV. 2.
109. *Enarr. in Psalm.*, XXXIV. 1.
110. See *De Civ. Dei,* X. 29; *Conf.*, IV. 1. 1; VII. 18. 24; *In Joann. Evang.*, XVIII. 1; XX. 5.
111. *Enarr. in Psalm.*, XXXVI. 15.
112. *Conf.*, XII. 10. 10.
113. *Conf.*, XI. 2. 4.
114. *In Joann. Evang.*, XXII. 6. '. . . he has made a passage, as it were, from the region of unbelief to the region of faith, by motion of the heart . . .
115. *De Trin.*, I. 13. 60.
116. *In Epist. Joann.*, III. 1.
117. *De Trin.*, XIV. 8. 11; cf. XV. 27. 49.
118. Ibid. XIII. 19. 24.
119. Ibid. VIII. 3. 4; cf. *Conf.*, X. 19.
120. *Conf.*, XIII. 12. 13.

-XII-

THE CREATION OF
THE WORLD

William A. Christian

'In the beginning God created heaven and earth.'

Few other passages of Scripture intrigued Augustine as much
as the first sentence of the book of Genesis. In the *Confessions,* in his treatises on Genesis, in the *City of God,* and elsewhere he dwells on it and recurs to it, as though he felt he could
not exhaust its suggestions and implications. His reflections on
this sentence are ample evidence of the acuteness, force, and
fecundity of his mind.

These reflections deserve attention not only as an index to
the quality of his mind but also because in his treatment of the
subject the main strands of his cosmology are knotted together.
Time and eternity, nature and human history, body and soul,
good and evil — all these themes are developed and interconnected in Augustine's thought about the creation of the world.

Two minor themes will appear as this study proceeds, namely (1) the role of Biblical revelation in Augustine's thought, and (2) the relation between Augustine the Neoplatonist and Augustine the Christian. These two topics are obviously connected, and our subject gives us a vantage point for getting some understanding of both. A brief preliminary word about each may be in order.

'In the beginning God created heaven and earth.' Here, for Augustine, was a truth mediated by a particular historical tradition with which he had identified himself. This truth he was not at liberty to ignore. He had to come to terms with it. Its claim on his mind was not the claim of a dictum of pure reason unconditioned by historical experience. Nor was it the claim of a fact immediately presented in the course of his observation of the world. It was the claim of a historical revelation, with which he was confronted in the Bible.

We shall see that Augustine took this sentence from Genesis quite seriously. It was for him a truth, not a fiction. It will be evident also that he took it in no simple sense, certainly not with a childish simplicity.[1] Its truth did not have for Augustine the kind of simplicity that puts an end to all questions. It was a productive truth, which made it possible to answer questions in a new and more adequate way. It was thus not a substitute for thinking. Rather, it stimulated thought by marking out a new direction for exploration. It was a source of truths, which illumined and set in a new and clearer perspective both the problems and all speculative attempts at their solution. In this way, from Augustine's point of view, the result of his acceptance of the Biblical revelation was a liberation, not an inhibition of thought.

It is in this light that we should look at the relation between Neoplatonism and the Christian faith in Augustine's thought. The contrast between these two did pose a problem for him. As he saw it, the problem was not how to reconcile two systems by judicious selections from each, the selections being determined by a perspective more fundamental than either. His aim was neither synthetic nor eclectic. The problem was to understand his world anew from a perspective determined by the Christian faith. In particular, his task was to rethink the meanings of time and eternity, nature and history, body and soul, good and evil, in the light of the truth that God is the Creator.

There can be no doubt that the mind he brought to this task had been formed by Neoplatonic habits of thought; the experience he now had to reinterpret had been shaped by Neoplatonic ideals. One may indeed doubt whether he was completely successful in rethinking his world from the new perspective of Christian faith. There can be little doubt that this was what he was *trying* to do. This was the pivotal movement of his mind as he reflected on the creation of the world.

How fruitful this adventure of ideas turned out to be the reader must judge. Some may feel that had Augustine possessed an 'outline of modern knowledge' he would have been able to avoid some pitfalls. Some may wish he had kept to the low road of common sense and simple faith and had not at times taken the high road of speculation. Some may wish that in his speculation he had freed himself more from Neoplatonic ways of thinking. Some will read him through medieval spectacles. To judge him fairly, we should look at him as a man of the ancient world, traversing the intellectual terrain of that world, a terrain whose features shift subtly and profoundly as he comes to see them with new eyes.

I. In the Beginning

Time and Eternity. The words, 'in the beginning,' Augustine takes in two ways: they have a figurative meaning and they have a literal meaning. Figuratively, the 'beginning' (*principium*) is the divine Word, the uncreated Wisdom, the eternal Son in whom and by whom God made all things.[2] Literally, 'the beginning' is the beginning of time. All things were made in the beginning of time. From this point of departure Augustine embarks on an exploration of the meaning of time and eternity, the results of which are profoundly original and suggestive.

Notice first, Augustine's thought runs, that creation is not in time. It is 'in the beginning.' In the beginning of what? Augustine would prefer to say simply, 'in the beginning.' One may say if one likes that the world was created in the beginning of time. For as in Plato's myth,[3] so for Augustine time comes into existence along with the world. 'Without doubt the world was not made in time, but with time.' [4] Creation does not fall within that series of successive events, each coming to be and ceasing to be, of which time is the measure. Creation is not an act in time. Creation is 'in the beginning.'

For time is a measure of change, a relation among changing things.

> Who does not see that time would not have existed had not some creature been made, which by some motion would bring about change, and that since the various parts of this motion and change cannot exist together (*simul*), when one passes away and another succeeds it in shorter or longer intervals of duration, time would be the result? [5]

Time is relative to changing things and exists where such things exist. Thus the original coming-into-being of the world of changing creatures 'begins' the temporal process and does not fall within that process. Creation is not in time but 'in the beginning.'

Nor, since there is no time where there is no created world, did the creation of the world take time. It had no temporal duration. We should not take the Genesis story, says Augustine,

> in a childish way, as though God exerted himself by working. For he spoke, not with an audible and temporal word, but with an intellectual and eternal word, and the things were done.[6]

God 'created all things at once,' [7] though, as we shall see later in this study, not all things were created in their present outward and visible forms. Living things were created in the beginning as 'hidden seeds' and later, in the providence of God, came to exist in the way we now know them.

Thus the beginning of the world and time, that is to say the coming into being of changeable things, was not itself in time.

Nor did it take time. For creation is an act of God's will, and God's willing is not in time, nor does it take time. God is eternal.

> Wherefore it is not true that he wills one thing at one moment and another thing at another moment, but once for all, and all at once, and always, does he will all things he wills.[8]

Augustine thinks that the six days of the Genesis story are to be understood 'in some other way' than as literal days, defined by the circuit of the sun.[9] The story of the six days is a dramatic representation of what took place at once and as a whole. God created all things at once (or, together). The author of the account of the creation in Genesis

> at first presents the creation as a whole, and then its parts are described in order according to the mystic number of the days.[10]

These 'parts' of the creation are not to be taken as temporal parts, one succeeding another in time; the things enumerated in temporal order in the story were all created 'together,' without any intervals of duration or periods of time.[11] The creation of the world did not have any temporal duration. It did not take time, nor was it in time. God created the world 'in the beginning.'

What was God doing before He created the world? A hoary answer to this ancient puzzle was that God was preparing hell for those who pry into mysteries. This answer John Calvin was later to approve,[12] and thus demonstrate a deficiency both in patience and in finesse. Augustine, more charitable and more sensitive to the problem, however crudely stated, rejected this short answer and took the question more seriously.

The real problem behind this crude question was stated more clearly by Immanuel Kant. Kant said it is a natural tendency of the mind to conceive that

> since the beginning is an existence which is preceded by a time in which the thing is not, there must have been a preceding time in which the world was not, *i.e.,* an empty time.[13]

And since in empty time nothing can come to be, it seems that the world has no beginning.

This problem Augustine is willing to face quite frankly and seriously. His answer is in effect that empty time has no real meaning. Time has meaning only in relation to changing things. Time apart from changing things, empty time, is not a notion we can really think. He says:

> If by the term 'heaven and earth' all the creation is understood, I confidently say that before God made heaven and earth he was not making anything . . . But if someone's flighty mind wanders backward through semblances of times, and wonders that thou, omnipotent and all-creating and all-sustaining God, maker of heaven and earth, shouldst have refrained from such a work for innumerable ages before thou didst make it, let him wake up and start to think, because he wonders at false things. For whence could innumerable ages pass by which thou didst not make, since thou art the author and founder of all ages? Or what times should there be which were not founded by thee? . . . If however before heaven and earth there was no time, why is it asked what thou wast doing then? For there was no 'then' when there was no time.[14]

So it is meaningless to speak of a time when the world was not. Any 'then' we can conceive presupposes some changing thing and hence the existence of a creation. However far we may remove such a 'then' into the past, we still think of some changing thing when we think of a 'then.' 'There was no "then" when there was no time.'

Hence the world has existed throughout all time. Does this mean the world has always existed? Yes, if 'always' means 'at all times,' then the world has always existed. To say that the world has always existed, and also to say that the world had a beginning, is not to fall into a contradiction, if 'always' means 'at all times.' For time began with the created world, and there was no time 'before' the created world.

Augustine returns to this conclusion when he ponders another theological puzzle, namely 'what God could be the Lord of, if there was not always some creature?' For he dares not speak as if 'the Lord God was ever not Lord,' that is to say as if there had not always been some responsible creatures who acknowledged God as Lord. Among the many thoughts that occur to his mind, the one that pleases him best is that the angels have at all times been subject to God. For, as we shall see later, man was created in the beginning 'potentially' and later came to have his present form, whereas the angels belong to that 'intellectual heaven' which was created perfectly formed in the beginning. And if this is so, 'then they have existed in all time, for time came into being along with them. And who will say that what was in all time, was not always?' God therefore has always been Lord of creation, and there has always been a creation over which God is Lord.[15]

At this point Augustine has to defend his suggestion against the charge that if the angels have always existed, then they are co-eternal with God, which would obscure the contrast between God and His creatures. His defense is that this contrast is not between what is earlier and what is later in time. It is a distinction between what is unchangeable and what is changeable. God's eternity is His unchangeableness, and in this sense the angels are not eternal. What God created is not co-eternal with Him, 'since he existed before it, although at no time did he exist without it, preceding it not by some passing duration but by an abiding perpetuity.'[16]

God is 'prior' to the world not by precedence in the dimension of time but by His eternity. By eternity Augustine does not mean an indefinite extension of time. He can say that the angels 'always' existed but are not eternal. The past 'eternal times' of which even the Apostle Paul speaks are not co-eternal with God.[17] By eternity he means unchangeableness. The world of created things including the angels changes; God does not. In God there is no passage; the created world and all things in it are in passage. Thus to say the world always existed would in no way blur the real contrast between God and His creatures.

> Nor dost thou by time precede time; otherwise thou wouldst not precede all times. But thou precedest all past times by the sublimity of ever-present eternity, and thou surpassest all future times, because they are yet to come and when they come they will be past; 'thou however art the same and thy years fail not.' [18]

When therefore we find Augustine speaking, as he often does speak, of a 'past' before the world was made, or of the nothingness in which things were 'before' they were created, we must understand him to mean by these terms a 'precedence' not by time but by eternity. The contrast between God and the world should not be described in such a way as to suggest a being who existed at a time when other beings did not exist. For not even the 'merest simpleton' would say there was a time when there was no time. It is rather a contrast between an unchangeable being and changing beings.

This contrast between time and eternity to which Augustine's thought has led him presents him with a knot he cannot untie. He is confronted, as Etienne Gilson says, with two modes of being which are not homogeneous but heterogeneous. We are subject, even in our thought, to the law of becoming. How then can we represent to ourselves the mode of being of that which is unchangeable? [19] Here is a problem indeed, and for it Augustine has no answer. What is worse, he is committed to saying that this unchangeable being, which he cannot adequately represent to himself, creates, knows, and administers a world of changing things. At this point Augustine is frank to say that no analogies can really help us. For example, he considers an analogy from the singing of a familiar psalm. As Augustine sings the psalm its parts succeed one another from beginning to end, yet while singing each of the parts he knows the whole of the psalm.

> But far be it that thou, creator of the universe, creator of souls and bodies, far be it, that thou shouldest in this way know all things future and past. Far, far more wonderfully and in a far more hidden way dost thou know them.[20]

How an unchangeable being can have any real relation to changing beings remains a mystery. What Augustine does is to locate the mystery, so to speak, and confess it.

Now if we take seriously what Augustine has said so far — if indeed a created world has 'always' existed, so there was no time when the world was not — then what meaning remains for the phrase 'in the beginning'? It would seem that instead of explaining the phrase Augustine has explained it away.

The Meaning of History. At this point some may say there are two Augustines. There is Augustine the Neoplatonist, and there is Augustine the Christian dogmatist. The former could have easily dispensed with the notion that the world had a 'beginning.' The latter, in retaining it, bowed blindly to the authority of the Scriptures. This interpretation would miss the point and distort the facts. In his thought about the creation of the world there is only one Augustine. This is the Augustine who found in the Bible a truth that illumined his experience and therefore became normative for his thought.

This can be discerned in his treatment of the Neoplatonic and Stoic theories of history. We shall see how the truth he found in Genesis enabled him to articulate a theory of the meaning of history different from theirs, a theory which has since been woven into the fabric of Western culture. We shall see also that the force of this truth for Augustine was in its suggestive power.

In the eleventh book of the *City of God* Augustine takes issue with the Neoplatonic view of God and the world. At first it seems that he quarrels with the Neoplatonists because they say the world always existed and was not created in time. But this can hardly be the point of his attack. For a little later in the same book this is precisely what he himself says, as we have seen, after explaining that time 'began' with the creation. As his argument develops we see that his real quarrel is with their view of the history and destiny of the soul.

The point Augustine wishes to drive home is that an understanding of the soul and its destiny requires a realistic view of history. What he is attacking is the Neoplatonic conception of time as a flux of shadowy forms in which there can be no decisively novel events. He is opposing their devaluation of the historical character of the world. His argument is that since the world, and within it human history, had a 'beginning,' it is a process within which novel and decisive events can and do occur. There are in this process events that never occurred before, and such events decide the future in a real and effective way, so that the same events could never recur.

The Neoplatonists, Augustine supposes, do not wish to say that the soul is co-eternal with God. For then they could not explain why the soul is now in a state of misery in which it was not before. If, on the other hand, they say that the soul ceaselessly undergoes an alternation of states of happiness and states of misery, they land in absurdity. For in each state of so-called happiness, either it would foresee its coming misery, or it would be deceived. In neither case could it be truly happy. The way out of their dilemma, says Augustine, is to recognize that both the soul's entry into its present state of misery and its entry into a future state of happiness are novel and decisive events.

The misery which is the soul's present lot, he says, is a 'new misery' which the soul had not experienced before; it is not a repetition of what the soul suffered in previous incarnations, as the Neoplatonists suppose. Likewise the happiness to which the soul looks forward, which will free it from its present misery, means that 'something new, and that an important and splendid thing, happens to the soul, which never in a whole past eternity had happened to it before.' [21]

Augustine knows the Neoplatonists hesitate to say there is genuine novelty in history because they fear this would contradict the unchangeableness of God. But this fear is unfounded. The apparent dilemma, 'God is unchangeable and history is unreal' or 'God is changeable and history is real,' is not a true dilemma. Augustine sees another possibility: God is unchangeable and history is real, for God created the world and with it time 'in the beginning.'

If therefore the Neoplatonists will acknowledge, as he thinks they must, that the soul like number has a beginning but no end and for that reason, once having experienced miseries, if freed from them will never afterward be miserable, they will certainly not doubt that this is done with the abiding immutability of the counsel of God. Let them then in like manner believe that the world could have been made beginning with time (*ex tempore*), and that notwithstanding this fact God did not change, in making it, his eternal counsel and will.[22]

For if the soul can have a real history, though God be eternal, so can the world. The process of history is not a mere reflection of timeless forms, a shadowy process in which no decisive changes are effected. Like the number series it has a beginning but no end.[23] It cannot run back or stop. In it something is decisively achieved. Yet, because God's creative act is not itself in time but 'in the beginning,' the unchangeableness of God is not called into question.

In this argument against the Neoplatonists we have an example of the way Augustine uses the truth brought to his mind by Genesis. 'In the beginning God created heaven and earth.' It is an instrument for detecting the fundamental defect in the Neoplatonic view of the world, wherein the history of the world, and particularly the history of the soul, becomes infected with unreality. And it is a source of illumination, suggesting that the eternal God wills that new things come to pass in the course of time.

Similarly Augustine confronts the Stoics, who held that the history of the world consists of ceaselessly recurring cycles of events, that, for example,

> just as in that [past] age the philosopher Plato taught disciples in the city of Athens and in that school which is called the Academy, so also the same Plato and the same city and the same school and the same disciples had been repeated through innumerable ages before, at long but determined intervals, and through innumerable ages thereafter are to be repeated.[24]

325

Augustine cannot believe this.

> For once Christ died for our sins. But rising up from the dead he dies no more, and death will no more have dominion over him. And we after the resurrection shall be ever with the Lord.[25]

Nothing, he says, more thoroughly explodes the theory of recurring cycles of history than the fact of the eternal life of the saints.[26]

There are events in the history of the world — for example the Fall, the Crucifixion, the Resurrection, our entrance into everlasting life — which happen once for all. Of these events, in the theater of the cosmos, there are no repeat performances. Such events never occurred before and will never occur again, for they decide the future. Historical time therefore proceeds not in circles but in a straight line. It proceeds in a straight line because it has a 'beginning,' as a circle does not.

The Stoics, like the Neoplatonists, had been concerned to maintain the immutability of God. They had argued that, since the world must have always existed, and since there must be a finite number of things in the world (for they said not even God's knowledge could comprehend the infinite), there must be recurring cycles of the events in which these things are combined. It is significant that in his argument against the Stoics Augustine does not deny the world 'always' existed. Nor does he deny the immutability of God. What he denies is their view of God's knowledge and their conclusion about the nature of history.

Here Augustine recurs to the analogy of the number series. The series of historical events, he says, is like the number series, in that new members of the series continually succeed earlier ones. Yet this does not compromise the immutability of God by requiring that God should have new thoughts, because

> the infinity of number, although there is no numbering of infinite numbers, is nevertheless not incomprehensible to him, of whose understanding there is no numbering.[27]

If therefore the Stoics corrected their view of God's knowledge, they could admit that new events continually come into being without new thoughts in God. Their misconception of perfection, namely their assumption that God's perfection requires that the world be a finite completion, has led them to deny the genuine novelty and decisiveness of historical events.

Contrary to their view Augustine says, 'The divinity can make things which, not to himself but to the world, are new.'[28] God can begin a 'new work'; He can make 'new things'; He can make His later works novel and unlike what went before them. Yet in all this He acts with the same eternal will.

> He brought it about by one and the same everlasting and immutable will that the things he created formerly did not exist, as long as they were not, and that afterward they did exist when they began to be.[29]

God is eternal. We live in a world in which genuinely novel and decisive events occur. Of this world God is creator. Augustine found it possible to think these three thoughts together, and to understand each in the light of the others. He was led to think them together by the truth he found in the Bible. 'In the beginning God created heaven and earth.'

It is notable that in neither of these confrontations with non-Christian views of history do we find Augustine's faith either in conflict with his reason or irrelevant to his thought. There are not two Augustines here, one blindly accepting the Bible, the other thinking as a philosopher. There is one Augustine, who finds in the Bible a new perspective and a new illumination of the meanings of time, history, and eternity, an illumination his thought must then explore and communicate.

We should not suppose that Augustine's exploration of these problems was conclusive and final, either for him or for us. I doubt whether he would have said he had a 'solution' in the sense that he 'saw' how an eternal being could be dynamically related to a world of changing things. Here as elsewhere his thought moves with a constant sense of the mystery of the world and God. Nor were these problems posed for him in quite the way they are posed in our time. For example, some modern philosophers, unlike the Neoplatonists and Stoics, question whether temporal events may not be in some way new for God as well as for us, so as to require a new definition of the unchangeableness of God.

In summary, how does the notion of a 'beginning' of the world function in Augustine's thought? It does not mean the world was created in time, for time was created with the world and not before it; hence the creation has existed at all times. Nor does it mean, on the other hand, simply that the world is dependent on God for its existence, for many ancient philosophers had said this, as Augustine well knew, without supposing a 'beginning.' Its function in Augustine's thought was to open to him a way of understanding and saying that though God is eternal, time is real, and that human history is neither a dreamlike appearance of eternity nor a perpetual cycle in which nothing is new. History is made up of events that are both new and decisive, as a 'beginning' is new and decisive. For it is the eternal will of the creator that in these events something real should be accomplished.

II. Heaven and Earth

In the beginning God created heaven and earth. Augustine is unwilling to 'strive about words' in interpreting 'heaven and earth.' By these words various things may be understood and yet all be true. He takes them to mean the 'intellectual heaven' and the 'formless earth.' [30]

The intellectual heaven is not the visible firmament. It is the perfectly formed realm of angels, the spiritual creation which is superior to all things save God. For the angels, though changeable creatures and hence not co-eternal with God, have a certain participation in eternity. 'By incessantly and unfailing cleaving' to him, they enjoy perpetually the vision of God.

This intellectual heaven which God made in the beginning is near to God. The formless earth is 'near to nothing,' though it is not nothing.[31] This 'formless earth' is not the visible world, it is that 'matter' from which all bodies, including the firmament, were formed. It is near to nothing because it is entirely unformed and without quality, though from it the qualities we perceive are formed. It is what the Greeks called ὕλη.[32]

This formless matter is the principle of change, not that it is an efficient cause of change, but in that it is the condition of change. Just what it is in itself Augustine finds it difficult to say.

> For the changeableness of changeable things is itself capable of all forms, into which changeable things are changed. And what is this changeableness? . . . If one might say, 'a nothing something,' an 'is, is not,' I would say, this is it. Yet it already had some sort of being, so that it was capable of receiving those visible and compound forms.[33]

Plato would have said we apprehend it by a 'bastard' kind of thought, though we are compelled to think it.

We should not think that God first created this formless matter and then, later in time, formed it into particular visible things. He created all things together: the intellectual heaven, the formless earth, and the visible world. All things were created at once. God's works were not made of previously existing matter,

> but of matter concreated, that is created at the same time by thee, because thou didst give form to its formlessness without any lapse of time. For since the matter of heaven and earth is one thing, and the visible form of heaven and earth another, thou madest matter of absolutely nothing, but the visible form of the world from unformed matter, yet both together, so that the form followed the matter with no interval of time.[34]

Matter is thus prior to determinate form not in respect to time, but in respect to 'origin,' as for example the sound is prior to the tune.[35]

Thus the world came into existence in the beginning. But not all things were created 'visibly and actually.' The living things which inhabit the earth were created 'potentially or causally' in the form of 'hidden seeds' or 'seminal causes' (rationes seminales).

From these seminal causes, or 'reasons,' they were to be brought forth later, in the providence of God and in due time, in the visible forms in which they are now known to us.

So the world may be likened to a tree, which develops in the course of time from its beginning in a seed.

> Just as in that seed there were together (*simul*) invisibly all the things which would in time develop into the tree, so the world itself is to be thought to have had together — since God created all things together — all the things which were made in it and with it when the day was made, not only the heaven with the sun and the moon and the constellations . . . and the earth and the abysses . . . but also those things which the water and the earth produced potentially and causally, before they should arise in the course of time in the way we now know them, through those operations which God carries on even till now.[36]

These seminal causes placed in the world in the beginning were not ordinary seeds or germ cells. They were 'hidden' seeds, potentials or matrices from which when the circumstances were appropriate individuals of various species would be brought forth. The species would then be propagated according to their kind.[37]

For example, Augustine thought that human beings as we know them have not existed from the beginning of the world. The human race as we know it began to exist in the course of time. Man was created in the beginning not in his visible form, but 'invisibly, potentially, causally, in the way in which things yet to be (in contrast to things which already exist) are made.' [38] Man was made in the beginning potentially, to be given actual form and visible existence 'in his time.' [39]

The seminal causes, according to Augustine, ordinarily give rise to living things according to determinate natural laws.

> That whole ordinary course of nature has what one might call its own natural laws, according to which even the spirit of life, which is a created thing, has what one might call its

own appetites determined in some way, so that even the evil will cannot go beyond them. And the elements of this corporeal world have their established power and quality, defining how much each one will flourish or not, and what may or may not become from what. Just as from these origins are all things which arise, so, each in its own time and of its own kind, they enter upon their comings forth and progressions and limits and decreasings.[40]

Still the supernatural intervention of God in the course of events is possible, though this intervention is not contrary to the potentialities God created in the beginning.

Above, however, this natural movement and course of things, the power of the Creator has in itself ability to act concerning all these things otherwise than their seminal causes, as it were, have — though this is not something he did not put into them [as a possibility] that it might be accomplished, at least by himself. For he is omnipotent not by thoughtless power, but by the strength of wisdom, and he does concerning each thing in its time that which he made in it before, that it might be possible for him.[41]

Finally, we should notice Augustine's warnings against crude and anthropomorphic images of God's act in creating heaven and earth. Let us not understand the creation, he says, as do the 'little ones and carnal' (who are not to be despised, though they are weak in understanding), who think that

God like a man, or like some powerful being, faced with an immense difficulty, did, by some new and sudden resolution, make heaven and earth outside himself, as if in a distant region.[42]

As there is no time before the world, when God might have existed and the world did not, so there is no place beside the world, where God might be exterior to the world.[43] God does not make the world as a carpenter makes a chest, because the carpenter is outside the chest and fashions it from without, but God, infused into the world, fashions it, being every-where present he fashions it, and does not withdraw to some other place. Nor does he, as it were, handle from without the mass which he fashions. By the presence of his majesty he makes what he makes; by his presence he governs what he made.[44]

III. Out of Nothing

Following a tradition which had long served the Church as a weapon against the Gnostics, Augustine finds in the Scriptures [45] the teaching that the world was created from nothing. By this he does not mean that there was a something, which is called 'nothing,' from which the world was made. He is not hypostatiz-ing. He means what he says: 'Thou wert, and nothing was there besides, from which thou createdst heaven and earth.' [46] The world was not made from God, as though God took some of His own substance and from it fashioned the world. Nor was it made from anything else. There was, and is, nothing else beside God and what God made. Unlike man, 'God had no need of any material he himself had not made, to assist his omnipotence.' [47] The world was brought into being out of nothingness.

No more than in the case of 'in the beginning' did this 'out of nothing' remain an inert and inhibiting foreign body, so to speak, in Augustine's mind. It functioned for him as an illuminating and liberating truth. This can be seen in two instances; first, his defense of the goodness of the body against the Neo-platonists and the Manicheans, and second, his attack on the Manichean view that the soul is of the same substance as God.

At the root of many of the errors of the Neoplatonists Augustine finds an aversion from the body. The Platonists, says Augustine, unlike the Manicheans, do not detest our present bodies as evil by nature. For they attribute all the elements of the visible world to God as maker.

Nevertheless they think that souls are so affected by the earthly body and its death-infected members, that from this source come the diseases of desires and fears and joy and sorrow in which . . . all the viciousness of human life is contained.[48]

This aversion from the flesh is itself 'fleshly,' for 'these feelings arise from human fancy, not from divine truth.' It prevents the Neoplatonists from confessing the truth of such Christian doctrines as the Resurrection and the final glorification of the body.

This aversion from the body which Augustine notices among the Neoplatonists is connected with an ambiguity about the formless matter which enters into the composition of all changeable things. Plotinus, for example, spoke at times of this formless matter or 'non-being' as 'the first evil,' even though this was not consistent with some of his own principles.[49]

Since, for Augustine, the world is made from absolutely nothing, even this formless matter was created by God, concreated with the individual natures for whose forms it is the matter. And since all that God made is very good, even this formless matter is good. Thus Augustine is enabled to be clearer in mind and firmer in conviction about the goodness of all that is not nothing than Plotinus seems to have been. The notion of creation from nothing clarified and strengthened Augustine's affirmative vision of universal good.

Hence the body is not of itself evil, or even a 'clog to the soul' as the Platonists say.

> It is not the body, but the corruptibility of the body, that is burdensome to the soul. . . [For] the soul is burdened, not by any body whatsoever, but the body such as it has become in consequence of sin.[50]

> And though the healthy and strong man feels heavier to other men carrying him than the thin and sickly man does, yet the man himself moves and carries his own body with less feeling of burden, when he has the greater bulk of vigorous health, than when his frame is reduced to a minimum by hunger or disease . . . And who can explain in words how much difference there is between the present state we call health and our future immortality?[51]

Nor are our souls locked up in our bodies as a punishment for evils done in some previous existence, as the Neoplatonists say. 'The soul is rather given to the body that it [i.e. the soul] may do good things.' [52] Therefore the goal of life is not that the soul escape from the body, but that the body as well as the soul should be saved from corruption and pass from sickness to health.

We should of course remember it was from the Neoplatonists themselves that Augustine had caught a vision of the goodness of all beings of whatever nature. What we now notice is that the notion of the creation of all things from nothing enables Augustine to clarify and maintain this vision, and to guard against the Neoplatonic flight from the bodily and the historical.

When we turn to Augustine's treatment of the Manichean view of the body, the contrast is even more striking. One might say the conception of creation from nothing completes Augustine's liberation from Manicheism, which Neoplatonism had begun before he became a Christian. Certainly it is clear in his anti-Manichean writings that this conception seems to him of fundamental importance in his argument.

The Manicheans supposed that there is 'some evil nature, brought forth and propagated by its own principle' in opposition to God.[53] This evil nature is matter. Hence bodies formed of matter are evil. All flesh is the work of the evil principle. But, says Augustine, this is not true. It is God alone who created from nothing all things both spiritual and corporeal. Hence matter is not something opposed to God, or contrary to God's will, for He created it. Hence bodies made of matter are not by nature evil and recalcitrant to good — because God created both matter and bodies from nothing, and their natures are due to Him alone. Therefore, as the apostle says, we should glorify God in our bodies. The Manicheans should

> learn that all natures God made and established are ordered in degrees of excellence from the highest to the lowest, and that all are good, though some are better than others, and that they all were made of nothing, though God their maker

made use of his own wisdom, so to speak, to give being to what was not, and that as far as it had being it might be good, but that as far as it was deficient, it might show that it was not begotten of God, but made by him from nothing.[54]

This passage gives us a second illustration of the way the notion of creation from nothing functioned in Augustine's thought. That the body is created from nothing, not from some evil matter, means the body is good. That the soul is created from nothing, not from God's own nature, means the soul is limited, changeable, and fallible.

The Manicheans said the soul is not created by God but begotten of God and is thus of God's own nature, and therefore, they thought, contrary to the evil principle in matter. This view of the soul, says Augustine, contradicts the soul's own witness to its nature as a changeable being, capable of falling away from the good, whereas God is unchangeable and unchangeably good. The Manicheans do not do justice to the facts.

> Let them think, in Christian sanity, that the soul, which can be changed for the worse by its own will and be corrupted by sin, and thus be deprived of the light of unchangeable truth, is not a part of God nor is it of the same nature as God, but has been made far different from its maker.[55]

It is true that the soul is created in the image of God, but it cannot be of the same nature as God. We know ourselves too well for that, his thought runs. Let us not deceive ourselves. We are not parts of God, nor are we begotten by God, so that we have His nature as a child has its parent's nature. We are created by God from nothing.

Both body and soul therefore are created by God from nothing. Since they are created by God they are, in their natures, good, for all that God creates is good.

> What alone is not from Thee is that which is not, and the motion of the will from Thee, who art, to that which is less than Thee, because such motion is a fault and a sin.[56]

Since body and soul are created from nothing they are, unlike God, changeable and capable of corruption.

In these ways the image of God's creation of the world from nothing meant for Augustine an illumination of his experience and a liberation from restrictive and confusing categories of thought. It also left him with a problem, just as the conception of the unchangeableness of God had left him with the mystery of the relation between eternity and time. Here the problem is in some ways an even more serious one. It is as follows. In creating, if God creates from nothing, God is absolutely unconditioned by anything other than Himself. Likewise the things created are not conditioned, in their natures as created, by anything other than God. Thus it becomes difficult to see how, if God is perfectly good, any motion away from God could have arisen in any of his creatures.

IV. 'And behold, it was very good'

The creation was very good, both in reason and in result. The reason of the creation was simply this, 'that the good God produced good things.' God was not driven by any necessity to create the world, for instance a necessity of doing so to repulse the evil power which, according to the Manicheans, warred against Him.[57]

There are others, Augustine says, who unlike the Manicheans do indeed believe in God as the only source of all things, and have yet refused to accept with a good and simple faith this good and simple reason for the creation of the world — Origen, for example. For Origen believed that this world was created not for the production of good things but for the restraint of evil, so that souls might be assigned to diverse stations in the universe and to diverse bodies as prison-houses, according to their respective merits. How could a man 'so learned and so well versed in the literature of the church' have thought these things? [58] Even Plato had seen that 'the most sufficient reason for the founding of the world' was 'that by the good God good works were made,' whether he had learned this directly or indirectly from Genesis, or whether he had, 'by his quick-sighted genius, perceived the invisible things of God, understood through the things which are made.' [59]

As in its reason so in its result, the creation is very good. This not only God but also man can see.

> Thanks to Thee, O Lord. We behold the heaven and earth . . . We see . . . this space of air through which wander the fowls of heaven between those waters which are borne in vapors above them, and in clear nights distil down in dew, and those heavier waters which flow along the earth . . . We behold the lights shining from above, the sun to suffice for the day, the moon and the stars to cheer the night; and that, by all these, times should be marked and signified. We behold on all sides a moist element, replenished with fishes, beasts, and birds . . . We behold the face of the earth adorned with living things, and man, created after Thy image and likeness (that is the power of reason and under-standing), set over all irrational creatures . . . These things we behold, and they are severally good, and altogether are very good.[60]

Augustine's thought about the creation of the world amounts to a searching and persistent exploration rather than a finished theory. And it is not surprising that we find, in his writings on the subject, unresolved tensions, unsolved problems, and con-stant confessions of mystery.

The old wineskins of classical and Hellenistic thought were strained, as all other philosophical systems have since been strained, when the wine of a new insight was poured into them. Nor was Augustine's handling of Scripture altogether free from bondage to ecclesiastical tradition — for example, his treatment of the formation of Eve. His confessions of confrontation with mystery certainly should not surprise us, when we consider the sort of questions he was asking, though they should not lead us to underestimate his intellectual courage. Only a false humility, which is timidity in disguise, talks of the limitations of the mind before those limits are reached.

But it is misleading to say, for example, as F. R. Tennant does, 'When the beginning of Time is dealt with, Augustine and, later, the schoolmen rely on revelation rather than philosophy.' [61] It is misleading because just at this point I find the contrast between Augustine's treatment of creation and that of Thomas Aquinas most striking. It is misleading also because of the more general suggestion that there is something intrinsically unphilosophical about Augustine's reliance on the Bible.

Augustine was a man who early in life had begun to think for himself, and he did not stop thinking when he became a Christian. When he became a Christian he began to think from a different point of view, and we have seen how from this new point of view he came to have a new understanding of his world. This new understanding was the product of thought, though certainly of thought guided by a new vision. In other words, it was for Augustine genuine, though partial, understanding, not acquiescence in unintelligibility.

It is true that Augustine relied on the Bible in the sense that he found there a new direction for his thought about the world and God. It is misleading to suggest, as Tennant seems to do, that this reliance was more external and unthinking, less concerned for clarity and comprehensiveness in thinking, that is to say, less 'philosophical' in this sense, than reliance on Plotinus or on Plotinus' vision would have been. It could be argued that Augustine, in his thought about God and the world, was no less philosophical than Plotinus, though the thought of each proceeded from a different initial vision. Without such a vision philosophy tells no tales about the world.

Augustine found in the Bible a new truth, which both fulfilled the promise of Neoplatonism and superseded it: God is the Creator of all things in heaven and earth. This new vision of the creativity of God was, in one sense indeed, the end of a search, but in another and more important sense, as I hope this study has illustrated, it was for Augustine a new beginning.

FOR FURTHER READING

M. J. McKeogh, *The Meaning of the Rationes Seminales in St. Augustine*, Washington, Catholic University, 1926.

E. C. Messenger, *Evolution and Theology: the Problem of Man's Origin*, New York, Macmillan, 1932.
A careful, thorough, and intelligent study.

Erich Frank, *Philosophical Understanding and Religious Truth*, Oxford University Press, 1945.
By a modern Augustinian philosopher.

NOTES

1. There is in the way the Scripture speaks, says Augustine, a loftiness which mocks at the pretensions of the intellectually arrogant, and a profundity which frightens away those who are mere pedants (*adtentos*). By its truth, however, it feeds mature minds, and by its gentleness it nourishes immature minds. *De Genesi ad Litteram*, v. 3; CSEL 28[1], 141.

   References are to the *Corpus Scriptorum Ecclesiasticorum Latinorum*, Vienna, 1866 and later, unless otherwise noted. The translations in *The Nicene and Post-Nicene Fathers* (First Series), except for the *Confessions*, where Pusey's translation was used, have been compared with the text and revised. I am grateful to Mr. David Coffin, of Phillips Exeter Academy, for his advice on translation, but any mistakes are my own.

2. *Conf.*, XIII. 5. 6; CSEL 33, 348.

3. Cf. *Timaeus*, 38B.

4. *De Civ. Dei*, XI. 6; CSEL 40[1], 519.

5. Ibid. XI. 6; cf. also XII. 16.

6. *De Civ. Dei*, XI. 8; CSEL 40[1], 521–2; cf. Ps. 148:5.

7. *De Gen. ad. Litt.*, VI. 6 (*creavit omnia simul*). Augustine quotes this Latin version of Ecclesiasticus 18:1 very often. The Septuagint reads ἔκτισεν τὰ πάντα κοινῇ. Cf. E. C. Messenger, *Evolution and Theology*, New York, Macmillan, 1932.

8. *Conf.*, XII. 15. 18; CSEL 33, 321.

9. *De Gen. ad Litt.*, III. 26; CSEL 28[1], 125.

10. *De Civ. Dei*, XI. 33; CSEL 40[1], 564.

11. *De Gen. ad Litt.*, v. 3; CSEL 28[1], 141.

12. Cf. *Institutes*, I, XIV, 1, and *Commentary on Genesis*, Edinburgh, 1847, 61.

13. *Critique of Pure Reason* (N. Kemp Smith, tr.), 397 (first antinomy, antithesis).

339

14. *Conf.*, x. 12–13. 14–15; CSEL 33, 290–91. Cf. also vii. 15. 21.
15. *De Civ. Dei*, xii. 16; CSEL 40¹, 592. He says he fears if he makes this reply he may be accused of recklessness, therefore he does not make it as a positive assertion. But his hesitation is not at saying there was no time when there was no time. He says it would be utter foolishness to deny this. His point is that the suggestion about the *angels* is speculation beyond what is clearly taught in Scripture. It is plain that as far as speculation goes he is inclined toward this suggestion.

  It should be kept in mind that the chapters in Book xii are numbered differently in the Benedictine edition (found in Migne, *Patrologia Latina*, and used by Dods in his English translation) from the CSEL. E.g. chapter 19 in CSEL is chapter 18 in NPNF.
16. Ibid. CSEL 40¹, 594.
17. *De Civ. Dei*, xii. 17; CSEL 40¹, 595. Cf. Titus 1:2.
18. *Conf.*, xi. 13. 16; CSEL 33, 291. Cf. Ps. 102:27 (101:28).
19. *Introduction à l'étude de saint Augustin*, Paris, Vrin, 1929, 246, 251. Cf. *Conf.*, xi. 11. 13.
20. *Conf.*, xi. 31. 41; CSEL 33, 309.
21. *De Civ. Dei*, xi. 4; CSEL 40¹, 516. Cf. also x. 30; xii. 21. Augustine excepts Porphyry, who acknowledged that the soul which found the happy life did not lose it again, and at this point refused to follow his teachers.
22. *De Civ. Dei*, xi. 4.
23. Though the drama of human life on this earth will have an end (cf. *De Civ. Dei*, xx. 7), this will be the end of the age (*saeculum*) but not the end of time. Presumably, time will exist as long as there are changing creatures.
24. *De Civ. Dei*, xii. 14; CSEL 40¹, 589.
25. Ibid. Cf. Rom. 6:9; 1 Thess. 4:16.
26. *De Civ. Dei*, xii. 20; CSEL 40¹, 601.
27. *De Civ. Dei*, xii. 19; CSEL 40¹, 599.
28. *De Civ. Dei*, xii. 21; CSEL 40¹, 605. Cf. also ch. 19.
29. *De Civ. Dei*, xii. 18; CSEL 40¹, 598.
30. *Conf.*, xii. 13. 16; CSEL 33, 320.
31. *Conf.*, xii. 7. 7; CSEL 33, 314.
32. *De Natura Boni*, 18; CSEL 25, 862. Cf. C. J. O'Toole, *The Philosophy of Creation in the Writings of St. Augustine*, Washington, Catholic University, 1944, ch. 3.
33. *Conf.*, xii. 6. 6; CSEL 33, 313. The association of formless matter with change leads Augustine to speak of a 'spiritual matter,' since angels and human souls, as well as bodies, are changeable. Cf. *Conf.*, xii. 20. 29, and *De Gen. ad Litt.*, v. 5; vii. 9, 10.
34. *Conf.*, xiii. 33. 48; CSEL 33, 385.

35. *Conf.*, XII. 29. 40; CSEL 33, 341.
36. *De Gen. ad Litt.*, V. 23; CSEL 28¹, 168.
37. Cf. M. J. McKeough, *The Meaning of the Rationes Seminales in St. Augustine*, Washington, Catholic University, 1926; E. C. Messenger, op. cit.; and C. J. O'Toole, op. cit.
38. *De Gen. ad Litt.*, VI. 6; CSEL 28¹, 177.
39. *De Gen. ad Litt.*, VI. 8; CSEL 28¹, 180. In the *City of God*, Augustine argues against those who hold that the human race always existed. He says, 'From the sacred writings we compute that six thousand years have not yet passed since the institution of mankind.' XII. 11. CSEL 40¹, 583. Dods' translation in NPNF is misleading since he leaves out an equivalent of *ab institutione hominis*. It seems probable that Augustine is not here arguing that the *world* is less than 6000 years old, as the editor of NPNF, J. E. C. Welldon in his edition (London, S.P.C.K., 1924), and V. J. Bourke, *Augustine's Quest for Wisdom*, Milwaukee, Bruce, 1945, 265, all seem to suggest. Later in the same book of the *City of God*, Augustine says, 'I confess I am ignorant what ages passed before the human race was instituted.' Chap. 17; CSEL 40¹, 595.
   Augustine was inclined to think that the human *soul* was not created 'causally' but 'actually' in the beginning, later to be united with man's body, though he was aware of the difficulties attending this view. CF. *De Gen. ad Litt.*, VII. 22–8, 33; Bourke, op. cit. 232–6; Messenger, op. cit. 177–8; and McKeough, op. cit. 87. He was torn between 'creationism' and 'traducianism' as explanations of the origin of the souls of subsequent human beings.
40. *De Gen. ad Litt.*, IX. 17; CSEL 28¹, 291.
41. Ibid.
42. *Conf.*, XII. 27. 37; CSEL 33, 338.
43. *De Civ. Dei*, XI. 5; CSEL 40¹, 517–18.
44. *In Joannis Evangelium*, II. 10; Migne, *Patrologia Latina*, 35, 1393.
45. In *De Nat. Boni*, 26, he cites Rom. 4:17, II Macc. 7:28, and Ps. 148:5. CSEL 25, 867–8. He uses *de nihilo*, as a more exact expression than *ex nihilo* would be. Cf. *De Nat. Boni*, 27; CSEL 25, 868.
46. *Conf.*, XII. 7. 7; CSEL 33, 314.
47. *De Nat. Boni*, 27; CSEL 25, 868.
48. *De Civ. Dei*, XIV. 5; CSEL 40², 10.
49. Cf. *Enn.*, I. 8. 3, 14; II. 4. 16 and W. R. Inge, *The Philosophy of Plotinus*, London, Longmans, 1918, I, 134. Porphyry reported that Plotinus was ashamed of being 'in the body.' Plotinus, nevertheless, does not assert that non-being (τὸ μὴ ὄν), which he distinguished from 'absolutely nothing' (οὐκ ὄν), is intrinsically evil so clearly and consistently as Etienne Gilson seems to suggest he does. Cf. *The Spirit of Mediaeval Philosophy*, New York, Scribner's, 1936, 111.

50. *De Civ. Dei*, XIII. 16; CSEL 40¹, 634.
51. *De Civ. Dei*, XIII. 18, CSEL 40¹, 640.
52. *De Civ. Dei*, X. 30; CSEL 40¹, 500. Cf. also XXII. 24, and *De Doctrina Christiana*, I. 24.
53. *De Civ. Dei*, XI. 22; CSEL 40¹, 543.
54. *Contra Epistulam Fundamenti*, 25; CSEL 25, 223. Cf. *De Nat. Boni*, 18.
55. *De Civ. Dei*, XI. 22; CSEL 40¹, 544.
56. *Conf.*, XII. 11. 11; CSEL 33, 317.
57. *De Civ. Dei*, XI. 22; CSEL 40¹, 543-4.
58. *De Civ. Dei*, XI. 23; CSEL 40¹, 545.
59. *De Civ. Dei*, XI. 21; CSEL 40¹, 542. Cf. *Timaeus*, 29E–30B.
60. *Conf.*, XII. 32. 47; CSEL 33, 383-5.
61. *Philosophical Theology*, Cambridge University, 1930, II, 132.

XIII

THE PERSON AND WORK

OF CHRIST

Albert C. Outler

THERE IS an interesting and complicated pattern in Augustine's long, devious, spiritual progress. As he traces it for us in *The Confessions,* we can observe that at each succeeding stage of his development, his acceptance of a new half-truth brought him liberty from the bondage of an old half-truth and thus led nearer the full vision of final truth. Still, in every progression, the old was never wholly discarded or the new wholly absorbed. The Manichees helped lead him out of his Punic provincialism; yet, both in speech and thought, he always kept something of the flavor of his early training at Tagaste and Madaura and Carthage. The Academics next gave him the critical tools by which he could break the spell of the Manichees; yet something of the Manichean preoccupation with the problem of evil remains even in the mature Augustine. Next, the Platonists taught him how to think of God in spiritual and rational categories and so gave him a firm base for a positive conception of truth and reality; yet the influence of the Academic skepticism continued to prod Augustine into deeper and deeper reflections about the nature of human knowledge. At long last, his Christian conversion led him beyond all these levels — even the highest level of Plotinian wisdom — and, moreover, broke the strongest fetters of all, the slavery to his lust and self-will. But even as a Christian, as we shall see, he never lost the imprint of his pre-conversion modes of thought.

In his new life as a Christian he was, however, able to retain the residues of all the past crises of his life, and also to refocus them; to reorder his enormous energy and vitality into an extraordinarily complex unity of mind and will and self. This complexity is an essential part of Augustine's genius and must be understood as one of the natural hazards of interpreting his thought. All of this is especially pertinent to remember when we try to delineate his teaching about the person and work of Jesus Christ, for there are many strands in his Christology and their weaving is neither simple nor neat.

I. The Development of Augustine's Christology

By the time of his climactic experience at Milan, Augustine had already achieved a highly developed doctrine of God, largely under the guidance of Plotinus and the Platonists. He had come to think of God as pure Spirit: the Infinite Mind which thinks the patterns of the intelligible world; the Ultimate Reality from whence all reals are derived; the dynamic Source of all power and action. God, so conceived, is utterly transcendent, sovereign, immutable.[1] All existence and all events are referable to God for their intelligibility and value — all save evil, which the Platonists had taught him to understand as privative, as loss or deficiency of good, with neither rational form nor positive power.[2]

Along with this philosophical idea of God, Augustine had also acquired, as he tells us, a 'pre-Christian' view of Jesus Christ

as of a man of marvellous wisdom, whom no other could possibly equal . . . I saw Christ as a complete man: not the

344

body of a man only, or an animating soul without a rational mind, but altogether man; and I thought he was to be preferred to all others, not as the very Person of Truth, but because of the great excellence of his human nature and his more perfect participation in wisdom.[3]

As a Platonist, he had a conception of the Logos which he reports in *The Confessions;* he contrasts the Platonic conception of the Word as the principle-of-connection between God and the world with the Christian Gospel of the Word-made-flesh, humble and suffering, effecting man's salvation. As a Christian, Augustine could see the fatal weakness of this philosophical doctrine of the Logos. It was incurably abstract, principally because the doctrine of God was so abstract. The Platonists understood that there had to be some sort of mediation between essence and existence, between eternity and history. But they had not seen, nor could they have ever conceived, the notion of the incarnate Logos as Lord of existence and history.[4]

The essential problem of Augustine's Christological development was the transformation of these two pre-Christian concepts to the point where he could really acknowledge that this 'man of marvellous wisdom' was actually and truly divine, could confess that this Word of God was actually and truly individualized in a full and real human life, in whom God revealed Himself and through whom God was reconciling the world unto Himself. He did not always succeed in this transformation. There are moments when we wonder whether Augustine's pre-conversion notions of God do not maintain themselves in spite of his new knowledge of God in Jesus Christ. His thought is clearly and constantly *theocentric;* it is not *always* so clearly and decisively *Christocentric.* But, at his normal best, he is a faithful and powerful interpreter of orthodox traditional Christian teaching concerning the mystery of the Incarnation and the saving work of Jesus Christ. There is little reflection in his thought of the ferment and confusion about the theoretical explanation of the Incarnation which kept the Eastern Church in such a prolonged uproar. He was a Chalcedonian before Chalcedon, largely because he was so representative a spokesman of the mind of the Latin Church, which had already begun to settle along the lines later stabilized at Chalcedon. In Augustine's thought, the vision of the Incarnate Lord had come as a climax and a capstone; it clarified and corrected his former thought about God and gave him a new perspective for interpreting the puzzles of life and destiny.

His Christological thought did not come clear all at once. In his earliest writings, after his conversion but before his ordination, the Platonic concept of the Logos remains the controlling notion, even when the Incarnation is also mentioned. The Word of God, in these dialogues, is regularly the 'principle' of Truth and Reason, the immanent aspect of the transcendent (and abstractly conceived) God.[5]

For its religious profundity and intensity, the opening chapter of the *Soliloquies* is one of the most moving passages in Augustine's writings. But in it the historical event of Jesus Christ is ignored; the book might almost as well have been written four years earlier.[6] Similarly, from this same period, we have the short but pregnant treatise *On the Teacher,* which outlines the thesis that both learning and teaching require Truth as the transcendent reference to which the teacher directs the learner, and to which the learner must attend. Christ is the true Teacher, the source of Truth and Light. This little treatise is the fountainhead of the famous Augustinian 'illuminism'; but there is no intimation of the actual Teacher portrayed in the Gospels, and no clear distinction between illumination as the dynamic of human knowledge in general and the self-disclosure of God's saving grace in the life and death and Resurrection of Jesus Christ.

A notable advance in his Christological thought is to be observed in the year 389 in a letter to Nebridius,[7] a brilliant fellow-philosopher who had shared Augustine's interest in Plato and Plotinus and who now sought his further help in understanding the Christian mystery of the Incarnation. In his reply Augustine begins, characteristically, with the problem of the

Trinity and then goes on to show that the Incarnation is a corollary of correct belief in the Triune God.

> The union of the Persons in the Trinity is in the Catholic faith set forth and believed, and by a few holy and blessed ones understood, to be so inseparable, that whatever is done by the Trinity must be regarded as being done by the Father and by the Son and by the Holy Spirit together.[8]

But only the Son is said to have assumed human nature and herein lies the paradox. Augustine proceeds to explain it by distinguishing between the order of God's being and the order of His being known to men. Men have three questions to ask about God: if He is, what He is, of what 'quality' He is (*an sit, quid sit, quale sit*). But, in the order of human knowledge, the crucial question is *what* God is. This question was answered

> by the divinely appointed method of the Incarnation, which is properly ascribed to the Son, in order that from it should follow our knowledge, through the Son, of the Father Himself (i.e., of the one first principle whence all things have their being) and a certain inward and ineffable charm and sweetness of remaining in that knowledge and of despising all mortal things (a gift and work properly ascribed to the Holy Spirit). Wherefore, although in all things the Divine Persons act perfectly in common, and without possibility of separation; nevertheless *their operations* behoved to be exhibited in such a way as to be distinguished from each other, *on account of the weakness in us, who have fallen from unity into variety.*[9]

Augustine was ordained in 391 and shortly thereafter he was invited to give an address before a council of bishops at Hippo, summarizing the cardinal articles of Christian doctrine. The framework of his exposition was the Apostles' Creed and the treatise is entitled *De Fide et Symbolo* (On Faith and the Creed). The text of the Creed is plainly that of the church at Milan, which he had doubtless learned in preparation for his own baptism six years earlier.[10] Here, as in the Cassiciacum dialogues and the letter to Nebridius, his chief concern is with the doctrine of God, but now the focus of his problem is on the relations between the divine Persons within the Godhead. He clearly and strongly affirms that Jesus Christ was truly God and truly man, but this belief is maintained with minimal attention to the historic revelation in the *earthly life* of Jesus of Nazareth.

After he became a bishop, Augustine's constant dual care was the instruction of Christians in their faith and the defense of that faith against all heresies and deviations. It is in this period, and especially in his sermons, that he developed a clearer and far more concrete conception of the Incarnation and of the relation between the man Christ Jesus and the eternal Word of God.[11]

But even in the mature Augustine, his Christology derived from his doctrine of the Trinity which he had taken, almost fully developed, from the the theological tradition of Latin Christianity. This constitutes an important reversal of the pattern of primitive and patristic Christianity, in which the doctrine of the Trinity is a derivation from the Christian confession of Jesus Christ as Lord and Saviour.[12]

II. The Mystery of the Incarnation

Augustine's doctrine of the Triune God is a truly impressive construction, subtle, massive, profoundly religious. For him, the prime literal truth is the unity of God.[13] This is one of his most insistent and unvarying motifs. Some of the most intricate dialectic in the whole of the Augustinian writings is devoted to the careful analysis of his thesis that Father, Son, and Holy Spirit are each respectively God, but the Father is not Son, nor Son Holy Spirit, nor Holy Spirit Father (although He does proceed from the Father *and the Son* [14]). God is not a triad but a Trinity. The Persons of the Godhead are personal modal functions of the the one integral divine Being, whose essence is known only as He reveals Himself and who cannot be conceived of in the categories of time, space, or individuality. The divine action, in whatever mode, is always the action of 'the entire Trinity, whose works are inseparable.'[15]

We have already observed that Augustine's earliest Christological notions, after his conversion, were concerned principally with the cosmic and un-incarnate functions of the Word of God. And, even though he took with absolute seriousness the Christian assertion that 'for us men and our salvation [the one Lord Jesus Christ] came down from heaven and was incarnate,' he frequently referred to God's redeeming grace at work prior to and apart from the historic revelation. There were righteous men *before* the Incarnation 'who were made whole by the *future* humility of Christ their King, revealed to them through the Spirit.' These men were 'saints' and they were 'members of Christ's Church,' although they lived before Christ our Lord was born according to the flesh.[16] There is a very interesting letter of Augustine's to a fellow-bishop, Evodius, in which he considers, in rather gingerly fashion, the reference in I Peter 3:19 to Christ's descent into hell. He takes the accuracy of the Scriptural statement for granted but then points out that the descent could not have had for its purpose the loosing of the bonds of the patriarchs, since they were already in Paradise (the proof of this being Jesus' reference to Lazarus in Abraham's bosom). We must suppose, he therefore concludes, that the patriarchs had already been redeemed by the power of the un-incarnate Word who was 'both in paradise and Abraham's bosom in his beatific vision, and in hell in his condemning power.'[17]

God's purpose to redeem a few elect souls to replenish the number of the fallen angels and to condemn the many to their just and irrevocable punishment is an eternal purpose, and God's reconciling grace has been manifest always and among all men, by signs and sacraments suitable to their times.[18] But the mystery of God's grace has been made fully plain and wholly effectual for the elect only with the historical advent of Jesus Christ.[19]

For his expositions of the mystery of the Incarnation, Augustine begins with the doctrine he had received on the authority of the Catholic Church.[20] A typical summary is in his sample 'instruction to a Christian catechumen':

God in His mercy, desiring to deliver men from this de-struction (i.e., from everlasting punishment) if only they be not enemies to themselves and resist not the mercy of their Creator, sent His only-begotten Son (i.e., His Word) equal to Himself, by which Word He created all things. And He, though abiding in His Godhead and neither departing from His Father nor being changed in anything,[21] yet by taking upon Himself human nature, and appearing to men in mortal flesh, came unto men; that as death entered into the human race by one man who was first created (i.e., Adam) because he consented to his wife, who had been led astray by the devil, so that they transgressed the commandment of God — so also through one man, who is also God, the Son of God, Jesus Christ, all who believe in Him, after their past sins had been utterly blotted out, might enter into eternal life.[22]

An interesting and important example of Augustine's typical manner in explaining the mode and manner of the Incarnation may be seen in his long epistle to Volusianus, the proconsul of Africa A.D. 412.[23] Volusianus' connection with the Church is not quite clear. His mother was a very devout and well-instructed Christian, but the proconsul seems to have been a sort of religious dilettante, still boggling over all the puzzles and paradoxes of the Christian preaching he had heard. He had submitted to Augustine a series of objections to the Christian doctrine of the Incarnation; these questions had apparently been raised in Carthage in a discussion group to which Volusianus belonged. Augustine takes considerable pains in his reply, not only because of the intrinsic merit of the questions but because of the importance of the questioner. He begins by the frank acknowledgment that the Incarnation *is* a mystery, veiled to the eyes of unbelief or to minds that seek to explain it away in terms of the space-time categories of physical existence.

Christian doctrine [Augustine explains] does not hold that the Godhead was so blended with the human nature in which He was born of the Virgin that He either relinquished or lost the administration of the universe or transferred it to that body as a small and material substance.[24]

The power of God formed a child in the Virgin's womb;

this same power associated with Himself a human soul, and through it also a human body — in short, the whole human nature to be elevated by its union with Him — without His being thereby lowered in any degree; justly assuming from it the name of humanity, while amply giving to it the name of Godhead.[25]

In the nature of the case, this was a unique miracle, not to be compared to other instances alleged to be similar or dissimilar.[26] The miracle occurred 'at the time which He knew to be most fitting and which He had fixed before the World began.' Its purpose was twofold. On the one hand, the Incarnate Lord came to instruct men and to reveal to them the living Truth which they had not known in their distorted and false approach to God — and thus to lead men into a progressive appropriation of Truth. On the other hand, Christ came to help men to their salvation, 'since without the grace of that faith which is from Him, no man can either subdue his vicious desires, or be cleansed by pardon from his guilt.'[27]

A similar, more dramatic, expression of the same point of view is found in *The Confessions:*

But our very life came down to earth and bore our death and slew it with the very abundance of His own life. And thundering, He called us to return to Him into that secret place from which He came forth to us — coming first into the virginal womb where the human creature, our mortal flesh, was joined to Him that it might not be forever mortal — and came 'as a bridegroom coming out of his chamber, rejoicing as a strong man to run a race' (Ps. 19:5). He did not delay, but ran through the world, crying out by words, deeds, death, life, descent, ascension — crying aloud to us to return to Him. And He departed from our sight that we might return to our own hearts — and find Him there! For He

left us, and behold, He is here. He could not be with us long,
yet He never left us. He went back to the place which He
had never left, for 'the world was made by Him' (Jo. 1:10).
In this world He was, and into this world He came, to save
sinners. To Him my soul confesses, and He heals it, for it
had sinned against Him [from Vol. VII of *The Library of
Christian Classics*].[28]

Augustine never varies this thesis that in the Incarnation the
Divine Person *assumed,* or joined Himself to, a whole human
nature, but that He did not thereby become a human 'person.'
Divinity is not rendered mutable by the assumption of humanity
but is rendered more effectually accessible to the experience of
the faithful elect. 'The meaning of the Word being made flesh is
not that the divine nature was changed into flesh, but that the
divine nature assumed our flesh . . . No part was wanting in
that human nature which He put on, save that it was a nature
wholly free from every taint of sin.' [29]

At the same time, 'all that is said of the man Christ Jesus has
reference, of course, to the unity of the person of the Unigen-
itus.' [30] The *persona* of Jesus Christ is divine. But is it not natural,
almost irresistible, for most moderns to think of human 'nature'
and 'personality' as mutually implicative? To be human is to be
a person. Not to have, or to be, a personality, is not to have, or to
be, a human nature whole and entire. Augustine is explicit in
declaring that the Word of God assumed not generic human
nature but a specific and individual human nature, created and
chosen for this mysterious union.[31] Christ's human nature, therefore, is that of a whole, real, individual man. But if He was
really 'like as we are, save without sin,' as Augustine steadfastly
maintains, was He not then a human person, as we are persons?
Augustine's answer is negative.

The clue to this apparent confusion is to be found in our
different connotations of the term 'person.' In modern thought,
generally, the term person refers to a discrete and individual
entity, having some sort of identity, continuity, and rationality.
For Augustine (and for the patristic fathers generally), the term

persona (cf. the Greek ὑπόστασις) signifies a principle or function of the *unity* of separate and often disparate elements. In *human nature,* the personal unity joins together a rational soul and a fleshly body; to be a human *person* is to have this kind of psychosomatic unity. This kind of unity is present also in Jesus Christ, in the highest measure. But there is also a higher unity in Christ. 'Christ is both the Word, *and* a soul and a body [i.e. the Word and a true human nature].' [32] The *persona* of Christ, then, is this *union* of the divine and the human natures; hence Christ's 'person' is specified by the highest principle of unity presented in His Incarnate Existence. 'Just as any man unites *in one person* a rational soul and a body, so Christ unites *in one person* the Logos and a man.' [33] Thus Augustine freely adapted the traditional formulas, coined by Tertullian and finally written into dogma at Chalcedon.[34]

The practical effect of this interpretation of the central figure in the Gospels is that Augustine asserts, without the slightest wavering, the real and actual human nature and historical career of Jesus Christ, and yet at the same time he tends to reduce his emphasis on that human nature and that historical career. The 'Divine Person' comes effectually to overshadow the 'human nature,' as it does not in the Gospels or in primitive Christianity.

This problem of the union of the two natures was, of course, to exercise the Church, and the Eastern sections of it particularly, for least two centuries after Augustine. The two main doctrinal tendencies are represented by the School of Alexandria (following Cyril) and the School of Antioch (following Theodore of Mopsuestia and Nestorius). The Alexandrines emphasized the *assumption* of human nature by the Logos, whereas the Antiochenes tried to interpret the union in terms of *moral harmony* and Jesus' human obedience to the Will of God. Characteristically, Augustine combines both emphases in his own way. One of the favorite metaphors of the Antiochenes [35] was the figure in Philippians 2:6–7 of Christ's taking 'the form of a servant.' Augustine also adopts this metaphor as a favorite explanatory notion for distinguishing the human nature of Christ from the divine in the Gospel references:

Christ Himself, therefore, the Son of God, equal with the Father because He was in the form of God, inasmuch as He emptied Himself, without losing the *form of God* but assuming *the form of a servant,* is greater even than Himself; because the unlost *form of God* is greater than the assumed *form of a servant* . . .

Let us acknowledge the twofold substance of Christ; to wit, the divine, in which He is equal with the Father, and the human, in respect to which the Father is greater. And yet at the same time both are not two, for Christ is one; and God is not a quaternity, but a Trinity. For as the rational soul and the body form but one man, so Christ, while both God and man, is one; and thus Christ is God, a rational soul, and a body. In all of this we confess Him to be Christ, we confess Him in each. Who, then, is He that made the world? Christ Jesus, but *in the form of God.* Who is it that was crucified under Pontius Pilate? Christ Jesus, but in *the form of a servant.* And so of the several parts whereof He consists as man. Who is He who was not left in hell? Christ Jesus, but only in respect of His soul. Who was to rise on the third day, after being laid in the tomb? Christ Jesus, but solely in reference to His flesh. In reference, then, to each of these, He is likewise called Christ. And yet all of them are not two, or three, but one Christ.[36]

Augustine's tremendous emphasis upon *unity* — the unity of God, the unity of the Person of Jesus Christ, the enhypostatic unity of the Persons of the Trinity — ruled out any temptation to the Nestorian heresy, but it did push him toward that kind of Christological doctrine in which the human nature of Jesus Christ is freely acknowledged and yet made radically subordinate to the divine nature.[37] The ecumenical councils of Chalcedon (451), II Constantinople (553), and III Constantinople (681) called the Church back again and again from monophysitism (a one-sided emphasis on the divine *nature* in Jesus Christ) and monothelitism (a one-sided emphasis on the divine *will* in Jesus Christ). But the tendency to exalt the Redeemer and to celebrate

354

His true deity was naturally very strong and the full mystery of the '*et homo factus est*' was not fully faced. Thus it was that in the prevailing Christological thought of the medieval Church the human nature of Jesus Christ was regularly confessed but its full import ignored — and 'the man Christ Jesus' (I Tim. 2:5) became the Heavenly Mediator (the Christus of the *grande portaille* of the Gothic cathedral) who must Himself be mediated to men by His human mother and the saints. Augustine was not the only, or chief, cause of this tendency, but he shared in it and his doctrine of God shows the effects of it.

As a bishop and a devoted son of the Catholic Church, Augustine was almost steadily embattled with the heretics who plagued the Church and distracted the faithful with their aberrant interpretations of Christ. In a treatise, about A.D. 397, which he called *The Christian Combat (De Agone Christiano)*, he identifies an even dozen Christological errors against which the orthodox Christian must defend the faith. Frequently throughout his writings he denounces the major heresies by name: Sabellianism (to which he regularly applies as synonym the term 'Patripassian'), Apollinarianism, Arianism, Photinianism, and Manicheism.[38] In one place he says that the orthodox Catholic doctrine of the two natures is midway between the extremes of Sabellius and Arius.[39] And in another very interesting passage, he lists the possible errors men make concerning Christ and suggests a line of refutation which he believes applies to them all.[40]

III. The Work of the Incarnate Lord

All of Augustine's theology grew out of his efforts to understand and interpret the faith he shared in common with his fellow Christians. The heart of Christian life and worship is faith's confession that 'Jesus Christ is Lord and Saviour.' Augustine believed this with profound sincerity and deep intellectual wonder. Moreover, he went on, in the sermons and treatises of his mature years, to work out a complex explanation of *how* the life and death and Resurrection of Jesus Christ suffice to redeem God's elect from the utter ruin into which mankind has fallen in sin and rebellion against God. The first premise of the theory

is that God, in sovereign justice and mercy, has purposed to offset the defections of the fallen angels and the first man by restoring a part of mankind to fill the gaps in the heavenly city.[41]
The second premise is that fallen man is irretrievably lost in the
tragic and vicious debility of his will and has nothing of merit
and no ability whatsoever to save or restore himself.[42] The conclusion follows that God must act, for man's redemption, through
a Mediator who is both God and man.[43] The work of the Mediator must reconcile the elect to God, must break the power of the
devil over human life, must demonstrate God's unmerited grace
and love, and, finally, must serve as exemplar of the Christian
life for all the faithful.[44] All this, required for man's salvation,
God has done, mysteriously but effectually, in the life and work
of Jesus Christ.

Augustine sees this divine mediation as a marvelous condescension on the part of God, which operates to beget human
faith, to humble human pride (the prod to sin), to bestir human
love, to break the devil's hold over human lives, and to inspire
Christians to humble and obedient and godly living.[45] The Incarnation reveals God's esteem for man, His unmerited favor
toward man [46]; and it calls forth, from the faithful, the fruits
of humility and obedience, thus ordering human love aright:

> Christ came chiefly for this reason that man might learn how
> much God loves him, and might learn this to the end that
> he might begin to glow with love of Him by whom he was
> first loved, and so might love his neighbor at the bidding
> and after the example of Him who made Himself man's
> neighbor by loving him, when instead of being His neighbor
> he was wandering far from Him.[47]

Moreover, God has suited the manner of man's redemption to
the specific needs and predicament into which sin had cast him:

> Our enlightening is the partaking of the Word, namely, of
> that life which is the light of men. But for this partaking we
> are utterly unfit, and fall short of it, on account of the un-
> cleanness of sins. Therefore we must be cleansed. And further

the one cleansing of the unrighteousness and of the proud is the blood of the Righteous One, and the humbling of God Himself; that we might be cleansed through Him, made as He was what we are by nature, and what we are not by sin, that we might contemplate God, which by nature we are not. For by nature we are not God: by nature we are men, by sin we are not righteous. Wherefore God, made a righteous man, interceded with God for man the sinner. For the sinner answers not to the righteous, but man answers to man. By joining therefore to us the likeness of His humility, He took away the unlikeness of our unrighteousness; and by being made partaker of our mortality, He made us partakers of His divinity. For the death of the sinner, springing from the necessity of condemnation, is deservedly abolished by the death of the Righteous One springing from the free choice of His compassion.[48]

In Christ's life and death Augustine saw a dramatic defeat of the devil. Man in his sinful state lacks either the will to righteousness or the power to realize his will; he is, in either case, a victim of the devil's unrighteous power. Christ's human nature was like all others — 'save without sin.' The devil blindly assumed he could dominate and ruin this life as he had done all others. But Christ — although possessed of divine power — emptied Himself of that power and challenged the devil's right purely on the basis of His righteousness and His devoted obedience to God's Kingdom as the rule of His life. The devil's response to this challenge was to loose his own unrighteous power on this human nature — and he was allowed to do so by Christ's abnegation of His divine power. Thus Christ suffered; and the devil seemed to carry the day, to prove once more that might can override the unarmored right. But, when Christ's human nature had humbly accepted — in righteous obedience — the worst the devil could do, God then reasserted the power of righteousness which overthrows the power of unrighteous might. 'The devil was conquered when he thought he himself had conquered Christ by slaying Him.'[49] The sufferings of Christ were, therefore, 'a

357

ransom by accepting which the devil was not enriched but bound.' [50] Christ's breaking the devil's power is the decisive objective proof that, even in human life, which is accustomed to the devil's domination, God's rule is ultimate and actual in the lives of His faithful and obedient children, who are joined to Christ in His Body, the Church, and who follow His example of humility and righteousness.

From yet another perspective, Augustine speaks of Jesus Christ as the Great Physician, come to heal men of their souls' infirmities; [51] the Great Restorer, who renews in man the lost *imago dei* and reconstitutes his true nature and existence. [52] Christ is the climactic manifestation of God's redemptive grace. [53]

Perhaps the most succinct summary Augustine gives of his understanding of this mystery of Christ's saving work is found in the conclusion of Book x of *The City of God:*

> The incarnation of Christ, and all those important marvels that were accomplished in Him, and done in His name: the repentance of men and the conversion of their wills to God; the remission of sins, the grace of righteousness, the faith of the pious, and the multitudes in all parts of the world who believe in the true divinity; the overthrow of idolatry and demon worship and the testing of the faithful by trials; the purification of those who persevered, and their deliverance from all evil; the day of judgment, the resurrection of the dead, the eternal damnation of the community of the ungodly, and the eternal kingdom of the most glorious city of God, ever-blessed in the enjoyment of the vision of God, — these things were predicted and promised in the Scriptures of this way; and of these we see so many fulfilled, that we justly and piously trust that the rest will also come to pass. As for those who do not believe, and consequently do not understand, that this is the way which leads straight to the vision of God and to eternal fellowship with Him, according to the true predictions and statements of the Holy Scriptures, they may storm at our position, but they cannot storm it. [54]

IV. Two Notions of God's Grace

Besides his emphasis on God's unity, Augustine always laid equal stress upon His unconditioned freedom, power, and grace. God's will is always triumphant and is never evil. He 'never does anything unless He wills it and does everything He wills.' [55] In relation to the world, then, all of God's action is *grace*. God creates, sustains, redeems, and consummates, not of necessity or because of human merit, but out of spontaneous love and goodness. Man's very being is a work of grace and his salvation is God's gracious gift. Augustine thus interprets the whole range of human existence in the light of this inclusive conception of the identity of God's action and His grace. It was not without warrant that the medieval Church assigned to him his honorific title, *Doctor Gratiae*.

But Augustine had two ways of talking about divine grace. On the one hand, there is his habit *within* the atmosphere of faith, inside the Christian community; it might be called his 'homiletical mood.' In this mode, grace is always spoken of in terms of man's gratitude to God and his joy in believing himself justified and reconciled by God's grace. Grace is wholly God's gift. But among the faithful Augustine emphasizes man's part in *responding* to God's gracious initiative, and he regularly presupposes that man has God-given freedom to respond. Grace, for the elect, is a glorious and wondrous mercy which they have received — for which they are thankful — but which they have by no means earned or merited. In his counsel to Deogratias on the art of catechizing, and in his own examples of catechetical instruction, there is a warm-hearted emphasis upon God's initiative in providing for man's salvation.[56] Augustine cautions the Christian catechist not to allow his suspicion that a candidate may not be of the elect to prevent his being treated as though he *might* be.[57] Elsewhere, in his sermons and expositions to persons who he could presume had been called to election by God's grace, Augustine's emphasis is one of wonder, love, and praise that such unmerited favor should have been bestowed upon sinful men. Being bestowed, it is the ground for a Christian confidence, security, and hope that energizes the will and transforms the whole of life.[58]

Even the casual reader will notice, however, that Augustine has another manner in which he speaks of God's power and grace. Against all who minimize grace or who assert man's abilities and power, after the Pelagian fashion, he opposes a harsh doctrine of God's omnipotence, which allows not the slightest qualification, or even paradox. In this 'polemical mood,' Augustine declares that God's grace is irresistible and inexorably effectual in accomplishing the divine purposes.[59] Salvation is a sheer miracle wrought by God's inscrutable will on behalf of a part of ruined mankind and is in no way congruent with human action or ability. Damnation is, likewise, sheer justice wrought by the same inscrutable will. God's mercy and justice are both alike beyond human questioning. The elect rejoice in God's mercy; the damned must acknowledge His justice. Both take their destiny from His choice and by His fixed decree.[60]

In his polemical mood, Augustine passes a verdict on the damned which is almost callous. The vast majority of mankind, so he thinks, goes in misery to its foreknown and foreordained doom,[61] terrible, endless — and 'just.' Augustine sharply decries any 'mere human sentiments' or 'feelings' which cause the tender-hearted to be 'perversely compassionate' and to 'deplore the eternal punishment and the unceasing and everlasting torments of the damned' or 'to tone down everything that seems harsh.' [62] Whatever apparent morality one observes among the non-elect is nugatory and inconsequential:

> God forbid that we should admit the existence of true virtue in anyone except he be righteous. And God forbid that we should admit anyone to be truly righteous unless he lives by faith: 'for the righteous lives by faith.' Who then of those who wish to be thought Christian (except the Pelagians alone, or perhaps you [i.e. Julian of Eclanum] alone even amongst the Pelagians) will apply the epithet of 'righteous' to an infidel? — even though such a one should be Fabricius, a Fabius, a Scipio or a Regulus! [63]

Nor does Augustine shrink from the further implication of this pitiless view of grace: the unbaptized, whether or not there is any reason for their state, are inevitably and justly damned.[64] This includes infants, although for them it is allowed that only the mildest punishments are reserved.

It may be asked whether these particular convictions of Augustine were derived from or validated by his knowledge of God in *Jesus Christ?* Are the notions of limited atonement, geminal predestination, irresistible grace, and the damnation of unbaptized infants directly taught or strictly implied in the New Testament? Actually, it would seem that these grim doctrines, extreme and almost mechanical, represent an unnatural and unnecessary distortion of Augustine's own central contention for the *sovereignty* of God's goodness and love and grace. It is as though, in order to preserve God's omnipotence, he had taken an abstract, speculative notion of it and drawn out the logical corollaries, without submitting his thought to the self-disclosure of God-in-Christ, of whom he speaks so well and so faithfully in his homiletical or constructive mood. One of the wisest and most discerning historians of Christian doctrine, Reinhold Seeberg, has appraised the matter thus:

> The profoundly religious spirit of Augustine is as manifest as is the fact that certain foreign and unevangelical threads have found their way into the texture of his thought. He had learned to present faithfully the *sola gratia* [salvation by grace alone] but his doctrine suffered from the fact . . . that the God whose fellowship his heart could so wonderfully portray was yet for his intellect not the God of the Gospel.[65]

Augustine's doctrine of God is a great complex prism which collected many rays of light from the patristic age and refracted them over the vast spectrum of medieval and Reformation Christianity. But, for all its massive scope and profundity, it was not at all points *fully* Christocentric. In his 'polemical mood,' he stands nearer to his pre-Christian 'Platonic' conception of deity than to the God of redemption, who 'sent His Son into the world, not to condemn the world, but that the world through Him might be saved.' [66]

It is instructive to observe that this part of Augustine's thought was, in fact, not accepted by the Church, which otherwise approved him as her most pre-eminent 'doctor.' Its too stark logic and its pitiless temper grated on Christian minds and hearts, and a reaction set in to modify and to reinterpret it. After a century of debate, amid the confusion that usually attends the birth of a dogma, the Second Council of Orange (529) drew up a series of canons which sought to draw a firm line between *sovereign* and *irresistible* grace and between single and double predestination. These canons were confirmed by Pope Boniface II and became normative for Catholic orthodoxy. They represent a modified Augustinianism (Augustine in his 'homiletical' vein), and they passed into the doctrinal framework of the whole of medieval theology.[67]

V. A Psychological Interpretation

It might be, however, that we should try to appraise Augustine's ideas of salvation and reprobation in psychological as well as theological terms. Windelband once remarked that Augustine's was 'a metaphysic of inner experience.' It may be that his understanding of Christ's work in human hearts is in some part a psychological reflection of his own inner, ethical experience.

Augustine had experienced a radical and permanent change of will and affection in his own turbulent spirit. This he could understand and explain only as a work of the mysterious and unmerited grace of God, 'who both readies the will to accept assistance and assists the will once it has been made ready.' [68] Similarly, it might be supposed that his statements about the damned are more significant as existential reflections on the manner in which *guilt and grace are humanly experienced* than as privileged reports on the actual state of affairs in hell and heaven.

To the sinner, in whose breast guilt feelings are aroused by an uneasy and unappeasable conscience, God's judgment must inevitably appear bleak and devoid of mercy — and yet, turn it as he may, this judgment must be faced and must be acknowledged as just. A man's sins may appear to have been unavoidable and necessitated — but they *are* his *own* sins and his conscience about them simply will not leave him in peace. To the saint, in analogous fashion, the experience of God's graciousness is inscrutable, wondrous, infallibly effectual. To feel himself reconciled to God is clearly not something he has merited or even prepared for. Salvation is the work of divine love; and this love has acted before, apart from, and beyond man's initiative or control. Hence, all righteousness is of faith. All faith is of grace; and the response of faith to grace is gratitude. If Augustine could have been content with some such phenomenological account of the experiences of alienation and reconciliation, modern men could recognize in his thought a more consistently evangelical doctrine of grace, and his concept of predestination would have resembled more fully those of Paul, the younger Luther, or Francis Thompson in 'The Hound of Heaven.' [69]

VI. Christology and Eschatology

The historical crises of his time drove Augustine to probing reflections about the form and meaning of history itself. More and more, he came to see the tapestry of time as patterned by God. Historical existence is not ruled by fate or fortune, nor does it turn round upon itself in an endless cycle. History stretches out from a beginning and toward an end. An immense cosmic drama, it has a plot, a denouement, and a resolution. The shape, the meaning, and the end of history are governed by God, whose 'commonwealth' (*civitas*) has an earthly career and a historical destiny. Human history is always the history of community, and the two ultimate divisions of human community are the community constituted by human self-love ('enlightened self-interest') and the community constituted by the love of God. This division can be discerned analogically in the careers of the empires of earth, on the one hand, and the covenant communities of Israel and Christ, on the other. The 'city of God' (God's "commonwealth," God's "kingdom") exists *in* time but its final reference points *beyond* time. The 'city of earth' (the always precarious and unstable commonwealth of human political striving) exists as a sort of concomitant sociological environment for the Church, but oriented to a vastly inferior end. While time shall last, the two cities must live together and neither can exclude the other wholly from the temporal scene. They 'both alike either enjoy temporal good things or are afflicted with temporal ills,' [70] but they have diverse faiths, diverse hopes, and diverse loves. This distinction will continue until they are finally and decisively separated in the consummation of God's good will and pleasure in the final judgment.

The City of God and the Catholic Church are not quite identified by Augustine, but they are not quite separated either. [71] Jesus Christ is Lord of history and Head of the Church. Thus He rules with revealing and redeeming power in and through the course of history. But it is at the *end* of history that He will stand forth most plainly as Judge of the living and the dead; and make an end to the struggle of the wicked — devils and men — who oppose and defy God's omnipotent will.

A very long section of *The City of God* (Books XIX–XXII) is devoted to Augustine's eschatology. In it he is concerned to show that the end of the good life (i.e. the life of the chosen, few elect) is 'the perfectly ordered and harmonious enjoyment of God, and of one another in God.' [72] But he feels that he must also show that in order to safeguard God's omnipotence, a condign and endless punishment must be wreaked on all the vast multitude of the non-elect. This requires a final Judgment and an implacable Judge. Jesus Christ, of course, is this judge. Augustine describes the 'final and strict judgment' and the eternal punishment of the wicked with a surprising wealth of detail and local color. But, again, we may ask if it is plausible to suppose that this particular conception of God's ultimate triumph is really derived from the central testimony of the New Testament and the revelation of God *in Jesus Christ*? It would seem that, in Augustine's eschatology, we have yet another instance of the unpurged residue of his abstract theomonism, which he had not yet fully submitted to the mind and heart of Christ. [73]

At the very end of *The City of God,* Augustine gives an intense and ardent description of the beatific vision and the perpetual felicity of the saints in heaven.[74] As we read this, and reflect upon the immense Augustinian corpus as a whole, it becomes plain that his prayer in the *Soliloquies* had been abundantly fulfilled. His particular theological forte was his knowledge of God and his psychological wisdom. They are unequaled and permanent resources for all subsequent Christian thinking, as the history of Christian doctrine clearly shows.

He came into the Christian community a Latin rhetor and a Platonic philosopher. In the tradition and cultus of the Church his heart and mind were reshaped by the vital presence of the Word of God, in liturgy, sacrament, and fellowship. He became an incomparably great interpreter of the Christian faith, and of the Christian life that springs from faith. In his complex theological system, we can, as I have suggested, mark out some segments that are not fully 'converted' by his knowledge of the person and work of the Incarnate Lord. Indeed, we may appeal from a worse Augustine, in his abstract and speculative moods, to a better Augustine, in his constructive, evangelical moods. Nevertheless, this system taken as a whole must be judged as one of the most remarkable of all Christ's triumphs in transforming the mind of genius. Thus Augustine remains a preeminent teacher for our time, as he was in his own, to all who can confess with him: 'We, therefore, who are called and are Christians, do not believe in Peter, but in Him whom Peter believed . . . Christ Himself, who was Peter's Master [and Augustine's] in the doctrine which leads to eternal life, is *our* Master, too.' [75]

FOR FURTHER READING

C. N. Cochrane, *Christianity and Classical Culture,* Oxford University Press, 1939, Part III.

A splendid general study of Augustine, with particularly important insights into the way in which Christology affected the Christian understanding of the problem of 'personality.'

Hugh Pope, *St. Augustine of Hippo,* The Newman Press, 1949.

A learned and wise interpretation of Augustine as bishop and theologian, with important incidental insights into his Christology.

Otto Scheel, *Die Anschauung Augustins über Christi Person und Werk,* Tübingen, 1901.

Still the 'classic' monograph on this particular aspect of Augustine's thought.

NOTES

1. *Confessions,* VII. 1, 9, 20; cf. IV. 11.
2. *Confessions,* VII. 3, 5, 12–16; compare his earlier statements of the doctrine in *Soliloquies,* I. 2 and *Concerning Order,* II. 7; and also his fully matured summary of the doctrine in *Enchiridion,* III–IV (9–15).
3. *Confessions,* VII. 19. 25.
4. VII. 21.
5. *Against the Academics,* II. 1. 2; III. 20. 43; *The Happy Life,* I. 4. 34, 35; *Concerning Order,* I. 8. 21; I. 10. 29; I. 11. 32; II. 5. 16; *Soliloquies,* I. 1; *On the Teacher,* I. 5, 11, 14.
6. Cf. the famous prayer in ch. II: 'I desire to know God and the soul . . . absolutely nothing more.'
7. *Epistle* XI.
8. Ibid. 2.
9. Ibid. 4. Italics not in the original.
10. Cf. Harold Smith, *St. Augustine: De Fide et Symbolo,* 7–9; see also Schaff, *Creeds of Christendom,* II, 47–56.
11. Cf. especially *On the Gospel of John* and *Selected Sermons.* See also *On the Trinity* and *Enchiridion.*
12. Cf. John Knox, *Christ the Lord,* 88f.; see also H. R. Mackintosh, *The Person and Work of Christ,* 509ff.
13. *On the Trinity,* VI. 6–9; *On the Gospel of John,* XXXVI. 9; XVIII. 3–5; XIX. 6; XX. 3–5; LXX. 1–7; LXXI *passim.*
14. On this issue, which would later divide the Latin and the Greek Churches, Augustine was already clearly on the side of the Latin 'filioque.' Cf. *On the Gospel of John,* XCIV; *On the Trinity,* XV. 26.
15. *Enchiridion,* XII. 38. Cf. *On the Trinity,* I. 9; V. 7–10; VI. 3–6, 9; XV. 27; *City of God,* X. 24; *On the Gospel of John,* LXXVII. 2; *Exposition of the Psalms,* LXIX. 5.
16. *On Catechizing the Uninstructed,* XIX. 33; later, in his 'narration' to the catechumens, he speaks of 'some unknown saints *who had obeyed* the first covenant of works,' XXII. 40. Cf. *City of God,* VII. 32–3; X. 25. None of this contradicts his agreement with Cyprian's dictum, 'No salvation outside the Church.' Instead, it is a significant redefinition of the Church: the church is *the number of the elect,* whenever and wherever found.

17. *Epistle*, CLXIV. 15–21.
18. The number of the elect corresponds to the number of fallen angels, *Enchiridion*, IX. 29; XVI. 61; *City of God*, XXII. 1; the elect are a minority and the damned a vast majority, *Enchiridion*, XXIV. 97; XXV. 99; *On Catechizing the Uninstructed*, XIX. 31; *On the Unity of the Church*, XIV. 36. God's grace always and everywhere effectual; cf. *City of God*, XII. 32–3.
19. *City of God*, X. 25.
20. Here, as in all the crucial issues, he illustrates the truth of his famous assertion to the Manicheans: 'For myself, I would not believe even the Gospel, unless moved thereunto by the authority of the Catholic Church.' *Against the Epistle of Manicheus*, 5. Cf. *On Catechizing the Uninstructed*, VIII. 12.
21. Cf. *Filius Dei non est mutatus per incarnationem, Sermon* XII (Migne, *P.L.*, V, 105–6).
22. *On Catechizing the Uninstructed*, XXVI. 52. See Christopher's excellent commentary on this passage in *St. Augustine: The First Catechetical Instruction*, 145–57.
23. *Epistle* CXXVII.
24. Ibid. II. 4.
25. Ibid. II. 8.
26. Ibid. III. 10.
27. Ibid. 12.
28. IV. 12.
29. *Enchiridion*, X, 34; *City of God*, XI. 2; '*Homine assumto; non Deo consumto*.' Chapters X–XI. 33–7 of the *Enchiridion* constitute an indispensable summary of Augustine's mature Christological teaching. This passage deserves the most careful study. For interesting contemporary variations on this same Christological position, cf. E. L. Mascall's *Christ, the Christian and the Church*, ch. III, and Emil Brunner, *The Mediator*, ch. XIII.
30. *Enchiridion*, XV. 56.
31. *Enchiridion*, XI. 39.
32. *Selected Sermons*, VII.
33. *Enchiridion*, XI. 36.
34. Cf. Tertullian, *Against Praxeas*, 37–8. *Deus est una substantia, tres personae* 'God is one substance, three persons.' *Christus est una persona, duae naturae*. 'Christ is one person, two natures.' Cf. the formulary of Chalcedon (451) in Schaff, *op. cit.* II, 62. 'One and the same Christ, Son, Lord, Only-begotten, to be acknowledged in two natures, inconfusedly, unchangeably, indivisibly, inseparably, the distinction of natures by no means taken away by the union, but rather the property of each nature being preserved and concurring in One Person and One Subsistence, not parted or divided into two

persons, but one and the same Son, and only-begotten, God the Word, the Lord Jesus Christ.'

35. As also in Hilary of Poitiers, who directly influenced Augustine. Cf. Hilary's *On The Trinity*, XI, 48.

36. *On John*, LXVIII. 2–3; Cf. *On the Trinity*, I. 7; II. 2; IV. 19–20; VII. 3; *Enchiridion*, XIII. 41–2; XIV. 51–3; *On John*, XXXVI. 2; XLVII. 13; *New Testament Sermons*, XXVI. 14. This is but a sampling of similar passages that might be cited.

37. There is no dearth of such assertions anywhere in Augustine's writings, notably *Confessions*, VII. 18–21; *On the City of God*, XIV. 9; XXII. 15–18. But note the passage in *City of God*, XIV. 9: 'But as He became man when it pleased Him, so, in the grace of His definite purpose, when it pleased Him He experienced those emotions in His human soul . . . In us, these emotions arise from human infirmity, but it was not so with the Lord Jesus; for even His infirmity was the consequences of His power.'

38. *On the Gospel of John*, XXIX, XL, XLVII, LXX, LXXI.

39. Ibid. XXXVII. 6.

40. Ibid. XCVI. 3–5.

41. *Enchiridion*, IX. 29: 'Thus it pleased God, Creator and Governor of the universe, that since the whole multitude of the angels had not perished in this desertion of Him, those who had perished would remain forever in perdition but those who had remained loyal through the revolt should go on rejoicing in the certain knowledge of the bliss forever theirs. From the other part of the rational creation—that is, mankind—although it had perished as a whole through sins and punishments, both original and personal, God had determined that a portion of it would be restored and would fill up the loss which that diabolical disaster had caused in the angelic society' [from Vol. VII of *The Library of Christian Classics*]. Cf. similar section in *City of God*, XII. 22.

42. *City of God*, XIII. 3, 10; *The Trinity*, XIII. 17; *Enchiridion*, IX. 30.

43. *Enchiridion*, XXVIII. 108.

44. Cf. *Enchiridion*, X–XV. 33–53; also, *The Trinity*, XIII. These are the most important summary sections of Augustine's soteriological theories.

45. *Enchiridion*, XIV. 49: 'Therefore, he [Christ] chose to be baptized in water by John, not thereby to wash away any sin of his own, but to manifest his great humility. Indeed, baptism found nothing in him to wash away, just as death found nothing to punish. Hence, it was in authentic justice, and not by violent power, that the devil was overcome and conquered: for, as he had most unjustly slain him who was in no way deserving of death, he also did most justly lose those whom he had justly held in bondage as punishment for their

sins' [from Vol. VII of *The Library of Christian Classics*]. Cf. *Sermons on the New Testament*, LXXVII. 17; LXIX. 5–6; *On the Psalms*, CXXVI. 3; *On Catechizing the Uninstructed*, 22, 40.

46. Augustine repeatedly states that the human nature assumed by the Word was not chosen because of any exceptional worthiness or antecedent merit. The act of assumption itself was as fully *sola gratia* as any of God's dealings with His human creatures. Cf. *The Trinity*, XIII. 17; *Enchiridion*, XI. 36.

47. *On Catechizing the Uninstructed*, IV. 8.

48. *The Trinity*, IV. 2. 4.

49. *The Trinity*, XIII. 15.

50. Ibid. 16: 'Why then should the death of Christ not have come to pass? Nay, rather, why should not that death itself have been chosen above all else to be brought to pass, to the passing by of the other innumerable ways which He who is omnipotent could have employed to free us; that death, I say, wherein neither was anything diminished nor changed from His divinity, and so great benefit was conferred upon men, from the humanity which He took upon Him, that a temporal death, which was not due, was rendered by the eternal Son of God, who was also the Son of man, whereby He might free them from an eternal death which was due? The devil was holding fast our sins, and through them was fixing us deservedly in death. He discharged them, who had none of His own, and who was led by him to death undeservedly. That blood was of such price, that he who even slew Christ for a time by a death which was not due, can as his due detain no one, who has put on Christ, in the eternal death which was his due.'

51. *On Matthew*, II. 58; *On John*, II. 1; III. 2; *On Christian Doctrine*, I. 14; *The Christian Combat*, XI. Cf. the long account, in *City of God*, XXII. 8, of the extraordinary miracles of healing which Augustine himself had witnessed or knew about in his own locality.

52. *On the Trinity*, XIV. 16.

53. *On John*, XXII; *On Catechizing the Uninstructed*, XXII. 39–40; *Enchiridion*, XIV. 48–55.

54. Ch. 32.

55. *Enchiridion*, XXVII. 103; cf. 102.

56. *On Catechizing the Uninstructed*, IV.

57. Ibid. XIV. 21.

58. *On John*, III. 15; XLV. 9; CIV. 3; *On the Psalms*, CXXVII. 3; *Sermons on New Testament Lessons*, LXXVI. 14; XCII; cf. *Confessions*, especially IX. 1 and X. 1–5.

59. *Enchiridion*, XXIV. 97; *On the Predestination of the Saints*, XIX. 10; *On the Gift of Perseverance*, 41; *On the Soul and Its Origin*, 16.

60. Compare the mood of the treatise *On Catechizing the Uninstructed*,

containing the assumption that the catechumen has the ability to respond to exhortation, with the mood of *On Admonition and Grace,* in which Augustine is defending, in extreme form, his doctrine of God's unconditional power.

61. That the majority of mankind are damned, see note 18. Normally, Augustine speaks of a single predestination of the elect and the divine preterition of the damned. But when the argument seems to require it, he does not shrink from the logical consequences of his position: double predestination. *On Catechizing the Uninstructed,* XVIII. 30; *Enchiridion,* VIII. 27; *On the Soul and Its Origin,* 16.

62. *Enchiridion,* XXIX. 112–13; cf. *City of God,* XIX. 17–25.

63. *Against Julian,* IV. 17; cf. *City of God,* XIX. 25.

64. *On Forgiveness of Sins and Baptism,* I. 21. 16; *Enchiridion,* XXIII. 93.

65. *Textbook of the History of Doctrine,* I, 352.

66. John 3:17.

67. One might cite in passing the episode of Gottschalk (810–70), where a naïve and literal revival of extreme, theomonistic Augustinianism reminded the Church yet once again of the havoc such a view will wreak upon the Gospel. Cf. Coulton, *Five Centuries of Religion,* I, 81–4.

68. *Enchiridion,* IX. 32.

69. In spite of superficial resemblances, there were important differences between the theologies of Augustine and Calvin on this point. Augustine's theology was derived from and dedicated to the cultic piety of the Catholic Church. His doctrine of grace is set in the framework of liturgy and sacrament and is almost always specifically a doctrine of *sacramental* grace; and the Church is the final authority in matters of faith and morals, in its custody of Scripture and the sacraments.

70. *City of God,* XVIII. 54.

71. Ibid. 47–8; XVII. 4.

72. XIX. 13.

73. For reference to Augustine's characteristic pattern of retaining his past 'residues,' see pages 343–4.

74. XXII. 29–30.

75. *City of God,* XVIII. 54.

XIV

THE CHRISTIAN ETHIC

Thomas J. Bigham and Albert T. Mollegen

T HOU HAST made us *toward* thyself,' one translation of the best-known saying of St. Augustine, makes clear the basic principle of his many-sided but unitary thought. For him ethics, theology, and philosophy are one, even as they also unite with, and give explanation to, the unity that exists in private virtue and public good, mystical prayer in its solitude and sacramental prayer in the Church, right thinking and holy thinking. Indeed, the whole universe of space and time on all levels of its being, physical, animate, rational, and in all aspects of its being, individual and social, theoretical and practical, good and evil — this whole ordered harmony and all things in it tend toward God, without whom nothing could exist at all.

The Augustinian theological ethic is a deep and real synthesis of Neoplatonism and the New Testament. Its influence in the history of the West and of Western Christianity can hardly be overestimated; it gathered up the thought of the Patristic Church (which was already a combination of Stoic views on the law of

nature and New Testament views on eschatology) and transmitted it to the coming feudal period, where it resulted in the
best features of medieval Catholicism, and to the Reformation
period, where it served as constant inspiration. Down to our own
day it gives us forms for our thinking. The massive unity of St.
Augustine's synthesis makes it possible to point out the chief
principles of his ethic and his way of vindicating them, and then
to illustrate these principles by his applications of them to the
two institutions of marriage and the state — which then, as now,
provided the most difficult ethical dilemmas.

To make a selection has its own dangers, however, especially
when on this basis some heirs of Augustinian thought address
themselves to other heirs. We all take St. Augustine differently.
Since the day that St. Thomas Aquinas made the Aristotelian
systematization of what is largely Augustinian teaching, Catholic
Christianity has been inclined to forget St. Thomas' debt and to
send St. Augustine himself into exile — as M. Gilson points out.
Reformation Christianity, likewise profoundly indebted to St.
Augustine, at the same time vigorously and sincerely rejects
much of his outlook. To the modern mind much of the Augustinian ethic seems very startling. His theoretical expositions
sound, of course, very much like what we have all learned from
the Bible and from Plato, those two great parents for our Western
life of right thinking and right character. But we ordinarily
assume that these two heritages are very similar to each other. It
startles us therefore to discover, as it were from the conversation
of an elder son of our family who also assumes their likeness,
that these two parents were very different indeed. This we see
most clearly in St. Augustine's practical applications of his theory,
but the differences can also be noted in the expositions of theory.

I. The Christian Answer to the Classical Ethical Question

St. Augustine, who sees that all things tend toward God, holds
caritas to be central. (We may call this 'charity,' as our word
used to be, or 'love,' as we generally say now.) *Caritas* toward God
is the goal of man's nature. Augustine frequently begins his
vindication of the Christian ethic with a frankly eudemonistic

principle. The argument in *On the Morals of the Catholic Church* begins: 'We all certainly desire to live happily; and there is no human being but assents to this statement almost before it is made.' A man is not happy if he does not have what he loves; or if he has what he loves and it is hurtful; or if he does not love what he has, even though it is perfect good. The happy life is 'when that which is man's chief good is both loved and possessed.' Man's chief good cannot be inferior to himself, for that would make him less than his nature; it must be God who is superior to man, even as man's soul is superior to his body.[1]

St. Augustine thus begins with the empirical element in man's love of unfulfilled desire or yearning, *amor appetitus*.[2] Then he states that what man loves determines the quality of his nature and whether his love is satisfied. If the object of man's love is lower than himself, his soul is dragged downward toward non-being and his love is frustrated and increasingly restless. By loving the creature, man grows into likeness to the world and cannot recognize the Incarnate Wisdom.[3] Of course, the natural creature does not experience this demotion by God as such, but as frustrated love and loss of being. Virtue, on the contrary, promises happiness. The soul seeks virtue, not in itself, where it is not, but in God, 'in following after whom we live well and in reaching whom we live both well and happily.'[4]

So far we may climb by reflection, reasoning, philosophy. Augustine himself began this ascent with his reading of Cicero's *Hortensius*. 'How did I burn to remount from earthly things to Thee . . . for with Thee is wisdom. But the love of wisdom is in Greek called "philosophy," with which that book inflamed me.'[5]

Philosophy, therefore, can take one from sensualism and hedonism on the ascent to the *summum bonum*. Neoplatonism can carry one, and did carry Augustine, to the vision of God's 'invisible things,' to the assurance 'that Thou truly art who art the same ever . . . and that all other things are from Thee, on this most sure ground alone, that they are.' The books of the Neoplatonists 'say whither they were to go, yet saw not the way'; the Scriptures of the Church tell of 'the way that leadeth not only to behold the beatific country but to dwell in it.' Neoplatonism admonished man to behold God but did not lead him to hold God. 'For it is one thing, from the mountain's wooded summit to see the land of peace . . . and another to keep to the way that leads thither.' [6] So for Augustine Neoplatonism gave place to Christianity. His *amor* was not satisfied with the Neoplatonist vision of God. *Amor* must come to hold God; our hearts are restless until they find rest in God. Desire must find rest in its object without fear of losing that rest and that object. At his conversion he found these in the God of Christ and His Church.

His own experience, he said, was universally true for two great reasons. First, love that begins its journey already corrupted by pride is never able to purge itself of pride. The *amor* of Adam before the Fall has now become *cupiditas,* that is, *amor* with *superbia.* Augustine does not always keep this exact language, but in view of his major uses it is justifiable to systematize his thought in this way. All human love is desire for happiness, for one's own self-fulfilling good. Self-sufficiency, however, has turned man from the one fulfillment that could give peace. In his present situation, when he tries to love above himself, he actually removes himself from God as he does so. God is not in the direction of the contemplative and mystical climb of the Neoplatonist; there is an unbridgeable gulf between its end and Himself. Like Icarus, the Neoplatonist ascends on the wax wings of pride, which melt and let him fall. 'And yet did I not press on to enjoy my God; but was borne up to Thee by Thy beauty, and soon borne down from Thee by mine own weight, sinking with sorrow into these inferior things.' [7] St. Augustine, the Christian, thinks of Neoplatonism as a pedagogue under whom God had set him to lead him to Christ, much in the same way as St. Paul thinks of the Law.

One thing was needed — humility — and that could not be achieved by man; only the Incarnate Word could achieve this in man. This is the second great truth Augustine discovered in his own experience. Only by surrender and confession of Christ and

His Church can presumption be undone. 'For where was that *caritas* building on the foundation of humility, which is Christ Jesus?' [8] Only by His love in taking our humanity and in dying for us can our true *caritas* be evoked. *Caritas* does not come by man striving but by God relating man to Himself. Charity toward God is produced by *gratia*, God's free gift of Himself to man through the charity of Christ, for *caritas* is *amor* with *humilitas*. 'Inasmuch as there is nothing more adverse to love than envy, and as pride is the mother of envy, the same Lord Jesus Christ, God-man, is both a manifestation of divine love toward us, and an example of human humility with us, to the end that our great swelling might be cured by a greater counteracting remedy. For here is a great misery, cured by a greater counteracting remedy. For here is a great misery, proud man! But there is a greater mercy, a humble God!' [9] In a sermon, Augustine wrote:

Whence doth iniquity abound? From pride. Cure pride and there will be no more iniquity. Consequently, that the cause of all diseases might be cured, namely, pride, the Son of Man came down and was made low. Why are thou proud, O man? God, for thee became low . . . For this is the commendation of humility, whereas pride doeth its own will, humility doeth the will of God. Therefore, 'Whoso cometh to Me, I will not cast him out.' Why? Because 'I came not to do my own will but the will of Him that sent me. I came humble, I came to teach humility, I came a master of humility: he that cometh to me is made one body with me; he that cometh to me becomes humble; he who adhereth to me will be humble, because he doeth not his own will, but the will of God, and therefore he shall not be cast out for when he was proud he was cast out.' [10]

Or again: 'Believe in the Crucified, and thou shalt be able to arrive thither. For thy sake He was crucified, to teach thee humility.' [11]

As Neoplatonism could be interpreted as a preparatory stage

for Christian conversion, so also even the futile search of *cupiditas* for a satisfying object can be spoken of as divine discontent. It is from this point of view that we are to understand Augustine's famous phrase, 'Thou hast made us toward Thyself, and our hearts are restless until they find rest in Thee.' [12] The very nature of our being as creatures has set us on the way back to the Creator; and the inevitable self-defeat that then comes from our pride in journeying onward is to be overcome by our surrender in love to the Redeemer who stooped in grace to raise man to Himself. God's *gratia* unites with man's *caritas*.

This experience of the religious and moral process has two aspects. Man by nature *does direct* himself toward God the Good, as philosophy and experience show. Also at the same time he *ought to direct* himself toward God the Governor, as Biblical commands and Christian experience show, summed up in the first law of God which commands man's *caritas:* Thou shalt love the Lord thy God. This one process is not arbitrary, as its legal and obligatory aspect might suggest if taken alone; nor is it simply aesthetic, a delight in harmony, as the rational affirmation alone might suggest. The seeking of man for his good is a fact that is to be stated in the indicative; it is the fact of man's present state that leads him on to his future. The good is what we would; man's seeking is man's hope. This aspect of our life is, however, reinforced because morality is also spoken of in the imperative. Man's hope and God's command coincide in the discovery of *caritas*.

This unity of 'tends to be' and 'ought to be' and of man's yearning and God's love is the great strength of the Augustinian ethic, combining Greek philosophy and Biblical religion to give Christian answer to the great ethical question of pagan antiquity. Yet the answer falls short of the New Testament ethic, because it turns out to be, after all, less Biblical than Neoplatonic. We may see this by examing three instances of Augustinian teaching: the description of the virtues, the reasons given for loving one's neighbor, and the description of the love of God.

II. The Limitations Placed by the
Question Upon the Answer

St. Augustine's ethics of individual life follows logically and surely from his *caritas* synthesis. He chooses the four Platonic and Aristotelian virtues, rather than the Old Testament laws, to guide love in personal relationships, society, and history. These pagan virtues need correction and completion, however, because pride uses their achievement to make them sinful. Therefore Augustine rightly does to the four virtues what Jesus did to the Jewish virtues of prayer, fasting, and alms-giving in the Sermon on the Mount. He shows that unless they be motivated by love of God, they are motivated by pride, being then but 'splendid vices.' [13] He sees *caritas,* God-given love of God, as being both the true motivation for the virtues and also the quality of the person who discerns how the virtues apply, that is, what to do.[14] Hence, 'temperance is love keeping itself entire and uncorrupt for God; fortitude is love bearing everything readily for the sake of God; justice is love serving God only, and therefore ruling well all else, as subject to man; prudence is love making a right distinction between what helps it toward God and what might hinder it.' [15] The four pagan virtues are transformed into Christian virtues only when faith (that by which we love God not yet seen) and hope (that by which we love what we have not yet reached) and love (which remains when faith has become sight, and hope has been realized) undergird them. Indeed, love is holiness, St. Augustine can say; therefore, 'Love and do what thou wilt . . . let the root of love be within, of this root can nothing spring but what is good.' [16] The virtues philosophy can talk about are given by grace to the Christian, and 'eternal life is the reward' for living the Christian virtuous life, says St. Augustine, and then adds, 'nor can the reward precede the desert, nor be given to a man before he is worthy of it.' [17]

The curious twist of thought at the end of this sentence may seem to be a doctrine of merited reward quite different from the emphasis St. Augustine elsewhere places upon St. Paul's doctrines of Christ dying for us while we were yet sinners and of the divine love seeking us out apart from any matter of merit. But St. Augustine really combines these two themes in the single view that God helps us to become virtuous in order to merit reward from Him.

Virtue then is defined as rewarded self-fulfillment. Such a definition is more Neoplatonic than Biblical. It is, to be sure, an effective answer to the classical question of pagan antiquity: What is the highest good? But because this is a Greek question, it receives an answer that does not do full justice to the Scriptural view. The New Testament will not allow this to be the central question; Jesus says, 'Why callest thou me good? There is none good save One.' The question St. Augustine answered is a genuinely rational one and important humanly. It is the question of the Prodigal Son, home-sick, yearning for fulfillment, seeking to come to himself; but the New Testament places all this to one side of the central goodness of that son's father who goes out to meet him. In the Scriptures the fundamental ethic is, Be ye merciful, even as your Father which is in heaven is merciful. To St. Augustine virtue is the *pattern* of human yearning fulfilled; to the New Testament virtue is the *person* through whom divine mercy is outpoured. After all, even to surrender one's self-seeking is not entirely to know the meaning of self-sharing; it does not quite enter into the self-sharing of God with man, or of a man with his neighbor. Self-giving has more outreach than self-fulfilling.

A second example of the Neoplatonic limitations to the ethic of St. Augustine is seen in his description of love for one's neighbor. In his treatise *On Christian Doctrine* he says that *caritas,* which fulfills the first law of God, fulfills also the command: Thou shalt love thy neighbor as thyself. 'Thus the end of the commandment is love and that twofold, the love of God and the love of neighbor.' *Caritas* gives the Christian the true virtues, for it gives him the discernment of the divine order of love. 'There are four kinds of things to be loved — first, that which is above us; second, ourselves; third, that which is on a level with us; fourth, that which is beneath us; no precepts need be given about the second and fourth of these.' [18] Augustine means that *amor sui* is man's nature in the fundamental sense that the soul seeks its good. If it seeks its good in itself, or even beneath itself, it nevertheless needs no command to love itself but only to love God and neighbor, which will correct its deformed *amor sui* into true *amor sui*. The command to love God and neighbor, therefore, includes the command to the proper love of self and all lovable things.

On Christian Doctrine is not very clear about why *caritas* should move toward neighbors as well as toward God, except that God loves us and also loves them. Those who love God are drawn into likeness to Him and desire earnestly to share 'the fellowship of the love of God' in which we live. This is St. Augustine's implicit answer.[19] The difficulty lies in the fact that it is so little explicit and emphatic. The most explicit passage in Augustine occurs where the plain meaning of Scripture in the words of Christ Himself demands it. In *Our Lord's Sermon on the Mount,* where *imitatio Dei* is expressly put by Jesus, Augustine follows faithfully. He understands 'that ye may be the children of your Father' as Johannine and Pauline 'adoption' [20] and gives the interpretation, 'But when He calls us to this [sonship] by means of the Only-Begotten Himself, He calls us to His own likeness.' [21]

St. Augustine is indeed increasingly Biblical as he grows older. It is, therefore, possible to make a case against the contention that Augustine does not so much fuse the Greek and the Biblical elements as put the Biblical into a Greek framework of the Platonic idea of Eros. St. Augustine quotes the Bible prolifically in all his later writings, and many of his works are simply expositions of Biblical books. Yet when all is said, the synthesis of Neoplatonism and the Bible has real limitations. Augustine never overcame his Neoplatonic roots. Augustine addresses God in dynamic, personal, passionate language, notably in the *Confessions;* yet for Augustine, God as it were never speaks this language as for example He does for the prophets of the Old Testament. Indeed, God according to Augustine's description seems to be above all that: He is therefore always pulling men away from historical realities and never sending them deep into

379

history. So also to St. Augustine our fellowship with our neighbor is never direct love for a unique person but a fellow feeling with someone who also is, or is to be, drawn up into a universal. For all of his great love for St. Paul, St. Augustine is far more Johannine, concerned for life 'in the world yet not of the world.' One has only to read his many passages on I Corinthians 13 to understand this, for he turns *agape,* moving outward to create fellowship and to discipline the chaotic gifts of the Spirit, into *caritas,* moving upward to God and drawing others into it. Despite his masterful insight into human personality, his basically Neoplatonic outlook made it possible for him to see only the Johannine meaning of Jewish and Christian love, and not that of the Synoptic Gospels and St. Paul, love for the other person who is my neighbor and for the Other who is fully Personal God. St. Augustine has no great sense of otherness. Indeed, 'man' is already a universal that overlooks the unique, historical reality of each man's being. Neoplatonic forms bind the Biblical ethic. The impersonality of philosophical questions and answers here inhibits the personal warmth of Church morality.

This is nowhere clearer than in the conception of God's love in its descent. 'God loves us. In what does He love us? As objects of use, or as objects of enjoyment [*ut nobis utator an ut fruatur*]? If he enjoys us, He must be in need of good from us and no sane man will say that; for all the good we enjoy is either Himself or what comes from Him. He does not enjoy us then, but makes use of us. For if He neither enjoys nor uses us, I am at a loss to discover in what way He can love us.' [22]

'To love,' it seems, is either *frui* or *uti.* One loves either because one seeks one's good in another and finds it (*frui*), or because one employs the other for the sake of one's good already found (*uti*). This language does not have to be translated by the prejudicial terms 'to enjoy' (*frui*) and 'to use' (*uti*). The point might be described by saying that, where A is one's chief good, one takes delight in B because A loves B, or B loves A, or B participates in A. Applied to God this pair of alternatives means that we cannot say that God enjoys us, that He completes Himself in us, for we are less than He and His gifts. We have to say that He makes use of us for His own goodness. In other words, God loves us because He loves Himself and we participate in His Goodness.

This conception is essentially Greek and in the Platonic tradition, although St. Augustine's God is three steps removed from Plato's. For Plato, 'the Good' was the vision of beauty along with truth and goodness, a vision attained by the aspiring soul through its own self-discipline. The first step was Aristotle's self-contemplating, self-enjoying unmoved mover, who (which) however moves the whole Cosmos by attracting it to himself (itself), even as a beauty awakens desire and as an ideal calls forth emulation and identification. The second step was Neoplatonic, for Plotinus, the overflow and downflow of Being, catching the soul in its own returning and upward movement; there in ecstasy beyond thought the soul beholds Being and becomes one with what it beholds, 'becomes God.' St. Augustine takes the third step and partly Christianizes this with the doctrine of Creation and Redemption. God creates us in His image and, for love of His goodness in us, descends the ladder of being to draw us up to vision and communion with Himself for our own good, which we yearn for and which He purposes. Because 'to love' for God cannot be *frui*, it seems logical that it must be *uti*. Similarly for man 'to love' God is for the ascending rational soul, not only to find God, but to make Him captive with its reason.

If the New Testament is not read through Neoplatonic lenses, it tells what St. Augustine was at a loss to discover. God's *agape* is beyond this dilemma of self-enjoyment and self-completeness, because *agape* is a characteristic of person moving toward persons, not a function of a *nature*. It has therefore a supernatural and a supra-rational quality that is not subpersonal. For Platonism to attain the good is a merging of natures in reason and in ecstasy; for Christianity to attain the good is a meeting as of persons. While a vision, it is more an action; while in one way an ascent to God, it is more 'to walk humbly with thy God.' For the Bible the God who commands *cares* for those who are commanded; the Father loves His children, because they are of his image but more because they are persons who respond in love.

When Jesus says, 'Come, follow me,' He is calling not especially to the contemplative and ecstatic life, except as that is part of the divine mission to all men, the movement of the divine love seeking out every person.

III. Marriage for the Christian

'Come, follow me' is not chiefly the call of a monastic and mystical Jesus, yet St. Augustine, because of the Neoplatonic questions constantly in his mind, hears it so. Perhaps nothing better illustrates St. Augustine's basic principles and presuppositions in Christian ethics and his brilliance and penetration in applying them than his works on virginity, marriage, and sex. By translating St. Paul's interim-ethic in the seventh chapter of I Corinthians into a Neoplatonic over-worldliness, Augustine makes the whole Bible give the counsel of celibacy and virginity in *caritas* to God. Everywhere in his works this basic attitude is affirmed, and he never seems to suspect for a moment that any New Testament witness could have meant anything else. Marriage is good, but celibacy now is always better. Marriage is good, for its goods are procreation, fidelity, fellowship between man and wife, the ruling of natural desire, the permanent sacramental bond.[23] But 'Christian doctrine, having diligent question made of it, makes answer that a first marriage also now at this time is to be despised, unless incontinence stand in the way . . . The good of marriage is indeed ever a good, but in the people of God it was at one time an act of obedience unto the law; now it is a remedy for weakness, but in certain a solace of human nature. Forsooth to be engaged in the begetting of children, not after the fashion of dogs by promiscuous use of females, but by honest order of marriage, is not an affection such as we are to blame in a man; yet this affection itself the Christian mind, having thoughts of heavenly things, in a more praiseworthy manner surpasses and overcomes.'[24] While Augustine admits that not all are able to receive this counsel, he insists that it is a universal divine counsel and that marriage is only a concession to unrestrained passion.

Augustine's views on sexual intercourse may be arranged as

follows. First, before the Fall, sexual conjunction was in obedience to the will, for the purpose of procreation only, and without shameful concupiscence. Here Augustine shows that to condemn the element of lust in sexual intercourse is not to condemn the goods of marriage or marriage itself. Second, marriage after the Fall was and is the same natural good for which God created sexual differentiation. The change is not in the nature of marriage but in the men and women. Shameful concupiscence came with the Fall. 'The devil has inflicted a heavy wound, not, indeed on marriage itself, but on man and woman by whom marriage is made.' [25] The divine command to be fruitful obtained from the Fall until Christ, because of the need for the propagation of the people of God.[26] Third, the coming of Christ and His Church makes procreation no longer a divine command but only a lesser good. Celibacy should be urged on all without fear of losing the lesser good, married life in the Body of Christ.

Augustine is nevertheless willing to pursue his logic to the end. If an opponent should argue, 'How shall the human race subsist, if all shall have been continent?' the answer is that 'this world is delayed' only in order that 'the predestined number of the saints be fulfilled, and were this sooner fulfilled, assuredly the end of this world would not be put off.' [27] If no man or woman marries, then it would mean only that the goods of marriage would already have been fulfilled in the fulfillment of Creation by the Church.

There is now, therefore, all other virtues being equal, a descending hierarchy of states of life in Christ in relation to sexuality, celibacy, and virginity: first, the life of 'angelic exercise here'; then, in order, absolute continence after early bereavement; absolute continence after late bereavement; monogamous marriage; then, also, one, two, three, or more marriages after bereavement. Beneath this are what are mortal sins for a Christian, fornication, adultery, and unnatural use of sex.

But the highest state must be 'in Christ' externally and internally in order to achieve its true value: a Catholic married woman is above a heretical virgin, and a humble Catholic wife above a proud or drunken Catholic virgin. Indeed inner virtue is greater than outer: fornication with the intent of lifelong union and without rejection of parenthood is better than social marriage only for the gratification of sexual appetite. Beneath even this is the use of contraception (even the rhythm method, he says, also proves the user to be simply gratifying passion) [28] and abortion, which he links with it.

The gratification of sexual desire in itself, if it does accept parenthood, is sinful but pardonably so, because one glory of marriage is that, if the partners love marriage more than disorders which may attend it, those excesses are overlooked. In the highest Christian marriage, procreation with a view to baptism is the only justification for sexual intercourse, and carnal concupiscence is only tolerated. [29]

This topic has been described in detail to show several of the major characteristics of Augustinian thought. First, he advocates celibacy because of a Neoplatonic reading of the Bible. No doubt his strong advocacy has its place in his own psychological history, and more in the vigorous polemic of the Church against the disordered sexual life of imperial Roman society. Indeed we must never forget that much of the Patristic sex ethic was a strong missionary effort to convert a society that, on the one hand, in Roman legal practice had reduced marriage from a lasting and religious union to a private arrangement of the contracting parties, and on the other hand, especially in Manichean teachings, had come to believe the body to be so corrupt as to be beyond hope of social usefulness or religious redemption. Yet we cannot but notice how much St. Augustine, as all the early Fathers, came close to agreeing with what he opposed. Because of the Christian doctrine of Creation by the good God, St. Augustine violently opposed the Manichees' Oriental belief that creation and procreation were evils that corrupted the soul by physical embodiment in the material world, and he opposed their delight in marriagelessness, whether virginal or debauched. Nevertheless, while his doctrine of marriage is Christian, his doctrine of sex is dubiously so. The difficulty seems to be that his opposition is based on a philosophy of Creation and Redemption more Neoplatonic than Biblical.

The doctrine of the Neoplatonists, stemming in part from the same Oriental sources, was that in the downflow of Being and the emanation of beings, as of rays from a light, there is an increasing admixture of darkness with light. The emanation of beings is therefore a primordial fall into guilt and sin as souls are entangled in matter. From that doctrine there follows the belief that the body is the prison house of the soul, and also there follows the Neoplatonic practices of asceticism and mystical ecstasy.

St. Augustine, when he became a Christian, could and did formally renounce these beliefs, but he continued to uphold the practices and to be influenced by them. Because of the Christian doctrine of Creation he believes in procreation, but because of his belief in Redemption he considers it unnecessary. Because of God's creation and command, marriage is for him a good; but because of the Fall, the results of which to his mind are transmitted through procreation, the act of procreation is always dangerously close to sin. Indeed, original sin is the mother of the excess of physical passion over and above the necessities of procreation and is also the daughter of that excess in the next generation.[30] Thus sexual feelings other than the conscious intention of parenthood and the parental impulses are sinful. With a doctrine of the Fall different from that of the Neoplatonists, Augustine is still able to think Neoplatonically of the body as a shackle and a shame, to be rescued by rational control for purposes of parenthood or, better, to be escaped by continence and meditation. This doctrine of the sinfulness in sex held sway until St. Thomas wrote his *Summa*. Celibacy, in St. Augustine's thought, was a means of escaping the body and the world, not, as for St. Thomas, the use of the body for particular work in the Church for the world, or, as for the Protestant reformers, a special individual vocation to bring the world to God. What to the modern mind perhaps stands out most in these views is the lack of concern St. Augustine shows both for wife and children and for the future of the human community. The Neoplatonic conditioning of the world view of the Bible makes men quite careless about the world's future; they give no hostages to fortune but stand in the hope of the completion of the City of God.

A second characteristic of St. Augustine's moral teaching, which can be briefly stated because it is easily understood, is his very Biblical understanding of the inwardness of sin and of the good life. He is unsurpassed as a moralist when he warns and admonishes with his special ability to see the way pride corrupts even the best and the way evils in men distort the good order of social life.

A third characteristic of his views on marriage is his philosophy of history, dividing the course of history into 'a time for marrying' and 'a time for continence.' Here he reflects a deep transformation of Greek philosophical views about cycles of time by a Biblical sense of time moving in one direction to fulfill the purposes of God. It may be claimed for St. Augustine that this insistence that history moves on irreversibly, which he learned from the Scriptures,[31] gave to Western civilization a characteristic outlook different from that of our Greek heritage. The Greeks, in common with all the ancient world, had sometimes held life to be recurring cycles of ages and had sometimes concentrated attention on empirical happenings within a given cycle. St. Augustine's teaching about the movement of history described only two dispensations of time, before Christ and after, but it opened the way for later Christians to see more fully the divine purposes working themselves out within history. In the sayings of Ecclesiastes about different occasions in the life of every man, including 'a time to embrace and a time to refrain from embracing,' St. Augustine saw a reference to the Old Testament period as a time for the natural good of marrying and to the Christian period as a time for transcending nature through continence. The high Scholastics, in whose sacramental doctrine marriage was raised from the natural to the supernatural order, went beyond the Patristic view to make full place for Christian family life, and at the same time they gave preeminence to monastic dedication as a social function within the Christian community and as an indivdual call to mystical devotion. Scholasticism, like Augustinianism, however, tends to think only in terms of *nature* and of God as Super*nature,* thus making use of Neoplatonic and Greek rational forms, rather than of Biblical historical forms that allow for individualization of persons and for particular vocations for all Christians. This is not so much wrong as it is inadequate; the vision of God above history is only a partial view of the Kingdom of God which is both in and above history. Properly, the eyes with which to see the New Testament are provided by the prophets rather than by Plotinus. To face our existence from the point of view of the normative and eschatological Christianity of the New Testament is to see our Lord as the Lord of a history in which the Kingdom has come, yet in its fullness is to come. In this approach to the New Testament from the Old, Luther saw family life as a particular vocation (even though he saw no place at all for monastic life), and Calvin centered ethical concern upon responsibility for the education of children to be worthy citizens and devout believers who could make the course of this world's affairs more Christian.

These teachings are all Christian, but no one of them is normative. As Reinhold Neibuhr has said,[32]

> . . . neither Catholicism nor Protestantism has ever completely realized the ideal of relating sexual life sacramentally to the whole of personality and to the whole of a loyal community of persons in the family partnership. Catholicism insists that sexual relationships, even in the family, except within the purpose of procreation, are wrong. And the Puritan heritage has continued a morbid and prurient attitude toward sex which is undoubtedly partly responsible for the inability of modern man to bring his sex life into a sane and healthy relationship to the whole of life.

Rationalism, legalism, and Puritanism are the three ghosts that haunt our ethic of Christian marriage, even as they haunted the ethic of St. Augustine. Normative Christianity seems to escape us as Protestants and Catholics; but it nevertheless appears among us as we witness with, and against, one another to the one Faith. On the ethic of sex, no one Christian seems to state Christian teaching definitively and inclusively; yet within the over-arching community of Christian thought the Christian teaching is made known, that marriage and sexuality are basically goods of Creation which become greater goods, corrected in their disorders and directed toward their deepest meanings, as they are touched by the divine work of Redemption. In the classical form in which St. Augustine put it, these goods are the bearing and raising of children in the love of the Lord, the loyalties of man and wife and of parents and children, and the sacramental unity of marriage.[23]

IV. The Christian in the State

We have only to apply Augustine's principles on love and marriage to world society in history to understand his conception of 'the City of God.' The transcendent city is among the angels who are fixed in their fulfilled love of God, not able to sin, and ordered according to their natures, and who receive their glory according to their due. At the end of the world, the world both passes away and passes into the love of God, which is its fulfillment, its obedience, and its perfect freedom. Here St. Augustine seems, and is in part, Biblical. While he does not see the transcendent city as impinging upon history to judge, destroy, and transform it, he does see it entering history, descending to pull it upward to God.

The transcendent city has its historical and social embodiment in the Catholic Church as a sociological institution, because the divine *caritas* descended in Christ, and still descends in the Spirit, and is brought forth as the virtue of *caritas* in the Catholic life. As Christ was born of the Virgin Mary, so Christians are born of the virgin-mother Church, a mother through loving charity. She brings forth many peoples, but they are members of One of whom she herself is both body and spouse.[33]

Alongside this City of God stands the City of Earth; alongside Jerusalem, Babylon. 'Two loves have created these two cities, namely, self-love to the extent of despising God, the earthly; love of God to the extent of despising one's self, the heavenly city.'[34] *Caritas* and *cupiditas* are the two loves.[35] But in history the two cities that express themselves in the historical Church and State are not identical with the Church and State:

> Observe two kinds of men . . . But these kinds of men are mingled. We see now a citizen of Jerusalem, a citizen of the Kingdom of Heaven, holding some office upon earth, as for example, wearing the purple, serving as magistrate, as aedile, as proconsul, as emperor, directing the earthly republic . . . Let us not therefore despair of the citizens of the Kingdom of Heaven when we see them engaged in the affairs of Babylon . . . nor again let us forthwith congratulate all men whom we see engaged in celestial matters, for even the sons of pestilence sit sometimes in the seat of Moses . . . But there will come a time of winnowing . . .[36]

In the Catholic Church the wicked are mingled with the good.[37]

There is, then, a true Church of the citizens of the Kingdom of Heaven within the sociological Church. So also it is possible for there to be a just State within the City of Earth. The implications of this are clearly drawn: 'The celestial kingdom groans amid the citizens of the terrestrial kingdom; and sometimes the terrestrial kingdom . . . exacts service from the citizens of the Kingdom of Heaven, and the Kingdom of Heaven exacts service from the citizens of the terrestrial kingdom.' [38]

The fact that the State properly exacts service from the members of the Church is clearly exemplified by the Christian soldier. 'Julian was an unbelieving emperor, nay, he was an apostate, unjust, an idolater. There were Christian soldiers in the service of the unbelieving emperor. Where the cause of Christ was at stake, they recognized only that Ruler who is in heaven. If the emperor desired them to worship idols, to throw incense on their altars, they put God before him; but when he said "form a line of battle" or "march against this or that nation" they at once obeyed.' [39]

Contrariwise, that the Church properly exacts service from the State appears in Augustine in the most extreme form with state persecution of schismatics.[40]

Originally my opinion was that no one should be coerced into the unity of Christ, that we must act only by words, fight only by arguments, and prevail only by force of reason, lest we should have those whom we know to be avowed heretics feigning themselves to be Catholics. But this opinion of mind was overcome not by the words of those who controverted it, but by conclusive examples to which they could point . . . Whole cities once Donatist are now Catholic, vehemently detesting that diabolical schism, and ardently loving the unity of the Church.

You now see therefore, I suppose, that what must be considered when anyone is coerced is not the mere fact of the coercion but the nature of that to which he is coerced, whether it be good or bad. Not that anyone can be good against his will, but that, through fear of suffering what he does not desire, he either renounces his hampering animosity, or he is compelled to examine a truth of which he had been ignorant; and under the influence of this fear repudiates the error which he was wont to defend, or seeks the truth of which formerly he knew nothing, and now willingly holds what he formerly rejected.[41]

The modern man who is not a Roman Catholic is affronted by St. Augustine's use of State coercion to abolish schism and heresy. To many, such an idea is a violation of Christian and civil liberties, and one of the most offensive of Roman teachings. Close examination of this in Augustine is therefore important. Several things must be clearly seen. First, Augustine did not believe that coercion could convert people to Christianity, and he was originally opposed to its use against schism 'lest we should have those whom we knew to be avowed heretics feigning themselves to be Catholics.' He did not change this original belief. For him, what alone could convert men was humility and love as they bear witness to the humble God and His *caritas*. The Church must 'be abased, scourged and crucified, its roots must be without the splendor of this world.' [42] Secondly, his judgment that it was right for the Church to use the State's arm against heresy, schism, and idolatry was based on empirical evidence and was purely a matter of strategy. Presumably, his conviction could be changed and the policy reversed when its results were bad. All he hoped for was that coercive action of the State would commend truth to the wayward. Thirdly, given the validity of his judgment that coercion works to these ends, a justification for coercion follows directly and logically — even inevitably — from his theology.

It is this last point that will be developed for a final criticism of Augustine. In modern categories, we are concerned with that aspect of his social ethics which deals with social action and stems from his doctrine of the Natural Law or the order of creation.

The order of nature, for St. Augustine, is the order of creation as all things tend toward God. This order is, as we have seen, love of God, love of self in God, and love of neighbor in God equally with self; and this *caritas* is also Eternal Law.[43] The order of nature was perfect order before the Fall of Adam. The Law of Love was obeyed by Adam without pride and with the help of grace. By nature and grace Adam was able not to sin and not to die, but he was also able to sin and die.[44] His disobedience was by will and not by nature; but in punishment God changed the nature of his body, making it subject to misery and death.[45] The social effects of Adam's Fall worked themselves out slowly as social history developed. The created good of marriage, as we have seen, became after the Fall a remedy, a solace, and an excuse. Originally a simple good, it is now practiced as a result of sin. So, too, the State, originally a simple order of common living, is now in existing states a result of sin and also a remedy for sin. In primitive times the original order was more nearly approximated by the nomadic peoples, when men were 'shepherds of cattle rather than kings of men.' That is, God intended men to be equal, having dominion over the irrational animals, not over other men.[46] But now private property, slavery, imperialism, the State itself, appear in post-Fall society as regulations of God to preserve nature, which is always being disrupted by sin.

We notice here the Augustinian pessimism about man and the orders of social life in history. We are perhaps ready to join in with this attitude in relation to the State, for we are as removed as was he, and for the same reasons, from any Oriental belief in the simple divine descent of rulers. As Americans and Augustinians we look cynically upon politics and we, too, see that power tends to corrupt — in our frontier culture we like to think that the less government there is the better. Were it not for our incurable romanticism about marriage — America being the country, according to many observers,[47] where it is most often held that marriage must be based on love — we might also agree with St. Augustine's pessimism about marriage.

Strengthening man's hope by its imperative, the divine decree, in order to preserve the fallen order against further disruption by sin, gives man the present orders *domus, civitas* (including empires), and *orbis terrae*, St. Augustine says. The rightness of coercive authority and inequality derives from a relative and necessary application of law to sin-disordered nature. Social institutions are the result of sin, yet they also maintain justice.[48]

The *paterfamilias* has his troubles in the household, the judge in the city, and the emperor in the larger city (the empire) and in the *orbis terrae*. 'The good man' as a ruler will not desire expansion of his dominion but, threatened by an imperialistic kingdom, may have to conquer and include it. 'Because it would be worse if the bad should get all the sovereignty, and so overrule the good, therefore in that respect, honest men may esteem their own sovereignty a felicity.' [49] A socially responsible man who wields power and punishes is like the *paterfamilias* who must punish; for 'it is not innocent to spare a man at the risk of his falling into graver sin.' To be innocent, we must not only do harm to no man but also restrain from sin or punish his sin, so that either the man himself who is punished may profit by his experience, or others be warned by his example. Masters, however, 'ought to feel their position of authority a greater burden than servants their service.' [50] The judge, aware that he ought to be omniscient and that he is not, cries out under social responsibility, 'From my necessities deliver Thou me,' but does not resign and become irresponsible.[51]

All of this is profound and freshly Christian. St. Augustine is brilliant in his interpretations of the structure of society, and his penetration of social problems is unparalleled. As he sees evils brought into the good orders of society by evil men, so he sees evils that good men must do within the disorders of social life. In him the Patristic Church, which did not think to be other than 'a society within a society' and could not hope to change the world, comes of age and takes social responsibility. The *City of God,* however, is uncertain in its theological ground for social responsibility. It was the first great attempt to relate the eschatological Christianity of the New Testament to culture, and a first grasp in the Church's groping toward a full social ethic. St. Augustine seems, however, never to have recognized a fundamental difficulty. From the Bible as a whole he received the command to love his neighbor as himself in the order of creation, and this was akin to the idea of Stoic equality in his own philosophical culture. But from Neoplatonism he received the doctrine of a self-enjoying God, and of a self-seeking man who could find his end in the vision of God, by climbing the hierarchy of being. He never broke through these latter presuppositions, although he radically transformed them. Social responsibility in Augustine never achieves the absoluteness of a command from the God whose Kingdom breaks into and transforms history. According to Augustine, our love for neighbor and our love for self, both in God, pull us away from *domus, civitas,* and *orbis terrae* toward the monastery or the desert, and to the Church as an angelic level of life. The celestial city is a higher level of *nature* to which we can climb by infused *caritas* and the exercise of the Christian version of the cardinal virtues. Grace helps the climber to merit the eternal reward, which is his self-fulfillment.

This view is the same one that underlies the exhortation to virginal dedication. St. Augustine sees celibacy not as a vocation in the Kingdom's warfare, not as a vocation that gives evidence of the social and personal value of chastity, not as an individual's strategy to govern a special problem of sexual passion, but as a higher level of Christian living to be counseled for all. Augustine recognizes pride in man's pretension to be God and in an angel's pretension to be God; but he does not see pride in man's pretension to live as an angel! He sees in that pretension only great temptations to pride.

For Augustine the peace of the Celestial City uses the peace of the terrestrial city only for its own ends. Citizens of the City of God are not passionately interested in achieving justice in the created order, because they can find the transcendent peace beyond secular society through the Church while they are in but not of secular society. In this, Catholicism follows Augustine and tends to think in terms of nature and supernature and of the transcendent vision of God. Classical Protestantism (where it is not quietistic) finds the divine justice and peace beyond but through the earthly order, for it thinks of the Kingdom of God as having come yet tarrying in its fullness. In Calvinism, for example, the transcendent city has its embodiment in a sociological Church, whose members enter it as the true meaning of their earthly citizenship. If we approach the New Testament from the Old Testament, we see that the City of God comes upon the City of Earth to judge it and to transform it, as well as to uplift it to God. Responsibility to the orders of creation is therefore commanded universally with vocational exceptions. We have not two citizenships but one citizenship. If all Christians sought vocational celibacy, the Churches would command many to marry (as St. Thomas, taking very seriously responsibility for society, also taught). This is not because the Churches love creation instead of God but because they love creation absolutely in God and have not the angelic pretension which is willing to let human history end by default. This is most clear in a truly Protestant culture. There the Church does not use the arm of the State for its own ends, but the State may use itself for Christian ends. Citizens or rulers of the terrestrial city choose its own good; but if they are also citizens of the celestial city, they will know what is best for it. The State is criticized by the Christian as citizen, not as Church official; the State is subordinated to God by its citizens, not by the sociological Church.

St. Augustine's theology makes for the Roman Catholic interpretation of his decision to use the State in the interests of orthodox Christianity. But this is not to say that the decision is itself wrong as an empirical judgment and a strategic move. It is only to say that a man should make that decision as a citizen in the interests of the State, not as a bishop in the interests of the Church. This is a real difference where two forms of Christianity oppose one another at their best. And neither, of course, is always able to maintain itself at its best.

FOR FURTHER READING

Erich Przywara, S.J., *An Augustine Synthesis*, New York, Sheed & Ward, 1936, chapters XII–XIV.

These excerpts from St. Augustine's writings give in a topical arrangement many references to his ethics not included in our chapter.

William Montgomery, *St. Augustine: Aspects of His Life and Thought*, London, Hodder & Stoughton, 1914, chapter VIII.

Standard and readable, it gives attention to the social ethic.

M. C. D'Arcy, S.J., *A Monument to St. Augustine*, London, Sheed & Ward, 1930, chapter VII.

This chapter by Bernard Roland-Gosselin, the author of *La Morale de St. Augustine*, describes and very little criticizes the Augustinian ethic.

Adolph von Harnack, *History of Dogma*, London, Williams & Norgate, 1898, V, chapters II–III.

A Protestant account of Augustine's ethics and his doctrine of man, from a standpoint more philosophical than theological and perhaps more critical than historical.

Anders Nygren, *Agape and Eros*, London, Society for Promoting Christion Knowledge, 1953, tr. P. S. Watson, II, pt. II.

With many quotations, here is an exposition of the relation of man and God in line with the central thesis of this controversial work—that Eros is foreign and antithetical to Christian love.

NOTES

1. *On the Morals of the Catholic Church*, III–VI (translation in Oates, *Basic Writings*). Except where Oates or Pusey is cited, all footnote references are to chapters in the translations provided in the *Nicene and Post-Nicene Fathers series*.

2. Anders Nygren, the modern Lutheran theologian, exaggerates this view in stating that 'all love is acquisitive love' (*Agape and Eros*, 476.)

3. *On Christian Doctrine,* I. 12; and *On the Morals of the Manicheans,* VII (9).

4. *On the Morals of the Catholic Church,* VI (Oates).

5. *Confessions,* III. 4. 8 (E. B. Pusey).

6. Ibid. VII. 20. 26; and VII. 21. 27.

7. Ibid. VII. 17. 23; and VII. 10. 16.

8. Ibid. VII. 20. 26. Cf. *City of God,* XI. 2; and W. Temple, *Nature, Man and God,* xv.

9. *On the Catechising of the Uninstructed,* IV. 8.

10. *On the Gospel of John,* Tract. xxv. 16.

11. Ibid. Tract. II. 4.

12. *Confessions,* I. I. 1 (Pusey).

13. *City of God,* XIX. 25; and v. 20.

14. *On Rebuke and Grace,* II (3).

15. *On the Morals of the Catholic Church,* xv and XIX–XXV (Oates).

16. *Epistle of St. John,* Homily VII. 8; *On Nature and Grace,* LXX (84); and *On Christian Doctrine,* I. 28 (42).

17. *On the Morals of the Catholic Church,* xxv. 46.

18. *On Christian Doctrine,* I. 26 (27); I. 23 (22).

19. Compare the treatment of love of enemies, ibid. I. 29 (30).

20. St. John 1:12, Romans 8:15, and Galatians 4:5.

21. *Our Lord's Sermon on the Mount,* I. 23. 78–9.

22. *On Christian Doctrine,* I. 31 (34).

23. *On the Good of Marriage,* 1–4; 15; cf. *On Marriage and Concupiscence,* I. 10 (11), and *On the Grace of Christ and on Original Sin,* II. 24 (39).

24. *On the Good of Widowhood,* 11.

25. *On Marriage and Concupiscence,* II. 31 (54).

26. *On the Good of Widowhood,* 10.

27. Ibid. 28; cf. *On the Good of Marriage,* 10.

28. *On the Morals of the Manicheans,* XVIII. 65.

29. *On Marriage and Concupiscence,* I. 8 (9); I. 15 (16); I. 18 (19).

30. Ibid. I. 8 (9); I. 24 (27).

31. *City of God,* XII. 13 and 19; and *On the Good of Marriage,* 15.

32. 'Sex Standards in America,' in *Christianity and Crisis,* VIII, 9 (24 May 1948), p. 65.

33. *Sermons,* CXCII. 2. (*PL,* vol. 39).

34. *City of God,* XIV. 28.

35. *Ennarations on the Psalms,* LXV (LXIV in *Patrologia Latina*). 2.

36. Ibid. LII (LI in *PL*). 2.

37. Ibid. C (XCIX in *PL*). 9.

38. Ibid. LII (LI in *PL*). 4. Cf. LXII (LXI in *PL*). 4; and LXV (LXIV in *PL*). 1–2.

39. Ibid. CXXIV (CXXIII in *PL*). 7.

40. W. Montgomery in his *St. Augustine*, pp. 238–42, traces the steps by which the Bishop of Hippo came to champion State persecution of schismatics. In the year 399, Augustine refused to appeal to civil power (*Ep.*, 237). In 404, at a Council in Carthage, he asked that the proposed fine on Donatists be exacted only in the districts where Donatist bishops did not attempt to repress the violence of the Circumcelliones. The Emperor, however, made the fine universal and banished Donatist clergy. The apparent success of this strategy in converting Donatists caused Augustine to change his mind.

41. *Epist.*, XCIII. 1. 3; 2. 4; 5. 16–17.

42. *Sermons*, XLIV. 1–2.

43. *City of God*, XIX. 13–14.

44. Ibid. XXII. 30. A similar status was enjoyed by the angels, XII. 9.

45. Ibid. XII. 8; and XIII. 3.

46. Ibid. XIX. 15. Here Augustine's *naturalis ordo* is identical with the *jus naturale* of Cicero, Seneca, and Ulpian, and also with that of St. Ambrose.

47. A. W. Calhoun, *Social History of the American Family*, III. 270; and Margaret Mead, 'What is Happening to the American Family?' in *Proceedings of the National Conference of Social Work 1947*.

48. *City of God*, IV. 4.

49. Ibid. IV. 15.

50. Ibid. XIX. 16.

51. Ibid. XIX. 6.

THE DEVOTIONAL LIFE

Roger Hazelton

I‍T is often and correctly said that Augustine set the course of Christian thinking for well over a thousand years. But it is not so generally recognized that he likewise marked the channels of Christian devotion, from his time to our own. His stamp upon the prayer-ways of the Christian West, both Catholic and Protestant, has been no less deep and enduring than his monumental theological influence. The great themes which recur in Christian worship, the images and metaphors by which the devotional spirit is perennially nourished, the very words and phrases by which Christians in public or in private recall themselves to God — these are still in large part indubitably Augustinian.

The primary reason for this tremendous and lasting impression is clear enough. Laying aside considerations of ecclesiastical history, we may find the cause first of all in the penetrating beauty and intimate directness of Augustine's own writing. Its appeal has been universal precisely because its point of view is so authentically personal. The fourth-century African bishop pictured his own spirit's search for God in bold strokes and deathless colors. His incisive mind and glowing heart found combined utterance in a great number of books covering a vast range of topics and issues. But present in them all, as a kind of dominant motif, is the movement of a human soul on its way to God.

In view of this constancy of the devotional theme and its great influence, it may seem at first surprising that there is no one book or group of books by Augustine which may properly be called devotional in the modern sense. He did not treat the devotional life as a special subject, for the good and simple reason that he did not regard it as an exceptional or separate type of Christian living at all. Anyone who lives as a Christian must live devotedly, in conscious, deliberate awareness of God and in steadfast adherence to him. So to live is the very texture of a Christian's work, the very presupposition of his thought. Thus the whole of Christian living, and not any part of it alone, displays the genuinely devotional quality.

In Augustine's writing, therefore, this quality appears throughout. Speech about God merges easily and almost imperceptibly into speech with God. Passages of acute theological or philosophical analysis are intertwined with those of the most intimate prayer and praise. So a work of Biblical commentary reveals the devotional temper quite as surely as the more celebrated *Confessions*; Augustine's characteristic religiousness is revealed in a controversial treatise no less than in personal correspondence; and his massive work on the Trinity may be fittingly read as the elaboration of a point of view assumed in the more slender *Soliloquies*. There are, of course, many places in which the high note of a life in God is struck and sustained more vibrantly than in others. Yet when the devotional life does come into the focus of explicit attention it represents but the distillation of a spirit that is everywhere present.

Similarly, for all his mystical temperament (Dom Cuthbert Butler calls him 'the prince of mystics'), Augustine seems not to have been so preoccupied as were the later mystics with the techniques and regimens of the life devoted to God. He was no

399

Loyola, setting forth spiritual exercises by the day and hour for the example of his followers. Nor was he a Bonaventura, crisply defining each path and promontory of the Christian life in the manner of a spiritual cartographer. Nor, again, was he a Jeremy Taylor, full of homely rules and sundry exhortations for the Christian caught in the tangles of a sad, bad, mad world. And surely he was not what might be termed today an 'authority on worship,' advocating this improvement or that program with well-advertised enthusiasm for the religious market. Augustine's authority was not that of the expert specialist or even that of the connoisseur; it sprang rather from his integrity as a human being toward One 'more inward to me than my most inward part, and higher than my highest.' [1] The modern reader may well miss in Augustine the specific recommendation, the 'practical help.' But if he reads him carefully he will certainly find something better — a profound and searching statement of what it is to live with God.

One further remark may be made by way of approach to Augustine's understanding of the devotional life, though to substantiate it fully would require at least another essay. It is that in Augustine's writings, as in his own experience, theology and devotion are the fused aspects of a single faith. Fortunately, the separation of theology from worship, which has proved so disastrous to modern thought, was unknown to him. The much-labored antithesis between love and logic, feeling and reason, in which our modern efforts to comprehend faith are confined had no meaning for him. To be sure, there were very real strains and oppositions which had to be faced and, if possible, resolved; yet T. R. Glover has spoken what is certainly a true word on this matter: 'Intellect and instinct have each their strength and their weakness, and in Augustine they correct each other. Emotion cannot lead where reflection will not approve, nor can thought rest where heart is dissatisfied.' [2] The point is that Augustine's theology is devotionally stimulated and oriented, just as his devotion is theologically sustained and controlled. His devotional utterances can be understood only in the light of his theological motivation; his theology is grasped only when its devotional rootage and direction are seen. For to know God is to love him, and loving demands knowing as its essential condition. Hence, for Augustine, the authenticity of a man's devotion is properly tested by the clarity and adequacy of his belief concerning God, and the thought of God is but a function of the life in God.

We shall inquire in this essay whether there can be found in Augustine's writings anything like a theology of devotion. Have we to deal simply with scattered biographical revealings, homiletical imperatives, rhapsodic outpourings of a full and eager heart? Or does some consistent pattern of interpretation, some rationale of the God-bestowed and God-directed life, run through these pages? If, as we have said, Augustine does not suggest techniques, may it not be maintained that he does enunciate principles guiding such a life? What possibilities of real attachment to God lie open to the human spirit and by what avenues may it come? Whatever the answers we may give to questions like these, we must, in any event, recognize at the outset that we are concerned with a vital togetherness of thought and experience bound by the cords of warm and living faith.

I. The Soul's Journey

We begin by adopting one of Augustine's own cherished images, speaking of the devotional life as a journey of the soul toward God. For Augustine, the Christian is always a pilgrim, *homo viator,* man on the march. Relatedness to God is not a position but a movement, not a point but a process. No static confrontation but a dynamic interaction of the soul and God is its substance, realized within a moving, growing experience. Prodded by burning desire and lured by unspeakable promise, the Christian wends his restless but determined way to God.

How shall we describe the nature of this journey? It is in the first place inescapably and basically personal. In all the changing landscape of the Christian's pilgrimage, and on its many different levels, the terms in relation are finally only two — the soul and God. Thus, when Reason asks Augustine what he desires to know, he replies that he wants to know God and the soul and nothing more. The meeting with God strips the soul to stark and naked selfhood; it is unmasked and defenseless, alone by itself. If one would enter upon the devotional journey he must be prepared to stand the scrutiny of God in the secret places of his own heart.

Not even Augustine's strong insistence upon Churchly authority or his profound sense of the commonwealth of faith can set aside this stern necessity. The doctor of the Church is at the same time the man who is a question to himself. It will not do to hold with Rufus Jones, Paul Sabatier, and others that there are really two Augustines, one the orthodox Churchman and the other the mystical individualist. The saint himself seems to be totally unaware of such a schizophrenic tendency on his part; his writings weave the two strands repeatedly together; and the notion can be defended only by contriving contradictions and ignoring contexts. The same mystical intimacy that breathes through the *Soliloquies* infuses also the corporate life described in the *City of God*. The doctrine of the Trinity is built of the same psychic substance as the *memoria* of the *Confessions*. Augustine is no more extreme an individualist than Paul of Tarsus, yet, like Paul, he underscores the indubitably personal nature of all Christian experience.

To call the devotional life personal, however, is not to label it as subjective. There is no way of a man with God which is not also a way of God with man. The spirit's journey to God is itself made possible by God, 'who has made modes of ascent in the heart.' [3] Relationship with God is marked by a kind of tension or polarity which is both inwardly felt and objectively given. To it belongs an ultimate otherness side by side with an intimate nearness. At every step of the way man is open upward to his God, who comes within the orbit of human devotion from above downward. Thus the life of devotion is basically *theandric*, to borrow a word from John Burnaby.[4] One may describe it either as an ascent by man to God or as a descent of God into the soul of man.

This second characteristic of the journey toward God cannot be overstressed. The soul's movement is both a seeking and a being found; both a human question, divinely urged, and a God-given answer, humanly acknowledged and obeyed. The passage in the exposition of Ps. 118 has many echoes elsewhere:

> He whom we desire to receive, causeth Himself to ask; He whom we wish to find causeth us to seek; He to whom we strive to attain causeth us to knock . . . And when He is received, He brings it about that he is besought by asking, by seeking, by knocking, to be more fully received.[5]

'Let us continue in Him Who continueth in us' is a characteristic exhortation of Augustine. And there is his eager prayer at the beginning of *Confessions,* x: 'Let me know Thee who knowest me, let me know Thee, even as I am known.'

Third, the soul's journey to God is a growth in intelligence. As faith is its condition, so understanding is its reward. This matter has been finely dealt with by Etienne Gilson.[6] Perhaps his division of the itinerary into a search via the intelligence and a search via the will may give the impression of a dichotomy which did not exist for Augustine. Yet Gilson states explicitly and often that the knowledge and possession of final truth is the necessary condition of blessed or happy life on Augustine's terms. In any case, it is clear that to come to God is to come to the truth. Understanding is the turning of one's self toward the changeless light of divine wisdom [7] and this means that one is brought into a more perfect life.[8] God truly illumines the minds of men with the light of truth, and the Christian travels by its radiance from faith to sight.

These marks of intelligent growth, theandric polarity, and intense personalness describe the whole course of the devotional life. But we must ask further what are the stages of the soul's approach to God, the right order which a Christian's spirit takes. These steps or levels are defined by Augustine in numerous and different ways. The well-known passage in *Confessions,* x, for example, follows the expected Neoplatonic pattern, advancing from perception of the outer created world to the introspective understanding of himself, then turning to the anticipation of blessedness which no self-knowledge but only God's gracious action can explain, and finally reaching the *gaudium de veritate* ('truth-given joy') which climaxes the whole course of the ascent.

There is a further account in the seven ages of the man who is 'interiorly reborn': he rises from the study of exemplary historical figures through rational search, the persuasion of virtue, spiritual competence, tranquil wisdom, and entrance into eternal life, concluded by the restful and blissful state of life after death.[9] Another instance of this step-by-step interpretation is Letter 181, where the Beatitudes are employed as a kind of spiritual ladder joining the Christian with the classical virtues.

A most noteworthy illustration is the statement of the 'powers of the soul' in the *De quantitate animae*. Augustine grades these powers in the following way: quickening, sensation, art (civilization and culture), virtue, tranquillity, entry, and contemplation. He tells us that these steps may be grouped in larger units in another way: 'the soul towards itself, the soul in itself, the soul towards God, the soul in God.'[10] This last designation we shall rely upon in setting forth Augustine's itinerary of the soul in motion toward its God.

II. Stages of the Journey

The 'journey not of feet' has four stages. Two of movement alternate with two of rest. The first pair is concerned with self as object, the last pair with God. Each stage is at once the condition and the preparation of the next. As each is attained, the next comes into view; approach becomes arrival, which in turn becomes a new approach. Thus each level of the ascent reveals the total bent and motive of the journey; yet each, except the last, exists only in order to be overcome by its successor. The whole forms an order of nature, in which anticipation precedes and brings on attainment, rather than of grace, in which God the goal becomes also the originating and sustaining cause of the journey.

Ultimately, of course, nature is but the sign and vehicle of grace, and a man's pilgrimage to God is but a return to where he started. If however, one would truly come to God he must start from where in fact he is. He must be *in via* before he may dwell *in patria.* While the Augustinian scheme emphasizes the proximate and provisional character of the human quest, it at the same time insists that it has a right temporal ordering. The itinerary thus set is therefore intended to be truly empirical, and Augustine means it to be taken seriously by those who would seek the living God with all their hearts.

The first step taken is that of the soul toward itself. Augustine speaks of it as a return or a restoring to one's self. This initial stage has both a purifying and a recollective aspect, each of which is preparatory in function. 'Man must be first restored to himself,' he writes, 'that, making in himself as it were a stepping-stone, he may rise thence and be borne up to God.' [11] The rule is frequently repeated: 'Recognize in yourself something within, within yourself. Leave abroad both your clothing and your flesh; descend into yourself; go to your secret chamber, your mind. If you are far from your own self, how can you draw near to God?' [12] Or again, 'Do not go outside yourself, but return to within yourself; for truth dwells in the innermost part of man.' [13]

In order to come to one's self, one must leave something behind. The soul must be purged from moral disorder and intellectual error, both of which, for Augustine, always involve an inordinate attachment to things of sensory appetite and perception. Only after such preliminary purification does the Christian enter upon recollection and introversion (the *memoria* of *Confessions,* x). The former is predominantly volitional, the latter primarily cognitive. At this first stage there is a vague yet intense longing for a state not clearly known but urgently desired. In it perceptive discrimination and deliberate desire are blended. This first step like all the others is both a willing and a knowing: a keen desire to know, a sensitive knowledge of what is truly desired. This interaction constitutes the very fabric of the devotional life.

Thus the initial stage discloses the motive and goal of the entire journey. The life of devotion is a quest for truth which has first of all to be sought in the inward parts. There is a truth in man which is the imaged reflection of truth in God. 'For not in the body but in the mind was man made in the image of God.

In His own likeness (*similitudine*) let us seek God, in His own image recognize the Creator.'[14]

As self-seeking becomes self-knowledge, the second stage of the soul's pilgrimage is reached. 'The soul in itself' is spirit's own consciousness that it is made in God's image. To be so made means that the spirit is capable of receiving and comprehending God's own truth, mirrored truly though never completely within man's own self. If reflection is not the same as reality, reflection nonetheless truly reflects reality. However clouded and broken the glass, it still mirrors in its own way the being and truth which are finally God's.

Augustine's doctrine of the divine illumination is to the point here. Philosophically it represents his revision of the Platonic theory of recollection, and thus it has sometimes been disparagingly termed 'Platonic' rather than 'Christian.' Yet it is clear enough that Augustine believed such a doctrine to be grounded firmly in Biblical faith. In commenting upon Ps. 118 he writes:

> God therefore of Himself, because He is the light (John 1:4, 9) enlighteneth devoted minds, that they may understand the divine truths which are declared or exhibited . . . God hath created man's mind rational or intellectual, whereby he may take in His light . . . and He so enlighteneth it of Himself that not only those things which are displayed by the truth, but even truth itself, may be perceived by the mind's eye.[15]

The road of faith is illumined at every step by the light of truth, else the Christian does not truly walk by faith. The knowledge of one's self, even of God's truth within one's self, is therefore a steppingstone rather than a resting place or, rather, a halt between marches on the Christian journey. In the long run, however, it is the stops which build up reserves of strength for new advances. So one who has come to himself must remain for a space within himself, living and tasting to the full the interior riches of the realm of spirit:

Do thou all within. And if perchance thou seekest some
high place, some holy place, make a temple for God within.
For the temple of God is holy, which ye are (I Cor. 3:17).
In a temple wouldst thou pray? Pray within thyself. Only
first be a temple of God, because He in His temple will hear
him that prayeth.[16]

The commentaries on the Psalms, being largely devotional in
temper, underscore this necessity and opportunity of living
interiorly. 'As this visible earth nourishes and preserves the exterior man, so does that invisible earth (God) the interior man.'
'The soul itself gives counsel from the light of God through the
rational mind, whereby it conceives the counsel fixed in the eternity of its Author.' [17]

As the second step follows the first, so the third succeeds the
second with a kind of devotional inevitability. 'The soul toward
God' is the stage at which the Christian becomes a pilgrim again,
beginning in confession and continuing in praise:

If thou wilt be brought from faith to the possession of the
reality, begin in confession. First accuse thyself, and having
accused thyself, praise God. Call upon Him whom as yet
thou knowest not, that He come and be known; not that He
come to thee Himself, but that He lead thee to Him.[18]

At this stage Augustine exhorts us to put aside all self-absorption:

Away with thee, away with thee, I say, from thyself. Thou
dost hinder thyself. If thou buildest thine own self, thou dost
build a ruin.

Flee thyself, and come to Him who made thee. For by
fleeing thyself thou followest thy true self, and by following thy true self thou cleavest to Him who made thee.

Remain not in thyself, transcend thyself also; put thyself
in Him who made thee.[19]

The whole course of the journey to this point is summarized in
another sermon in this way:

Return to thyself; but when, again facing upwards, thou hast returned to thyself, stay not in thyself. First return to thyself from the things that are without, and then give thyself back to Him who made thee.[20]

God, momentarily and partially an object of enjoyment, now becomes once again the object of search. The pilgrim seeks not knowledge but forgiveness, because he knows himself so well. So Augustine writes:

If thou wouldst have Him turn away His face from thy sins, do thou turn away thy face from thyself, and do not turn away thy face from thy sins. For if thou turn away thy face from them, thou art thyself angry with thy sins, and if thou turn not away thy face from thy sins, thou dost confess them and God will pardon them.[21]

And the promise thus offered soon becomes a principle of devotional guidance: 'Those who wish to follow God, allow Him to go before, and they follow; they do not make Him follow while they go before.'[22]

Many passages recast the same devotional imperative in other words. Particularly does the work on the Trinity give added content to it. When the mind knows itself, it knows itself *as seeking*. It is enjoined to know itself simply in order that it may live according to its own nature, which is to be 'under Him by whom it ought to be ruled, above those things which it ought to rule.' For 'the true honor of man is the image and likeness of God, which is not preserved save in relation to Him by whom it is impressed. The less therefore he loves what is his own, the more he adheres to God.'[23]

The last transition, from life under God to life with God, is of course the culmination of the whole devotional movement. One of Augustine's favorite texts is Ps. 72:28: 'It is good for me to adhere unto my God.' *Haerere, adhaerere, cohaerere* — the words hammer out a kind of victory march of the soul. To cleave to God is more than to set one's course in the direction of God, more even than to cling to God with all one's powers; it is to be lifted up into the circle of God's own most intimate concern, to be made participant in His very life. To determine precisely what the theological import of this conviction is would carry us far from the matter of this essay. Is it an actual apotheosis which Augustine envisages or a mystical rapport or enraptment? All that can be said here, and it may be stated emphatically, is that Augustine conceives the possibility of man's search for God as being abundantly fulfilled. Here, finally, the yearning for truth is satisfied, the craving for love is answered, spirit is possessed by Spirit.

A passage in the treatise on Catholic morals helps to make Augustine's meaning plainer:

> The striving after God is therefore the desire of beatitude; the attainment of God is beatitude itself. We seek to attain God by loving Him; we attain to Him, not by becoming entirely what He is, but in nearness to Him, and in wonderful and sensible contact with Him, and in being inwardly illuminated and occupied by His truth and holiness. He is light itself; it is given to us to be illuminated by that light.[24]

The last stage of the devotional journey, then, is not only the climax of an intellectual process but also the satisfaction of longing and desire. Augustine, as he himself declared and as Burnaby and Nörregaard emphasize, believed himself not merely to have demonstrated a proposition but to have felt the holy presence of God 'in the flash of a trembling glance.' [25] It is vision of the most intense and exalted sort, but possession, too — a possessing and a being possessed. To apprehend God and be apprehended by Him is a gift, not an achievement [26]; the soul's journey is one which we could not ourselves make had not 'the Way itself come down to us.' [27] Thus at journey's end the soul recognizes that it is God, and not itself, which has guided all its steps. This distinguishes Augustine's itinerary sharply from the Neoplatonic ecstasy of contemplation, as Augustine himself is well aware.[28]

In most of the passages in which this final resting place of the soul in God is mentioned, it is spoken of in the future, not the present, tense. Typical of these passages is the following:

> Peace there will be there, perfect peace will be there. Where you wish you shall be, but from God you will not depart. Where you wish you shall be, but wherever you go you shall have your God. With Him, from whom you are blessed, shall you ever be.[29]

Is this rest, this peace passing understanding, a state available to people this side of death? There is a baffling ambivalence about Augustine's statements on the matter. Perhaps all that can safely be said is that to us, in this life, are vouchsafed genuine foretastes of eternal blessedness, though transient and fragile; and, what is still more important, that the Christian's life is continuous from earth to heaven, and the homeland of eternity casts its shadow before upon the temporal journey as *patria* to the Christian's *via*. The ambivalence of meaning is quite certainly deliberate and is well calculated to underscore the nature of the Christian journey as an anticipated attainment. 'Some sweet odor of the divine praise and of that peace reaches us, but for the greater part mortality weighs upon us,' [30] writes Augustine. To us, working and striving on earth, such a foretaste signifies 'the activity of our rest.'

> O the happy Alleluias there! . . . There praise to God and here praise to God, but here by those full of anxious care, there by those free from care; here by those whose lot is to die, there by those who are to live eternally; here in hope, there in hope realized; here on the way, there in our fatherland. Now therefore my brethren, let us sing, not for our delight as we rest, but to cheer us in our labor. As wayfarers are wont to sing, sing, but keep on marching . . . If you are progressing, you are marching; but progress is good, progress in true faith, progress in right living; sing, and march on.[31]

III. Defining the Orientation

With these stages of the soul's journey before us, we have finally to ask whether they constitute a distinctively Christian statement of the devotional itinerary or only a fusion — perhaps a confusion — of Neoplatonic with Christian elements, as is often claimed. It cannot be denied that throughout Augustine's treatment the distinctively Platonic combination of the intellectual with the spiritual life is employed. Are we forced to say, then, that the devotional theology of Augustine is merely a composite, a blending of purposes and methods that are essentially diverse and irreconcilable? Can the search for God by way of the intelligence actually be regarded as the same as the search by way of the loving will, or not?

In order to answer these questions we may make use of Augustine's own statements of contrast between the Platonist and the Christian experience of rapport with God. The basic difference which he emphasizes is that whereas the Platonist believes union with God to be the direct and achieved result of the soul's intellectual pilgrimage, the Christian knows that his life in God is rather caused by God's own free and gracious gift. Although Augustine's account of his own experience of God is everywhere involved with Neoplatonic terminology and conceptions, nevertheless he finds its source, sustenance, and goal always in the love of God for men, inspiring and guiding men's love for God. He continually opposes 'a barren intellectualism which cannot give life,' according to E. I. Watkin, and admits 'only whatever studies are *directly* serviceable to the knowledge of God.'[32] In spite of the fact that he is constantly under the influence of the Platonic longing for a vision of God in this life, he nonetheless insists upon interpreting Moses' sight of God and Paul's enrapment into the third heaven, as well as his own experience of communion, as but foretastes of the beatific, heavenly vision, not themselves final and consummatory moments of deification.[33] Such transient experiences are more like the perceiving of an odor than the grasping and eating of spiritual food, more taste than sight, more a passing touch than a permanent possession.

As far as Augustine's theology of devotion is concerned, then, it may be maintained that his Christian instinct and insight have always the last word. However close to mystical pantheism the bishop seems at times to come, he again and again recoils from its logical conclusion. Though he may seem at other times to give comfort to the intellectualist who would make the contemplative intuition of God a substitute for loving obedience to God, Augustine never travels with him the whole way. The check upon mystical or intellectualist enthusiasm is provided in Augustine's thought, as in his life, by his vivid and inescapable sense of the love of God.

God is to be loved simply and solely because He is love. It is His love that calls forth our own and leads it home to him. This is how Augustine understands the predominant restlessness, the straining after blessedness, which marks the whole journey of the Christian spirit:

> Give me a lover, he will feel what I speak of; give me one who longs, who hungers, who is the thirsty pilgrim in this wilderness, sighing after the springs of his eternal homeland; give me such a man, he will know what I mean.[34]

In the context of Christian dedication and faith, love is always the soul's movement toward God (*motus animi ad Deum*). It is the guiding energy of the Christian's will leading him from desire into delight, from need to satisfaction, from longing to belonging.

Considered purely on the human plane, love is of course a neutral term. It may become either an inordinate affection or a holy longing. The 'two cities' are the corporate crystallization of 'two loves,' each of which lies within the scope of human motivation. But the Christian motive is always for Augustine to be found within an energy of man's will which is ours only by virtue of God's gift. Thus Augustine interprets Romans 5:5 (mistakenly, to be sure) by saying that the 'love of God' there mentioned is not 'the love wherewith God loves us, but that by which He makes us His lovers.' [35] He even interprets the Pauline question, 'Who

shall separate us from the love of Christ?' in the same manner.
But it would be quite as wrong to understand Augustine's rendering of love in purely subjective terms as it would be to understand Paul's in merely objective terms. From first to last, Augustine views the love wherewith man loves God as the intended
outcome of God's own love for man.

And yet this is no divine determinism. There is freedom as well
as grace within a Christian's loving. Man ought to love *because*
God loves; he cannot love *as* God loves, simply because he is not
God. Man's love of God will always have the character of *Sehn-
sucht*, longing, even craving; whereas God's love for us is purely
charitable, spontaneous, impartial, and 'unmotivated.' The
stream of love is not the source of love. It is forever in man response, not stimulus, effect, not cause. The divine transcendence
is thus preserved even here, where Augustine might most un-
derstandably ignore it.[36]

This doctrine makes possible a directive. Everything is to be
loved, even one's self, 'for the sake of God' or 'in God.' Hence
the celebrated beatitude of *Confessions*, iv. 9: 'Blessed is the
man who loves Thee, O God, and his friend in Thee, and his
enemy for Thee. For he alone loses no one that is dear to him,
if all are dear in God, who is not lost.' The seemingly solitary
journey of the soul to God is thus actually a brotherly love as
well as a private longing. *Caritas Dei* implies and indeed demands the love of the neighbor; and it does so because God
is truly present in the neighbor:

> The love of God cometh first in the order of commanding,
> but the love of our neighbor first in the order of doing
> . . . Because thou dost not yet see God, thou dost earn the
> seeing of Him by loving thy neighbor. By loving thy neigh-
> bor thou purgest thine eyes for the seeing of God . . .
> Love therefore thy neighbor; and behold that in thee where-
> by thou lovest thy neighbor; there wilt thou see, as thou
> mayest, God.[37]

This is as far from a 'flight of the alone to the Alone' as could
possibly be imagined. It bears the unmistakable stamp of

Christian teaching and trust. It is animated and shaped by the *caritas Christi:*

> In Christ thou hast all. Dost thou wish to love God? Thou hast Him in Christ . . . Dost thou wish to love thy neighbor? Thou hast him in Christ.[38]
>
> Lo, thou art far from God, O man, and God is far above man. Between them the God-man placed Himself. Acknowledge Christ; and through Him as Man ascend to God.[39]

The path on which the Christian journeys is Christ; Christ is the head, whose body we are. He is our way, our truth, and our life, and all these may be comprehended in the word 'love.'

It is a long way home to God, and Augustine never allows us to forget it. One must leave the created world of outer things behind and enter into one's own depths; then, in humility, he may see a Light which is above him because it made him, which he can see even while he knows that he is not the man to see it; and after that the journey begins again, the pilgrim feeling through the darkness of his mind what he is not yet actually able to see; until the widening radiance dissipates the darkness and brings strength and growth, so that the wayfarer may do God's bidding and know that it is God who gives the power to obey.

A long way, yes, but a way illumined and guided by the love of God in Christ. 'We are Christians, we belong to Christ.'

> Thou wast walking in thy own ways a vagabond, straying through wooded places, through rugged places, torn in all thy limbs. Thou wast seeking a home . . . and thou didst not find it . . . There came to thee the Way itself, and thou wast set therein . . . Walk by Him, the Man, and thou comest to God. By Him thou goest, to Him thou goest . . . I do not say to thee, seek the way. The Way itself is come to thee; arise and walk.[40]

FOR FURTHER READING

John Burnaby, *Amor Dei: A Study of the Religion of Saint Augustine*, London, Hodder, 1938.

The most reliable full-length treatment of the devotional theology of Augustine available in English.

Edward Cuthbert Butler, *Western Mysticism*, London, Constable, 1922, pp. 23–88.

The preface to this work should also be read, as it defines the perspective within which Augustine's contemplative mysticism is interpreted. A very helpful discussion.

A Monument to Saint Augustine, London, Sheed and Ward, 1930.

See particularly the essay by E. I. Watkin, 'The Mysticism of Saint Augustine,' pp. 103–19. Somewhat marred by contentiousness, but manages to convey with insight and empathy Augustine's inner religious nature.

R. L. Ottley, *Studies in the Confessions of Saint Augustine*, London, Robert Scott, 1919, pp. 88–111.

This chapter, while not especially original or brilliant, is nevertheless useful in summarizing competently and clearly a great mass of written material, both from Augustine himself and from his interpreters.

NOTES

1. *Confessions*, III. 11.
2. *Life and Letters in the Fourth Century* (Cambridge, Eng.: The University Press, 1901), 196.
3. *Enarrations on the Psalms*, 122. 3.
4. See his very helpful volume *Amor Dei: A Study of the Religion of St. Augustine* (London: Hodder & Stoughton, 1938).
5. *Enarrations on the Psalms*, 118.
6. In *Introduction à l'étude de S. Augustin* (Paris: J. Vrin, 1929), especially ch. I.
7. *De Gen. ad Lit.*, I. 5.
8. *De Lib. Arb.*, I. 7. 17.
9. *De Vera Relig.*, 26. 48–9.
10. *De Quant. Animae*, 33. 70–76; 35. 79.
11. *Retractations*, I. 7. 3.
12. *In Joan. Evang.*, XXIII. 10.
13. *De Vera Relig.*, 39. 72.
14. *In Joan. Evang.*, XXIII. 10.
15. *Enarrations on the Psalms*, 118.
16. *In Joan. Evang.*, XV. 25.
17. *Enarrations on the Psalms*, 1. 4; 145. 5.

18. Ibid. 146. 14.
19. *Serm. de Script. N.T.,* 169. 9; *Serm.,* 29. 4; *Serm. de Script. N.T.,* 153. 7.
20. *Serm.,* 330. 3.
21. *Enarrations on the Psalms,* 122. 3.
22. Ibid. 124. 9.
23. *De Trin.,* XII. 11.
24. *De Moribus Eccl.,* I. 11.
25. Burnaby, op. cit. 31–2; J. Nörregaard, *Augustins Bekehrung,* 65.
26. *De Civitate Dei,* X. 29.
27. *De Doctr. Christ,* I. 10. 11.
28. See, among others, the passage in *De Trin.,* V. 10.
29. *Serm.,* 242. 7.
30. *Serm.,* 252. 9.
31. *Serm.,* 256. 3.
32. In *A Monument to Saint Augustine* (New York: MacVeagh, 1930), 114.
33. See Butler, *Western Mysticism,* 77–88; *Confessions,* VII. 16. 23.
34. *In Joan. Evang.,* XL. 10.
35. *De Spir. et Litt.,* 56.
36. For a discussion of the basic issues involved, see Anders Nygren, *Eros and Agape,* Part II, Vol. II, ch. ii; and Burnaby, op. cit., 15–19, 92–3, 117–18.
37. *In Joan. Evang.,* XVII. 8; see also *De Trin.,* VIII. 8.
38. *Serm.,* 261. 8.
39. *Serm. de Script. N.T.,* 81. 6.
40. *Enarrations on the Psalms,* 70; *Serm. de Script. N.T.,* 141. 4.

Index